# THE POVERTY OF DISASTER

The eighteenth century in Britain is often understood as a time of commercial success, economic growth and improving living standards. Yet during this period, tens of thousands of men and women were imprisoned for failing to pay their debts. *The Poverty of Disaster* tells their stories, focusing on the experiences of the middle classes who enjoyed opportunities for success on one hand, but who also faced the prospect of downward social mobility on the other. Tawny Paul examines the role that debt insecurity played within society and the fragility of the credit relations that underpinned commercial activity, livelihood and social status. She demonstrates how, for the middle classes, insecurity took economic, social and embodied forms. It shaped the work people did, their social status, their sense of self, their bodily autonomy and their relationships with others. In an era of growing debt and the squeeze of the middle class, *The Poverty of Disaster* offers a new history of capitalism and takes a long view of the financial insecurities that plague our own uncertain times.

TAWNY PAUL is Senior Lecturer in the Department of History at the University of Exeter, where her research focuses on the economic and social history of eighteenth-century Britain. She has published widely on the history of economic life as well as in the field of heritage studies. She is the author of numerous journal articles and the co-editor of *Art and Public History: Approaches, Opportunities, and Challenges* (2017) with Rebecca Bush.

CAMBRIDGE STUDIES IN EARLY MODERN BRITISH HISTORY

SERIES EDITORS

MICHAEL BRADDICK
*Professor of History, University of Sheffield*

ETHAN SHAGAN
*Professor of History, University of California, Berkeley*

ALEXANDRA SHEPARD
*Professor of Gender History, University of Glasgow*

ALEXANDRA WALSHAM
*Professor of Modern History, University of Cambridge,
and Fellow of Trinity College*

This is a series of monographs and studies covering many aspects of the history of
the British Isles between the late fifteenth century and the early eighteenth
century. It includes the work of established scholars and pioneering work by
a new generation of scholars. It includes both reviews and revisions of major
topics and books which open up new historical terrain or which reveal startling
new perspectives on familiar subjects. All the volumes set detailed research within
broader perspectives, and the books are intended for the use of students as well as
of their teachers.

*For a list of titles in the series go to*
www.cambridge.org/earlymodernbritishhistory

# THE POVERTY OF DISASTER

*Debt and Insecurity in Eighteenth-Century Britain*

TAWNY PAUL

*University of Exeter*

CAMBRIDGE
UNIVERSITY PRESS

# CAMBRIDGE
## UNIVERSITY PRESS

University Printing House, Cambridge CB2 8BS, United Kingdom

One Liberty Plaza, 20th Floor, New York, NY 10006, USA

477 Williamstown Road, Port Melbourne, VIC 3207, Australia

314–321, 3rd Floor, Plot 3, Splendor Forum, Jasola District Centre, New Delhi – 110025, India

79 Anson Road, #06–04/06, Singapore 079906

Cambridge University Press is part of the University of Cambridge.

It furthers the University's mission by disseminating knowledge in the pursuit of education, learning, and research at the highest international levels of excellence.

www.cambridge.org
Information on this title: www.cambridge.org/9781108496940
DOI: 10.1017/9781108690546

First published 2019

Printed in the United Kingdom by TJ International Ltd, Padstow Cornwall

*A catalogue record for this publication is available from the British Library.*

ISBN 978-1-108-49694-0 Hardback

*To Aaron*

# Contents

# Figures

# Tables

# Acknowledgements

It seems only appropriate that in writing a book about debt, I have accrued many debts of my own. Over the years, I have relied on encouragement, help and support from many friends, colleagues and institutions, all of whom helped to make this project possible.

This book started as a PhD thesis. My greatest debt is to my PhD supervisor, Adam Fox, for his insights and for the clarity that he brought to my research, and to my second supervisor, Stana Nenadic, who always pushed me to think strategically about my work. My external examiner, Craig Muldrew, encouraged me to shape a project originally about credit into a book about the debtors' prisons. The School of History at the University of Edinburgh provided me an academic home for many years. I benefitted from the mentorship of many academic faculty in economic and social history, including Richard Rodger, Martin Chick, Louise Jackson and Nualah Zahedieh, and my postgraduate colleagues and friends contributed to a brilliant ten years in Edinburgh. I would like to thank Harriet, Sherice, Jess, Rosi, Gail, Andy, Leigh, Keith, Tricia, Devon, Jeff, Vanessa and Michael for distractions and decadent Saturdays.

In carrying out the research for this book, I have relied extensively on the knowledge of archivists, librarians and curators. In particular, I would like to thank the staff at the Edinburgh City Archives, the National Records of Scotland, the Lancashire Archives, the London Metropolitan Archives, the National Archives at Kew, the Huntington Library and the Clark Library. I have also relied on institutional support in the form of grants and fellowships from the Economic History Society, the Huntington Library, the National Endowment for the Humanities and the William Andrews Clark Library.

Since my postgraduate studies, this project has travelled with me in my residencies at three institutions. I am grateful to my colleagues and students at Northumbria and Exeter for their intellectual companionship and for providing supportive environments for carrying out my work. I wrote

xi

much of this book while I was a long-term fellow at the Huntington Library in California. I owe much to Steve Hindle for his encouragement and support over the years. I would also like to thank the members of my writing group who joined me in companionate silence every morning, and the gardeners at the Huntington whose work I appreciated every day.

Portions of this book have appeared in part in K. Tawny Paul, 'Credit, Reputation and Masculinity in British Urban Commerce: Edinburgh c. 1710–1770', *The Economic History Review* 66, no. 1 (2013), 226–48; K. Tawny Paul, '"A Polite and Commercial People"? Masculinity and Economic Violence in Early Modern Scotland', in Lynn Abrams and Elizabeth Ewan (eds.), *Nine Centuries of Man: Manhood and Masculinity in Scottish History* (Edinburgh, 2017), 203–22; and K. Tawny Paul, 'Accounting for Men's Work: Multiple Employments and Occupational Identities in Early Modern England', *History Workshop Journal* 85, no. 1 (2018), 26–46. The material extracted from these publications is reprinted here with kind permission, respectively, from the Economic History Society, John Wiley and Sons, Edinburgh University Press and Oxford University Press.

A wise woman once told me that writing is a collaborative process, and drafting this book has convinced me that she was right. Draft chapters were read by Carole Shammas, Karen Harvey, Keith Pluymers, Alexandre Dubé, Mark Hailwood, Lisa Cody, Vanessa Wilkie and Michael Meranze. Jeremy Boulton did me the honour of reading and commenting on the entire draft. This book is better for their input, and any mistakes or idiosyncrasies are of course my own. I presented earlier versions of chapters of this book to numerous conferences and workshops. I would like to thank the organisers and audience members at: the Early Modern Economic and Social History Seminar (Cambridge), the Society, Culture and Belief, 1500–1800 Seminar (IHR), the Wealth and Debt Accumulation in Early Financial Markets Symposium (Stockholm School of Economics), the Ideas of Poverty in the Age of Enlightenment Conference (KCL), the Berkshire Conference of Women Historians (Hofstra), the USC-Huntington Early Modern British History Seminar, the North American Conference on British Studies (Denver), the Pacific Coast Conference on British Studies (Huntington), the American Historical Association Annual Conference (Denver), the Maritime Studies Seminar (Exeter), the Western Society for Eighteenth Century Studies (UC Riverside), the Gender in the European Town Conference (Odense, Denmark), the Markets, Law and Ethics Conference (Sheffield) and the Department of History Seminar at Aberystwyth University. I would like to thank the series editors of the Early

Modern British History Series at Cambridge University Press and my general editor, Liz Friend-Smith, for providing such insightful comments on previous drafts and for their enthusiasm for this project.

Long before I began to write this book, or even to pursue an academic career, my professors at Vassar College introduced me to the study of history. I received especially important training and mentorship from Jim Merrell, Miriam Cohen, Bob Brigham and Lydia Murdoch. Though my approach to studying the past has grown and changed over the years, my interest in writing history from the bottom up and from the perspective of gender was cultivated at Vassar. I write this book with a keen interest in social justice and a firm belief that the past is crucial to understanding the social and economic problems that we face today. The long history of debt matters.

Finally, I would like to thank my family for their emotional support. My parents have always believed in me and supported my ambitions. From thousands of miles away, my dad provided pep talks at key moments. Aaron encouraged and supported me through the process of completing this book, right down to meticulously copy-editing the manuscript. He has taught me the true meaning of partnership. This book is for him.

# Introduction

Archibald How was, in most respects, an unremarkable character. An ordinary tradesperson in Edinburgh, he spent his days working as a glover. How's lineage afforded him a semi-independent status. He was the son of a skinner and a burgess of Edinburgh, which gave him access to training through the Incorporation of Skinners, the right to trade under an occupational title and the privilege of citizenship. In 1736, How inherited his father's shop on the High Street, a space from which he manufactured and sold gloves. As a master craftsman, he succeeded in his first decade in business. He was elected an officer of his kirk (parish), and his wife became a governess of the Trades Maiden Hospital, a charity school established by the Craftsmen of Edinburgh to educate the daughters of impoverished craftsmen. The couple rented a house on the High Street and spent £6, a considerable amount of money at the time, purchasing new sets of furniture, including a mahogany bedstead and a chest of drawers, for their new home.

In many ways, Archibald How looks like a familiar eighteenth-century social type, a member of the burgeoning middling sorts. He was upwardly mobile. He was not rich, but he was independent. He worked for himself rather than depending on a wage. He and his wife held positions of civic responsibility in their community, and the consumer purchases of their household allowed them to display the material trappings of middling status. How was in many ways the archetypal eighteenth-century figure popularised by Adam Smith: the independent, economic man who has become the marker of modernity and selfhood in the scholarly literature today. But as was true for many of his social rank, How's relative affluence was tinged with insecurity.

If the circumstances of How's life were in many ways ordinary, his position in the urban landscape provides an extraordinary reminder of the porous boundary between success and failure. How's glove shop adjoined the east wall of the city's debtors' prison. This meant that he worked only feet away from men confined for debt. In 1750, he began to experience financial trouble that would land him on the other side of the prison wall. In December, the brewer Daniel McFarlane imprisoned How for a debt of £2. While How was imprisoned, his wife managed the household's assets and debts. She negotiated with the creditor and secured her husband's release within three days. But the public nature of imprisonment made others aware of How's financial status, and his creditors became anxious that How would not be able to pay them. A local surgeon stepped forward for 15s. to cover a debt for attending How's wife when she was ill the previous month. A tanner demanded payment of a debt for leather, one of the raw materials of How's trade. Unable to meet all of these obligations at once, How was imprisoned a second time by a local stabler for a debt of £1 11s. This time, How languished in prison for more than a month. He lost his civic position in the church, and more creditors stepped forward. Despite selling off the household furnishings and the goods in his shop, How's wife was unable to negotiate terms that satisfied the creditors. With little property left, How eventually petitioned the city court to release him because he was too poor to pay his debts.[1]

Archibald How's ill fate was not unusual, but rather was typical of the precariously positioned middling sort. He stands as a testament to the fragility of middling people's financial and social security. Debt and social identity were closely intertwined. By the early eighteenth century in Britain, as many as one in four men of How's class spent time in debtors' prison. In contemporary thought, this loss of liberty was the paradigmatic opposite to independence. Not only did How lose his property, but he also lost his autonomy, his social status and his reputation as an independent tradesperson, all of which were closely intertwined with his gender identity as a middling man. Those who never went to prison saw it as a tangible threat. It is nearly impossible to find a lower-middling diary or letter book that does not contemplate failure or express anxiety over debt. This kind of precariousness, a form of perennial insecurity that threatened both purse and personhood, was different than being poor in the traditional sense of the word. As Daniel Defoe made clear, there was a distinction between the 'Poverty of Inheritance' that characterised a permanent class of 'People born to Labour' and the 'Poverty of Disaster' that threatened mostly 'the middling Sorts of People, who have been Trading-Men, but by Misfortune

---

[1]  National Records of Scotland (hereafter NRS), Edinburgh Tolbooth Warding and Liberation Books (hereafter ETWLB), 1746–50, HH11/23; Sheriff Court Productions, 'Miscellaneous Legal Papers Related to the How Family', SC39/107/8.

or Mismanagement, or both, fall from flourishing Fortunes into Debt, Bankruptcy, Jails, Distress, and all Sorts of Misery'.[2] The eighteenth-century world was structured by insecurity, far more than historians have previously acknowledged. This book is about that world and what it was like to live in it. It is about the fragility of the credit relations that under-pinned commercial activity, livelihood and social status in eighteenth-century Britain.

## Insecurity

Archibald How sits in a historical blind spot. His story and the stories of incarcerated middling tradespeople like him remain invisible because their experiences fail to resonate with an economic culture characterised by success, development and economic growth. There is a broad consensus that the long eighteenth century was a period of transition in the culture of capitalism. Britain experienced sustained economic growth and modernisation.[3] As the economy quickened, markets developed and became more integrated. Technological innovations and the diffusion of useful knowledge contributed to improvements in the organisation of agriculture, production and manufacturing.[4] Domestic and international commerce expanded. Material standards of living improved, especially for the middle ranks. Improvements in agricultural productivity and trans-portation alongside more integrated markets increased the food resources available to the majority of the population, contributing to a decline in adult mortality.[5]

---

[2] Daniel Defoe, *Review of the State of the English Nation* 4 (3 April 1707), 91.

[3] N. F. R. Crafts, *British Economic Growth during the Industrial Revolution* (Oxford, 1985); Phyllis Deane and W. A. Cole, *British Economic Growth, 1688–1959: Trends and Structure* (Cambridge, 1962), 8; Stephen Broadberry, Bruce M. S. Campbell, Mark Overton, Alexander Klein and Bas van Leeuwen, *British Economic Growth, 1270–1870* (Cambridge, 2015); E. A. Wrigley, *The Path to Sustained Growth: England's Transition from an Organic Economy to an Industrial Revolution* (Cambridge, 2016).

[4] Joel Mokyr, *The Enlightened Economy: An Economic History of Britain, 1700–1850* (New Haven, CT, 2009); Margaret C. Jacob, *The First Knowledge Economy: Human Capital and the European Economy, 1750–1850* (Cambridge, 2014).

[5] For contrasting interpretations of food availability and nutrition, see Craig Muldrew, *Food, Energy and the Creation of Industriousness: Work and Material Culture in Agrarian England, 1550–1780* (Cambridge, 2011); Roderick Floud, ed., *The Changing Body: Health, Nutrition, and Human Development in the Western World since 1700* (Cambridge, 2011); Morgan Kelly and Cormac Ó Gráda, 'Numerare Est Errare: Agricultural Output and Food Supply in England before and during the Industrial Revolution', *Journal of Economic History* 73, no. 4 (December 2013): 1132–63; Cormac Ó Gráda, 'Neither Feast nor Famine: England before the Industrial Revolution', in *Institutions, Innovation and Industrialization*, ed. Avner Greif, Lynne Kiesling and John Nye (Princeton, NJ, 2015), 7–32; Gregory Clark, *A Farewell to Alms: A Brief Economic History of the*

Recent histories of Britain's transition to capitalism have focused predominantly on goods and on financial instruments. As part of the Consumer Revolution, men and women came to own more things. Luxuries, including consumer durables and non-essential foodstuffs, became more accessible, allowing individuals to consume for pleasure and comfort rather than out of mere necessity. These changes had profound consequences for individuals' material lives, but they were also crucial to the formation of social identity. Consumption and the display of objects was an important means of signalling taste and status.[6] The Financial Revolution from the late seventeenth century invented new forms of credit and financial instruments, with new institutions to regulate and manage them. These changes made lending more secure and facilitated long-distance trade, but they also had a significant impact on how people imagined the market. New ways of investing, borrowing and lending changed how people conceptualised money and value.[7]

This book puts some of the people back into the history of capitalism: the middling people who purchased consumer luxuries, who invested in new financial instruments and who are often regarded as the entrepreneurs of the industrial age. When we focus on their stories, we see neither a narrative of unbridled success nor a story of exploitation emphasised by social histories of class and labour.[8] Rather, a group of people emerges for whom insecurity was the defining feature of commercial experience. Middling people had opportunities for success, but many of them experienced downward mobility. In their eyes, financial failure and commercial success were not mutually exclusive. Insecurity, a condition that was as unremarkable as it was pervasive, was compatible with national economic growth. As Julian Hoppit and others have recognised, failure and success

---

World (Princeton, NJ, 2007). For agricultural improvements, see Mark Overton, *Agricultural Revolution in England: The Transformation of the Agrarian Economy, 1500–1850* (Cambridge, 1996), 23; E. A. Wrigley, 'British Population during the "Long" Eighteenth Century, 1680–1840', in *The Cambridge Economic History of Modern Britain*, ed. Roderick Floud and Paul Johnson (Cambridge, 2003), 79–86.

[6] Carole Shammas, *The Pre-industrial Consumer in England and America* (Oxford, 1990); Lorna Weatherill, *Consumer Behaviour and Material Culture in Britain, 1660–1760* (London, 1988); Mark Overton, *Production and Consumption in English Households, 1600–1750* (London, 2004).

[7] Peter Temin and Hans-Joachim Voth, *Prometheus Shackled: Goldsmith Banks and England's Financial Revolution after 1700* (New York, 2013); Ann Murphy, *The Origins of English Financial Markets: Investment and Speculation before the South Sea Bubble* (Cambridge, 2012); Larry Neal, 'How It All Began: The Monetary and Financial Architecture of Europe during the First Global Capital Markets, 1648–1815', *Financial History Review* 7, no. 2 (2000): 117–40; Carl Wennerlind, *Casualties of Credit: The English Financial Revolution, 1620–1720* (Cambridge, MA, 2011).

[8] E. P. Thompson, *The Making of the English Working Class* (New York, 1964); John Rule, *The Labouring Classes in Early Industrial England, 1750–1850* (London, 1986).

had a close relationship. Bankruptcy rates in England increased in the second half of the eighteenth century, just as the economy expanded and drifted into early industrialisation. Entrepreneurship and business enterprise drove the developing economy, but innovation required risk taking. Some innovations succeeded, while others naturally failed.[9] While many entrepreneurs failed, many more lived insecure financial lives, facing the constant threat of downward mobility even if failure never materialised. By taking failure into account, it becomes clear that national prosperity is not necessarily synonymous with security and well-being for the majority of the population.[10] Without disputing trajectories of macroeconomic growth, *Poverty of Disaster* joins a modest but growing body of literature that recognises failure as central to understanding commercial culture, business practices and economic change in the British and Atlantic worlds.[11]

Failure, defined as a degree of indebtedness that prevented an individual from paying his or her obligations, has until now been made visible through analysis of bankruptcy. While this legal process left an extensive record, it was restricted to a narrow group of users. Bankruptcy was available only to traders owing debts over a certain threshold, which limited the number of people who pursued this process.[12] However, the threat of ruin reached far beyond these individuals, permeating eighteenth-century society. *Poverty of Disaster* considers the implications of insecurity for the broader population. Rather than going bankrupt, individuals occupying the middle ranks of society were committed to debtors' prisons. They were incarcerated because they defaulted on their debts, or because they were insolvent. Middling people confronted the prisons in staggering numbers. Thirty-three thousand businesses went bankrupt during the eighteenth century.[13] At least 10 times as many people were imprisoned for debt. Like bankrupts, their experiences were shaped by a precarious economy characterised by an unstable business environment and problems

---

[9] Julian Hoppit, *Risk and Failure in English Business, 1700–1800* (Cambridge, 1987), 1, 11, 52, 174.

[10] Joseph A. Schumpeter, *Business Cycles: A Theoretical, Historical, and Statistical Analysis of the Capitalist Process*, vol. 1 (New York, 1939), 140; T. S. Ashton, *Economic Fluctuations in England, 1700–1800* (Oxford, 1959), 29–30.

[11] Hoppit, *Risk and Failure*; Thomas Max Safley, ed., *The History of Bankruptcy: Economic, Social and Cultural Implications in Early Modern Europe* (London, 2013); Edward J. Balleisen, *Navigating Failure: Bankruptcy and Commercial Society in Antebellum America* (Chapel Hill, NC, 2001); Scott A. Sandage, *Born Losers: A History of Failure in America* (Cambridge, MA; London, 2005); Jennifer Aston and Paolo Di Martino, 'Risk, Success, and Failure: Female Entrepreneurship in Late Victorian and Edwardian England', *The Economic History Review* 70, no. 3 (2017): 837–58.

[12] Hoppit, *Risk and Failure*, 18, 29–41.    [13] Hoppit, *Risk and Failure*, 43.

of credit and competition, and punctuated by the occasional crisis. Unlike bankrupts, uncertainty for these types was compounded by additional insecurities associated with life cycle, gender and erratic employment.[14]

Throughout this book, I discuss middling people's lives through a framework of insecurity rather than in relation to risk. Risk, a term that came into use from the late seventeenth century, is more familiar to historians. It is a form of uncertainty that can be measured, calculated and managed, and by the eighteenth century, it was part of a technical, professional vocabulary belonging to traders.[15] In the new capitalist marketplace, risks were understood as threats as well as opportunities. By taking risks, commercial actors could profit, and in negotiating these uncertainties, they exercised their freedom and agency.[16] In contrast to risk, insecurity is a form of uncertainty that cannot be quantified or estimated. Thus, it had more of a blind immediacy than risk. While risks can be chosen as part of a business calculus, insecurity is something that individuals are subjected to unwillingly, and it has an impact upon economic life beyond the commercial sphere. In early modern Britain, notions of security were fundamental to understandings of the social order and the state. Insecurity's emotional and social consequences related not only to commercial endeavours, but also to notions of selfhood and identity, or in the words of Anthony Giddens, 'ontological security'.[17] In Thomas Hobbes' thinking, one of the primary purposes of law and state power was to ensure social security.[18]

---

[14] Hoppit, *Risk and Failure*, 176.

[15] Emily Nacol, *An Age of Risk: Politics and Economy in Early Modern Britain* (Princeton, NJ, 2016), 2; John Vail, 'Insecure Times. Conceptualising Insecurity and Security', in *Insecure Times: Living with Insecurity in Contemporary Society*, ed. John Vail, Jane Wheelock and Michael Hill (London, 1999), 1–20; Mary Douglas and Aaron B. Wildavsky, *Risk and Culture: An Essay on the Selection of Technological and Environmental Dangers* (Berkeley, CA, 1983).

[16] John Vail, 'Insecurity', in *The Elgar Companion to Social Economics*, ed. John Bryan Davis and Wilfred Dolfsma (Cheltenham, 2010), 45; Douglas and Wildavsky, *Risk and Culture*; Vail, 'Insecure Times', 6; Jane Wheelock, 'Who Dreams of Failure? Insecurity in Modern Capitalism', in *Insecure Times: Living with Insecurity in Contemporary Society*, ed. John Vail, Jane Wheelock and Michael Hill (London, 1999), 23–4; Nacol, *An Age of Risk*, 125; Peter Mathias, 'Risk, Credit and Kinship in Early Modern Enterprise', in *The Early Modern Atlantic Economy*, ed. John J. McCusker and Kenneth Morgan (Cambridge, 2000), 15–35.

[17] Vail, 'Insecurity', 45–6; Anthony Giddens, *The Consequences of Modernity* (Cambridge, 1991); Douglas and Wildavsky, *Risk and Culture*; Thomas Hylland Eriksen, 'Human Security and Social Anthropology', in *A World of Insecurity: Anthropological Perspectives on Human Security*, ed. Thomas Hylland Eriksen, Ellen Bal and Oscar Salemink (London, 2010), 1–19.

[18] Stanley Williams Moore, 'Hobbes on Obligation, Moral and Political: Part Two: Political Obligation', *Journal of the History of Philosophy* 10, no. 1 (1972): 29–42.

## Credit and Debt

The story of insecurity is closely bound with the dynamics of credit and debt. It is difficult to exaggerate credit's economic importance. By the eighteenth century, the exchange of credit underpinned commercial activity, social status and livelihood, as it had since at least the fourteenth century.[19] Due to shortages of coin and problems with 'deep monetisation', men and women from across the social spectrum relied on credit to carry out their everyday purchases and to engage in commerce.[20] Without institutional intermediaries, most of this credit took the form of interpersonal lending or sales credit, extended by shopkeepers to their customers or exchanged between individuals and households. Because of the way in which credit was exchanged, it was understood in deeply social and cultural terms. It was based upon trust. 'Credit' or 'trustworthiness', used interchangeably by contemporaries, was defined socially in terms of an individual's honesty and moral character. When deciding whether to lend credit, a tradesperson had to trust that the person s/he lent to had both the ability and the disposition to repay the debt. Trustworthiness was based upon a variety of personal attributes, from thrift to diligence, industry and, for women, chastity. According to Craig Muldrew, because social character was so important to economic exchange, a household's reputation for fair and honest dealing actually became a kind of currency.[21]

Accounts of credit tend to emphasise the ways in which it was successful. At a macro level, credit facilitated commercial growth and oiled the wheels of industry.[22] Daniel Defoe wrote that credit 'encreases commerce, so I may add, it makes trade, and makes the whole kingdom trade for many millions more, than the national specie can amount to'.[23] In the wake of the Financial Revolution, there was considerable contemporary enthusiasm for credit, which, like magic, could create something out of nothing to solve the nation's fiscal crises.[24] At a micro level, credit was the glue that bound communities together. The mutual exchange of credit between

[19] Chris Briggs, *Credit and Village Society in Fourteenth-Century England* (Oxford, 2009).

[20] Craig Muldrew, *The Economy of Obligation: The Culture of Credit and Social Relations in Early Modern England* (Basingstoke, 1998); Jan Lucassen, 'Deep Monetisation: The Case of the Netherlands 1200–1940', *The Low Countries Journal of Social and Economic History* 11, no. 3 (2014): 73–121.

[21] Muldrew, *Economy of Obligation*, 148.

[22] Martin J. Daunton, *Progress and Poverty: An Economic and Social History of Britain, 1700–1850* (Oxford, 1995), 247.

[23] Daniel Defoe, *The Compleat English Tradesman, in Familiar Letters: Directing Him in All the Several Parts and Progressions of Trade* ... (London, 1726), 337.

[24] For the associations between credit and magic, see Wennerlind, *Casualties of Credit*.

households created 'tangled webs of economic and social dependency'.[25] For individuals, credit could be emancipatory and even facilitate social mobility.[26] Because nearly everyone acted as both a lender and a borrower, credit introduced a degree of equality to exchanges and cut through the strict hierarchies of class.[27] Moral and social virtues generated credit, rather than notions of status based upon birth or inherited title.[28] It was therefore theoretically possible for a person with few material resources but who possessed a reputation of working hard and being trustworthy to outstrip the credit of individuals with greater financial reserves.[29]

For women, credit is celebrated as having facilitated economic agency. Laws of coverture limited married women's ability to own property, but they had legal access to credit through the law of necessaries.[30] Credit facilitated consumption, and indeed, women have often been portrayed as the consumers of the eighteenth-century world. But through their access to credit, single, widowed and married women also ran businesses at local, regional and international levels. They acted as brokers, borrowers, lenders and investors, and they appeared in the legal system as both creditors and debtors.[31] Though married women's credit practices have traditionally been portrayed as small, informal and community driven, more recent studies have found that female enterprise could be substantial and profit driven.[32] Women were not 'acted upon' by capitalism, but were

---

[25] Muldrew, *Economy of Obligation*, 97, 123, 150.

[26] Keith Wrightson, 'The Social Order of Early Modern England: Three Approaches', in *The World We Have Gained: Histories of Population and Social Structure: Essays Presented to Peter Laslett*, ed. Lloyd Bonfield and Peter Laslett (Oxford, 1987), 182; Keith Wrightson, '"Sorts of People" in Tudor and Stuart England', in *The Middling Sort of People: Culture, Society and Politics in England: 1550–1800*, ed. Jonathan Barry and Christopher Brooks (Basingstoke, 1994), 28–51; Keith Wrightson, 'Estates, Degrees and Sorts: Changing Perceptions of Society in Tudor and Stuart England', in *Language, History, and Class*, ed. P. J. Corfield (Oxford, 1991), 30–52.

[27] Muldrew, *Economy of Obligation*, 97.      [28] Muldrew, 'Class and Credit', 151.

[29] Muldrew, 'Class and Credit', 151; Sarah M. S. Pearsall, *Atlantic Families: Lives and Letters in the Later Eighteenth Century* (Oxford; New York, 2008), 116.

[30] Margot C. Finn, 'Women, Consumption and Coverture in England, c. 1760–1860', *The Historical Journal* 39, no. 3 (1996): 709.

[31] Judith M. Spicksley, '"Fly with a Duck in Thy Mouth": Single Women as Sources of Credit in Seventeenth-Century England', *Social History*, no. 2 (2007): 187; Amy M. Froide, *Silent Partners: Women as Public Investors during Britain's Financial Revolution, 1690–1750* (Oxford, 2016); Cathryn Spence, *Women, Credit, and Debt in Early Modern Scotland* (Manchester, 2016); Alexandra Shepard, 'Crediting Women in the Early Modern English Economy', *History Workshop Journal* 79, no. 1 (Spring 2015): 1–24; Nicola Phillips, *Women in Business, 1700–1850* (Woodbridge, 2006); Hannah Barker, *The Business of Women: Female Enterprise and Urban Development in Northern England 1760–1830* (Oxford, 2006).

[32] Beverly Lemire, 'Petty Pawns and Informal Lending: Gender and the Transformation of Small-Scale Credit in England, circa 1600–1800', in *From Family Firms to Corporate Capitalism: Essays in Business and Industrial History in Honour of Peter Mathias*, ed. Christine Bruland and Patrick O'Brien

capitalism's actors, and credit is celebrated as the instrument that facilitated their agency.

While emphasising credit's influence on early modern economy and society, we have thought rather little about the moments when it went wrong. It is crucial that we focus on these moments because by the eighteenth century, credit seems to have been increasingly fragile. In the decades leading up to the Industrial Revolution, credit was arguably as important and ubiquitous as it had been for centuries. However, it was becoming less rather than more secure over time. As the economy quickened, credit networks expanded. Intricate chains of debt developed. New, imaginary forms of paper money created in the Financial Revolution made wealth more easily transferable, but credit also had 'casualties': indeterminacy, precariousness and violence.[33] Furthermore, as Alexandra Shepard's recent account of worth shows us, the components of individual credibility changed significantly. Once founded on assessments of moveable wealth, by the early eighteenth century, credit came to rely on what people *did* and who they *were* rather than on what they *had*. Credit now depended upon the unstable language of reputation.[34] Because historical approaches to credit in the eighteenth century have been predominantly cultural in nature, we have little understanding of how credit was structured, how structures changed over time and what the consequences of these changes were after the early part of the century.[35] By tracing economic structures of debt and assessing the position that credit assumed within household assets, it is possible to see that by its very ubiquity, credit became a pervasive force that threatened families with downward social mobility. Reflecting these fragilities, a record number of people ended up in debtors' prisons, their names advertised to the increasingly literate world in the new *London Gazette*.

The ubiquity of imprisonment for debt suggests a need to reconsider the eighteenth century's 'culture of credit'. While credit was the stuff of growth, agency and community bonds, it also had a dark side: debt.

(Oxford, 1998), 112–38; Alexandra Shepard, 'Minding Their Own Business: Married Women and Credit in Early Eighteenth-Century London', *Transactions of the Royal Historical Society* 25 (2015): 53–74.

[33] Wennerlind, *Casualties of Credit*; J. G. A. Pocock, 'The Mobility of Property and the Rise of Eighteenth-Century Sociology', in *Virtue, Commerce, and History: Essays on Political Thought and History, Chiefly in the 18th Century* (Cambridge, 1985), 103–23.

[34] Alexandra Shepard, *Accounting for Oneself: Worth, Status, and the Social Order in Early Modern England* (Oxford, 2015), 279.

[35] Margot C. Finn, *The Character of Credit: Personal Debt in English Culture, 1740–1914* (Cambridge, 2003).

Credit was Janus-faced. Recent histories have begun questioning credit's emancipatory power by disputing the components of worth. Shepard's assertion that early modern credit was based upon assessments of a household's moveable goods rather than reputation alone indicates that credit was perhaps not as emancipatory as we have assumed, but rather that a person's credibility could be a function of inherited wealth.[36] Integrating debt into our conceptions of credit further complicates credit's role in solidifying community cohesion. As Avner Offer suggests, the 'bonds' created by reciprocal exchange can be conceptualised in three ways: as contractual obligations, as emotional links and as fetters or forms of oppression. Relationships of exchange and reciprocity can drive the weaker party into permanent subordination, so that the market produces social 'bads' as well as goods.[37] In the eighteenth century, because most people were simultaneously creditors and debtors, the economic choices they made drew on both perspectives. When faced with the insecurity of their own debts, individuals did not necessarily negotiate credit in ways that bolstered positive relations of neighbourliness. In a highly competitive commercial environment, relationships of indebtedness could be coercive rather than consensual. Credit and debt constantly orbited each other and cannot be disentangled. While credit and debt tend to be cast in very different terms, economic anthropologists emphasise that they form an inseparable dyadic unit.[38]

## Social Identities and Class Formation

*Poverty of Disaster* tells the story of debt insecurity through the eyes of middling people, normally understood to be the main beneficiaries of the eighteenth century's commercial, financial and consumer developments, but who were in fact one of the economy's structural victims. The majority of prisoners for debt came from the middle ranks of society, and their encounters with the prison left far-reaching marks on their economic and social lives. If their stories allude to a broader set of experiences, focusing on their encounters with debt makes clear that insecurity was not only economic; it was also social. Economic insecurities created precarious

---

[36] Shepard, *Accounting for Oneself*.
[37] Avner Offer, 'Between the Gift and the Market: The Economy of Regard', *The Economic History Review* 50, no. 3 (1997): 455; Marcel Mauss, *The Gift: The Form and Reason for Exchange in Archaic Societies* (New York, 2000), 37.
[38] Gustav Peebles, 'The Anthropology of Credit and Debt', *Annual Review of Anthropology* 39 (2010): 226.

identities as well as precarious balance sheets. Debt complicates the stable categories that have come to define eighteenth-century social identities, including what it meant to be a member of the 'middling sort'.

The rise of a middling sort of people is regarded as one of the most significant historical developments in early modern Britain, and an extensive historiography has been devoted to defining this social group. Society's new 'stout midriff' included a broad swath of individuals, from merchants and lawyers to petty traders and artisans, whose wealth, occupations and life experiences were intimately tied to processes of commercialisation and economic expansion, and to the myth of upward mobility.[39] Middling people have been characterised according to a number of intertwined categories. For some, middling status was defined by wealth-holding, and required an income of at least £40–50 per year.[40] Wealth, in turn, facilitated participation in consumer culture, allowing middling people to distinguish themselves through material social display.[41] Further, middling identity had a close relationship to power. As self-described 'chief inhabitants', middling people participated in governance and occupied positions of civic authority within their parishes.[42] Projections of power supported independent status. In contrast to the gentry, the middling sort had to work for their living and traded with the products of their hands or their skill, but they worked for themselves and frequently employed others.[43]

Most histories of the middling sort have focused on the successful members of this broad group.[44] Characterisations tend to emphasise aspirations towards upward mobility. Middling status is often positioned against an upper boundary of gentility. But rather than being characterised

[39] Wrightson, 'Estates, Degrees and Sorts'; Wrightson, '"Sorts of People"'.

[40] Peter Earle, *The Making of the English Middle Class: Business, Society, and Family Life in London, 1660–1730* (London, 1989), 81.

[41] Maxine Berg, *Luxury and Pleasure in Eighteenth-Century Britain* (Oxford, 2005), 199–246; Neil McKendrick, John Brewer and J. H. Plumb, *The Birth of a Consumer Society: The Commercialization of Eighteenth Century England* (London, 1982), 1; Peter Borsay, *The English Urban Renaissance: Culture and Society in the Provincial Town, 1660–1770* (Oxford, 1989), 284–306; Helen Berry, 'Polite Consumption: Shopping in Eighteenth-Century England', *Transactions of the Royal Historical Society* 12 (2002): 375–94.

[42] Henry French, *The Middle Sort of People in Provincial England 1600–1750* (Oxford, 2007), 26–7, 105–7.

[43] Shani D'Cruze, 'The Middling Sort in Eighteenth-Century Colchester: Independence, Social Relations and the Community Broker', in *The Middling Sort of People: Culture, Society, and Politics in England, 1550–1800*, ed. Jonathan Barry and Christopher Brooks (Basingstoke, 1994), 181–207.

[44] French, *The Middle Sort of People;* Margaret R. Hunt, *The Middling Sort: Commerce, Gender, and the Family in England, 1680–1780* (Berkeley, CA, 1996); Earle, *The Making of the English Middle Class.* Notable exceptions include Hannah Barker, 'Soul, Purse and Family: Middling and Lower-Class Masculinity in Eighteenth-Century Manchester', *Social History* 33, no. 1 (2008): 12–35.

as rising, the middling sort might be more accurately depicted as falling, positioned against a lower boundary that separated the middling ranks from the poor. The middling sort were profoundly insecure. The trappings of middling identity were built on unstable foundations, and their experiences suggest that insecurity was existential and social as well as more obviously financial and material. First, middling households were not as materially secure as they might at first appear, and many experienced downward mobility. Craig Muldrew's reading of tax records suggests that most families were unable to sustain their position over generations and that wealth was highly mutable. Downward mobility was therefore a definite possibility for many households.[45] Descent into poverty was a regular feature of the life course. It was common for rate payers to fall on poor relief in old age.[46] Claims to independence were fragile. Traditional sources of social mobility, such as guild apprenticeship, were failing to create security, and increasing numbers of journeymen found themselves unable to achieve the status of masters.[47] Adam Smith's theory of moral sentiments emphasised a fear of downward mobility. The Society for Equitable Insurance on Lives, the first life assurance company, was founded in 1762 with the promise that 'a man who is rich today will not be poor tomorrow.'[48] Insecurity asserted itself in different temporal thresholds. While families might lose their wealth over the course of generations, people constantly transitioned between the categories of creditor and debtor, making demarcations of status insecure. Aspirations towards success were therefore tempered by the pervasive threat of ruin, creating what Michael Mascuch terms 'attenuated horizons of expectation' and driving a quest for 'modest competency' rather than success.[49]

If insecurity challenges what it meant to be middling, it also expands how we might define and conceptualise poverty. By the dawn of the

---

[45] Craig Muldrew, 'Class and Credit: Social Identity, Wealth and the Life Course in Early Modern England', in *Identity and Agency in England, 1500–1800*, ed. Henry French and Jonathan Barry (Basingstoke, 2004), 151–2; Muldrew, *Economy of Obligation*, 294, 303; Hoppit, *Risk and Failure*, 43; Earle, *The Making of the English Middle Class*, 129–30; Barker, *The Business of Women*, 128; Maxine Berg, 'Small Producer Capitalism in Eighteenth-Century England', *Business History* 35, no. 1 (1993): 17–39.

[46] Samantha Williams, *Poverty, Gender and Life-Cycle under the English Poor Law, 1760–1834* (Woodbridge, 2011), 126–7.

[47] Ilana Krausman Ben-Amos, 'Failure to Become Freemen: Urban Apprentices in Early Modern England', *Social History* 16, no. 2 (1991): 155–72.

[48] Gareth Stedman Jones, *An End to Poverty? A Historical Debate* (London, 2004), 32–3.

[49] Michael Mascuch, 'Social Mobility and Middling Self-Identity: The Ethos of British Autobiographers, 1600–1750', *Social History* 20, no. 1 (1995): 45–61; Daniel Vickers, 'Competency and Competition: Economic Culture in Early America', *The William and Mary Quarterly* 47, no. 1 (1990): 3–29.

eighteenth century, a large social class called 'the poor' existed in British society. The culmination of a century of changing agricultural practices and forms of landholding led to an increase in the wage-dependent population. Being poor was both an economic condition and a form of identity. Historians now recognise that the poor were not an undifferentiated mass, but that variations in experiences and identities existed, from the vagrant and settled poor to Paul Slack's conception of 'deep' and 'shallow' poverty.[50] Most studies, however, focus on institutionalised poverty and on the labouring poor. The swelling debtors' prison population makes visible a further form of economic distress in the eighteenth century: those who experienced downward mobility. These different forms of poverty were distinctive and did not necessarily overlap. By including downward mobility in our definition of poverty, material insecurity emerges as a condition that threatened a much wider group of people than we might imagine. While insecurity has always been recognised as an aspect of the lives of the labouring poor, it was part of the lived experience of the middling sorts as well.

While recognising a new social category of poverty, *Poverty of Disaster* builds on recent histories of class formation which conceptualise class identity as a language or a discourse open to constant negotiation rather than a stable category.[51] The development of class categories including the 'poor' to the 'middling' was murky and partial. The mutability of wealth made social identities and social structures unstable, turning social status into a precarious process of constant achievement rather than a fixed identity. Given the insecurity of financial status, traditional valuations of wealth and status are not necessarily the best guide to individual outcomes. By the eighteenth century, given the fragility of credit, people who might have seemed economically stable in fact were not. At the same time, individuals could feel poor or insecure without being poor according to traditional metrics. Insecurity was structured by belief, perception and projection.[52]

---

[50] Steve Hindle, *On the Parish? The Micro-Politics of Poor Relief in Rural England, c. 1550–1750* (Oxford, 2004); Paul Slack, *Poverty and Policy in Tudor and Stuart England* (London; New York, 1988); Paul Slack, *The English Poor Law 1531–1782* (Basingstoke, 1990); Tim Hitchcock and Robert B. Shoemaker, *London Lives: Poverty, Crime and the Making of a Modern City, 1690–1800* (Cambridge, 2015), 5; Williams, *Poverty, Gender and Life-Cycle under the English Poor Law, 1760–1834.*

[51] Wrightson, '"Sorts of People"', 38; Shepard, *Accounting for Oneself,* 6; David Rollinson, 'Discourse and Class Struggle: The Politics of Industry in Early Modern England', *Social History* 26 (2001): 166–89.

[52] Vail, 'Insecure Times', 20.

Class was supported by the assertion of difference. Most histories describe the social dynamics of class formation as playing out between people of unequal status. In the seminal theoretical texts on social distinction, Veblen and Bourdieu emphasise the communication of class and income differences between people of different social positions.[53] Keith Wrightson's account of the rise of the language of sorts suggests that the language of social differentiation which elites used in early modern England involved terminologies of dissociation with those below them.[54] Similarly, middling status was positioned against an upper boundary of gentility.[55] Marxist social histories emphasise the crystallisation of a working class through the exploitation of labour by those who owned capital.[56] In contrast to these histories, the culture of debt involved competition within the burgeoning middle class and struggles over fine gradations of status. For middling people facing insecurity, status was solidified by their attempts to shift the burdens of precariousness sideways. In the shadow of the debtors' prison, middling people protected their own solvency by shifting the burdens of debt onto others like themselves, contributing to processes of social distinction.

## Gender and Economic Man

Middling economic identities were closely bound with notions of gender through the trope of the economic man. The figure of *homo economicus*, an ideal type invented by John Stuart Mill in the nineteenth century, was foregrounded by economic thinkers in the eighteenth century, and came into its own as part of a watershed of industrial, scientific, financial and consumer revolutions which reorientated society towards being more acquisitive, industrious and driven by the desire for profit.[57] As a central figure in this transition, the modern economic man was defined by his self-interest and his rationality, in other words, his tendency to

---

[53] Thorstein Veblen, '"Conspicuous Consumption"', in *The Theory of the Leisure Class: An Economic Study of Institutions* (New York, 1902), 68–101; Pierre Bourdieu, *Distinction: A Social Critique of the Judgement of Taste* (London, 1979).

[54] Wrightson, '"Sorts of People"', 38–9; Wrightson, 'Estates, Degrees and Sorts', 46–7.

[55] French, *The Middle Sort of People*, 20, 29.

[56] Thompson, *The Making of the English Working Class*.

[57] Karl Polanyi, *The Great Transformation: The Political and Economic Origins of Our Time* (Boston, MA, 2001); Mokyr, *The Enlightened Economy*; Jacob, *The First Knowledge Economy*; P. G. M. Dickson, *The Financial Revolution in England: A Study in the Development of Public Credit, 1688–1756* (London, 1967); Wennerlind, *Casualties of Credit*; Berg, *Luxury and Pleasure in Eighteenth-Century Britain*.

make decisions based upon perceived utility. Adam Smith articulated the economic man's interests in his *Wealth of Nations*, where in a famous passage invoking the desires of the butcher, the brewer and the baker, he suggested that individuals were motivated to participate in the market out of self-love, and made decisions based upon 'the mechanics of utility'.[58] Similarly, Daniel Defoe wrote that men in trade were 'bound by their Interest; Gain is the end of Commerce'.[59] As a rational, selfish actor, economic man was relatively devoid of emotion. His behaviour was governed by virtues, especially prudence, but he acted without the passions of his predecessors, instead making decisions according to 'interest'.[60] He was also characterised by his autonomy and independence. Through his self-interest, he was atomised and able to choose and act in ways that were free from social obligation.

Since the foundational texts of Smith, Mills and others, neoclassical economists have searched for and celebrated rational, calculative behaviour and self-interest, and these features have come to define economic modernity. Yet there are numerous reasons to question the applicability of rational choice and self-interest to eighteenth-century culture. Intellectual histories argue that concepts of self-interest were prevalent well before Smith's time, and that his concept of 'self-love' was tempered by the need for sympathy and regard.[61] Furthermore, if contemporary economic writers emphasised profit and autonomy, in practice these ideas constituted only one strand of economic thought. Non-economic writers expressed concern over unstable risk taking and indebtedness.[62] Generations of scholars, led by E. P. Thompson's articulation of the 'moral economy', have traced how individuals made decisions based upon ethics and social relations, rather than on the desire for pure profit.[63] Credit

---

[58] Mary S. Morgan, 'Economic Man as Model Man: Ideal Types, Idealization and Caricatures', *Journal of the History of Economic Thought* 28, no. 1 (2006): 1–27; Albert O. Hirschman, *The Passions and the Interests: Political Arguments for Capitalism before Its Triumph* (Princeton, NJ, 1997).

[59] Adam Smith, *An Inquiry into the Nature and Causes of the Wealth of Nations*, ed. R. H. Campbell, Andrew S. Skinner and William B. Todd (Oxford, 1976), 21, 22–3, 35–6, 82–104, 526–7; Daniel Defoe, *An Essay upon Loans: Or, an Argument Proving That Substantial Funds Settled by Parliament, . . . Will Bring Inloans of Money to the Exchequer, in Spight of All the Conspiracies of Parties to the Contrary; . . . By the Author of the Essay upon Credit* (London, 1710).

[60] Hirschman, *The Passions and the Interests*.

[61] Pierre Force, *Self-Interest before Adam Smith: A Genealogy of Economicscience* (Cambridge, 2003); Patrick Neal, 'Hobbes and Rational Choice Theory', *The Western Political Quarterly* 41, no. 4 (1988): 635–52; Offer, 'Between the Gift and the Market', 451.

[62] Julian Hoppit, 'Attitudes to Credit in Britain, 1680–1790', *The Historical Journal* 33, no. 2 (1990): 305–22.

[63] E. P. Thompson, 'The Moral Economy of the English Crowd in the Eighteenth Century', *Past & Present*, no. 50 (1971): 76–136.

remained predominantly social. Individuals in the eighteenth century continued to emphasise a social rationality of trust in preference to self-interest.[64] Even by the nineteenth century, the shift to contract asserted by narratives of economic individualism was partial at best. Personal credit remained central to market relations, and credit was, according to Margot Finn, 'contingent upon dress, manner, verbal facility and connection', and drew upon 'the perceived verities of social capital rather than upon the monetary values of the cash nexus alone'.[65] Scholars have therefore argued for alternative models of 'homo-socius' or 'individuals-in-relation'.[66] Furthermore, economic individualism was tempered by Christian ethics.[67] Affluence and material wealth created challenges that contemporaries mitigated through charitable action and spiritual activity. In Matthew Kadane's account, one of the predominant concerns of merchants and tradespeople was to achieve a middle course between profit and piety.[68] Insecurity, with its emotional and social dimensions, further tempered the emergence of modern commercial practices. Insecurity and its emotional implications shaped the decisions that middling people made as they carried out their day-to-day work, engaged in commerce, extended credit and collected their debts.

*Homo economicus* provides an impoverished framework for understanding eighteenth-century economic life from the perspective of gender. Through this figure, the characteristics most highly valued in economics, including objectivity, separation and individual accomplishment, have come to be coded as masculine, while emotions, dependence and informal relations are associated with femininity.[69] Behavioural theories built around economic man emphasise choice while ignoring the legal, institutional and social constraints placed upon women, and they tend to ignore life cycle

---

[64] Craig Muldrew, 'Interpreting the Market: The Ethics of Credit and Community Relations in Early Modern England', *Social History* 18, no. 2 (1993): 163–83.

[65] Finn, *The Character of Credit*, 320.

[66] Paula England, 'Separative and Soluble Selves: Dichotomous Thinking in Economics', in *Feminism Confronts Homo Economicus: Gender, Law, and Society*, ed. Martha Albertson Fineman and Terence Dougherty (Ithaca, NY, 2005), 49.

[67] Brodie Waddell, *God, Duty and Community in English Economic Life, 1660–1720* (Woodbridge, 2012).

[68] Muldrew, *Economy of Obligation*, 127; Matthew Kadane, *The Watchful Clothier: The Life of an Eighteenth-Century Protestant Capitalist* (New Haven, CT, 2013).

[69] Michael Roberts, 'Recovering a Lost Inheritance', in *The Marital Economy in Scandinavia and Britain, 1400–1900*, ed. Maria Ågren and Amy Louise Erickson (Aldershot, 2005); Julie Nelson, 'Feminism and Economics', *Journal of Economic Perspectives* 9, no. 2 (1995): 133; Julie Nelson, 'Fearing Fear: Gender and Economic Discourse', *Mind and Society: Cognitive Studies in Economics and Social Sciences* 14, no. 1 (2015): 129.

experiences.[70] The idealisation of a 'separatist self' has devalued concern for nurture and community.[71] Thus, it fails to recognise and to account for forms of care, historically undertaken by women in the eighteenth-century household, as forms of legitimate work and as economically valuable activities. *Homo economicus* therefore fails to describe women's lives. But as this book argues, the trope of the independent, autonomous subject is not much better at describing men's gendered commercial experiences.

*Poverty of Disaster* applies gender analysis to male experiences, motivations and attitudes as they unfolded in the context of debt negotiation. It probes the limits of the eighteenth century's economic man and seeks to provide a more nuanced account of male lives. In so doing, it draws on methodologies and insights developed by studies of female economic practices. A gendered critique exposes the fictions of patriarchal autonomy. The independence of the male householder was fragile and rested on 'hidden dependences', including the labour of household members, and as Chapter 4 argues, men recognised their interdependence.[72] A gendered perspective also exposes the importance of the life cycle to male experiences. By envisioning the individual as an adult subject, *homo economicus* fails to describe life cycle stages that subjected men to forms of vulnerability and dependency, particularly in young and old age. Young men, who might later become household heads, occupied positions of subordination and claimed only semi-independent status. Early in adulthood, they were subjected to patriarchal authority rather than being recipients of its dividends.[73] Furthermore, models of economic manhood create a false dichotomy between men's autonomous, self-interested behaviour and women's connected, socially oriented behaviour.[74] Just as women ran businesses and made investments for profit, so men could be more orientated towards the social and the domestic, and their capacity for 'rational' choice was limited by family and social obligations. Finally, financial status, including both success and failure, was expressed in profoundly gendered terms for *both* men and women.[75]

---

[70] Jane Humphries and Carmen Sarasua, 'Off the Record: Reconstructing Women's Labor Force Participation in the European Past', *Feminist Economics* 18, no. 4 (2012): 57, 59.

[71] England, 'Separative and Soluble Selves', 32–8.

[72] D'Cruze, 'The Middling Sort in Eighteenth-Century Colchester', 182.

[73] Alexandra Shepard, 'Manhood, Credit and Patriarchy in Early Modern England c. 1580–1640', *Past & Present* 167, no. 1 (2000): 75–106.

[74] Nelson, 'Feminism and Economics'.

[75] Toby L. Ditz, 'Shipwrecked; or, Masculinity Imperiled: Mercantile Representations of Failure and the Gendered Self in Eighteenth-Century Philadelphia', *The Journal of American History* 81, no. 1 (1994): 51–80; Sandage, *Born Losers*.

## Middling Economic Culture

By telling the story of insecurity through middling eyes, facets of eighteenth-century economic culture, to which middling people were central, take on a different hue. One of these is the Consumer Revolution. Using probate inventories, historians have convincingly argued that eighteenth-century people came to own more material goods, filling their houses with furniture, china and other consumer durables which became cheaper and more widely accessible.[76] Middling people were the consumers of the eighteenth century. In pursuit of pleasure and luxury, they filled their houses with the plethora of new 'baubles' that became available during the Consumer Revolution. Shopping emerged as a form of leisure. Consumerism was central to cultural life.[77]

The pleasures of the material world have dominated accounts of consumer culture, but the recognition that most people lived in an insecure world contributes to recent efforts to question the experiences and motivations that we ascribe to consumption. Narratives of desire, pleasure and luxury have been questioned by studies that examine the limits of consumer empowerment and that recognise goods as financial resources.[78] Alexandra Shepard has recently argued that in a specie-poor economy, goods were conceptualised as forms of savings, and that female participation in consumption might be reconceptualised as a form of investment rather than as a cultural pastime.[79] By extension, experiences of distraint temper the characterisation of goods as emotional objects, showing instead their position in non-elite households as repositories of value.[80] The constant struggle to remain solvent and routine exposure to procedures of default meant that individuals experienced the world of goods through the process of loss as much as through the pleasures of acquisition.

Insecurity provides a framework to reinterpret the social context of consumer and commercial practices. One of the most important of these was politeness, defined by one contemporary writer as the 'dextrous

---

[76] Shammas, *The Pre-industrial Consumer*; Weatherill, *Consumer Behaviour*; Overton, *Production and Consumption*.

[77] McKendrick, Brewer and Plumb, *The Birth of a Consumer Society*.

[78] Julie Hardwick, 'Parasols and Poverty: Conjugal Marriage, Global Economy, and Rethinking the Consumer Revolution', in *Market Ethics and Practices, c.1300–1850*, ed. Simon Middleton and James E. Shaw (New York, 2018).

[79] Shepard, 'Crediting Women in the Early Modern English Economy'.

[80] Sarah Pennell, 'Happiness in Things? Plebeian Experiences of Chattel "Property" in the Long Eighteenth Century', in *Suffering and Happiness in England 1550–1850: Narratives and Representations: A Collection to Honour Paul Slack*, ed. M. J. Braddick and Joanna Innes (Oxford, 2017), 208–26.

management of our words and actions, whereby we make other people have better Opinion of us and of themselves'.[81] This prescriptive set of manners, which marked a shift from older prescriptions of civility and honour, was subscribed to especially by the middling sorts – Langford's famous 'polite and commercial people'.[82] It allowed those providing commercial and professional services to interact with different sorts of people and let people who did not know each other trade and resolve disputes without resorting to violence. Not only did politeness facilitate the ascent of the middling sorts, but as the 'rules by which the economic game is played', it helped to create a civil economy that allowed unprecedented economic expansion in Britain despite a lack of formal institutional regulation. These institutionalised behaviours were not externally enforced, but relied instead upon the functions of reputation, penalising those who deviated through damage to their credit.[83] The putative, aggressive form of interaction represented by the debtors' prison, however, might lead us to question polite economic culture and the civilising process of which it was a part, contributing to understandings of alternative forms of behaviour.[84]

## The Embodiment of Debt

Incarceration was not merely an abstract legal process. It was a deeply physical and visceral experience. Attending to that experience is crucial to understanding the nature of insecurity. As Lyndal Roper wrote, 'corporeal facts' are worth attending to because they 'have consequences for the experience and subjectivity of people in history'.[85] Insecurity not only impacted individuals' notions of selfhood and status, but also had deep implications for their corporeal experiences. Negotiations over credit and debt were embodied. During the processes of obtaining credit, the body

---

[81] Abel Boyer, 'On Conversation, Society, Civility, and Politeness', in *The English Theophrastus; or, Manners of the Age* (London, 1702), 108.

[82] Paul Langford, 'The Uses of Eighteenth-Century Politeness', *Transactions of the Royal Historical Society* 12 (2002): 316; Paul Langford, *A Polite and Commercial People: England 1727–1783* (Oxford, 1989); Lawrence Klein, 'Politeness for Plebes. Consumption and Social Identity in Early Eighteenth-Century England', in *The Consumption of Culture, 1600–1800: Image, Object, Text*, ed. Ann Bermingham and John Brewer (London, 1995), 362–82.

[83] Mokyr, *The Enlightened Economy*, 368–71; Avner Greif, *Institutions and the Path to the Modern Economy: Lessons from Medieval Trade* (Cambridge, 2006), 8.

[84] Helen Berry, 'Rethinking Politeness in Eighteenth-Century England: Moll King's Coffee House and the Significance of "Flash Talk"', *Transactions of the Royal Historical Society* 11 (2001): 65–81; Tawny Paul, 'A "Polite and Commercial People"? Masculinity and Economic Violence in Scotland, 1700–60', in *Nine Centuries of Man*, ed. Elizabeth Ewan and Lynn Abrams (Edinburgh, 2017), 203–22.

[85] Lyndal Roper, 'Beyond Discourse Theory', *Women's History Review* 19, no. 2 (1 April 2010): 317.

served as a means of communicating individual worth. By the eighteenth century, individuals conveyed character through their outward appearance. Adornment and clothing communicated status and identity, and hence they helped their owners to establish credit. As a young man newly arrived in London, James Boswell wrote of the 'effect of my external appearance and address' in establishing credibility. He recounted how through dress and behaviour, he convinced a tradesman to sell him a sword worth five guineas on credit.[86] While sartorial practices marked respectability and credibility, they also signalled debt and poverty. In Scotland, a law passed in 1669 required those individuals who had been in the debtors' prison to emerge wearing a 'dyvours' habit' (debtors' habit), a yellow and brown garment that covered their clothing and head. This cloak, which physically marked the body of the debtor, was still in use in 1771.[87] For the poor, clothing could serve as a marker of status or as a marker of discredit, if for example a person owned only his or her clothes. Clothing was generally discounted from assessments of a person's worth and was exempt from insolvency proceedings.[88]

When credit failed, the body assumed a central position in the interactions between creditors and debtors as a site where relationships of power and obligation were negotiated. Imprisonment served as a means for creditors to coerce their debtors into paying. The body was also a site of punishment, and punishing debtors was a means of deterrence, echoing the Foucauldian logic of corporeal punishment that was applied to criminals.[89] Inflicting harm on debtors became an accepted and functional means of negotiating indebted relationships in a way that counters more consensual and socially positive images of credit that have tended to dominate the historiography.

Finally, in the culture of credit, the body assumed a concrete rather than a symbolic form of value. The worth of people within the credit economy is normally understood in terms of ephemeral forms of reputation, their labour capacity or the goods they owned. But by the early eighteenth century, bodies also had concrete value. The consequence of the shift from material wealth to reputation as the basis for credit, described by Alexandra Shepard, was the commodification of the debtor's body. Men and women contracted credit on their personhood. If a debtor failed to

---

[86] James Boswell, *Boswell's London Journal, 1762–1763*, ed. Frederick A. Pottle (New Haven, CT, 1992), 59–60.
[87] Hugh Hannah, 'The Sanctuary of Holyrood', *Book of the Old Edinburgh Club* 15 (1927): 85.
[88] Shepard, *Accounting for Oneself*, 120–2.
[89] Michel Foucault, *Discipline and Punish: The Birth of the Prison* (New York, 1977).

repay that obligation, their body was taken to stand in for the debt, much like the object submitted to the pawnshop. The debtors' prison transformed people into forms of collateral, blurring the distinction between persons and things.[90]

## The Debtors' Prison

*Poverty of Disaster* reconstructs the insecurities of purse and person through the lens of Britain's debtors' prisons. By the eighteenth century, incarceration for failure to pay one's obligations became routine practice. Despite the recent emphasis on institutional economics, the debtors' prison has never been considered for its impact upon commercial life. Histories of the prison focus almost exclusively on penal incarceration, even though debtors made up the majority of Britain's prison population.[91] The prison fits into a longer history of institutions, which were central to how individuals related to one another and negotiated their economic and social relationships.[92] Middling people developed and used institutional resources like the courts and the parish to protect and defend their interests and to draw social boundaries. Legal courts have been described as the 'parliaments of the middling sort'.[93] Yet institutional histories prioritise organisations that facilitated commercial development, the exchange of knowledge and the establishment of trust through positive means, such as coffee houses and civil societies, rather than institutions of punishment or incarceration. Even court litigation is interpreted as representing a culture of reconciliation.[94] By contrast, histories of property crime suggest that institutions which performed punitive functions could be integral to

---

[90] Finn, *The Character of Credit*, 10; Amanda Bailey, *Of Bondage: Debt, Property, and Personhood in Early Modern England* (Philadelphia, PA, 2013).

[91] Michael Ignatieff, *A Just Measure of Pain: The Penitentiary in the Industrial Revolution, 1750–1850* (New York, 1978); Michael Meranze, *Laboratories of Virtue: Punishment, Revolution, and Authority in Philadelphia, 1760–1835* (Chapel Hill, NC, 1996); Peter Linebaugh, *The London Hanged: Crime and Civil Society in the Eighteenth Century* (Cambridge, 1992); Michele Lise Tarter and Richard Bell, eds., *Buried Lives: Incarcerated in Early America* (Athens, GA, 2012); Foucault, Discipline and Punish.

[92] See for example Mokyr, *The Enlightened Economy*. [93] French, *The Middle Sort of People*, 20.

[94] For accounts of neighbourly reconciliation, see J. A. Sharpe, '"Such Disagreement betwixt Neighbours": Litigation and Human Relations in Early Modern England', in *Disputes and Settlements: Law and Human Relations in the West*, ed. John Bossy (Cambridge, 1983), 167–88; Craig Muldrew, 'The Culture of Reconciliation: Community and the Settlement of Economic Disputes in Early Modern England', *The Historical Journal* 39, no. 4 (1996): 915–42. This vision has been contested by Tim Stretton, who suggests that litigation over penal bonds eroded neighbourly relations. See Tim Stretton, 'Written Obligations, Litigation and Neighbourliness, 1580–1680', in *Remaking English Society: Social Relations and Social Change in Early Modern England*, ed. Steve Hindle, Alexandra Shepard and John Walter (Woodbridge, 2013), 189–210.

economic policy and commercial life. The Bloody Codes sought to protect new forms of financial property, and Carl Wennerlind has convincingly argued that the imposition of the death penalty for counterfeiting was intended to restore confidence in the monetary system.[95] *Poverty of Disaster* builds upon this line of thinking, offering a new portrait of an institution that has rarely been considered, arguing that this putative resource helped to shape economic culture in the eighteenth century, but also that the lack of broader institutional regulation shaped the culture of debt.

## Book Structure

Debtors' prisons generated an extensive archival record, and they provide the historian with access to the fragile credit of a large and diverse population of individuals. As prison populations swelled, Parliament passed periodic Acts for the Relief of Insolvent Debtors. In the wake of these acts, the name of every man and woman who applied for release was published in the *London Gazette*, and an inventory of his or her wealth and debts was drawn up and lodged with the local Quarter Sessions. While the *Gazette* provides a broad, quantitative picture of the prison population, individual prisons also kept records of their populations in the form of commitment books and lists. The debt disputes that led to incarceration were preserved in local courts and discussed in surviving personal papers and diaries. Because imprisonment for debt was a controversial political issue, reform movements generated an archive of pamphlets and printed materials that provide insights into attitudes towards indebtedness and incarceration.

My methodology in approaching the legal archive related to debt differs from previous social history approaches. Social historians have developed a strong tradition of reading against the grain of legal records to access the everyday practices of ordinary individuals, using records generated by unusual moments of conflict and failure. Indeed, much of the historiography of credit practice has drawn upon records

---

[95] Carl Wennerlind, 'The Death Penalty as Monetary Policy: The Practice and Punishment of Monetary Crime, 1690–1830', *History of Political Economy* 36, no. 1 (1 March 2004): 131–61; J. M. Beattie, 'London Crime and the Making of the "Bloody Code" 1689–1718', in *Stilling the Grumbling Hive: The Response to Social and Economic Problems in England, 1689–1750*, ed. Lee Davison, Robert B. Shoemaker, Tim Keirn and Tim Hitchcock (Stroud, 1992), 49–76; Simon Devereaux, 'England's "Bloody Code" in Crisis and Transition: Executions at the Old Bailey, 1760–1837', *Journal of the Canadian Historical Association* 24, no. 2 (2013): 71–113; Randall McGowen, 'Making the "Bloody Code"? Forgery Legislation in 18th-Century England', in *Law, Crime and English Society 1660–1830*, ed. Norma Landau (Cambridge, 2002), 117–38.

of debt litigation.[96] While these methodologies have been essential to uncovering the complex world of credit and social relations, the scale of incarceration points towards a need to consider these records for their intended purposes: as institutional mechanisms through which people negotiated their debt relationships. By reading *along* rather than *against* the grain of debt litigation, the coercive apparatus that generated these records becomes apparent.[97]

*Poverty of Disaster* draws on records from both English and Scottish localities, including Edinburgh, Lancaster and London, chosen for the wealth of their extant evidence. The Edinburgh Tolbooth and Lancaster Castle were both important regional prisons, and they are two of the best-documented carceral institutions outside of London. English and Scottish case studies normally receive separate treatment because of their different legal and institutional systems. However, comparative analysis is both appropriate and fruitful. After the Union of 1707, Britain's economy and culture became slowly integrated. The urban experience in Britain was increasingly unified. Provincial capitals shared growing populations of middling people, movements towards Improvement and institutional resources. Common architectural, social and cultural trends meant that by the late eighteenth century, a recognisable 'urban culture' was evident across Britain. Cross-border commerce, participation in imperial trade, similar consumer practices and universal reliance on credit facilitated a broadly common British economic culture.[98] Yet despite these similarities, Scotland is often left out of British economic histories.

Comparative study of urban economic culture is especially productive because England and Scotland's distinctive legal systems generated different forms of evidence. These forms of evidence offer contrasting perspectives and insights into the core themes of this book. English records like the *London Gazette* facilitate a broad overview of the incarcerated population across multiple prisons, while legal records associated with Debtor Relief Acts provide access to trends in prisoner wealth. Scottish records, including prison commitment books, are more localised and attentive to the

---

[96] See for example Muldrew, *Economy of Obligation*; Spence, *Women, Credit, and Debt in Early Modern Scotland*.

[97] For a similar approach, which reads litigation for its antagonistic rather than neighbourly functions, see Stretton, 'Written Obligations'.

[98] Borsay, *The English Urban Renaissance*; R. H. Sweet, 'Topographies of Politeness', *Transactions of the Royal Historical Society* 12 (2002): 355–74; Robert Harris and Charles McKean, *The Scottish Town in the Age of Enlightenment 1740–1820* (Edinburgh, 2014); Stana Nenadic, 'Middle-Rank Consumers and Domestic Culture in Edinburgh and Glasgow 1720–1840', *Past & Present* 145, no. 1 (1994): 122–56.

imprisonment process and to individual narratives of distress. They facilitate better insights into the perspectives of the creditors responsible for
incarceration than do the English records, as well as opportunities for
gendered comparison of the components of credibility. These varying
perspectives provide the means for assessing the social mechanics of incarceration, the breadth of the prison population and the gendering of debt,
offering a window into the broad system of insecurity that was present
throughout Britain.

In tracing lives of insecurity, my focus is on the first three quarters of the
eighteenth century. While significant economic and social change has
traditionally been located in the late eighteenth and early nineteenth
centuries, Britain's industrialisation and economic growth are now understood to have been slower and more protracted. The late seventeenth and
early eighteenth centuries are now understood as a crucial moment of social
and economic change. Economic expansion placed pressure on credit,
pressure that was little relieved by the invention of new credit instruments
as part of the Financial Revolution. These years witnessed a profound
change in how individual credit and debt were assessed.[99] They saw the
culmination of shifts in legal culture, which drew litigants away from
common law. These changes caused a significant decline in civil litigation
throughout England, but they also placed increasing emphasis on the
prisons as spaces of negotiation.[100] *Poverty of Disaster* considers the culture
of debt in the decades between the culmination of these changes and 1770,
a period that would bring in a new era of change and a period of prison
reform that would change the landscape of failure. At the same time, these
decades witnessed marked improvement in living standards.[101] Narratives
of improvement provide a surprising backdrop to increasing insecurity,
calling into question the relationship between economic growth and
prosperity.

This book is structured in three parts which attend to the different forms
of insecurity that middling people faced: economic, social and corporeal. It
begins with an account of the structures of insecurity. Chapter 1 outlines
the demographics of imprisonment, revealing that incarceration for debt

---

[99] Shepard, *Accounting for Oneself.*
[100] Muldrew, *Economy of Obligation*, chapters 1–3; W. A. Champion, 'Recourse to the Law and the
Meaning of the Great Litigation Decline, 1650–1750: Some Clues from the Shrewsbury Local
Courts', in *Communities and Courts in Britain, 1150–1900*, ed. Christopher Brooks and
Michael Lobban (London, 1997), 179–98; Christopher Brooks, *Lawyers, Litigation and English
Society since 1450* (London, 1998).
[101] Broadberry et al., *British Economic Growth, 1270–1870*, 232.

was a routine practice and that middling people were especially vulnerable. Large numbers of middling men were incarcerated for debt during their lifetimes, and their imprisonments affected their households, neighbourhoods and business networks, so that imprisonment rippled through middling communities. Chapter 2 explains why middling people were so vulnerable to imprisonment through analysis of structures of credit and wealth. Drawing on debtors' schedules, or inventories of wealth generated by the imprisonment process, the credit networks and patterns of wealth-holding of middling households are reconstructed. I argue that the portions of middle-ranking wealth bound up in credit, changing structures of credit and middling people's positions within credit networks rendered them vulnerable to failure.

While financial structures made middling people vulnerable to imprisonment, they were not the only reasons for their insecurity. Imprisonment was also social and circumstantial. As a civil process, imprisonment for debt was the result of decisions made by creditors, based upon perceptions of a debtor's credibility and the shifting sands of reputation. Chapter 3 attends to the perspectives of creditors, a perspective not often attended to in studies of the debtors' prisons, which tend to focus on the plight of the incarcerated. Yet the positions and reasoning of those who used the prison as a tool are crucial to understanding insecurity. The chapter considers why creditors chose to send their debtors to prison and how it was in their interests to do so. Imprisonment depended upon how economic failure was perceived, as well as upon creditors' entangled financial, social and emotional positions. While imprisonment could provide a useful tool for enforcing contracts within an economy that offered little protection to those who lent money, the importance of emotion and social perceptions of failure tempers the weight that we afford to 'rational' decision-making within the modernising economy. Like credit, debt was understood as part of a moral economy.

The second section of this book attends to how notions of worth and failure were articulated and mobilised in a precarious economy. Insecurity is the starting point for understanding how individuals accounted for themselves and judged the debts of others. Chapters 4 and 5 turn to how debtors articulated their own sense of worth, and to the identity consequences of insecurity. The fragility of credit had implications for notions of selfhood and worth. In the eighteenth century, character was increasingly important in economic settings because a person's financial credibility depended upon his or her social reputation. A good name constituted a kind of currency. This was an economy of circulating selves. Yet the trappings of selfhood were highly unstable. Default was a function of belief and perception. Chapter 4 draws on defamation litigation from Edinburgh, making use of evidence generated by Scotland's unique legal context to compare the components of credibility for men and women and to explore the ways in which reputation was constructed and upheld, highlighting the importance of collective and interdependent notions of reputation and status within households. Strategies for mitigating risk and uncertainty involved the cooperation of husbands, wives and household dependents.

Chapter 5 focuses on constructions of occupational identity, which was central to constructions of selfhood. Drawing on diaries, it considers the precariousness of work not only as a function of maintenance, but also as a problem of identity. In an insecure economy, people took on multiple forms of employment in order to make ends meet. But because cultural constructions of male identity were closely tied to occupation, multiple employments complicated traditional associations between masculinity and work. The chapter investigates how men and their households established stable work identities while undertaking multiple forms of labour. For these types, work was not defined only as monetised labour, but also as an activity that was productive or that generated status and credit.

The final section of this book turns to the debtor's body. Experiences of insecurity were profoundly physical, borne out through the threat of confinement and the loss of liberty. Read through the lens of the prison, the life cycle of debt, from contracting credit, to insecurity, to default, was an embodied experience, and the ways in which debtors' bodies were treated have important implications for the characterisation of economic culture during Britain's transition to capitalism. Chapter 6 describes the body as a site for negotiated relations of power and obligation. By uncovering how creditors inflicted different forms of harm on debtors, from the denial of liberty to violent physical assault, it reveals the coercive nature of credit. Failure to abide by the rules of credit was dealt with by incarceration and physical punishment. In an era normally characterised by politeness and the decline of violence, the treatment of debtors instead reveals an economy tinged with aggression and even violence.

Chapter 7 anchors reputation and individual worth to the body. The transformation of bodies, from the able working body to the corpse, into forms of transmutable value, placed middling people's liberty at risk. Though being in debt was a ubiquitous feature of life for most individuals, debt became embodied especially at the moment of default. When a debtor failed to pay, British law gave creditors the power to arrest their debtors'

persons, and during that moment of arrest, the debtor's body was substituted for the value of the debt owed, temporarily transforming it into
a form of value.[102] Thus, the confinement of debtors created a conceptual
slippage between persons and things, with significant implications for
notions of selfhood and independence and for experiences of mobility.

Together, the following chapters offer a new vision of economic culture
during Britain's transition to capitalism. During a period of sustained
economic growth, the eighteenth century was, for many, a period of
insecurity. This insecurity had broad consequences for their social, economic and physical experiences. It shaped how they worked, produced and
consumed, and it shaped how they thought about themselves. If there was
one feature of life that defined the social experience of commerce in the
eighteenth century, it was the insecurity of being in debt.

[102] Finn, *The Character of Credit*, 10; Bailey, *Of Bondage*.

# PART I

## *Structures of Insecurity*

CHAPTER I

# The Scale of Incarceration
## Debt and the Middling Sort

For men and women in eighteenth-century Britain, financial failure seemed like a definite possibility. People read about it in the news-papers on a regular basis. In England, Daniel Defoe wrote in 1727 of the 'many Bankrupts and broken Tradesmen now among us, more than ever were known before'. In Scotland, James Boswell noted in 1759 that bankruptcies 'do actually happen almost every day, as must be known to every man who has been much conversant in the low or middling state of mankind'.[1] Edmund Burke would describe Britain in the later eighteenth century as 'a commonwealth of prisoners'.[2] The *London Gazette* was filled with notices of bankruptcy commissions and lists of imprisoned debtors released by Parliamentary Insolvency Acts, and these notices were as widely attended to and as sensationalised as foreign news.[3] Six thousand names were listed in 1712 alone. More than 8,000 names were listed in 1729. Popular prints depicted moments of distress, of debtors harassed by their creditors, of families unable to pay the rent and of men suddenly unable to support the household.[4] Diarists fretted in pen and paper about their financial obligations and expressed fears of falling into debt. The stonemason Thomas Parsons of Bath wrote in 1769 of being 'harrass'd and perplex'd for money', and worried 'am in debt and know not how to pay'. Diarists, from Samuel Pepys to the shopkeeper Ralph Josselin, recorded dreams about falling into debt and being arrested. John

---

[1] Defoe, *The Compleat English Tradesman*, v; *Scots Magazine*, April 1759, 675.
[2] 'Mr Grey's Motion for a Committee on the Effects of Imprisonment for Debt, May 12, 1791', in *Cobbett's Parliamentary History of England*, vol. 29 (London, 1817), 513–14.
[3] Natasha Glaisyer, '"A Due Circulation in the Veins of the Publick": Imagining Credit in Late Seventeenth- and Early Eighteenth-Century England', *The Eighteenth Century* 46, no. 3 (2005): 263.
[4] See for example William Hogarth, *The Distrest Poet*, 1737; *The Bubblers Mirrour: Or England's Folly*, 1720; Moses Vanderbank, *A Noted Bard. Writing a Poem in Blank Verse to Lay before Sr R – on the Great Necessity at This Time for an Act of Insolvency*, 1737.

Cannon   recounted   the experiences of creditors 'coming on me so fast that I could not answer immediately and was arrested'.[5]

Being in debt was a completely normal part of life in eighteenth-century Britain. Credit provided the lynchpin of the economy. People borrowed for many reasons. Shortages of coinage meant that men and women completed their day-to-day purchases by using credit. Others relied on credit to sustain themselves while they waited for their wages to be paid. Those who borrowed for trade or manufacture took on debt as a form of risk and relied on credit to sustain their business enterprises. Given credit's wide circulation, most people were in debt most of the time. Most of these debts were paid, cancelled out through the reciprocal exchange of credit, renegotiated or forgiven. However, sometimes debtors 'broke' or became unable to honour their obligations.

If insecurity felt like a pervasive threat to many eighteenth-century men and women, quantifying it is an endeavour fraught with difficulty. Unlike other forms of financial distress, which can be measured using institutional determinants such as tax and poor law records, insecurity took varied and inconsistent forms, and it was characterised as much by social perception as it was by strict financial thresholds. As Scott Sandage suggests, 'success or failure often depended on the story that a man could tell about his own life – or that others could tell about him.'[6] Failure was impressionistic and fuelled by a climate of economic anxiety.[7] Yet previous studies suggest that many households were unable to sustain financial security. Julian Hoppit's research on bankruptcy calculated that 33,000 businesses went bankrupt in the eighteenth century. Peter Earle suggests that in the 1710s and 1720s, 15 per cent of the big bourgeoisie in London failed, and that financial instability put as many as half of middling urban households 'at risk' of failure. Craig Muldrew's analysis of probate accounts from the late seventeenth century reveals that one quarter of households in England had moveable assets worth less than their debts and were thus spending more than they were earning. Hannah Barker's analysis of trade directories from northern cities in the late eighteenth century discovered that at least 10 per cent of businesses disappeared from the record, and that small

---

[5] Henry E. Huntington Library, San Marino, California (hereafter HEH), Thomas Parsons, 'Diary, 1769, Jan.–Aug.', 27 January 1769, f. 20, HM 62593. John Money, ed., *The Chronicles of John Cannon, Excise Officer and Writing Master* (Oxford, 2010), 174.

[6] Sandage, *Born Losers*, 9.

[7] Julian Hoppit, *A Land of Liberty? England, 1689–1727* (Oxford, 2000), 4–5.

family firms were the most vulnerable.[8] According to these determinants, contemporary fears seem to have been realised.

Bankruptcy, probate material and tax records have provided useful sources for examining downward mobility.[9] An examination of the debtors' prison makes visible an additional population experiencing insecurity. Eighteenth-century commentators considered incarceration to be a form of poverty and an important marker of downward social mobility. Defoe's concept of the 'poverty of disaster' was echoed in Haine's treatise on governing the poor, which classed prisoners for debt alongside vagrants and beggars.[10] Meanwhile, a prison relief society considered prisoners to be people 'reduced to poverty' and described how the imprisoned debtor, his property confiscated, was 'turned into the world in a state of poverty and misery'.[11] This was the institution through which the middle ranks of society experienced economic distress.

By the eighteenth century, incarceration for debt was a routine practice rather than an exceptional experience. Yet debtors are rarely recognised in histories of imprisonment. Histories of incarceration have been written largely from the perspective of crime and penal reform, even though debtors were by far the largest group of prisoners in eighteenth-century Britain.[12] They made up the majority of prison populations, even during the seasons when local assize courts met (which should have resulted in a temporary increase in penal incarceration). John Howard's survey of the English prisons in the 1770s counted 4,084 prisoners, 2,437 of whom were debtors. In the Edinburgh Tolbooth, Scotland's largest prison, debtors made up 69 per cent of the prison population during the period 1720–70.[13]

---

[8] Hoppit, *Risk and Failure*, 43; Earle, *The Making of the English Middle Class*, 129–30; Muldrew, *Economy of Obligation*, 294, 303; Barker, *The Business of Women*, 128; Berg, 'Small Producer Capitalism in Eighteenth-Century England'.

[9] See Hoppit, *Risk and Failure*, 43; Bruce H. Mann, *Republic of Debtors: Bankruptcy in the Age of American Independence* (Cambridge, MA, 2002); Balleisen, *Navigating Failure*; Safley, *The History of Bankruptcy*; Barker, *The Business of Women*, 128–30.

[10] Richard Haines, *A Model of Government for the Good of the Poor and the Wealth of the Nation . . . the Stock Rais'd and Presented, All Poor People and Their Children for Ever Comfortable Provided for, All Idle Hands Employed . . . All Beggars and Vagrants for the Future Restrained, Poor Prisoners for Debt Relieved, and Malefactors Reclaimed* (London, 1678). Thanks to David Hitchcock for this reference.

[11] Society for the Discharge and Relief of Persons Imprisoned for Small Debts, ed. *An Account of the Rise, Progress and Present State of the Society for the Discharge and Relief of Persons Imprisoned for Small Debts throughout England and Wales* (London, 1774), xlviii, 32.

[12] Ignatieff, *A Just Measure of Pain*; Meranze, *Laboratories of Virtue*; Linebaugh, *The London Hanged*; Tarter and Bell, *Buried Lives*; Foucault, *Discipline and Punish*.

[13] Randall McGowen, 'The Well-Ordered Prison, England 1780–1865', in *The Oxford History of the Prison: The Practice of Punishment in Western Society*, ed. Norval Morris and David J Rothman (Oxford, 1998), 73–81; Hitchcock and Shoemaker, *London Lives*, 103; NRS, ETWLB, 1720–70, HH11/11–28.

Furthermore, debtors and criminals had distinctive experiences of incarceration. In the unreformed prisons, debtors were the only class of long-term prisoner. They were normally held for a period of at least months, if not years, while those accused of crimes normally remained in prison for a period of several days or weeks.[14] Debtors were also the only prisoners for whom incarceration could be considered punitive. Prior to the development of the penitentiary, which introduced the prison as a form of reform and solitary punishment, prisons served primarily as spaces where individuals were held before trial.[15] Debtors, however, were incarcerated because they failed to pay a debt.[16] The numerical dominance of debtors in British prisons, the functions of these spaces and the social dynamics that surrounded them might lead us to see these institutions less as tools to attack criminality, and more as forms of economic sanction. The eighteenth-century debtors' prison was not, as Foucault has suggested, primarily a response to disquiet about public punishment.[17]

This chapter establishes the prominence of the debtors' prison to eighteenth-century economic life, and focuses on three central questions: How did individuals end up in prison, who were they, and how common were their stories? The answers to these questions provide a framework for understanding the role that failure and insecurity played in shaping middling identities and in recasting how we might characterise the economic culture of eighteenth-century Britain. In an economy based upon credit, the debtors' prison defined a middling world of debt insecurity.

## The Legal Context of Failure

Not everyone who was indebted could not pay, and not everyone who could not pay went to prison. The prison population was shaped by the law. Incarceration was the result of specific legal processes of insolvency, and it fit within a wider legal universe that involved multiple and changing institutions and processes. The risk of imprisonment varied depending on the kinds of activities debtors engaged in, how much they owed, and because debt laws differed in England and Scotland, where they lived.

---

[14] NRS, ETWLB, 1720–70, HH11/11–28.

[15] Hitchcock and Shoemaker, *London Lives*, 325–30. The exception was the use of the prisons by local magistrates, who could hand down prison sentences for minor offenses such as vagrancy in summary sessions without a jury.

[16] My interpretation differs from that of Finn, who sees prisons primarily as spaces for the safe custody of inmates' bodies. Finn, *The Character of Credit*, 110.

[17] Michel Foucault, *Discipline and Punish: The Birth of the Prison* (New York, 1977).

A debt could be enforced in many ways. However, by the eighteenth century, recent changes in legal procedure made arresting a debtor one of the cheapest and most expedient ways for creditors to pursue what they were owed.

Early modern England has often been characterised as a litigious society. Going to law was a normal and preferred means of resolving disputes, and most of the cases heard at court were cases of debt.[18] However, from the 1680s, England witnessed a sharp decline in civil lawsuits in both central and local courts, which reached its nadir by 1750.[19] Rising costs in the form of lawyer fees and new court charges put the law beyond the reach of many litigants.[20] Inefficiency made settling conflicts through litigation much less desirable. The traditional common law procedure used to pursue commercial debts and informal transactions, called assumpsit, was lengthy and gave defendants significant scope to delay proceedings. Furthermore, it kept significant portions of debtor property off limits to creditors. The process most commonly used to pursue debtors' property, the writ of elegit, allowed creditors to pursue a debtor's goods and chattels; however, it protected immoveable property. Wages could not be garnished. New and increasingly prevalent forms of property in the eighteenth century, such as money, annuities, bonds and stock in funded companies, were exempt from the process of default, as were landholdings and debts owing to debtors. A debtor's bed, bedding, clothing and tools of trade were also protected.[21]

As commerce and credit expanded, litigants and their legal counsel sought out new ways of enforcing their debts. From the late seventeenth century, they turned increasingly to a combination of writs called *latitat* (also known as the mesne process), which enabled plaintiffs to arrest and hold defendants to bail before their cases had gone to trial. This mode of procedure had been available from the early sixteenth century, but only became a regular feature of Common Pleas practice after the introduction of new writs by Chief Justice Francis North in the 1670s, and was soon

---

[18] Muldrew, *Economy of Obligation*; Sharpe, "'Such Disagreement betwixt Neighbours'"; Martin Ingram, *Church Courts, Sex and Marriage in England, 1570–1640* (Cambridge, 1990).

[19] Muldrew, *Economy of Obligation*, 237; Brooks, *Lawyers, Litigation, and English Society*, 31–2; Champion, 'Recourse to the Law', 180.

[20] Brooks, *Lawyers, Litigation, and English Society*, 46–9.

[21] Paul Haagen, 'Imprisonment for Debt in England and Wales' (PhD thesis, Princeton University, 1986), 30; Paul Haagen, 'Eighteenth Century English Society and the Debt Law', in *Social Control and the State: Historical and Comparative Essays*, ed. Stanley Cohen and Andrew Scull (Oxford, 1983), 225; Christopher Brooks, *Law, Politics and Society in Early Modern England* (Cambridge, 2008), 318–19; Brooks, *Lawyers, Litigation, and English Society*, 34.

matched in local jurisdictions.[22] As creditors turned increasingly to these processes, arrest became the preferred means of bypassing common law procedure to enforce debts. In addition to being faster and less expensive, arrest circumvented the protections afforded to certain kinds of property. By arresting a debtor, a creditor could coerce him or her into handing over property against which the creditor had no legal claim.

The system of bypassing lengthy court processes and turning immediately to arrest was not matched north of the border. In Scotland, the process of incarceration involved a longer and more complicated series of procedures. Debtors tended to be imprisoned at different points in the legal process. In Scotland, a creditor could not pursue a debtor's body until he or she had been charged to pay a debt by the court and a period of 15 days had passed, allowing the debtor to fulfil the court's judgement. Only then could a creditor obtain a 'warrant of poinding' from the court, authorising execution against a debtor's property, or initiate an 'act of warding', which authorised execution against a debtor's body. Scottish legal processes did not incentivise arrest, as did the law in England. Imprisonment before judgement was rare because the law required creditors to prove with substantive evidence that a debtor was actively preparing to flee, and could become liable for damages if the court deemed the evidence submitted to be inadequate.[23]

The ways in which creditors could handle debtors' failure to repay also depended upon the size of the debt and the activity or occupation of the debtor. Incarceration fit within a tripartite division of debt, in which debtors were classified as bankrupts, insolvents or petty debtors. At the higher end of the financial spectrum in England, after the passage of the Bankruptcy Act in 1706, bankruptcy was available to 'traders' owing debts of at least £100 to a single individual.[24] By allowing traders to submit their effects to be distributed amongst creditors, the key point of bankruptcy was to limit imprisonment of the merchant's body. In Scotland, there was no process of bankruptcy until 1772, but a related process called *cessio bonorum* allowed insolvent debtors to 'submit their all' to creditors in return for the safety of their bodies. Unlike in England, there were no debt thresholds or limits based upon debtors' activity.[25]

[22] Brooks, *Law, Politics and Society*, 318–19; Brooks, *Lawyers, Litigation, and English Society*, 34; Champion, 'Recourse to the Law', 191.

[23] George Joseph Bell, *Commentaries on the Laws of Scotland, and on the Principles of Mercantile Jurisprudence. Considered in Relation to Bankruptcy; Competition of Creditors; and Imprisonment for Debt* (Edinburgh, 1810), 577, 596; Anthony Macmillan, *Forms of Writings Used in Scotland, in the Most Common Cases*. The second edition, with considerable additions (Edinburgh, 1786), 204.

[24] Hoppit, *Risk and Failure*, 32, 18, 36, 142.　　[25] Bell, *Commentaries on the Laws of Scotland*, viii.

At the opposite end of the financial spectrum, petty debts were enforced in equity courts called 'Courts of Conscience' in England or the 'Ten Merk Court' in Scotland. These local courts, which dispensed summary justice, normally dealt with obligations of less than 40s., or in Scotland 10s. 9d. (10 Scottish 'merks').[26] Developed from the mid-eighteenth century, they were a response to the proliferation of consumer credit. Summary courts facilitated the easy collection of consumer debt by shopkeepers and trades-people, and they often involved litigants at the lower ends of the social spectrum, primarily labourers and those without substantial property.[27] Summary courts developed a system of installation payments, thus secur-ing creditors' interests while protecting the poor from ruinous and punitive forms of debt collection.[28] By bypassing formalities and limiting the role of legal professionals, these courts made access to justice more affordable and the process of law more efficient.

In England, those debtors in the middle, who owed 40s. or more and less than £100, and who were unable to meet the occupational criteria for bank-ruptcy, were subject to insolvency law, in which creditors were given access to debtors' bodies as one means of resolving disputes over debt. Common law insolvency processes put the middling debtor's body at much higher risk of being imprisoned than the bankrupt merchant or the petty debtor. Debtors who owed between 40s. and £100 ended up in prison in the highest numbers, forming 86 per cent of incarcerated debtors (Table 1.4). The mesne in 'mesne process' even meant 'middle'.[29] In contrast to bankruptcy or summary justice, insolvency made the coercive power of the prison the most attractive option available to creditors. While English law gave creditors very limited power over their debtors' property, they were afforded broad powers to arrest debt-ors' bodies and nearly unregulated power to hold their debtors in prison.[30]

Being a middling person, then, was not only a social status defined by indicators of wealth, work or appearance. It was a legal status defined by an absence of regulation, which created insecurity. Middling people ended up in prison because two other forms of law failed to protect their bodies, and middling creditors used the prisons because debt laws failed to protect their financial interests. While bankruptcy reform and the establishment of summary courts established systems to regulate the conflicts over debt at

---

[26] Finn, *The Character of Credit*, 202–3; Hoppit, *Risk and Failure*, 32; David M. Walker, *A Legal History of Scotland, Vol. 5, The Eighteenth Century* (Edinburgh, 1998), 599. Edinburgh City Archives (hereafter ECA), Edinburgh Town Council Minutes, 13 May 1795, SL1/1/123.
[27] Hoppit, *Risk and Failure*, 33.  [28] Brooks, *Lawyers, Litigation, and English Society*, 43–4.
[29] Jerry White, *Mansions of Misery: A Biography of the Marshalsea Debtors' Prison* (London, 2016), 7.
[30] Haagen, 'Imprisonment for Debt', 28.

the high and low ends of the financial spectrum, Parliament did very little
to reform and restructure the insolvency laws that affected middling
people. Legislative attempts to modify the impact of arrest included
a 1725 statute which restricted arrest on the mesne process to cases where
the amount in dispute was more than £10, thereby depriving creditors of
the cheapest means of coercing the payment of small sums of money, thus
forcing creditors to pursue cases through to verdict, and ensuring that there
was a high cost to pursuing smaller debtors.[31] Rather than reforming debt
laws, lawmakers passed periodic and controversial insolvency acts that
cleared the prisons of their swelling populations.[32] Periodic declarations
of amnesty, echoing the biblical process of 'jubilee', thus became a feature
of how the eighteenth-century credit economy was practised.[33]

The eighteenth-century economy is often characterised by the rise of
institutional intermediaries, which facilitated a less emotive and more abstract
code of market ethics, improving market efficiency and facilitating commercial expansion.[34] Despite the recent emphasis on institutional economics, for
middling debtors, economic experience was shaped rather by a lack of
institutional regulation. Britain's middling tradespeople, who were central
to the eighteenth century's commercial expansion, were remarkably ill served
by the legal system. Personal papers provide glimpses of creditors attempting
to keep debt disputes out of the legal system so that they could be more
equitably resolved. The shopkeeper William Stout recounted in his diary how,
when it became evident that his neighbour William Godsalve 'could not
continue to trade or answer his crediters', Stout and other creditors devised
a resolution to keep Godsalve out of debtors' prison by persuading him to
assign his creditors to manage. Stout saw the solution as effective because it
ensured 'the payment of his just debts . . . and not to suffer them to be spent in
suit by atturneys, whereby some got all and others got nothing'.[35]

## The Mechanics of Imprisonment

The experience of incarceration was shaped not only by legal and institutional structures, but also by individual decisions and social negotiation.

---

[31] Brooks, *Lawyers, Litigation, and English Society*, 34.
[32] Haagen, 'Eighteenth Century English Society and the Debt Law', 223.
[33] David Graeber, *Debt: The First 5,000 Years* (Brooklyn, 2014), 2, 82, 390.
[34] See for example Mokyr, *The Enlightened Economy*; Greif, *Institutions and the Path to the Modern Economy*.
[35] J. D. Marshall, ed., *The Autobiography of William Stout of Lancaster, 1665–1752* (Manchester, 1967), 156–7.

Imprisonment for debt was part of a civil process enforced by creditors upon their debtors, and facilitated by semi-privatised state institutions. Incarceration involved a complex arrangement of formal and informal actions involving multiple spaces, multiple actors and complex motivations on the part of those people involved. Though historians tend to see imprisonment as the endpoint in a relationship of debt, prison is more accurately characterised as part of a longer progression. The debtors' prison was not merely a building, but was rather a process that included all the actions, reactions and behaviours of different actors, leading ultimately to the confinement of the debtor's body.

'Desperate debts', or debts that creditors understood that their debtors would be unable to pay, were a typical part of the credit system. Every account book included debts listed as 'desperate' or 'forgiven', and debtors described as 'broke'. The middling diarist John Cannon noted when balancing his accounts that he held debts 'from ten or a dozen particular persons not worth a penny'.[36] Anticipating that not all debts could be collected, tradespeople built an element of bad debts into their pricing.[37] Unpaid debts, however, could also become intolerable, and could constitute a significant loss of savings for the average creditor. When they did, creditors dealt with recalcitrant debtors in a range of ways. Imprisonment took place within a wider context of recourse that included different formal legal options, as well as informal, para-judicial and infra-judicial actions.[38] As the most common legal form of debt collection, arrest assumed a similar role to that played by litigation a century earlier, wherein the threat of incarceration could force different forms of reconciliation.[39]

The long descent to the debtors' prison normally began with a 'dunning'. Often carried out by women, and traditionally on Saturdays, dunning meant calling on the debtor and requesting that he or she honour the debt. Being dunned was the first step in losing one's credit and gaining a reputation for being unable to pay. As Defoe made clear, the timely payment of debts was an important component of honour, and a tradesperson would 'suffer in reputation by every day's delay'. By contrast, the person who paid 'tolerably well, and without dunning, is a good man, and in credit; shall be trusted any where, and keeps up

---

[36] Money, *Chronicles of John Cannon*, 173.
[37] Anthony Trollope, *London Tradesmen* (London; New York, 1927), 8–9.
[38] Benoît Garnot, 'Justice, infrajustice, parajustice et extra justice dans la France d'Ancien Régime', *Crime, Histoire & Sociétés / Crime, History & Societies* 4, no. 1 (2000): 103–20.
[39] For comparisons with early modern litigation, see Muldrew, 'The Culture of Reconciliation'; Sharpe, '"Such Disagreement betwixt Neighbours"'.

a character in his business'.[40] Individuals therefore went to great lengths to honour and to keep track of their debts.[41] If after dunning, the debtor still failed to honour the obligation, the creditor might resort to other informal means of exerting pressure. This could include threatening legal action or threatening to harm the debtor's reputation. The objective was to force debtors to hand over moveable wealth, or if they had little property of their own, that they might call on friends or family to pay the debt for them. The options pursued varied according to individual circumstances, mitigated by social relations and obligations and knowledge of a debtor's circumstances. Normally, only failing informal pressure would creditors begin to pursue the formal legal options that led to imprisonment.

As creditors pursued the formal and informal means of collecting debts, debtors faced multiple but circumscribed options as well. As their financial situations worsened, they might consider fleeing either abroad or to a debtors' sanctuary like the London Mint or Holyrood Abbey in Edinburgh. The physical mobility forced by debt was in fact so common that after Parliament passed the Mint Act in 1723, which gave amnesty to those inside, 4 per cent of London's adult male population applied for relief. In England, debtors could evade arrest by remaining locked in their own homes, as the law prevented bailiffs from forcibly entering private dwellings.[42] If a bailiff arrived at their house, debtors had three immediate options. First, they could pay the debt and the arrest fees, an unlikely route given that most of their resources were drained in the negotiations leading to imprisonment. Second, they could secure their liberty by paying bail and finding the support of two householders to act as cautioners. However, the bail demanded was normally up to four times the value of the debt, and thus was impossible for most debtors to pay. Third, they could submit to imprisonment.[43]

The experience of being arrested varied from place to place, from prison to prison and from person to person. In larger towns, debtors and creditors negotiated complex urban geographies of debt that included a matrix of different institutions and spaces of semi-confinement that offered debtors different degrees of liberty and opportunities for evasion. In the period

[40] Defoe, *The Compleat English Tradesman*, 350, 357.

[41] Jeremy Boulton, 'Microhistory in Early Modern London: John Bedford (1601–1667)', *Continuity and Change* 22, no. 1 (2007): 117–18, 128.

[42] Haagen, 'Imprisonment for Debt', 300, 20.

[43] William Blackstone, *Commentaries on the Laws of England*, vol. 3 (Oxford, 1765), 353. For a fuller description of the process of arrest, see Nicola Phillips, *The Profligate Son: Or, A True Story of Family Conflict, Fashionable Vice, and Financial Ruin in Regency Britain* (New York, 2013); Haagen, 'Imprisonment for Debt', 1–6.

leading to imprisonment, recently arrested debtors were taken to lockup houses, 'sponging houses', private residences or taverns where they could pay for accommodation while attempting to secure bail and negotiate with creditors. Those committed to prison might purchase partial liberty by paying bail to the gaoler for the privilege to reside in the 'Rules', defined areas around the prison in which debtors could move about freely.[44] Outside of London, however, the option to inhabit spaces of partial confinement was more limited. According to John Howard's survey, Rules existed in only two prisons outside of London.[45] As one contemporary traveller wrote, the difference between York and King's Bench was that 'at York a Prisoner never goes without the Walls; but from the Fleet and Kings Bench, in a Hackney Coach, one may go privately anywhere.'[46]

Prisons subjected debtors to a variety of conditions, depending upon their social status and their location. London and some provincial capitals, including York and Lancaster, had dedicated debtors' prisons. These institutions often contained distinctive spaces where prisoners with means could rent separate accommodations and purchase a relative degree of comfort. For example, the Fleet and Marshalsea prisons in London had different spaces known as the 'masters' side' and the 'common side'. Those in the masters' side rented and furnished their own apartments. They could receive visitors and entertain, and they could spatially demarcate themselves from the more desperate and lower-status debtors in the common side.[47] By contrast, most provincial debtors were sent to town gaols or tolbooths where they were incarcerated along with vagrants and criminals (although they were normally housed in separate rooms). Of the 300 known spaces of confinement in eighteenth-century Britain, most were little more than a gatehouse or cellar.[48] Even those towns with larger prisons lacked dedicated institutions to house debtors. In Edinburgh, for example, the Tolbooth was a building 62 feet long by 33 feet wide adjoining the city's main cathedral. Its four stories were divided into 14 small

---

[44] Finn, *The Character of Credit*, 116–17; John Howard, *The State of the Prisons in England and Wales, with Preliminary Observations, and an Account of Some Foreign Prisons and Hospitals*, 2nd edn (Warrington, 1780), 386, 468.

[45] Howard, *State of the Prisons*; Haagen, 'Eighteenth Century English Society and the Debt Law', 227.

[46] John Macky, *A Journey through England: In Familiar Letters from a Gentleman Here, to His Friend Abroad* (London, 1722), 208.

[47] Finn, *The Character of Credit*, 120; Joanna Innes, 'The King's Bench Prison in the Later Eighteenth Century: Law, Authority and Order in a London Debtor's Prison', in *An Ungovernable People: The English and Their Law in the Seventeenth and Eighteenth Centuries*, ed. John Brewer and John A. Styles (London, 1980), 265–6.

[48] McGowen, 'The Well-Ordered Prison, England 1780–1865', 73.

apartments that separated men from women and debtors from felons, and also included a common hall and a taproom.[49]

English and Scottish law gave debtors different means of avoiding confinement and obtaining release. In England, those arrested before trial could pay the amount demanded or put up bail. Debtors imprisoned on the mesne process were automatically released under a *supersedeas* unless their creditors chose to pursue the case further. However, most were never able to apply for release because of the cost of obtaining the appropriate writ. The mesne process only kept debtors in prison until they were tried (although this period could last up to one year), but creditors could also choose to imprison debtors after trial through a writ of *capias ad satisfaciendum*, which allowed them to hold their debtors in prison indefinitely until the debt was paid.[50] Those imprisoned after trial were therefore theoretically subjected to indefinite incarceration and released at the consent of their creditors, but prisoners could also apply for release under Acts of Grace or the 1729 and later 'Lords' Acts', wherein the court could order the creditors of destitute debtors to pay 4d per day for the debtors' subsistence (known as 'groats'), and release the debtors after six weeks if the creditors failed to pay.[51] Others were released by Parliamentary Acts for the Relief of Insolvent Debtors, passed periodically between 1695 and 1824, in which debtors were released in return for drawing up an inventory of their estate to be sold and distributed amongst creditors.

In Scotland, three primary mechanisms were available for release. The first, as in England, was satisfaction of the debt or the consent of creditors, usually indicating an informal agreement. Second, debtors could apply for the Act of Grace, which was akin to England's Lords' Acts. Enacted by the Scottish Parliament in 1696, the Act of Grace charged the creditors of those deemed too poor to aliment themselves with the responsibility of maintaining their imprisoned debtors or consenting to the debtors' liberty.[52] The third mechanism for release in Scotland was the process of *cessio bonorum* or 'submitting their all'. Effectively a precursor to bankruptcy,

---

[49] Robert Miller, *The Municipal Buildings of Edinburgh. A Sketch of Their History for Seven Hundred Years Written Mainly from the Original Records ... With an Appendix Suggesting Improvements and Extensions to the Present Buildings in the Royal Exchange* (Edinburgh, 1895), 37.

[50] Haagen, 'Eighteenth Century English Society and the Debt Law', 225.

[51] Haagen, 'Imprisonment for Debt', 6; Haagen, 'Eighteenth Century English Society and the Debt Law', 226.

[52] Act of Parliament 1696 c. 32 anent the alimenting of poor prisoners. English debt legislation, including periodic Insolvent Debtor Relief Acts, did not apply in Scotland. See *An Abridgment of the Public Statutes in Force and Use Relative to Scotland, from the Union, ... to the Twenty-Seventh ... George II. ... In Two Volumes* (Edinburgh, 1755).

Table 1.1 *Incarceration time, Edinburgh, Lancaster and London, 1720–1770*

| Incarceration time | London Fleet and King's Bench | | Lancaster Castle | | Edinburgh Tolbooth | |
|---|---|---|---|---|---|---|
| | *N* | % | *N* | % | *N* | % |
| < 1 month | *146* | 13.0 | *8* | 3.5 | *521* | 81.8 |
| 1–6 months | *356* | 31.8 | *58* | 25.3 | *98* | 15.4 |
| 6 months–1 year | *277* | 24.8 | *78* | 34.1 | *8* | 1.3 |
| > 1 year | *340* | 30.4 | *85* | 37.1 | *10* | 1.6 |
| Total | *1,119* | | *229* | | *637* | |

*Sources:* TNA, Fleet Prison Commitment Books, 1736, 1745–8, 1770–2, PRIS 1/6, PRIS 1/10, PRIS 10/21; King's Bench 1747–8, PRIS 4/2; Lancashire Record Office (hereafter LRO), Preston, Lancashire Courts of Quarter Sessions (hereafter LCQS), Insolvent Debtor Papers, Lists of Debtors in Lancaster Castle, 1724, 1736, 1742, 1755, QJB/10, QJB30/1–3, QJB/31, QSP/1243/7; National Records of Scotland (hereafter NRS), Edinburgh Tolbooth Warding and Liberation Books (hereafter ETWLB), 1720, 1730, 1740, 1740, 1750, 1760, 1769, HH11/11, 12, 17, 20, 23, 24, 26, 28

*cessio bonorum* allowed debtors to secure their personal liberty by surrendering their effects to their creditors. But unlike bankruptcy, *cessio bonorum* was not limited to tradespeople, and there was no upper or lower debt threshold.[53]

With a wide variety of routes to prison and mechanisms for release available, debtors could expect to remain incarcerated for periods ranging from a month to several years, depending on their particular circumstances, their geographical location and the prison in which they were housed (Table 1.1). Most prison stays were in fact much shorter than the images portrayed in novels and reform literature. Though the image of the debtor languishing in prison indefinitely was a popular trope, prison commitment books reveal a constantly evolving prison community and a substantial population of short-term inmates. In England, only about one third of prisoners were incarcerated for more than one year. In the Fleet and King's Bench prisons, 45 per cent of incarcerated debtors were released within six months. In the London Woodstreet Compter prior to 1770, 28 per cent of debtors were released within 100 days.[54] The short-term prison population was shaped by local variations. Prison stays in London tended to

---

[53] Macmillan, *Forms of Writings Used in Scotland*, 167.
[54] Alexander Fensome Wakelam, 'Imprisonment for Debt and Female Financial Failure in the Long Eighteenth Century' (PhD thesis, University of Cambridge, 2019), 107, 241.

be slightly shorter than those in the provinces. In Lancaster Castle, nearly three quarters of debtors were held for longer than six months, as compared to 55 per cent of London prisoners. Prisoners in Scotland carried out shorter prison terms than those in England. There, more than 80 per cent of prisoners were released within one month, as compared to 13 per cent in London.

## A Commonwealth of Debtors: The Prison Population

Across Britain, the mechanics of imprisonment repeated themselves thousands of times every year, creating an economic culture that was framed by the pervasive threat of incarceration. By using the surviving commitment books for two London prisons, the Fleet and King's Bench, alongside lists of debtors applying for relief under the Insolvency Acts published in the *London Gazette*, an impressionistic sense of the size of the prison population in one city is possible. In London, between 140 and 486 people, or an average of just under 300 debtors, were committed to both the Fleet and King's Bench prisons every year. According to *London Gazette* lists, these institutions together made up 55 per cent of London's total prison population. Thus, the number of people committed annually to debtors' prisons in London between 1710 and 1770 would have ranged from 570 to 1,549 individuals per year.[55] Some 80 per cent of these prisoners were London residents. The rest listed provincial residences in their insolvency papers.[56] In these cases, indebtedness led them to London in search of opportunity before they were incarcerated, or they had transferred to the Fleet or King's Bench by writs of habeas corpus from provincial prisons.

Very many people went to debtors' prison. When incarceration rates are placed in the context of London's total population, we gain an indication of the proportion of urban residents who would see the inside of the prison walls (Table 1.2). Imprisonment fell most heavily on adult men, who, according to data published in the *London Gazette*, accounted for an average of 93 per cent of imprisoned debtors. Estimates of London's population between 1710 and 1770 range from 575,000 to 730,000, and

---

[55] This is most likely a low estimate because minor local prisons like the Woodstreet Compter incarcerated more debtors than indicated by the *London Gazette* lists. See Wakelam, 'Imprisonment for Debt and Female Financial Failure'.

[56] Lists of prisoners applying for the benefit of Parliamentary Acts for the Relief of Insolvent Debtors, *London Gazette*, 1728–9, 1748–9, 1761.

Table 1.2 *Incarceration rate of adult males, London*

| | Total urban population (N) | Total adult male urban population (N) | Annual commitments of adult males (N) | Annual incarceration rate of adult males, lower-bound commitments (N per 1,000) | Annual incarceration rate of adult males, upper-bound commitments (N per 1,000) | Generational chance of incarceration for an adult male, low bound (%) | Generational chance of incarceration for an adult male, high bound (%) | Generational chance of incarceration for an adult male, middle bound (%) |
|---|---|---|---|---|---|---|---|---|
| Lower Bound | 575,000 | 193,510 | 424 | 2.2 | 6.0 | 4.4 | 11.9 | 8.1 |
| Upper Bound | 730,000 | 245,674 | 1,152 | 1.7 | 4.7 | 3.5 | 9.4 | 6.3 |
| Middle Bound | 652,500 | 219,592 | 779 | 1.9 | 5.2 | 3.9 | 10.5 | 7.1 |

Low- and high-bound commitment rates are based upon total annual commitments of between 570 and 1,549, based upon Fleet and King's Bench Prison commitment books. These have been adjusted based upon a prison population composed of 93 per cent men and 80 per cent London residents. The population of adult males in London is based upon an age profile of 71 per cent adults over age 20 and an urban sex ratio of 90:100.
*Sources:* TNA, King's Bench Commitment Books, 1748–78, PRIS 4/2–6; Fleet Prison Commitment Books, 1708–13, 1719–21, 1725–48, PRIS 1/2–10, PRIS 4/1; population figures from Schwartz, *London in the Age of Industrialization*, 28, 131

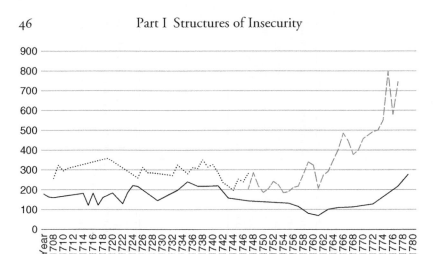

Figure 1.1   Prison populations, Fleet, King's Bench and Edinburgh Tolbooth,
1707–1790
Sources: NRS, ETWLB, 1707–80; HH11/11–28; TNA, King's Bench Commitment
Books, 1748–78, PRIS 4/2–6; Fleet Prison Commitment Books, 1708–13, 1719–21,
1725–48, PRIS 1/2–10, PRIS 4/1

adult men made up about one third of the total population.[57] The prison
population fluctuated from year to year (Figure 1.1). Based upon high and
low commitment rates and estimates of the growing urban population,
a range of incarceration rates between upper and lower bounds becomes
apparent. Annually, between 2 and 6 adult men per 1,000 inhabitants
living in London were committed to prison. Calculated generationally,
adult men had between a 4 and 12 per cent chance of being incarcerated for
debt during their lifetime. In other words, as a high bound, as many as 1 in
8 men would experience incarceration during their lifetime, while at the
very lowest estimate, 1 in 28 men would end up in debtors' prison. Using
the average annual commitment rate and an urban population of 650,000,
a middle ground estimate suggests that some 1 in 14 men would experience
incarceration for debt during their lifetime.

[57] E. A. Wrigley, 'Urban Growth and Agricultural Change: England and the Continent in the Early
Modern Period', *The Journal of Interdisciplinary History* 15, no. 4 (1985): 686–8; L. D. Schwarz,
*London in the Age of Industrialisation: Entrepreneurs, Labour Force and Living Conditions, 1700–1850*
(Cambridge, 1992), 28, 131; Vanessa Harding, 'The Population of London, 1550–1700: A Review of
the Published Evidence', *The London Journal* 15, no. 2 (November 1990): 111–28; John Landers,
*Death and the Metropolis: Studies in the Demographic History of London, 1670–1830* (Cambridge,
1993), 180.

Table 1.3  *Incarceration rate of adult males, Edinburgh*

|  | Total population (N) | Adult population (N) | Adult men (N) | Male prisoners resident in Edinburgh (N) | % adult male urban residents in prison | Generational chance of incarceration for adult men (%) |
|---|---|---|---|---|---|---|
| 1720 | 23,455 | 18,060 | 8,298 | 149 | 1.8 | 36.0 |
| 1755 | 31,000 | 23,870 | 10,967 | 149 | 1.4 | 28.0 |
| 1775 | 47,480 | 36,560 | 16,798 | 178 | 1.1 | 22.0 |

*Sources:* NRS, ETWLB, 1720, 1755, 1775, HH11/11–13, 25, 29; James Gray Kyd and Alexander Webster, *Scottish Population Statistics, Including Webster's Analysis of Population, 1755* (Edinburgh, 1952); Helen M. Dingwall, *Late Seventeenth-Century Edinburgh: A Demographic Study* (Aldershot, 1994); R. A. Houston, *The Population History of Britain and Ireland, 1500–1750* (Basingstoke, 1992); R. A. Houston, *Social Change in the Age of Enlightenment: Edinburgh, 1660–1760* (Oxford, 1994)

In Scotland, without the help of the mesne process, the lengthy and expensive process of incarceration should have deterred creditors from using the prisons as their primary means of enforcing unpaid debts. Parliamentary Insolvency Acts did not apply to Scotland, and there are therefore no comprehensive data akin to the lists published the *London Gazette*. However, when Edinburgh Tolbooth prison commitment books are compared to the total urban population of adult men in Edinburgh, it seems that between 1 and 2 per cent of the city's adult male population was confined in the Tolbooth for debt annually (Table 1.3). As many as one third of men in Edinburgh could expect to be incarcerated during their lifetime, as compared to 12 per cent in London.[58] John Howard's comment that the prison population of Scotland was smaller due to the shame associated with incarceration was not accurate, at least as it applied to the country's urban population.[59]

---

[58] Adults made up 77 per cent of Edinburgh's population, and the sex ratio of men to women was 85:100 in the late eighteenth century. *The New Statistical Account of Scotland. v. 6* (Edinburgh, 1845), 563; R. E. Tyson, 'Contrasting Regimes: Population Growth in Ireland and Scotland during the Eighteenth Century', in *Conflict, Identity and Economic Development: Ireland and Scotland, 1600–1939*, ed. S. J. Connolly, R. A. Houston and R. J. Morris (Preston, 1995), 65; R. A. Houston, *Social Change in the Age of Enlightenment: Edinburgh, 1660–1760* (Oxford, 1994), 255–6; Houston, *The Population History of Britain and Ireland, 1500–1750*, 20.

[59] John Howard, *Appendix to the State of the Prisons in England and Wales, Containing a Farther Account of Foreign Prisons and Hospitals, with Additional Remarks on the Prisons of This Country* (Warrington, 1780), 104.

Because the populations of debtors' prisons were constantly in flux, the static prison population, meaning the number of individuals in prisons at any given time, could differ substantially from the annual commitment rate. In Scotland, where prisoners tended to remain incarcerated for very short periods of time, the number of people in prison at any given time was much smaller than the annual commitment rate. In England, the opposite was true. For example, in 1729, 300 debtors were committed to the Fleet, but at least 785 individuals applied for relief under the 1728 Insolvency Act. Similarly, in 1748, 204 debtors were committed to the King's Bench, but 404 applied for relief. Based upon the total number of prisoners who applied for relief in London during those years, and if some 30 per cent of prisoners were released during Act years, then the population of London's incarcerated debtors might have numbered more like 9,500 individuals in 1729 and 5,000 individuals in 1748. The static prison population was so large, in fact, that significant numbers of debtors lived outside of the prison. A prison list composed by the keeper of the Fleet in 1748 noted that 46 per cent of the prison population lived in the Rules. Thus, only just over half of those incarcerated for debt in the Fleet actually resided within the prison walls.[60] By comparison, London's 38 workhouses built in the 1720s housed some 5,000 paupers. The population of incarcerated debtors during the same decade was therefore nearly twice the size of the workhouse population.[61] In a city known for exceptionally high mortality rates, the figures given earlier represent one third the total number of burials in London during the same years.[62]

Though striking in themselves, these figures are substantially lower than contemporary estimates. By the 1720s, eighteenth-century commentators believed that the prison population had reached a point of crisis. The efficacy of imprisonment for debt was a topic of political debate, even before the period of prison reform in the 1780s. Reformers estimated that England's population of imprisoned debtors ranged from 20,000 to

---

[60] London Metropolitan Archives (hereafter LMA), 'Lists from the several prisons of insolvent debtors in the prisons on certain dates, sworn to at the Sessions, for the debtors to take benefit of the Insolvent Acts'. Fleet Prison, 1747–8. CLA/047/LJ/17/001.

[61] Hitchcock and Shoemaker, *London Lives*, 122.

[62] *A Collection of the Yearly Bills of Mortality, from 1657 to 1758 Inclusive. Together with Several Other Bills of an Earlier Date* (London, 1759), 180, 220. My figures are much higher than Haagen's estimates. Because his figures were generated using *London Gazette* data, which described only a portion of the prison population, they substantially underestimate the incarcerated population. According to Haagen, incarceration rates for adult males ranged from between 1 in 260 to 1 in 1,000. Generationally, between 3 and 8 per cent of adult males in England were imprisoned. The static prison population ranged from between 2,000 and 4,000, reaching a high point of 6,000 in the 1720s. See Haagen, 'Imprisonment for Debt', 55–9.

100,000. Daniel Defoe wrote in 1709 that 80,000 individuals were in prison for debt. Another pamphlet in 1732 suggested that 'there are about sixty thousand miserable debtors perishing in the prisons of *England* and *Wales*, where Hundreds die weekly of want and infectious Diseases'. In 1759, Samuel Johnson wrote that one quarter of the prison population died every year. If true, this meant that imprisonment led to more deaths than did war.[63] The population figures published by Defoe, Johnson and others were much higher than the numbers suggested by analysing surviving quantitative sources. Perception and fear might have inflated contemporary estimates. Even if inaccurate, contemporary figures are valuable because they illustrate the perceived scale of the problem at the time. People in the eighteenth century believed that the incarcerated population was massive, and that the lives of those debtors caught in confinement were at risk. Fear of the debtors' prisons shaped life for the eighteenth century's urban inhabitants.

## The Social Composition of the Prisons

The burden of incarceration for debt depended upon a person's occupational status, gender and place of residence. Men of the urban middling sorts had the highest chances of ending up in debtors' prison. Analysis of prisoner occupations listed in the *London Gazette* during three sample years, compared with those listed in Scottish prison registers, shows that throughout Britain, most prisoners held occupations in craft, manufacturing or petty trade. Few of those imprisoned came from the higher and lower ends of the social spectrum (Table 1.4).[64] In England, less than 2 per cent of people applying for relief under the Insolvent Debtor Acts called themselves gentlemen or gentlewomen. In Scotland, only 1 per cent of prisoners were self-defined members of the gentry. Similarly, those performing unskilled occupations form a disproportionately small portion of the debtors' prison population. In England, less than 1 per cent of those listed in the *London Gazette* described themselves as labourers, while

---

[63] Haagen, 'Eighteenth Century English Society and the Debt Law', 228. Daniel Defoe, *Review* 5 (1 March 1709), 379–80; Thomas Baston, *Observations on Trade, and a Publick Spirit* ... (London, 1732), 93; *The Debtors Glory; And the Gaolers Lamentation, for His Majesties Act, Concerning the Imprisonment of Insolvent Debtors* ... (London, 1727), 10; Samuel Johnson, *The Idler*, no. 38, 6 January 1759.

[64] Occupations described in Table 1.4 include men and women. Thirty per cent of women in the London Fleet and King's Bench prisons and 22 per cent in the Edinburgh Tolbooth provided an occupational designation, while 48 per cent of women in Edinburgh described themselves by their civic status as 'resident' or 'indweller'. Women are included in the life cycle status category in cases where they provided only their marital status and no occupation.

Table 1.4 *Occupational status of imprisoned debtors, Edinburgh and London*

| | London | | Edinburgh | |
|---|---|---|---|---|
| Occupation | N | % | N | % |
| **Agriculture** | 171 | 3.8 | *35* | 5.6 |
| *Gardener* | *31* | | *7* | |
| *Yeoman/tenant* | *41* | | *16* | |
| *Farmer/husbandman* | *78* | | *6* | |
| *Other* | *21* | | *6* | |
| **Artisan/Manufacturer** | 2,039 | 44.8 | *188* | 30.0 |
| *Building* | *301* | | *50* | |
| *Clothing* | *486* | | *39* | |
| *Textile production* | *285* | | *11* | |
| *Leather* | *156* | | *18* | |
| *Metal* | *282* | | *17* | |
| *Printing* | *66* | | *19* | |
| *Wood* | *238* | | *9* | |
| *Barber/surgeon* | *59* | | *15* | |
| *Other* | *166* | | *10* | |
| **Food, Drink, Accommodation** | 1,015 | 22.3 | *49* | 7.8 |
| *Brewer/distiller* | *99* | | *5* | |
| *Food production* | *377* | | *31* | |
| *Innkeeper/victualler* | *533* | | *13* | |
| *Other* | *6* | | *0* | |
| **Trade/Retail** | 613 | 13.5 | *103* | 16.5 |
| *Merchant* | *150* | | *4* | |
| *Shopkeeper/petty trade* | *424* | | *86* | |
| *Vintner* | *39* | | *13* | |
| **Services** | 326 | 7.2 | *66* | 10.5 |
| *Domestic service* | *18* | | *10* | |
| *Land transport (carrying trades)* | *145* | | *34* | |
| *Water transport (including mariner)* | *146* | | *6* | |
| *Military/city guard* | *17* | | *16* | |
| **Professions** | 99 | 2.2 | *63* | 10.1 |
| *Lower professional/clerical* | *40* | | *18* | |
| *Civic or legal official* | *9* | | *5* | |
| *Schoolmaster* | *21* | | *3* | |
| *Lawyer* | *4* | | *34* | |
| *Other* | *25* | | *3* | |
| **Gentleman/ Gentlewoman** | 72 | 1.6 | *6* | 1.0 |
| **Labourer** | 8 | 0.2 | *9* | 1.4 |
| **Resident/Citizen** | 3 | 0.1 | *82* | 13.1 |
| **Persons Identified by Life Cycle Status Only** | 203 | 4.5 | *25* | 4.0 |

Table 1.4 (*cont.*)

| Occupation | London | | Edinburgh | |
|---|---|---|---|---|
| | N | % | N | % |
| *Wife* | *1* | | *4* | |
| *Widow* | *148* | | *15* | |
| *Daughter* | *0* | | *3* | |
| *Son* | *0* | | *3* | |
| *Spinster* | *54* | | *0* | |
| **Total** | **4,549** | | **626** | |

*Source:* Lists of insolvent debtors applying for relief under the Insolvent Debtors' Relief Acts, published in the *London Gazette*, 1729–31, 1748–50, 1761; NRS, ETWLB, 1720, 1730, 1740, 1750, 1760, 1769, HH11/11, 12, 17, 20, 23, 24, 26, 28

unskilled occupations, such as carrying trades like carters and watermen, were similarly under-represented in the prison population.

Compared to the general population of England, those in commercial occupations were disproportionately represented in the prisons (Table 1.5). In the occupational structures described by contemporary observers Gregory King (1688) and Joseph Massie (1759), adjusted by Lindert and Williamson, artisans and manufacturers made up between 19 and 24 per cent of the English population, yet they made up nearly half of incarcerated debtors in London.[65] Similarly, retailers made up between 7 and 12 per cent of the general population, but nearly one third of prisoners. Middling people, according to Gregory King's analysis, accounted for about one quarter of the general population, but they made up three quarters of imprisoned debtors.[66] When the life chances of incarceration for adult men are controlled for occupation and social rank, the burden of imprisonment upon the middling sort becomes even more apparent (Table 1.6). While London men had between a 4 and 12 per cent chance of ending up in prison, middling men had between an 11 and 37 per cent chance of incarceration. In other words, at a low estimate, one in nine middling men, and at a high estimate, one in three middling men, experienced the debtors' prison. A conservative estimate using the average incarceration rate and a population of 650,000

[65] Peter H. Lindert and Jeffrey G. Williamson, 'Revising England's Social Tables 1688–1812', *Explorations in Economic History* 19 (1982): 388–9, 396–7.

[66] For King's outline of England's occupational structure, see Thirsk and Cooper, *Seventeenth-Century Economic Documents*, 780–1.

Table 1.5 *Occupations of imprisoned debtors compared with occupational structure of the general population*

| Occupation/Status | King 1688 | | Massie 1759 | | London Prison Population (1729, 1748, 1761) | |
|---|---|---|---|---|---|---|
| | N (households) | % | N (families) | % | N (persons) | % |
| Gentleman/titled | *19,626* | 1.4 | *18,070* | 1.2 | *72* | 1.6 |
| Agriculture | *227,440* | 16.4 | *379,008* | 24.6 | *171* | 3.8 |
| Professions (including persons in offices, persons in the law, clergymen, naval and military officers) | *51,960* | 3.7 | *65,000* | 4.2 | *99* | 2.2 |
| Retailing and petty trade (including shopkeepers, innkeepers, petty traders) | *101,704* | 7.3 | *187,500* | 12.2 | *1,478* | 32.5 |
| Artisans and manufacturers | *256,866* | 18.5 | *366,252* | 23.8 | *2,039* | 44.9 |
| Merchants | *26,321* | 1.9 | *13,000* | 0.8 | *150* | 3.3 |
| Labourers and the poor (including menial services, common seamen and common soldiers) | *706,669* | 50.8 | *510,310* | 33.2 | *334* | 7.3 |
| Women identified by marital status only | *n* | N | *n* | N | *203* | 4.5 |
| Total population | *1,390,586* | | *1,539,140* | | *4,549* | |

*Sources:* Lindert and Williamson, 'Revising England's Social Tables', pp. 388–9, 396–7; Joan Thirsk and John Phillips Cooper, *Seventeenth-Century Economic Documents* (Oxford, 1972), 780–1; lists of insolvent debtors applying for relief under the Insolvent Debtors' Relief Acts, *London Gazette*, 1729–31, 1748–50, 1761.

suggests that one in four middling men in London could expect to be incarcerated for debt during their lifetime.

Most imprisoned debtors were heads of their households and legally responsible for household debts by the strictest definitions of the law. Thus, nearly half of incarcerated women in London and one quarter in Edinburgh were widows (Table 1.7). Wives were surprisingly under-represented in prison records, especially given recent scholarly emphasis on the roles they played in brokering credit.[67] Life cycle data on

[67] Shepard, 'Minding Their Own Business'; Spence, *Women, Credit, and Debt in Early Modern Scotland*, 34.

Table 1.6 *Incarceration rate of middling adult males, London*

| | Total urban population | Total adult male urban population | Annual commitments of middling men | Lower incarceration rate, middling men (n per 1,000) | Upper incarceration rate, middling men (n per 1,000) | Generational chance of incarceration for an adult male, low bound (%) | Generational chance of incarceration for an adult male high bound (%) |
|---|---|---|---|---|---|---|---|
| Lower Bound | 143,750 | 48,378 | 331 | 6.8 | 18.6 | 13.7 | 37.1 |
| Upper Bound | 182,500 | 61,419 | 899 | 5.4 | 14.6 | 10.8 | 29.3 |
| Middle Bound | 163,125 | 54,898 | 608 | 6.0 | 16.4 | 12.0 | 32.7 |

Middling incarceration rates are based upon a middling population that comprised some 25 per cent of London's population, and a prison population composed of 78 per cent middling sort.
*Sources*: As Table 1.2.

Table 1.7 *Status of women incarcerated for debt, London and Edinburgh*

| | London | | Edinburgh | |
|---|---|---|---|---|
| | N | % | N | % |
| Single woman | 1 | 0.2 | 0 | 0.0 |
| Spinster | 122 | 19.7 | 0 | 0.0 |
| Widow | 301 | 48.7 | 15 | 23.8 |
| Wife | 6 | 1.0 | 4 | 6.3 |
| Occupational designation | 188 | 30.4 | 14 | 22.2 |
| Resident/indweller | 0 | 0.0 | 30 | 47.6 |
| Total | 618 | | 63 | |

*Sources:* As Table 1.4

incarcerated men, where available, suggest that they tended to be married with children. A survey of London's prisoners undertaken by the Thatched House Society in 1774 found that 996 debtors had between them 382 wives and 1,125 children.[68] Similarly, parliamentary investigations in the 1790s found that at least two thirds of incarcerated men in England were married

---

[68] James Halifax, *A Sermon Preached at the Parish Church of St. Paul, Covent-Garden, on Thursday, May 18, 1775, for the Benefit of Unfortunate Persons Confined for Small Debts. Published by Request of the Society* (London, 1775), 15.

and that many had children.[69] Age data support the notion that prisoners were of middle age and probably house-holding, and indicates something of the place that debt occupied in the life cycle. For men, the risk of incarceration increased with age. Contemporary wisdom suggested that young men setting up business were more fragile than those who had accumulated wealth after years of trading. The authors of diaries and advice books noted that young men tended to be too easy in their credit and were often at risk of default. The shopkeeper William Stout wrote in his diary that the problem of extending too much credit was 'frequent with young tradesmen', while Daniel Defoe directed much of his advice on how to increase and keep credit to 'the young Tradesman . . . setting up with the ordinary stock'.[70] But although younger men tended to take on riskier debts, they were less likely to go to prison. Creditors more frequently targeted middle-aged men. While debtor age was not routinely noted in prison registers, Parliamentary Insolvency Relief Acts passed in 1696 and 1702 stipulated that debtors under the age of 40 were eligible to gain their liberty only if they joined the English Navy or Army.[71] Prisoner lists compiled in the wake of those Acts therefore noted debtor age. The ages of 454 debtors from the Marshalsea who appeared before the Surrey Court of Quarter Sessions ranged from 24 to older than 70. However, 70 per cent of incarcerated debtors were older than age 40, and incarcerated men tended to be clustered between ages 40 and 59 (Table 1.8). Young men may have been the most reckless with credit, but in order to face incarceration, debtors also had to have enough accumulated wealth for it to be worth creditors' resources to pursue them using arrest.

Given the life cycle and household status of most debtors, we might conceptualise the burden of imprisonment in terms of households rather than individuals. The household served as early modern Britain's primary economic unit. Both King and Massie constructed their occupational analyses according to the number of families in England. Householders ended up in prison in the highest numbers because the law saw them as responsible for the debts of the entire household unit, though credit contracts might not have been of their own making. Male and female householders were made responsible for debts contracted by dependents, including servants, children and apprentices. Property law made husbands

---

[69] *Journals of the House of Commons*, vol. 47, 2 April 1792, 647.

[70] Marshall, *The Autobiography of William Stout of Lancaster, 1665–1752*, 96; Defoe, *The Compleat English Tradesman*, letter xxiv, 345.

[71] 1695–6: 7&8 Will 3 c.12, 'An Act for Relief of Poor Prisoners for Debt or Damages'; 1702: 1 Anne stat. 1 c. 19, 'An Act for the Relief of Poor Prisoners for Debt'.

Table 1.8 *Age profile of prisoners applying*
*for release from the Marshalsea, 1696–1704*

| Age Range | Prisoners | |
|---|---|---|
| | N | % |
| 24–29 | 12 | 2.6 |
| 30–39 | 31 | 6.8 |
| 40–49 | 131 | 28.9 |
| 50–59 | 84 | 18.5 |
| 60–69 | 48 | 10.6 |
| 70– | 3 | 0.7 |
| < 40 (no age specified) | 91 | 20.0 |
| > 40 (no age specified) | 54 | 11.9 |
| Total | 454 | |

*Source:* Surrey History Centre, Debtors
Appearance Books, 1696–1704. QS3/2/12

liable for their wives' contracts and gave women the power to assume
'reasonable' debts under their husbands' names.[72] This dynamic was confirmed by parliamentary investigations, which found that at least two
thirds of incarcerated debtors were married and that many had
children.[73] If we assume, therefore, that each case of imprisonment repre-
sents a household rather than an individual, then in the 1720s, when the
annual incarceration rate was some 6,000 per year (involving approxi-
mately 4,200 middling people), then just under 2 per cent of England's
261,000 middling households experienced the debtors' prison. Over a 20-
year generation, 40 per cent of lower-middling households would send
a member to debtors' prison.

Patterns of social and occupational vulnerability were so strong that the
prison populations were very similar in England and Scotland despite
different legal frameworks. Unlike England, Scotland lacked debt thresholds for incarceration. Cases of higher value and those involving litigants
who were traders would not have been siphoned off into bankruptcy
processes. We might therefore expect the Edinburgh prison to have confined a broader occupational range of debtors. Yet with some minor
differences that reflect variations in Edinburgh's occupational structure,

[72] Amy Louise Erickson, *Women and Property in Early Modern England* (London; New York,
1993), 100.
[73] *Journals of the House of Commons*, vol. 47, 2 April 1792, 647.

the social composition of imprisoned debtors in London and Edinburgh was nearly identical (Table 1.4). Individuals of broadly middling social status, practising occupations that were skilled but not of elite status, and concentrated in secondary and tertiary trades in manufacturing, retail and service, were particularly vulnerable to debt. Though legal and institutional frameworks shaped the prison population, debtors were vulnerable because of the trades they practised. These trades afforded them middling social status, but also subjected them to high risks of incarceration.

People at the time were aware of the middling character of the prisons. The names and occupations of incarcerated debtors applying for relief were printed in the *London Gazette* and available for public consumption, and discussions of the prison population in newspapers as well as in Parliament recognised incarcerated debtors as individuals drawn from the 'honest and useful callings of life'.[74] Subscribers to *The Morning Post* read that London's prison population was made up predominantly of tradesmen, and a parliamentary report inquiring into the state of the prisons described those in gaol as 'About Two-thirds Manufacturers and Labourers'.[75] The economic impact of confining working populations came to form one of the main arguments waged by reformers against imprisonment for debt. One pamphlet blamed the poor state of trade in the early eighteenth century on the confinement of skilled workers. According to the author, commercial stagnation 'may be alleviated by easing the Nation of the Burthen of so many poor Prisoners, who, in a little Time, might become rich, or at least useful Subjects: For, but the Industry of so many thousands as are now confin'd, Trade would become more brisk and flourishing, Credit encourag'd, and the Strength of the Nation better supported'.[76] Imprisonment for debt, therefore, was not just a problem facing those whose bodies were confined. It was a problem that affected the productive capacity of the nation.

While broad middling social patterns characterised the national prison population, imprisonment was experienced unevenly across Britain and was shaped by region, town and neighbourhood. It was very specifically an *urban* middling phenomenon, centred on London. London was home to about half of England's imprisoned debtors, but accounted for only 10–11 per cent

[74] 'Debate in the Lords on the Insolvent Debtors Bill, March 27, 1792', in *Cobbett's Parliamentary History of England*, vol. 30, 649.

[75] *Morning Post and Gazetteer*, 22 August 1801; *Report from the Committee Appointed to Enquire into the Practice and Effects of Imprisonment for Debt* (London, 1792), pp. 89, 25, quoted in White, *Mansions of Misery*, 4.

[76] *The Honour and Advantage of Great Britain, in a General Act of Redemption for Insolvent Debtors ...* (London, 1707), 12.

of England's national population.[77] In the provinces, those who resided in towns were almost twice as likely as those from rural counties to end up in debtors' prison. Counties with the highest urban populations had the highest committal rates. As Paul Haagen has shown, 6 of the 10 counties in which more than one fifth of the inhabitants lived in towns of more than 10,000 persons had an annual debtor committal rate of more than 1 per 2,000 inhabitants.[78] Similar patterns of urban concentration existed in Scotland. John Howard calculated in 1780 that the Edinburgh Tolbooth accounted for about one quarter of the national prison population, though it was home to only a fraction of the national population.[79]

## Incarcerated Women

The prison population was predominantly male, but women constituted a significant minority of prisoners, with some variations from prison to prison, and with variations according to the records consulted (Table 1.9). The *London Gazette* tended to under-represent women's presence, listing them as constituting only 7 per cent of the prison population, while institutional commitment records and prison lists suggest that women made up closer to 10 per cent of the prison population. However, even at this higher figure, women seem under-represented in the prisons, especially given the roles they are known to have played in credit and debt relations. In comparison to the incidence of female litigants in debts cases, the imprisonment of female debtors was low. Women constituted just over 10 per cent of prisoners in the Edinburgh sample, but comparable studies of urban debt litigation in seventeenth-century Scotland show that single women and widows alone were involved in one fifth of debt cases in borough courts.[80] Similarly, while women made up only 10 per cent of the prisoners in London prisons, or 7 per cent of the *London Gazette* lists, Craig Muldrew has shown that as many as 36 per cent of litigants in English debt cases were women.[81] Women at all stages of the life cycle

---

[77] Wrigley, 'British Population', 90.      [78] Haagen, 'Imprisonment for Debt', 65–6.

[79] Howard, *Appendix to the State of the Prisons*.

[80] Karen Sander Thomson and Gordon DesBrisay, 'Crediting Wives: Married Women and Debt Litigation in the Seventeenth Century', in *Finding the Family in Medieval and Early Modern Scotland*, ed. Elizabeth Ewan and Janay Nugent (Aldershot, 2017), 92–4; Spence, *Women, Credit, and Debt in Early Modern Scotland*.

[81] Craig Muldrew, 'Credit and the Courts: Debt Litigation in a Seventeenth-Century Urban Community', *The Economic History Review* 46, no. 1 (1993): 28–9; Craig Muldrew, '"A Mutual Assent of Her Mind"? Women, Debt, Litigation and Contract in Early Modern England', *History Workshop Journal* 55, no. 1 (1 January 2003): 55.

Table 1.9   *Gender composition of imprisoned debtors and creditors*

| | Prisoners | | Creditors (plaintiffs) | |
|---|---|---|---|---|
| Prison Lists and Commitment Books | Male (%) | Female (%) | Male (%) | Female (%) |
| Edinburgh Tolbooth | 89.6 | 10.4 | 89.3 | 10.7 |
| Lancaster Castle | 94.2 | 5.8 | 84.7 | 15.3 |
| Fleet | 89.7 | 10.3 | 91.7 | 8.3 |
| Ludgate | 92.8 | 7.2 | 88.7 | 11.3 |
| Newgate | 92.7 | 7.3 | 88.9 | 11.1 |
| Poultry Compter | 90.6 | 9.4 | 89.6 | 10.4 |
| Woodstreet Compter | 86.3 | 13.7 | 91.3 | 8.7 |
| *London Gazette* | | | | |
| All London Prisons | *92.2* | *7.8* | - | - |

*Sources:* NRS, ETWLB, 1720–80, HH11/11–28; LMA, 'Lists from the several prisons of insolvent debtors', London Fleet 1724, 1728, 1742, 1748, 1760; Ludgate 1724, 1737, 1755, 1760; Newgate 1728; Poultry Compter 1728, 1737, 1748, 1755, 1760; Woodstreet Compter 1724, 1728, 1736, 1755, 1761 CLA/047/LJ/17/001–2; Lancaster Castle 1725, 1736, 1742, QJB30/1–3

were involved in trading with credit, making coverture little more than a 'legal fiction', yet laws of coverture seem to have been strictly observed in cases of imprisonment.

The character of the incarcerated female population was broadly comparable to that of the male prison population in terms of occupational status, life cycle status and the character of their indebtedness. One third of incarcerated women in London listed occupational designations in the *London Gazette*, providing a glimpse of the range of occupations undertaken by urban women. More than 40 per cent worked in trades related to craft and manufacturing, a figure almost identical to the general prison population (Tables 1.4 and 1.10). Three quarters of those who worked as artisans were employed in clothing trades, for example as milliners and dressmakers. Imprisoned women, like men, were also clustered in tertiary occupations in retail, service, victualing and innkeeping. Incarcerated women could be found in all occupational sectors. Three women in the sample listed occupations at butchers. In 1761, Elizabeth Everard described herself as a bookkeeper. Some women listed more than one occupation. Hannah Glasse, who applied for release from the Fleet in 1761, claimed occupations as both a habit-maker and a warehousewoman.[82] While it

---

[82] *London Gazette*, issues 10088 and 10089.

Table 1.10  *Occupational status of female debtors applying for relief*

|                          | N   | %    |
|--------------------------|-----|------|
| Craft and manufacturing  | 82  | 43.6 |
| Retail/trade             | 34  | 18.1 |
| Gentlewoman              | 17  | 9.0  |
| Innkeeping               | 28  | 14.9 |
| Service                  | 9   | 4.8  |
| Food production          | 8   | 4.3  |
| Medical                  | 5   | 2.7  |
| Labour                   | 3   | 1.6  |
| Agriculture              | 1   | 0.5  |
| Professional             | 1   | 0.5  |
| Total                    | 188 |      |

*Source: London Gazette*, 1728–9, 1748–9, 1761

would be inaccurate to characterise female prisoners' debts as petty and informal, women tended to be over-represented in debts of less than £2, and under-represented in debts of more than £100.[83] Female prisoners also tended to be released more quickly than men. Women spent an average of 250 days in prison, while men spent 350.

In cases of incarceration, women were more prominently represented as creditors than as debtors, reflecting their roles as lenders and as brokers of credit.[84] Where prison lists noted the names of the plaintiffs or creditors who had initiated the suits leading to incarceration, women made up an average of 11 per cent of creditors (Table 1.9). In some institutions, their presence as creditors far exceeded their presence as debtors. In Lancaster Castle, women made up less than 6 per cent of the prisoner population but constituted more than 15 per cent of creditors. Similarly, in London's Ludgate and Newgate prisons, women made up just 7 per cent of incarcerated debtors, but 11 per cent of creditors. Female participation in pursuing unpaid debts began far outside of the prison registers as those who traditionally dunned the household's debtors. As the first step in debt collection, dunning meant that women often set the legal process of debt collection in motion. The diary of the wigmaker Edmund Harrold

---

[83] Lemire, 'Petty Pawns and Informal Lending'.
[84] Shepard, 'Minding Their Own Business'; Shepard, 'Crediting Women in the Early Modern English Economy'; Spence, *Women, Credit, and Debt in Early Modern Scotland*.

describes how his wife's participation in dunning the household's debtors contributed to his solvency and ensured his liberty. He also reflected on the experience of being dunned by other women, recounting in one diary entry how 'Edward Oake's wife dun'd me for £3 10s, set me agrieving at my folly'.[85] As an extension of the process of collecting debts, women used the prison as a strategic tool to force repayment.

## Networks of Failure

If women constituted a significant minority of the prison population, they were integrally involved in the process of incarceration behind the visibility of the formal records. Female participation reveals that the impact of imprisonment ran deep into middling households and broader urban communities. Histories of crime, prison reform and prison writing portray the incarcerated as unrooted persons. They are imagined as marginal, deviant or lonely characters, isolated from social networks. Prisoners in the eighteenth century have been described as 'poor', 'low in life' and 'friendless'. [86] A parliamentary debate suggested that those emerging from prisons were unlikely 'to gaigne so much credite from any honest householder as to enterteyn them'.[87] However, in contrast to penal incarceration, individuals imprisoned for debt were incarcerated precisely *because* they were enmeshed within social and economic communities. Imprisonment was the result of a series of individual decisions made as part of interpersonal relationships. For every person confined, a household, a family, a social community and a trading network were implicated. Numerous individuals were affected financially, socially and emotionally by each debtor's imprisonment. Because of the sheer number of middling imprisoned debtors, nearly everyone would have known someone who had been to prison. Just as credit involved networks of people and relationships of trust, so did failure.

The household members and dependents of incarcerated debtors were intimately affected by imprisonment. Women were hardly passive victims, but they constituted part of an unrecognised population forced into

---

[85] Craig Horner, ed., *The Diary of Edmund Harrold, Wigmaker of Manchester 1712–15* (Aldershot, 2008), 30, 69.

[86] Ignatieff, *A Just Measure of Pain*;; McGowen, 'The Well-Ordered Prison, England 1780–1865'; Foucault, *Discipline and Punish*; J. M. Beattie, *Policing and Punishment in London 1660–1750: Urban Crime and the Limits of Terror* (Oxford, 2001); Hitchcock and Shoemaker, *London Lives*, 249.

[87] Commons Debates, 1621. Quoted in J. A. Sharpe, *Judicial Punishment in England* (London, 1990), 260.

downward mobility by debt incarceration. Contemporary reformers were concerned about the ability of prisoners to labour and the ethics of individual liberty, but paid very little attention to the wives who were left to single-handedly manage their households' livelihoods and care for dependents. John Howard's magisterial account of the debtors' prisons mentioned women only twice. Of the starving debtors in Chesterfield Gaol, Howard wrote that 'each had a wife; and they had in the whole thirteen children, cast on their respective parishes.'[88] He later opined that 'man and wife should not be totally separated' and that there was 'little probability . . . of an industrious woman being much service to her family in a prison'.[89]

In contrast to Howard's statement, legal records suggest that women played very critical roles in managing and carrying out the labour necessary to maintain households during periods of insolvency and debt crisis. Women, especially wives, collected debts, secured the liberty of prisoners and brokered household wealth. They negotiated relationships with creditors and organised the repayment of debts to secure the release of male householders. For example, while he was in prison, the wife of the glover Archibald How wrote a letter to his cousin Henrietta Dunbar, asking her to pay an account that would secure his release. She ensured Dunbar of her husband's credibility, noting that by 'his keen honesty and fondness he keeps credit up even now'.[90] When William Robertson, a bell maker, was liberated, the creditor noted that his wife had given 'assurances of payment owed this week'.[91] Women's roles were noted inside and outside the courtroom. In Hogarth's famous series 'Rake's Progress', which depicts Thomas Rakewell's descent into debt through extravagant spending, Rakewell is saved from arrest by his lover, Sarah Young. In plate IV, when stopped by two bailiffs who present a paper marked 'arrest', Young produces a purse and offers to pay the demand and ensure Rakewell's safety.[92]

Women managed the process of household loss. Though they have been afforded central roles in processes of material acquisition as shoppers and consumers, for the indebted household, women played a key role in strategically negotiating the disposal and dispersal of assets, extending their roles as the brokers of moveable property.[93] After a person was

---

[88] Howard, *State of the Prisons*, 286.    [89] Howard, *State of the Prisons*, 34.
[90] NRS, Sheriff Court Productions, 'Miscellaneous Legal Papers and Correspondence Relating to How Family', 1708–77, SC39/107/8.
[91] NRS, ETWLB, 1748, HH11/23.
[92] William Hogarth, *A Rake's Progress*, Plate 4, 'Arrested for Debt', 1735. British Library, 18,801,113.21.
[93] Shepard, 'Minding Their Own Business'.

incarcerated, the household continued to support both household members and the incarcerated debtor, so prison was not the end point in a household's flow of credit, but rather one step in an ongoing process. After a household lost the income of an individual to imprisonment, careful disposal of moveable assets became essential to household maintenance and the repayment of debts. During incarceration, it was normal for households to lose significant amounts of property. Women managed this process by strategically selling household goods or using them as forms of payment. Their roles were recognised in debtors' schedules, when prisoners referred to their wives' knowledge when accounting for their wealth. Timothy Roberts, a wine cooper imprisoned in the Fleet, testified in his schedule of wealth that 'All the household goods beds Bedding plate and other furniture whatsoever belonging unto me in my late dwelling house' was 'now in the possession of my wife'.[94] Oliver Lomax, imprisoned in Lancaster Castle, testified that most of his household goods had been sold by his wife, and that 'the money ariseing by the said sale hath been expended to maintain my wife and family and to subsist me in my imprisonment.'[95] Others referred to goods disposed of by their wives, or expressed a lack of knowledge of household assets. One debtor confined in Lancaster described the household wealth as 'in my wifes possession'.[96]

While entire households were affected by incarceration, individuals and institutions outside of the household were also drawn into cases of imprisonment. The experience of incarceration was negotiated at the levels of the community and the neighbourhood. Most imprisoned debtors were residents of the cities where they were confined. In Edinburgh, more than 90 per cent of prisoners claimed residence in the greater urban area, and most of these from within the walls of the old city. In Lancaster Castle, 86 per cent of prisoners came from towns within Lancaster County, and 9 per cent from towns in adjacent counties, while only 4 per cent came from further afield. Even in London's King's Bench and Fleet prisons, where debtors imprisoned elsewhere had the right to be moved by writs of habeas corpus, provincial prisoners never made up more than 18 per cent of the total prison population.[97] Few debtors would have found it expedient to remove themselves from local communities. Imprisoned debtors were

---

94 LMA, CLA/047/LJ/17/025/002/122.
95 LRO, LCQS, Insolvent Debtor Papers, July–September 1725, QJB/12/27.
96 LRO, LCQS, Insolvent Debtor Papers, July–September 1725, QJB/12/23.
97 Haagen, 'Imprisonment for Debt', 65–6.

people who continued to be enmeshed in local social, family and occupational networks, and who depended on these networks for support.

Friends and family provided food and charity and helped to secure prisoners' release. The legal documents that survive from disputes with creditors often involved the names of third parties who stepped in to pay or who were involved in negotiating with creditors. For example, in 1769 in Edinburgh, James Oliphant, imprisoned for a debt of 6s. by a shopkeeper, was released when William Forbes paid the sum.[98] John Baptist Grano received charitable gifts from friends in the form of clothing and money while he was incarcerated in the Marshalsea.[99] Incarceration was a well-known form of leverage creditors used to extract payment from the friends, family and associates of a debtor. As a parliamentary debate suggested, 'it was well known that the creditor often proceeded against the unfortunate debtor to the utmost severity of the law, with a view to torture the compassion of his relations or acquaintances into a subscription for his relief.'[100] The judge Lord Mansfield described how 'the feelings of the friend were often tortured to administer to the resentment or interest of the creditor.'[101]

For families, friends and commercial communities, helping an imprisoned debtor was not only a matter of social obligation or concern. Acquaintances intervened because their own bodies were implicated by the financial failures of others. Imprisonment followed the complicated webs of obligation that characterised early modern credit. The exchange of reciprocal obligations between households could bind communities together, but also placed entire networks at risk. Chains of credit meant that failure could have a rippling or domino effect through a community, and one person's default could cause others to default and fail as well.[102] Chains of default are evident in local cases of small debt. In the bailie court of Edinburgh in February 1750, William Lauder, a coach maker, was sued in the sheriff's court by John Durymure, a merchant. In order to protect his own interest in Lauder's estate, another creditor, Harry Miln, sued Lauder in July. Without the liquid assets to fulfil obligations to both creditors at the same time, Lauder was forced to call in one of his own debts. Later in

---

[98] NRS, ETWLB, 1769, HH11/28.
[99] Bodleian Library, John Baptist Grano, 'A Journal of My Life in the Marshalsea', MS. Rawlinson d. 34.
[100] 'Debate in the Lords on the Practice of Imprisonment for Debt, 27 March 1797', in *Cobbett's Parliamentary History of England*, vol. 33, 181.
[101] 'Debate in the Lords on the Insolvent Debtors Bill', in *Cobbett's Parliamentary History of England*, vol. 30, 648.
[102] Muldrew, *Economy of Obligation*, 150, 180.

July, he sued Robert Blackwood, an advocate, in the bailie court. Blackwood, in order to fulfil the obligation demanded by Lauder, sued James Haly, a goldsmith.[103] Thus, Lauder's indebtedness implicated four other people within the formal record, and perhaps many more informally. Sequences of debt and litigation could carry on in a seemingly indefinite manner.

Networks of failure also emerged in diaries and journals, where authors noted the fortunes and failures of others in their communities. The Manchester wigmaker Harrold wrote about when debtors fled, noting in 1712 that 'Thomas Abram brought word that he [Jones] was flown is overrun the towne' and later that 'John Prince [is] gone. Asked advice of paying debts.'[104] Financial predicaments seemed to be one of the characteristics most often discussed when describing others. These stories reflected contemporary concerns over the fleeting nature of wealth, but also the extent to which diarists' own fortunes and reputations were tied to others. After finding out that his debtor John Midmire was 'keeping out of sight' for debt, the shopkeeper Thomas Turner exclaimed, 'Sure I am a most unfortunate man! What will become of me I cannot think. I must certainly fail and leave off trade.'[105] Similarly, Harrold worried about the effect that another's predicament would have on his own credit. He wondered whether the debtor would avoid an obligation, putting it 'off to a [lawsuit], and so have run it on till he had made his, and so I should had all the charges left to pay'. When another debtor with whom Harrold had done business fled town, he worried about the effects this association would have on his own reputation. He regretted his judgement in having been 'so overseen in ye man as to hurt myself by him' and lamented 'I'm thought ill on for his knavery.' For Harrold, the unpredictable nature of other people's actions was the underlying cause of insecurity, creating 'such a world as this of troubles, sorrow, losses and crosses and disapointments'.[106]

## Conclusion

Incarceration in eighteenth-century Britain was a routine practice rather than an exceptional experience. Britain was home to a substantial

---

[103] ECA, Bailie Court Processes (hereafter BCP) 1750, Box 119, Bundles 302, 304.
[104] Horner, *Diary of Edmund Harrold*, 3, 54.
[105] David Vaisey, ed., *The Diary of Thomas Turner, 1754–1765* (Oxford; New York, 1984), 171.
[106] Horner, *Diary of Edmund Harrold*, 3.

population of people living on a thin line between competency and failure. As a consequence, a significant portion of the national population was incarcerated for failing to pay its personal debts. The prison population was not composed of the indigent poor, for whom insecurity was a well-recognised condition. Rather, it was an experience borne out by middling commercial types. Prisoners were clustered in occupations as petty traders and craftspeople. A middling man in eighteenth-century England had a one in four chance of going to prison during his lifetime, and every generation, nearly half of middling households would send one of their members to prison. Middling people in eighteenth-century Britain, a period normally characterised by commercial development and growth, were extremely insecure. To some extent, vulnerability to financial failure and downward mobility, borne out through the prisons, shaped what it meant to be middling. This condition was shaped by the debt laws, which failed to protect individuals with middle levels of wealth and middle-sized debts. While processes of bankruptcy and petty debt courts provided a means of negotiating the largest and the pettiest debts, the population of tradespeople with middle-sized debts, as both creditors and debtors, were underserved by the legal process. Arrest became a normal means for creditors to negotiate the debts of those in between.

Middle-rank householding men were the most vulnerable to confinement, but incarceration impacted a much broader group of people. Behind every imprisoned debtor was a household, a family, a trading community and a neighbourhood. Because incarceration bound people into networks of failure, members of an imprisoned debtor's community were drawn into the process, providing relief and paying off the debtor's obligations in order to maintain their own credit security. Households struggled to maintain themselves during periods of incarceration. The deficit of one income drove many into processes of loss, normally managed by wives, in which material wealth was sold and disposed of in order to maintain the household.

The case of imprisonment for debt in eighteenth-century Britain suggests a need to reframe how we characterise the economy and commercial culture of a place and a time period normally defined by success, growth and rising living standards. The degree of failure and insecurity represented by the prisons might not be incompatible with growth, but as Julian Hoppit recognised more than two decades ago, might rather be one of its consequences. Failure and success had a close relationship, and the debtors' prisons make clear that failure had broad implications. Normally thought of as the lubricant of commerce, and liberating for individuals, credit also made households highly insecure. Credit may have fuelled growth and prosperity, but for a surprising number of households, credit was also failing. The next chapter investigates why.

# CHAPTER 2

# Credit and the Economic Structures of Insecurity

In 1731, the brewer Walter Hepburn was imprisoned for debt. While confined, he made a list of all the debts he owed, and a list of all the people who owed him money. Hepburn's debts amounted to £98 due to five individuals. His credits were worth £477, owed by 151 households. This long list of debts, which amounted to an average of just over £3 each, had accumulated by the shilling over a period of years as Hepburn extended credit to customers for pints of ale. Collecting these debts would require a significant amount of time as Hepburn dunned his debtors one by one. He initiated legal proceedings against some of them, but the legal process was slow and expensive.[1] Like many middling tradespeople in the eighteenth century, Hepburn found himself caught between a merchant and a mass of small debtors. By eighteenth-century standards, he was a moderately wealthy man. But most of what Hepburn was worth took the form of IOUs. He did not lack wealth, but he lacked a way of making his wealth transferable in order to pay his own debts.

Hepburn's situation illustrates some of the reasons why so many middling people ended up in the debtors' prison. A household's solvency and its ability to pay its debts was dependent upon more than merely possessing wealth.[2] That wealth needed to be held in forms that could be easily mobilised when debts were called in. The ways in which households held or 'invested' their wealth were therefore crucial to their relationship with debt. Imprisonment was frequently the consequence of the eighteenth century's financial structures. The insecurity of middling people was entangled with structures of credit. Though new and more secure technologies of credit emerged with the Financial Revolution from the 1690s, including paper money, these new forms of credit were not nearly as important as trade debt or simple financial accommodation. Carole

---

[1] NRS, List of Debts Due to Walter Hepburn, Brewer in Edinburgh, 1730, GD113/4/117/133.
[2] Shepard, *Accounting for Oneself*, 35–6.

Shammas estimates that deferred payments (or 'simple debt' as contemporaries called it) accounted for some 47 per cent of investments in the 1720s.[3] The majority of this wealth was accounted for in the ledgers of tradespeople and in the verbal promises of consumers. New technologies did little to secure the credit of ordinary, day-to-day consumer practices. Thus, while credit provided opportunities for growth, it also created risks for the middling people who were the main sources of consumer credit. As Brewer, McKendrick and Plumb assert, 'the widespread entanglement of almost all tradesmen in the snare of trade indebtedness not only facilitated business but created a new set of economic and social problems . . . the ease with which credit in its different forms could be obtained exacerbated the situation.'[4]

This chapter reconstructs middling patterns of wealth-holding and networks of credit in order to explain why middling people were so vulnerable to imprisonment. It draws upon samples of small debt litigation from Edinburgh and debtors' schedules from London and Lancaster. These inventories of a household's assets were created when prisoners applied for release under the eighteenth century's periodic Insolvent Debtor Relief Acts. When compared to probate inventories, which illustrate the wealth and credits of the general population, schedules provide an indication of the specific circumstances that led to imprisonment. The constitution of middling wealth, the position of households within credit networks and changes in broader structures of credit made middling households insecure.

## The Middling Constitution of Wealth

Most eighteenth-century households held their wealth in a combination of household goods, trade stock and production equipment, credit (debts owing to the household), money and livestock. Additionally, some people had land, and in rural areas, leases could be included in inventories. In the eighteenth century, forms of wealth-holding amongst the middling sort were diversifying. In the wake of the Financial Revolution, men and women invested their wealth in new financial instruments, including annuities and government stocks.[5] In port cities, it was common for middling tradesmen to invest in mercantile trade, and in some cases, the bodies of slaves and bound labourers.[6]

---

[3] Shammas, *The Pre-industrial Consumer*.
[4] McKendrick, Brewer and Plumb, *The Birth of a Consumer Society*, 204.
[5] Murphy, *The Origins of English Financial Markets*; Neal, 'How It All Began'; Froide, *Silent Partners*.
[6] Diana E. Ascott, Fiona Lewis and Michael Power, *Liverpool 1660–1750: People, Prosperity and Power* (Liverpool, 2006), 94–108.

Previous studies of the constitution of wealth, drawing especially upon probate inventories, categorise property in three ways. The inventory total, a measure of an estate's complete value, including all types of assets (excluding land), indicates a household's financial position within a community.[7] By contrast, domestic wealth focuses only on the value of household goods, and provides a useful measure of a household's standard of living.[8] Measures of material wealth combine work-related and household goods, but omit real estate and financial assets.[9] Within this category, household assets have often been grouped according to consumer or occupational function in order to measure household work and consumption habits.[10] In order to account for the dynamics of credit and solvency, categorising a household's assets in terms of moveable wealth and non-moveable wealth provides an indication of the extent to which a household's wealth was liquid or transferable. Material wealth was moveable and could be transmuted into other forms of value, allowing a household to pay its debts. Additionally, in a credit economy, goods could circulate as forms of cash, and as such, they constituted a form of savings and the security for credit.[11] By contrast, non-material wealth, including land, leases, some financial instruments and debts owing to the household, might be secure but were less fungible. A household could be wealthy in terms of the total value of its assets, but could default on debts if those assets were held in forms that could not be easily mobilised and used to pay debts. Because probate inventories reveal assets but not liabilities, they can paint a misleading picture of a household's net worth and financial position.[12] However, they do provide useful data on the distribution of household assets. A comparison of debtors' schedules and probate material indicates that the precariousness of middling people and their vulnerability to imprisonment in the eighteenth century was due in part to

---

[7] Carole Shammas, 'Constructing a Wealth Distribution from Probate Records', *The Journal of Interdisciplinary History* 9, no. 2 (1978): 297–307.

[8] Sebastian A. J. Keibek and Leigh Shaw-Taylor, 'Early Modern Rural By-Employments: A Re-examination of the Probate Inventory Evidence', *Agricultural History Review* 61, no. 2 (31 December 2013): 279.

[9] Overton, *Production and Consumption*, 137.

[10] Weatherill, *Consumer Behaviour*; Shammas, *The Pre-industrial Consumer*; Overton, *Production and Consumption*; Hannah Barker, *Family and Business during the Industrial Revolution* (Oxford, 2016), 17–52; Geoffrey Crossick, 'Meanings of Property and the World of the Petite Bourgeoisie', in *Urban Fortunes: Property and Inheritance in the Town, 1700–1900*, ed. Jon Stobart and Alastair Owens (Aldershot; Burlington, VT, 2000), 50–78.

[11] Shepard, 'Crediting Women in the Early Modern English Economy', 16.

[12] Margaret Spufford, 'The Limitations of the Probate Inventory', in *English Rural Society, 1500–1800: Essays in Honour of Joan Thirsk*, ed. John Chartres and David Hey (Cambridge, 1990), 151–3.

the changing relationship between moveable and non-moveable forms of worth.

Middling ownership of household goods and consumer products was on the rise during the eighteenth century, and these forms of material wealth made up a significant portion of household assets. The ratio of moveable to non-moveable assets depended upon a household's location, productive activity and social status. Households of lower social status tended to hold proportionally more of their wealth in goods than households of higher social status, due to the fixed costs of household necessities such as kitchen equipment, which all households purchased. Lorna Weatherill's study of probate accounts from England between 1675 and 1725 revealed that mariners held 35 per cent of their wealth in the form of household goods, while members of the craft and dealing trades held 20 per cent of their wealth in that form.[13] Similarly, labourers in London and Worcester held the highest proportion of wealth of all occupational categories in the form of household goods, while members of urban trades, craftspeople and professionals held their wealth in the form of debts owed to them.[14] Amongst middling people, the proportion of wealth made up by consumer goods was lower than the general population. Henry French's analysis of wealth constitution according to office holding (which marked out middle-status individuals as 'chief inhabitants'), shows that non-office-holding individuals in North-West and South-West England were likely to have higher proportions of household goods in their inventories than those who held office.[15] Thus, while the purchasing habits of the middling sorts are said to have fuelled the Consumer Revolution, and while material goods were crucial to displays of status, if considered purely in terms of their financial worth, goods occupied a less important place in the middling household than we might expect. Probate inventories suggest that household and consumer products made up a minority of their total wealth, supporting Alexandra Shepard's conclusion that from the late seventeenth century, goods held a less prominent place as forms of investment than they had several decades earlier.[16]

By the eighteenth century, middling people held more of their wealth in non-productive forms of material property and in virtual forms of wealth, primarily credit and financial instruments. Probate inventories show that the credit of (or debts owing to) people in trading and manufacturing occupations made up significant portions of their assets, with variation

---

[13] Weatherill, *Consumer Behaviour*, 184.     [14] Shammas, *The Pre-industrial Consumer*.
[15] French, *The Middle Sort of People*, 156–7.     [16] Shepard, *Accounting for Oneself*, 35–6, 232, 303.

depending upon location and occupation. In rural households, the median value of personality, including bonds and debts owed to the deceased, increased by 2.5 times between 1600 and 1750.[17] While previous studies of wealth in rural England have noted an increase in lending and borrowing secured by bonds, in the estates of ordinary tradespeople, most of this credit was not extended in the form of formal loans, but as a part of normative, everyday market sales and services. Most of the obligations owing to merchants, middlemen and retailers were held in the form of petty short-term credit which had been extended to customers and clients on account. In probate inventories, the value of these short-term credits was often four to five times greater than a household's fixed assets.[18] Similarly, Peter Mathias' analysis of the capital structure of firms shows 'how small a proportion of their total assets, even for the most capital intensive business such as a large iron-works, or a London porter brewery, lay in fixed assets'.[19] Middling people held the majority of their wealth in the form of obligations owed to them by other people, including consumers or other traders, and relatively small proportions of their assets in the form of moveable wealth.

Amongst the imprisoned debtor population, the relationship between moveable and non-moveable wealth was exaggerated, indicating higher levels of vulnerability to default (Figure 2.1). The composition of wealth reflected in debtors' schedules shows that goods amounted to an even smaller proportion of total household worth than the levels evident in probate material. In schedules from both London and Lancaster, obligations made up more than half of household wealth, while household goods accounted for less than 11 per cent of wealth amongst London debtors, and 17 per cent of the wealth of Lancaster prisoners. Eighty per cent of debtors listed their household goods as being below the legal £10 threshold that required them to itemise these goods in schedules (even if their other assets were substantial). Like probate inventories, debtors' schedules show that individuals in trading occupations had high levels of non-material wealth. Thus, when Joshua Wainwright, incarcerated in Lancaster, drew up his schedule, he revealed that his goods, sold for house rent, amounted to a value of £3, and he valued his wearing apparel at £2. His total assets, however, were worth £22, of which

[17] Overton, *Production and Consumption*, 140.
[18] Peter Spufford, 'Long Term Rural Credit in Sixteenth and Seventeenth Century England: The Evidence of Probate Accounts', in *When Death Do Us Part: Understanding and Interpreting the Probate Records of Early Modern England*, ed. Tom Arkell, Nesta Evans and Nigel Goose (Oxford, 2000), 217–25; Muldrew, *Economy of Obligation*, 95.
[19] Spufford, 'Long Term Rural Credit in Sixteenth and Seventeenth Century England', 217–25; Peter Mathias, 'Capital, Credit and Enterprise in the Industrial Revolution', *Journal of European Economic History* 2, no. 1 (1973): 126.

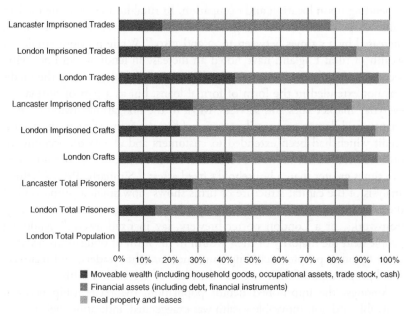

Figure 2.1  Comparison of wealth constitution amongst imprisoned and free
occupational groups, 1720–1760

Source: Probate inventories, London East End, 1720–9. Data collected by Carole
Shammas, *Wealth, Household Expenditure, and Consumer Goods*. Many thanks to
Prof. Shammas for providing access to these data; LRO, LCQS, Insolvent Debtor
Papers, 1725 QJB10-13; LMA, Debtors' Schedules, Fleet, Poultry Compter, and
Ludgate Prisons, 1720, 1749, 1760, CLA/047/LJ/17/020, 024, 025, 030, 043, 046

nearly 80 per cent was held in obligations owed by other people.[20] James
Maude, a chapman and merchant, declared his household goods to be worth
less than the legal threshold of £10, yet his total assets (consisting predominantly of credit) amounted to £283.[21]

The exceptionally low proportions of material goods in debtors' schedules were partially a result of the process of material loss that occurred
prior to and during imprisonment. As a debtor defaulted, goods, as the
most fungible form of wealth, were disposed of first. Samuel Randall,
confined in the Fleet, testified in his schedule to having no household
goods, his landlord 'having seized all my household furniture'.[22] Frances

[20] LRO, LCQS, Insolvent Debtor Papers, June 1725, QJB/10/24.
[21] LRO, LCQS, Insolvent Debtor Papers, June 1725, QJB/10/11.
[22] LMA, Schedule of Samuel Randall, 1761, CLA/047/LJ/17/046.

Johnson, a yeoman imprisoned by his landlord, declared in his schedule that 'goods at the house have been traded and sold for arrears of rent' and that no effects remained other than 'a bed, bedstocks, a copper and a chest'.[23] Similarly, Lawrence Walmesley, a surveyor in Martin Mere, declared in 1725 that the value of his remaining household goods was less than £10, 'he having given the rest of his goods away to secure house rent'.[24] Household estates continued to lose wealth after an individual was incarcerated. Prisoners were responsible for their own maintenance, so that though income generated by the imprisoned individual no longer flowed into the household, the estate continued to support the prisoner as well as household dependents. Thomas Slap, a debtor confined in the Fleet, explained to the court that he had the right to a legacy of £10 from his mother's will, but that he had 'since his confinement to support his family been obliged to assign the same some time ago to Thomas Fountain, Broker'.[25]

Though schedules might under-represent material wealth, the process of loss was at least partially mitigated by the legal status of imprisonment. English law required creditors to choose between pursuing debtors' bodies and pursuing their wealth. Prison protected assets.[26] A household estate was theoretically 'frozen' by imprisonment. Furthermore, the significant place that debt and obligation occupied in the constitution of middling worth is corroborated by other sources. Household accounts reveal that the repayment of debts could account for an extensive portion of a family's annual budget. Lorna Weatherill's analysis of the Pengelly and Latham households shows that both spent significant portions of their income repaying loans and gifts as well as interests on loans. These repayments could amount to as much as 80 per cent of the household's total outgoings in a given year.[27] Peter Earle has shown that for a quarter of middling households, liabilities were worth more than half of the value of their assets. For another 50 per cent of middling households, liabilities accounted for 10 to 50 per cent of their gross worth.[28] Similarly, Mark Overton calculated that mean indebtedness accounted for nearly 60 per cent of households' total wealth in the south of England, while Craig Muldrew has shown that in the late seventeenth century, the majority of households had more debts

[23] LRO, LCQS, Insolvent Debtor Papers, June 1725, QJB/10/75.
[24] LRO, LCQS, Insolvent Debtor Papers, June 1725, QJB/10/65.
[25] LMA, Schedule of Thomas Slap, 1761, CLA/047/LJ/17/046.    [26] Innes, 'King's Bench', 256.
[27] Weatherill, *Consumer Behaviour*, 116–17, 124–5.
[28] Earle, *The Making of the English Middle Class*, 119.

than credits. One quarter of householders were spending more than they were earning.[29]

### Insecurity and the Value of Goods

The ways in which households held their wealth made them precarious. Moveable and non-moveable assets vested households with different capacities to mobilise their assets. Holding wealth in the form of goods was an advantage in a debt economy because goods were highly fungible forms of property. Though histories of consumption have emphasised the function of material objects for comfort and social display, material objects also had important utility as mechanisms of exchange. Alexandra Shepard has charted a shifting away from moveable goods as a mainstay in perceptions of worth from the late seventeenth century. Witnesses in church courts came to rely less on what they had as indications of credibility.[30] This shift contributed to financial insecurity.

In a specie-poor economy, goods functioned like cash. Even by the eighteenth century, money may have been involved in less than 10 per cent of exchanges.[31] Coins were scarce enough that probate and debtor inventories listed them alongside goods. William Meadow's schedule, for example, listed wood boxes, iron keys, linen cloth, a silver watch and 'in cash thirty two pounds twelve shillings and nine pence'.[32] Diarists described ready money as 'a good commodity', and reflected that for business, the possession of coin was 'very necessary'.[33] Without cash, the transfer of goods from one hand to another was often the most expedient way to make a payment. Thomas Turner's diary recorded paying servants in goods, as well as paying for consumer products in kind. In January 1760, he exchanged goods for butter with Mrs French, then used the butter to barter for wigs for himself and his brother. In 1755, he bartered rags collected in his neighbourhood for paper with two paper mills in Kent. As a parish officer, Turner noted that people paid their parish rates in kind. Elizabeth Browne settled her rate of 24s. 'not in cash, but a coffin' used for a pauper's funeral. A fee of 7s. due to Thomas German was settled by giving him a hat.[34]

---

[29] Mark Overton, 'Household Wealth, Indebtedness, and Economic Growth in Early Modern England'. International Economic History Congress. Helsinki, Finland, 2006, 134; Muldrew, *Economy of Obligation*, 118.

[30] Shepard, *Accounting for Oneself*, 232.   [31] Muldrew, *Economy of Obligation*, 100–1.

[32] LRO, LCQS, Insolvent Debtor Papers, 1755–6, QJB/32.

[33] Horner, *Diary of Edmund Harrold*, 64.

[34] Vaisey, *The Diary of Thomas Turner, 1754–1765*, 198, 10, 293, 341.

As moveable assets and forms of payment, goods formed part of a flow of wealth between households, and could constitute the foundations of credit. Moveable and non-moveable forms of wealth were related. At the front end of the credit life cycle, goods could provide the basis for loans. While using goods to secure credit was a common strategy amongst the poor, and has long been recognised as part of the economy of makeshifts, it was also employed by a variety of middling consumers.[35] A wine merchant confined in the Fleet testified to having deposited in the hands of his creditor 'a quantity of silver plate which to the best of my judgement might amount in value to about the sum of sixty pounds (but the particular prices thereof I cannot set forth) as a security for about eighty pounds in mony which I had borrw'd of Michael Thirkle Esq'.[36] Another prisoner in the Fleet borrowed £70 from his creditor, 'for securing the payment of which I left in his hands one suit of figured velvet cloths with a brocaded waistcoat' as well as a watch, a gold chain and a silver dish.[37] Just as the borrowing networks that were crucial to plebeian consumption strategies made goods highly mobile, so the material worth of middling people could circulate.[38] Within credit networks, goods were temporarily placed in the possession of other households, where they served as security and as the basis of trust until a debt was paid. For example, the wealth assessment of Thomas Hindle, a chapman from Preston incarcerated in Lancaster Castle, included items ranging from a fire iron to pans to bedsteads, which were 'set over unto my brother John Hindle of Blackburne'.[39] Timothy Jackson, yeoman, gave 'husbandry gears stock on hand and other things' to Mr William Birdsworth in Lancaster.[40]

[35] Jan de Vries, *The Industrious Revolution: Consumer Behaviour and the Household Economy, 1650 to the Present* (Cambridge, 2008), 175–6; K. Tawny Paul, 'Credit and Social Relations amongst Artisans and Tradesmen in Edinburgh and Philadelphia, c. 1710–1770' (PhD thesis, University of Edinburgh, 2011), 70–1; Laurence Fontaine, 'The Circulation of Luxury Goods in Eighteenth-Century Paris: Social Redistribution and an Alternative Currency', in *Luxury in the Eighteenth Century: Debates, Desires and Delectable Goods*, ed. Maxine Berg and Elizabeth Eger (London, 2002), 95–6; Elizabeth C. Sanderson, 'Nearly New: The Second-Hand Clothing Trade in Eighteenth-Century Edinburgh', *Costume* 31, no. 1 (1997): 41–2.

[36] LMA, Schedule of Samuel Jacomb, 1748, CLA/047/LJ/024/14.

[37] LMA, Schedule of Henry Drake, 1748, CLA/047/LJ/17/024/09.

[38] Lynn MacKay, 'Why They Stole : Women in the Old Bailey, 1779–1789', *Journal of Social History* 32 (1999): 631; Alannah Tomkins, 'Pawnbroking and the Survival Strategies of the Urban Poor in 1770s York', in *The Poor in England, 1700–1850: An Economy of Makeshifts*, ed. Alannah Tomkins and Steven King (Manchester, 2003), 181–2.

[39] LRO, LCQS, Insolvent Debtor Papers, 1755–6, QJB/31/21.

[40] LRO, LCQS, Insolvent Debtor Papers, June 1725, QJB/10/71.

The amount of credit an individual was able to obtain was in part a function of his or her assets.[41] Borrowing and lending continued to be a function of a household's stock of material goods, as moveable wealth provided the basis of credit. Though the proportion of goods in the estates of middling people was lower than that in other social groups, if measured in terms of absolute value, middling people had significantly more moveable wealth than those further down the social scale (Table 2.1). The absolute value of the household goods of imprisoned tradespeople and craftspeople was 30 to 50 per cent more than that of labourers. If occupational assets are included, then those in commercial occupations had on average over seven times the mean value of the moveable wealth of labourers. Meanwhile, the average obligations of tradespeople in London were worth 17 times the obligations of labourers. A stock of goods allowed individuals to access virtual forms of wealth. This had implications for middling people's potential to succeed or to fail because potential wealth was based upon a stock of assets.[42] Households that possessed more absolute moveable wealth had more potential to increase that wealth via credit. If this was the case, it made sense for households to invest heavily in material wealth, fuelling the Consumer Revolution.

The consequence of a credit economy where material wealth facilitated flows of assets and exchange was that households lacking a stock of goods to underpin credit could become vulnerable to default. Credit may have pushed forward economic growth, but holding wealth in the form of credit also made households vulnerable.[43] When debts were called in, those households lacking easily mobilised material wealth that could be used for payment were placed at risk. Prison records show that debtors were not poor; rather they lacked a means to transfer their assets to their creditors. In Edinburgh, London and Lancaster, prisoners tended to have a positive balance of accounts. The assets that prisoners claimed exceeded the debts that led to their incarceration. In London, in cases where both the assets and the obligations of prisoners are known, nearly 70 per cent of debtors had a positive balance of assets. The unpaid debts that led to their incarceration amounted on average to 17 per cent of their total worth. Problems with illiquidity seemed to become exacerbated over time as the

---

[41] Shepard, *Accounting for Oneself*, 35–6; Overton, 'Household Wealth, Indebtedness, and Economic Growth in Early Modern England', 13.

[42] For a modern equivalent, see Thomas Piketty, *Capital in the Twenty-First Century*, trans. Arthur Goldhammer (Cambridge, MA, 2014).

[43] On the notion that economic growth was pushed forward by credit, see Muldrew, *Economy of Obligation*, 118.

Table 2.1 *Constitution of household wealth of imprisoned debtors, Lancaster and London, 1725–1755*

| Occupation | Total wealth (mean value £) | | Household goods (mean value £) | | Real property and leases (mean value £) | | Occupational assets (mean value £) | | Obligations (mean value £) | | Financial Instruments (mean value £) | |
|---|---|---|---|---|---|---|---|---|---|---|---|---|
| | London | Lancaster | London | Lancaster | London | Lancaster | London | Lancaster | London | Lancaster | London | Lancaster |
| Whole sample | 156.7 | 62.4 | 6.8 | 6.4 | 23.5 | 14.3 | 5.4 | 3.2 | 84.9 | 34.2 | 36.0 | 4.2 |
| Farming | 158.7 | 62.2 | 5.4 | 3.6 | 0.0 | 4.3 | 0.0 | 1.9 | 153.4 | 46.9 | 0.0 | 4.3 |
| Crafts | 128.1 | 47.8 | 6.0 | 8.1 | 5.3 | 16.9 | 0.8 | 0.5 | 93.9 | 22.3 | 22.2 | 0.0 |
| Trades | 253.6 | 118.2 | 8.3 | 5.0 | 65.0 | 25.6 | 41.7 | 14.0 | 120.3 | 50.3 | 18.4 | 15.0 |
| Labour | 12.2 | 5.2 | 5.4 | 3.9 | 0.0 | 0.0 | 0.0 | 0.8 | 6.9 | 0.5 | 0.0 | 0.0 |
| Gentry and professional | 378.9 | 30.0 | 12.0 | 18.3 | 115.0 | 0.7 | 0.0 | 0.0 | 30.0 | 11.1 | 221.9 | 0.0 |

*Source:* LRO, LCQS, Insolvent Debtor Papers, 1725 QJB10-13; LMA, Debtors' Schedules, Fleet, Poultry Compter and Ludgate Prisons, 1720, 1749, 1760, CLA/047/LJ/17/020, 024, 025, 030, 043, 046

gap between the debts leading to incarceration and prisoner worth widened (Table 2.2). In 1725 in London, the debts prisoners owed accounted for some 85 per cent of their total wealth. By 1760, debts were worth only about 20 per cent of total assets.

Most imprisoned debtors might be described as illiquid rather than insolvent. Though the total household worth of imprisoned debtors amounted to more than the debts they owed, the possession of this wealth made little difference during insolvency proceedings if it could not be mobilised and used as payment. This was especially the case where prisoners held large proportions of their assets in the form of credit. In 66 per cent of London schedules, credit made up all their household worth. Similar dynamics are evident in Lancaster and Edinburgh. Henry Waldgrave, a comedian in Edinburgh incarcerated in 1751 by the merchant William Clapperton, was owed £96 from various debtors.[44] William Kendle, a slater, was owed £37.[45] In other cases, prisoners held assets in the form of real property or financial instruments that could not be liquidated. James Higham, a trunk maker, was incarcerated in the Ludgate prison in London in 1757 for a debt of £240. His total household worth amounted to £454. Susannah Read, a widow incarcerated in the Ludgate, made investments that could not be easily mobilised. When she was incarcerated for a debt of £83 in 1724, her assets included £92 due by five debtors as well as possession of a dwelling house and one quarter ownership of a ship in Virginia. By most accounts, Read would be considered a wealthy woman, but the forms her property took led her to the debtors' prison.[46]

For widows like Susannah Read, the risks posed by the constitution of middling wealth merged with vulnerabilities associated with life cycle position. Many middling people were at risk of default, but insolvency was also gendered. Insolvency was often the consequence of the need to quickly liquidate assets, a task which could be nearly impossible if wealth was held in the forms of debts owing to an estate. Most men experienced illiquidity as a sustained risk precipitated by a crisis which required them to transfer assets unexpectedly. Women faced an additional risk associated with life cycle position. When a woman was widowed, the household estate had to be settled. Assets were liquidated and credits, debts, stock and flow reconciled. The probate process exposed the problem that household assets were held in the form of obligations. When settling estates, women stood

[44] ECA, BCPA, Petition of Henry Waldgrave, 3 May 1751, Box 285, Bundle 40.
[45] ECA, BCPA, Petition of William Kendle, 8 July 1751, Box 285, Bundle 40.
[46] LMA, Schedule of Susannah Read, 1725, CLA/047/LJ/17/020A.

Table 2.2 *Comparison of assets and debts owed by imprisoned debtors, London*

| Year | Debt owed (£) | | Total wealth (£) | | Debt owed as percentage of total wealth (%) | |
|---|---|---|---|---|---|---|
| | mean | median | mean | median | mean | median |
| 1725 | 20.00 | 8.00 | 23.26 | 8.00 | 85.97 | 100.00 |
| 1748 | 54.79 | 10.00 | 229.89 | 70.55 | 23.83 | 14.17 |
| 1760 | 31.04 | 6.00 | 143.27 | 36.69 | 21.67 | 16.36 |

*Source:* As Table 2.1

to lose their financial worth. Debts died with a person, but a significant portion of an estate could be taken up to satisfy the deceased's debts. Unless it was legally secured, even a widow's own property could be taken to cover her husband's obligations. As a consequence, one quarter of probate accounts ended in debt and as many as one fifth of widows who chose to administer their estates were left in debt or with nothing. As Amy Erickson has argued, because laws of coverture denied women legal rights to property, financial ruin threatened women when their husbands died.[47]

The financial risks associated with widowhood brought women into close proximity with the debtors' prisons. By the eighteenth century, the consequences of a negative estate settlement included incarceration, as creditors used the prisons as leverage to force payment of their obligations. Widows made up about half of the population of female prisoners in Britain. Of the debtors released in the wake of the 1728 Insolvency Act in England, 52 per cent of female prisoners self-identified as widows, while 45 per cent claimed this status in 1748.[48] Furthermore, significant numbers of widows fled their debts. The majority of female debt fugitives who returned to England to take advantage of Insolvent Debtor Relief Acts in the eighteenth century were widows.[49] Of course not all widows were made insolvent as a consequence of their widowhood. Women failed in business just as men did, and their incarceration serves as a reminder that credit was not only a means of female agency, but that relying on credit could also lead to ruin. However, the dynamics of the prison expose the risks women faced as a consequence of demographic dynamics and legal status. While men faced failure as a consequence of a broad set of factors, for women, debt insecurity was a routine feature of life cycle status.

[47] Erickson, *Women and Property in Early Modern England*, 101, 174–5.
[48] *London Gazette*, 1748, issues 8747–8933.   [49] Haagen, 'Imprisonment for Debt', 352.

## The Architecture of the Market and Involuntary Credit

Middling households were made precarious not only by the constitution of their wealth, but also by the nature of the debts that they were owed and the positions that they occupied within the architecture of the eighteenth-century credit market. Middling people were the credit brokers of the eighteenth-century world. Nearly everyone was dependent upon credit to engage in trade and to make everyday purchases, but shopkeepers, trades-people, small masters and retailers stood at the centre of webs of credit. As Defoe explained, credit 'takes its beginning in our manufactures'. He described how a clothier might

> appear to be four or five thousand pounds in debt. But then look into his books, and you shall find his Factor at Blackwell-hall, who sells his Cloths, or the Warehouse-keeper, have two thousand pounds worth of goods in hand left unsold; and has trusted out to Draper and Merchants, to the value of four thousand pounds more.[50]

Success or failure depended upon the 'credit matrix', meaning the balance of credit extended and received.[51] For some, a central position in structures of credit was profitable. Shopkeepers could bury interest rates in their prices and profit by accruing interest, making consumers 'pay warmly' for credit.[52] Others have suggested that credit was the stuff of leverage for small businesses. According to Martin Daunton, 'the mutual indebtedness of traders and producers created a pyramid of credit which could prop up smaller men, such as in the drink trade where shopkeepers were in debt to innkeepers, who were in turn in debt to maltsters, brewers, and wine-merchants.'[53] But for most, enmeshment in credit networks was a point of insecurity rather than an opportunity for profit.

Tradespeople and manufacturers tended to be net creditors. They took on trade debts to obtain goods and raw materials from suppliers. They then sold finished products and services in smaller quantities to consumers on credit. Paying their own creditors depended upon collecting debts from their consumers. In a liquidity crisis, they found it difficult to realise their assets because this required customers to pay their bills.[54] As the individuals who extended the pettiest credit to consumers, tradespeople were fre-quently stuck with bad debts that would never be honoured. The diarist

---

[50] Defoe, *The Compleat English Tradesman*, 341–2.    [51] Daunton, *Progress and Poverty*, 237.
[52] Defoe, *The Compleat English Tradesman*, 413.    [53] Daunton, *Progress and Poverty*, 247.
[54] Daunton, *Progress and Poverty*, 247–52; McKendrick, Brewer and Plumb, *The Birth of a Consumer Society*, 212.

John Cannon's career as a maltster ended in part because of his accumulation of bad debts, including many from individuals who had 'become entirely insolvent', while the shopkeeper William Stout recorded that bad debts were worth nearly 20 per cent of his profits.[55] Notes made in debtors' schedules about the status of obligations show that nearly 60 per cent of the debtors imprisoned in Lancaster Castle had at least some debts marked as uncollectable. The inventory of the linen draper William Worden of Manchester, valued at £34, included £4 worth of debts which Worden 'looked upon to be desperate debts'.[56] In London samples, 15 per cent of all debts noted in schedules were desperate. These numbers were much higher than the rates of uncollectable debt amongst non-imprisoned creditors. J. A. Johnston's study of a Worcester parish in the long eighteenth century found that about 5 to 8 per cent inventories included desperate debts, and that these amounted to some 1 to 2 per cent of the value of estates.[57] Peter Earle's study of elite London inventories at death from the eighteenth century calculated that desperate debts amounted to 7 per cent of the value of the total assets of the deceased.[58]

Debts went bad for various reasons (Table 2.3). The most common was the decease of a debtor. In the carpenter Andrew Clarke's schedule, 32 per cent of the debtors were marked as dead. Richard Wilson, an innkeeper, had outstanding obligations of £54 owed by 30 debtors. The largest single debt of £30 was owed by Jonathan Nichols, a cheese factor marked as deceased, alongside another £8 and 6s. from seven other people marked as dead. Seventy per cent of Wilson's debts were therefore uncollectable.[59] Other debtors had been transported, imprisoned or faced their own financial ruin. Of the 12 people who owed debts to William Morrow, a pedlar, 3 had been imprisoned and 2 had been transported.[60] Some debtors ended up alongside one another in prison. Brian Wildman, a joiner in Lancaster Castle, claimed money 'due to me from Samuell Hall my fellow prisoner'.[61] The debts owing to prisoner Robert Bygrave included £10 owed by fellow prisoner Andrew Clarke 'remaining on the balance of accounts between us for business done and money paid out and expended'.[62]

[55] Money, *Chronicles of John Cannon*, 173; *Autobiography of William Stout of Lancaster*.
[56] LRO, LCQS, Insolvent Debtor Papers, June 1725, QJB10/60.
[57] J. A. Johnston, 'Worcester Probate Inventories 1699-1716', *Midland History* 4, no. 3 (1978): 204.
[58] Earle, *The Making of the English Middle Class*, 118–23.
[59] LMA, Schedule of Andrew Clarke, CLA/047/LJ/17/024; LRO, LCQS, Insolvent Debtor Papers, 1755–6, QJB/31/8.
[60] LRO, LCQS, Insolvent Debtor Papers, 1755–6, QJB/31/16.
[61] LRO, LCQS, Insolvent Debtor Papers, July–September 1725, QJB/12/23.
[62] LMA, Schedule of Robert Bygrave, 1748, CLA/047/LJ/17/024/004.

Table 2.3 *Status of desperate debts due to London*
*prisoners*

| Debtor Status | N | % |
| --- | --- | --- |
| Abroad | *14* | 13.0 |
| At sea | *6* | 5.6 |
| Dead | *30* | 27.8 |
| Bankrupt | *2* | 1.9 |
| Moved residence | *24* | 22.2 |
| Prisoner | *32* | 29.6 |
| Total | *108* | |

*Source:* As Table 2.1

Tradespeople were made vulnerable by the nature of the credit they extended. Debtors' schedules show that obligations owed to middling individuals were small, lingering and long term, and that their credit networks were extensive. Sixty-five debtors imprisoned in Lancaster Castle and released by the 1725 Insolvency Act collectively had 631 debtors of their own. Consumer accounts accumulated over time, forcing shopkeepers to extend what they referred to as 'long credit'. The ability to extend this kind of credit, which allowed consumers to buy now and pay later, was not only a feature that made tradespeople attractive and competitive within the marketplace, it was also a necessity for doing business. Often the length of this credit was claimed by consumers rather than arranged under contract. As the shopkeeper Guy Green wrote, 'The very long credit taken by most of my customers, tho' contrary to agreement makes it difficult to fix a price where a profit will arise worth one's while – and without credit I am in doubt if any considerable business can be carried on.'[63]

The obligation to extend credit as a requirement of business would seem to temper the heavy emphasis historians have placed on trust as the basis of credit, and on creditors' careful assessment of worth. Numerous studies have charted the components of individual credibility and the kinds of information trust were built upon, whether that be personal reputation, the appearance of a moveable estate or trust in intermediaries. In such accounts, problems with trust are often blamed upon information

[63] Guy Green to Josiah Wedgewood, 2 April 1775. Quoted in McKendrick, Brewer and Plumb, *The Birth of a Consumer Society*, 208–9.

asymmetries.[64] The conception of risk that underlies such studies assumes that tradespeople had a substantial capacity for choice in deciding whether they would extend credit. But in a consumer economy that demanded credit, a tradesperson's calculations may have been less about whether they *could afford* to extend credit, and more about whether they *could afford not to*. Extending credit was an obligation rather than a risk to be calculated. Hence, the information that tradespeople collected and maintained about their debtors in making these calculations, as outlined in schedules, appears sparse. Tradespeople seemed to know remarkably little about the people to whom they extended credit. Robert Anderson Martin, an inn holder in the Parish of St Sepulcher in London, knew the occupation of only 5 of his 36 debtors, and could state a residence for only 16 of them. In some cases, he could not even remember a name. For example, he was owed 14s. by 'a person at Stamford Hill near Stoke Newington whose name I cannot recollect'.[65] Others had little sense of the value of debts they were owed. The prisoner Elizabeth Foden had a debt owing of £12 for lent money and also mentioned 'some small debts' that she could not specify.[66]

One of the challenges within the credit market was a problem of timing. While consumers accumulated lingering debts over time, tradespeople and manufacturers took on up-front costs in large lump sums for goods and raw materials from wholesalers. There could be a significant gap between the credit terms set by wholesalers and the credit expected by consumers. Pat Hudson's study of the West Riding Wool Textile Industry shows the discrepancies between manufacturers' credits and debts. While weavers purchased wool from growers and dealers at 3 to 6 months credit, they sold finished cloth at 8 to 18 months credit. This gap forced them either to retain large quantities of capital to use as payment, or to sell their bills on to third parties and lose profit.[67] Cases for debt brought before the bailie court of Edinburgh reveal similar gaps between the length of credit tolerated by wholesalers and retailers. Brewers and merchants, who sold large quantities of goods or ale to retailers who in turn worked directly with consumers, gave credit ranging from 1 to 3 months. By contrast, bakers, tailors and

---

[64] Muldrew, *Economy of Obligation*, 128–57; K. Tawny Paul, 'Credit, Reputation, and Masculinity in British Urban Commerce: Edinburgh, c. 1710–70', *The Economic History Review* 66, no. 1 (2013): 226–48; Shepard, *Accounting for Oneself*, 35–81; Philip Hoffman, Jean-Laurent Rosenthal and Gilles Postel-Vinay, *Dark Matter Credit: Peer to Peer Lending and Banking in France* (Princeton, NJ, 2019).

[65] LMA, Schedule of Robert Anderson Martin, 1748, CLA/047/LJ/17/025/001/093.

[66] LMA, Schedule of Elizabeth Foden, 1725, CLA/047/LJ/17/020A.

[67] Pat Hudson, *The Genesis of Industrial Capital: A Study of the West Riding Wool Textile Industry, c. 1750–1850* (Cambridge, 1986), 191–3, 195.

wigmakers who dealt directly with consumers extended credit for between 2 and 10 months, and waited even longer before pursuing debts in the legal system. Tailors, for example, waited up to an average of 28 months before pursuing debts in court.[68] This position in credit networks placed middlemen's own financial solvency at risk. If consumers defaulted or took too long to pay, the credit of tradespeople suffered, and their bodies stood at risk of imprisonment.

In extending consumer credit, middling tradespeople were stuck between suppliers and two groups of customers who were widely recognised for failing to pay their debts: the elites and the poor. Elite consumers, especially those who patronised the sellers of luxury goods, were notorious for wracking up exorbitant debts and delaying their bills. As Defoe noted,

> we see very considerable families who buy nothing but on trust; even Bread, Beer, Butter, Cheese, Beef and Mutton ... I have known a family, whose revenue has been some thousands a year, pay their Butcher, and Baker, and Grocer and Cheesemonger, by a hundred pounds at a time, and be generally a hundred more in each of their debts, and yet the tradesmen have thought it well worth while to trust them.[69]

By refusing to pay on time, customers forced tradespeople to extend 'hidden' loans as involuntary creditors to their social superiors, using their social standing to delay payment.[70] The dissolute aristocrat failing to pay his debts became a common trope in popular print and was reflected in tradespeople's diaries. Thomas Turner wrote in 1763 of being 'so confined with ... some large debtors in my parish that I hardly know which way to act or extricate myself out of so great a dilemma'. He lamented the need to show wealthy customers favour, reflecting that 'for what by our extravagant living and an indolent way of life we are got into, makes custom so prevalent that rather than retrench our expenses, we too often see people run out of their estates and defraud their creditors.'[71] Similarly, William Stout recounted the financial failure of a man in Lancaster, William Godsalve, as being the consequence of 'being too forwards in creddit' and becoming involved with members of the gentry, to whom he gave 'large creddit' and became 'bound with them to others for large summes, and drew him into costly treats, which much reduced his creddit'.[72]

[68] ECA, BCP, 1730–70.    [69] Defoe, *The Compleat English Tradesman*, 340.
[70] McKendrick, Brewer and Plumb, *The Birth of a Consumer Society*, 212.
[71] Vaisey, *The Diary of Thomas Turner, 1754–1765*, 266, 286–7.
[72] Marshall, *The Autobiography of William Stout of Lancaster, 1665–1752*, 156–7.

In such cases, the mutual exchange of credit did not necessarily lead to mutual interests or mutual obligation because consumer and customer were not equal partners in risk. For elite customers, failure to pay on time could be a way of ensuring loyalty, setting prices and forcing price reductions, which ultimately could lead to wage stagnation. The higher a client's account, the more the merchant's own survival depended upon eventual repayment of the debt. In the world of fashion and consumer goods, this increased the merchant's stake in delivering goods that would expand the client's social credit.[73] If they delayed payment for long enough, elite consumers could exempt themselves from legal proceedings. In Scotland, for example, a variety of obligations, including debts on account, became obsolete three years after the last article was delivered.[74] For middling tradespeople, everyday commerce could therefore involve, in Claire Crowston's words, a 'tyranny of credit'. Some tradespeople occupied 'a strikingly inferior position in credit dealings with their clients'.[75]

While many tradespeople were caught in cycles of debt with elite customers, others were caught in webs of indebtedness created by extending small credit to labourers and the poor. Referred to as 'low credit' by contemporaries, shop credit was offered to labourers at high interest rates which were buried in the prices of goods, consequently ensuring that the poor paid a premium for consumer products. A new class of small retailers, who were often just starting in business, specialised in retailing of this kind. By dealing almost exclusively with the poor, who lacked credit and who often failed to pay up, shopkeepers offering low credit placed themselves at considerable risk. If their customers failed to pay, these tradesmen defaulted on their obligations. As Charles Townshend described in 1751, the proprietors of 'little shops',

> as they buy chiefly on credit and consequently dear, they must also sell dear, and do generally sell on credit. They rarely receive money for what they sell, and being as backward in their payments of what they owe, find a quick transition from these shops to a prison. The poor are their only customers ... and it very often happens, that many of these customers, when they have raised their score to any height, abscond and run away ... it

[73] Clare Haru Crowston, *Credit, Fashion, Sex: Economies of Regard in Old Regime France* (Durham, NC; London, 2013), 176–9.
[74] Andrew MacDowall Bankton, *An Institute of the Laws of Scotland in Civil Rights: With Observations upon the Agreement or Diversity between Them and the Laws of England*, vol. 2. Stair Society 42 (Edinburgh, 1994), 169.
[75] Crowston, *Credit, Fashion, Sex*, 194. For further French comparisons of the troubled credit relationship between tradespeople and elite consumers, see Natacha Coquery, *L'hôtel Aristocratique. Le Marché Du Luxe à Paris Au XVIIIe Siècle* (Paris, 1998).

is plain that the credit, which they give for small sums, does but accelerate the ruin of those who deal with them.[76]

In extending credit to labourers, tradespeople absorbed debts forced onto workers by wealthier employers. Workers waited considerable amounts of time to be paid for their labour.[77] One of the consequences of the scarcity of coinage was that employers lacked a means to pay cash day wages. In the 1750s, when about half of English households were earning income in the form of wages and small payments, a weekly cash wage of 7s.–8s. would have required £221,000–254,000 in circulation. Yet no more than £4,000 was minted every year.[78] Because labour was often the most flexible item in the costs of a business, employers effectively borrowed credit from their workers through 'truck', by delaying the payment of wages or by paying in tokens (offering company credit) rather than coin.[79] Occasionally, these debts are alluded to in prison registers, especially when they related to payments owing to skilled artisans or labourers working for larger firms. For example, 92 per cent of the £209 owed to the glassmaker Joseph Henzey was described as 'wages' owed by firm Thomas Cockburn and Co. Richard Rothwell, a corn dealer imprisoned in Lancaster Castle, was owed £16 for two years' worth of wages.[80] James Lando, imprisoned in the Fleet, was owed money for 'wages due to me as Chaplain on board his majesties ship the Falkland Man of War from the 10th day of June 1744 til January 1746'.[81] In turn, workers like Lando and Henzey, who were paid irregularly, depended upon the availability of credit to make purchases. Irregular payment of wages therefore meant irregular payment of debts to tradespeople. A variety of employers, including elite households, larger manufacturers and even the British Navy, therefore passed their debts on to labourers, and labourers passed them on to traders, so that middling individuals were positioned at the culmination of long lines of debt. In effect, tradespeople financed the early modern equivalent of float and became the ultimate recipients of the eighteenth century's liquidity crisis.

[76] Charles Townshend, *National Thoughts, Recommended to the Serious Attention of the Public. With an Appendix, Shewing the Damages Arising from a Bounty on Corn. By a Land-owner* (London, 1751), 10.
[77] Judy Z. Stephenson, '"Real" Wages? Contractors, Workers, and Pay in London Building Trades, 1650–1800', *The Economic History Review* 70, no. 1 (2018): 116.
[78] Craig Muldrew, 'Wages and the Problem of Monetary Scarcity in Early Modern England', in *Wages and Currency: Global Comparisons from Antiquity to the Twentieth Century*, ed. Jan Lucassen (Bern, 2007), 392–7.
[79] Daunton, *Progress and Poverty*, 247.
[80] LRO, LCQS, Insolvent Debtor Papers, 1755, QJB31/11; QJB12/12.
[81] LMA, Schedule of Rev. James Lando, 1748, CLA/047/LJ/17/025/001/87.

Because tradespeople assumed roles as credit brokers to labourers, towns with large industrial workforces had high middling imprisonment rates. Eighteenth-century Newcastle, a city with a large population of labourers in the coal trade, had one of the highest imprisonment rates in England. There, adult men had a one in four chance of being imprisoned during their lifetime. In Norwich, a town dominated by the worsted industry, 38 per cent of the adult male population saw the inside of the debtors' prison during the 1720s.[82] During this period, worsted faced competition with new and cheaper fabrics such as calicoes. As domestic markets contracted, wages fell by 25 per cent, leading workers to depend more heavily upon credit.[83] In the north-west of England, a region with a large industrial workforce also dominated by textile industries, the concentration of credit risk amongst tradespeople supplying goods and necessaries to workers was alluded to in debtors' schedules. John Nichols, a butcher in Oldham, a centre of fustian production, was imprisoned with assets composed of 80 per cent obligations. Of Nichols' 35 debtors, 13 were weavers. Another six worked in other forms of labour, including coal mining and carrying. More than half of Nichols' debtors would have been subjected to seasonal or irregular wage payments representing the indebtedness of their employers. Those debts were then transferred to Nichols' account book.[84]

As the credit of tradespeople like John Nichols was put increasingly at risk, appeals for eighteenth-century legal reform specifically targeted the problems experienced by urban tradespeople. In 1728, the House of Commons received petitions from gentlemen in Yorkshire, Wiltshire and Devon complaining that it was impossible to use the royal courts to recover small debts. Petitions specifically cited the concentration of credit amongst communities of shopkeepers and other traders who dealt directly with consumers, and described a dynamic wherein delayed payments from consumers prevented these middlemen from paying their own debts, forcing them into poverty. As one petition explained,

> there is in [this] Part of the Kingdom a great Number of industrious Manufacturers, and other poor labourious People, who are often intitled to receive small Sums of Money from Persons they deal with, and labour for; which just Debts they cannot in many Cases recover, without considerable

[82] Haagen, 'Imprisonment for Debt', 67–70.
[83] Penelope J. Corfield, 'The Social and Economic History of Norwich, 1650–1850: A Study in Urban Growth' (PhD, London School of Economics and Political Science (University of London), 1976), 55–7.
[84] LRO, LCQS, Insolvent Debtor Papers, 1755, QJB3/2; Geoffrey Timmins, *Made in Lancashire: A History of Regional Industrialisation* (Manchester, 1998), 17–18.

> Expenses of Suit … whereby they are rendered less able to support their Families.[85]

The solution to the problem seemed to be the establishment of summary courts to facilitate the collection of small consumer debts. Thus, towns with large industrial workforces petitioned Parliament to establish Courts of Request.[86] In 1763, traders in the towns of Bradford, Trowbridge and Melksham submitted a petition to Parliament explaining that in their towns,

> there is a large and extensive trade of superfine Cloth, and other woollen Manufactures, which employs many thousand people, who are perpetually contracting many small Debts; and alleging, that from the Difficulties their Creditors lie under, by the Expence they are unavoidably put to, and the Delays they meet with in suing them, many of those People, though well able, refuse to pay their just Debts.[87]

Without the means to collect the accumulating small debts of consumers, credit became increasingly concentrated in middling communities. As the landed and labourers brought their debts to tradespeople, tradespeople were obliged 'to take credit of one another'.[88] When payment failed to materialise, the bodies of middling people ended up in prison.

## Changing Structures of Credit

Because credit was so important to their wealth and business structures, middling households were the first to be impacted by broader transformations in credit structures. Debt litigation records and debtors' schedules show that from the 1720s, networks of obligation became more dispersed. Debt networks became larger both in terms of the number of individuals involved and in terms of their geographical diffusion. In Lancaster schedules from 1725, prisoners had an average of 6 people owing them obligations. By 1755, they had an average of 17 debtors. In London, prisoners in 1725 had on average 4 debtors, while those submitting schedules in 1748 had 13. Debts were also contracted across longer distances, especially in rural communities, as revealed by the residences of prisoners compared to

---

[85] *Journals of the House of Commons*, vol. 21, 20 Mar 1728, 274. Quoted in Brooks, *Lawyers, Litigation, and English Society*, 45.

[86] For a fuller account of the establishment of Courts of Request, see Finn, *The Character of Credit*, 197–235.

[87] *Journals of the House of Commons*, vol. 29, 4 Feb 1763, 433–4.

[88] Defoe, *The Compleat English Tradesman*, 413.

their debtors. In 1725 in Lancaster, credit networks extended up to 90 miles from prisoners' home residences. By 1755, they extended up to 200 miles.

The extension of credit networks placed pressure on customary means of balancing debt. The mutual exchange between households that characterised early modern credit involved face-to-face contracting the cancellation of mutual debts. Traditionally, this face-to-face credit accumulated over time. For households engaged in reciprocal trade, the bulk of debts eventually cancelled out. For example, the wigmaker Harrold noted 'swapping' debts and goods in his diary. In one entry, he 'swap'd away 5 wig[s] with Roger Gordon for hair for £4 10s and hood and [I] swapped with PBs and Mr Thropes a note for 30s for a fine lock'.[89] Business, personal and household debts, which were not necessarily conceptualised as entirely distinct, could be interchanged. Harrold put 'beer for Mee and Hulme', to whom he owed money for wig-making products, on his account at a local alehouse as a means of cancelling business debts. On 23 August 1712, he 'spent 4d on them at the Fox, so we paid all debts bor'wd'.[90] Households let reciprocal debts accrue for long periods of time, then met to compare their mutual obligations in an act described as 'reckoning'. In theory, good trade practices involved balancing accounts annually. William Stout described his desire to balance and 'clear accounts yearly'.[91] In practice, however, tradesmen and households let debts accrue for years. Most creditors pursued unpaid debts in court in one to two years, but some waited as long as six years before initiating litigation.[92]

As credit jumped the bounds of face-to-face contracting, households that did not engage in direct trade arranged to cancel debts through the accounts of mutual creditors and debtors. In 1730, the Edinburgh slater Alexander Ramsay accepted from John Nairn a promise 'to paynt the breen [brewery] which Baillie Gilepsie posseses' as payment. By doing so, Ramsay effectively used Nairn's debt to satisfy a debt that he owed to Gilepsie.[93] Gnarled webs of debt could entangle multiple households as they attempted to reckon their obligations. John Whitehead, a clothier from York, owed 19s. 'for money and goods laid out for Thomas Coal's use for which said Walmsley and Madam Coal promised to pay'.[94] In 1720, William Burrell, a sailor in Edinburgh, was incarcerated for one year for

---

[89] Horner, *Diary of Edmund Harrold*, 74.      [90] Horner, *Diary of Edmund Harrold*, 29.

[91] Marshall, *The Autobiography of William Stout of Lancaster, 1665–1752*, 96.

[92] Muldrew, *Economy of Obligation*, 201; Paul, 'Credit and Social Relations amongst Artisans and Tradesmen in Edinburgh and Philadelphia, c. 1710–1770', 56–7.

[93] ECA, BCP, *Ramsay v Nairn*, 1730, Box 86, Bundle 213.

[94] LRO, LCQS, Insolvent Debtor Papers, 1755–6, QJB/31/10.

a debt in the form of a bill 'accepted by the said William Burrell payable to Alex Williamsone dated the 6 Sept 1715 and by him indorsed to the said David Tod'.[95]

Over time, increasingly complex chains of debt developed, involving higher numbers of secondary debts, meaning debts that circulated beyond the parties who originally contracted them. Secondary debts usually took the form of bills of exchange or promissory notes, written promises of payment made by one person to another, signed by the maker and engaging to pay the bearer either on demand or at a specified date. Creditors left holding bills could liquidate them before they were due either by 'discounting', which meant giving the bill to a purchaser, normally a bank or an attorney who would offer less than the face value, or by passing it in payment of a claim to another creditor. This creditor would normally buy the debt at a discount, with the intent either of reselling it at a profit, or of collecting the full debt from the debtor, thus profiting in the difference between the full debt and the discounted price. By selling a debt, a tradesperson accepted a reduction in profit in exchange for gaining payment more quickly. The process effectively turned the bill into a kind of paper currency. These paper artefacts of verbal obligation were drawn directly from creditor to debtor, then passed from person to person with each party endorsing the back. The robust legal status of bills facilitated their use as a form of currency. From 1765 in England, bills could be payable to the bearer and completely separate from the original transaction.[96] Evidence from court cases suggests that contemporaries thought of bills as cash. As one litigant claimed, in passing on a bill, 'the one gives and the other receives the bill as a good bill as it were ready money or a bank note.'[97]

Diaries, debt litigation and schedules all provide glimpses of the lives of secondary debts as they circulated from person to person.[98] The London watchmaker William Lloyd described £1 14s. being 'due on a note of hand of the said David Berry and indorsed by the said Isaac Huet to the said William Lloyd'.[99] In one case from Edinburgh, a bill drawn by William Murray against Archibald McEwen, keeper of Parliament House, was passed to John Young, servant to the Earl of Hopetoun, then to Robert Dickson, a writer. Dickson protested the bill in court in 1730, causing the arrest of Robert Pollock, a merchant, who was in debt to Archibald

[95] NRS, ETWLB, 1720, HH11/13.     [96] Daunton, *Progress and Poverty*, 248.
[97] ECA, *Hunter v McNight*, 1730, Box 85, Bundle 212.
[98] Vaisey, *The Diary of Thomas Turner, 1754–1765*, 341–3.
[99] LMA, Schedule of William Lloyd, 1761, CLA/047/LJ/17/046.

Table 2.4  *Frequency of direct and secondary debts pursued*
*in Edinburgh bailie court*

| Type of debt | 1730 (% cases) | 1750 (% cases) | 1770 (% cases) |
|---|---|---|---|
| Direct | 81.2 | 72.6 | 65.0 |
| Secondary | 18.8 | 27.4 | 35.0 |

*Source:* ECA, BCP, 1730, 1750, 1770

McEwen for £20 Scots for shop rent in Parliament House, who then protested a bill of John Simpson, who was indebted to him for £20 Scots. Thus, one bill implicated the credit of five individuals. Over time, as secondary debts became more common, cases involving them appeared in the legal system more frequently. The number of debts at least two degrees removed from the people who originally contracted them increased by 16 per cent between 1730 and 1770 in Edinburgh (Table 2.4). By 1770, more than one third of cases pursued in court were for secondary debts.

Debts could be passed from party to party as a means of reckoning, but their increasing numbers in the legal system are also indicative of a burgeoning secondary credit market and the rise of professional moneylending. Sources occasionally reference moments when debts were explicitly sold. Edmund Harrold noted in 1713 in his diary that 'This day brother Crossley sold part of his 5s promise to John Barlow.'[100] Samuel Hussey, a stationer in London, accounted in his schedule for a note of hand with a balance of £18, which he had given to Mr James Goldsbrough 'to Balance the account'.[101] Secondary debts appeared in diaries and court cases during the same period when the practice of professional 'discounting' within the textile industry, normally undertaken by lawyers or merchants, has been traced by John Smail.[102] In provincial towns, tradespeople who were already central to networks of credit often became the brokers of secondary credit. For example, the shopkeeper Abraham Dent of Kirby Lonsdale offered credit, supplied loans and became a major

---

[100]  Horner, *Diary of Edmund Harrold*, 92.
[101]  LMA, Schedule of Samuel Hussey, 1761, CLA/047/LJ/17/046.
[102]  John Smail, 'The Culture of Credit in Eighteenth-Century Commerce: The English Textile Industry', *Enterprise & Society* 4, no. 2 (2003): 306–8; John J. McCusker, *Money and Exchange in Europe and America, 1600–1775: A Handbook* (Chapel Hill, NC, 1978), n. 21.

discounter of bills.[103] As credit lending was professionalised, lawyers appeared more frequently as plaintiffs in debt cases. In Edinburgh by 1770, lawyers accounted for 9 per cent of the plaintiffs in debt cases that reached the city court.[104]

Women were active participants in professional and secondary credit markets, where they served as guarantors and as facilitators of loans. In schedules, women frequently appeared as the witnesses to debts. Elizabeth Gregory proved the moneylending activities of Paul Marchant, a peruke maker in the Fleet, including a £3 note of hand for money lent by him claimed as part of his household worth.[105] Debts owing to the prisoner John Ravenscroft, a silverware dresser, were all proven by his wife.[106] Finding intermediaries to buy up debts constituted an extension of the roles that women had long assumed in brokering credit relations and trust. As Beverly Lemire has argued, women assumed responsibilities for household credit transactions and played a wider role in facilitating the credit of other households.[107] In the pages of debtors' schedules, single, married and widowed women also lent out money for use.

Female lending is apparent in schedules especially where it involved taking goods as security, and when prisoners claimed ownership of goods in the custody of women who had lent them money. James Lando claimed in 1748 that Mrs Ann Williams had 'in her possession or custody a parcel of linen clothes and wearing apparel (Which I am informed she hath pawned) and for which I have a note of her hand'.[108] Henry Smith, a clothwork dealer in London, claimed in 1761 that Miss Francis Vines had 'some of my wearing apparel which she claims on account of a debt of £36.15.5 I owe her'.[109] Female lending also included the early modern equivalent of payday lending to wage labourers. For example, when one prisoner's wages remained unpaid by the British Navy, Mrs Priscilla How of Great Marlborough Street in London purchased the debts that he owed to several creditors, leaving him instead indebted to her for £130.[110] While female lending has often been characterised as a form of small, informal,

[103] Thomas Stuart Willan and John Waller, eds., *An Eighteenth-Century Shopkeeper: Abraham Dent of Kirkby Stephen* (Manchester, 1970).
[104] NRS, ETWLB, 1740, HH11/20; ECA, BCP, 1730, 1750, 1770, Boxes 85, 86, 119, 120, 122, 144, 145.
[105] LMA, Schedule of Paul Marchant, 1748, CLA/047/LJ/17/024.
[106] LMA, Schedule of John Ravenscroft, 1748, CLA/047/LJ/17/025/002/119.
[107] Lemire, 'Petty Pawns and Informal Lending'; Beverly Lemire, *The Business of Everyday Life: Gender, Practice and Social Politics in England, c.1600–1900* (Manchester, 2005).
[108] LMA, Schedule of Rev. James Lando, 1748, CLA/047/LJ/025/001/87.
[109] LMA, Schedule of Francis Vines, 1761, CLA/047/LJ/17/046.
[110] LMA, Schedule of Rev. James Lando, 1748, CLA/047/LJ/025/001/87.

'unassuming enterprise', schedules confirm female participation in formal lending.[111] Women secured their debts on bond and drew upon legal forms such as indentures. Henry Burdyn's schedule, for example, described an indenture contracted with the widow Elizabeth Reeve, who he described as 'one of my principal creditors'.[112]

## Conclusion

High numbers of prison commitments in eighteenth-century Britain were a direct consequence of economic structures. These structures placed middling people at particularly high risk of default. Middling people's wealth was built upon credit. When we assess how they held their wealth using probate inventories, it becomes clear that high proportions of their wealth were held in the form of debts owing to the household. These debts normally took the form of consumer credit. Often, they had accumulated over long periods of time, and they were insecure, 'simple' debts. Inventories of wealth generated by the Insolvency Acts reveal similar but exaggerated dynamics. Holding large amounts of wealth in the form of credit was a problem because this wealth could not be easily mobilised. By contrast, material property could be more easily liquidated, or even directly transferred through networks of debt. Goods could serve as a form of cash. If households held their wealth in the form of obligations owed to them, they were illiquid and stood at high risk of default.

Middling households were also at risk of default because of the positions they occupied within networks of credit. Increasingly, to be a middling person meant to sit in the middle of long chains of debt. Tradespeople, shopkeepers, craftspeople and the providers of consumer services were obliged to give credit to their customers. They also took on loans from suppliers. In order to meet their own financial obligations, they relied on consumers to pay their debts on time. They often became stuck within long chains of credit, holding worthless IOUs and long lists of accounts that did little to satisfy their own creditors. Tradespeople complained of carrying the debts of labourers (small debtors) and the elite, but in fact, the problems they faced with these two groups were symptomatic of broader structural issues. Despite the Financial Revolution, which generated new forms of secure credit, the problem seemed to get worse before it improved.

[111] Lemire, 'Petty Pawns and Informal Lending'. For an argument for women's substantial and profit-driven lending, see Shepard, 'Minding Their Own Business'.
[112] LMA, Schedule of Henry Burdyn, 1748, CLA/047/LJ/17/024/03.

Over time, credit networks became more extensive and more diffuse. They became creditors to people they did not know, and whom they could not easily pursue when their own debts were called in.

The view that imprisonment was a consequence of endemic structural insecurities stands in contrast to how many contemporaries and subsequent historians have made sense of financial failure. Economic writers pointed to the ethics by which individuals managed their wealth and the role played by unforeseen events and business cycles. According to one contemporary writer, 'Losses by Sea, Disappointments in Trade, during the War; and the Mortality amongst the Horned Cattle, have been the Ruin of many Thousands, who are now confined in Prisons.'[113] Recent histories have tended to link financial failure with unforeseen crises. Hoppit attributed bankruptcies to war, business cycles, local economic conditions, financial crises and weather.[114] Other accounts have emphasised recurrent crop disasters producing volatile prices, inflation, government-imposed fluctuations in the value of coin and financial crises such as the South Sea Bubble.[115] By contrast, the evidence drawn from schedules and debt litigation suggests that middling people were subjected to sustained structural insecurities, punctuated by life events and short-term economic fluctuations, and grounded in a growing and fragile credit market.

---

[113] *Reasons Humbly Offered for an Act for Relief of Insolvent Debtors, and Fugitives for Debt* (London, 1753), 1.
[114] Hoppit, *Risk and Failure*.    [115] Crowston, *Credit, Fashion, Sex*, 168–9.

# CHAPTER 3

# Social Structures of Insecurity

When the glover Archibald How was sent to the debtors' prison for the third time in 1755, the circumstances of his financial failure were contested. How's creditor, Alexander Williamson, framed him as a morally bankrupt debtor. Williamson told the court that he offered How credit on the understanding that he was a person with both the means and the disposition to repay the loan, but How broke his promise. According to Williamson, 'had the prisoner any inclination to pay his just debts he could easily do the same.' He knew that in addition to possessing valuable household goods, How had a salary of £5 sterling yearly as a church officer and as an officer to the Incorporation of Skinners and Furriers.[1]

How's version of the story was, unsurprisingly, quite different. Like many middling tradespeople, he was caught in a long chain of obligation. He depended upon payment from his own debtors in order to satisfy his creditors. In court, he produced an unpaid bill. It included three names: David Mudie, a brewer who owed him 18s. as the balance of an account for gloves; James Nasmith, a brewer, indebted to the extent of £1 1s. 1d., also for gloves; and William Jackson, a city resident of unspecified occupation who had borrowed 5s. in ready money. The total owed to How's household amounted to 13s. more than the £1 11s. that led to his incarceration. But despite the clearly structural nature of his default, How, like Williamson, appealed to a language of morality to defend his case. He claimed that he had 'fairly given in a condescendence of his whole effects and even the inventory of debts'. Yet though he behaved in an 'upright manner', Williamson made the decision to incarcerate him out of vindictiveness and spite. How described his creditor as litigious and claimed that he deliberately 'endeavoured to deprive him', rendering his family 'destitute of all subsistence in all time coming'. He framed Williamson's decision to

---

[1] NRS, Sheriff Court Productions, 'Miscellaneous Legal Papers and Correspondence Relating to How Family', 1708–77, SC39/107/8; NRS, ETWLB, 1755, HH11/17.

incarcerate him as a violation of the ethics of the marketplace. For creditors, imprisonment was a game of power. As one of How's fellow prisoners claimed in a petition, incarcerating a debtor 'may be sport to [his creditors] who now carry everything before them, but it is death to the [debtor]'.[2]

Like most incarcerated debtors, How defaulted because he was disadvantaged by structural complications within the credit market. But default resulted in incarceration because of his creditor's decisions. The system of imprisonment was interpersonal. Debtors were imprisoned because their creditors decided to put them there. The prison population comprised many kinds of debtors. Some were poor and had no means to pay. Others had assets but were illiquid, and still others had the means to pay but refused to honour their obligations. British law made no distinction between misfortune and malfeasance in cases of insolvency. Instead, the law empowered creditors to decide how to treat their debtors, giving them seemingly limitless power. The sheer number of people who experienced the prison would seem to suggest that incarceration was a routine practice. Yet of all the complex questions surrounding the debtors' prisons, why someone would choose to imprison their debtor remains perhaps the most perplexing and elusive. In Williamson's case, imprisonment could be conceptualised as a form of revenge waged against a debtor who he trusted, and who later slighted him by failing to honour a promise. Likewise, it could be part of an economic calculus to extract How's dwindling wealth. Creditors like Williamson chose imprisonment for a variety of complex and entangled reasons. Decisions relied heavily on perceptions of debtors, and the ways in which their creditors understood them to have failed. How's case provides a glimpse at how the people who spent a portion of their lives in debtors' prison were perceived by their communities and how their failures were understood and framed.

The choices made by creditors can be interpreted in relation to economic theories of rationality. Neoclassical economic theory interprets the market as a space of modern and 'rational' behaviour, where individuals make decisions based upon perceived utility, self-interestedness and the calculation of future profit. While theories of self-interest and reason have long histories, the shift towards utility-maximising behaviour is seen to have crystallised in the eighteenth century.[3] The eighteenth-century man of letters was said to have 'invented an economics emancipated from

---

[2] NRS, Court of Session, *Charles Cock v Hammermen of Kinghorn*, 1771, CS271/14459.
[3] Force, *Self-Interest before Adam Smith*; Milton L. Myers, *The Soul of Modern Economic Man: Ideas of Self-Interest, Thomas Hobbes to Adam Smith* (Chicago, 1983); Muldrew, 'Interpreting the Market'.

history and politics and assigned himself the position of exemplary economic man'. This man was motivated by self-interest, 'whose own history
was a career designed to correspond in all its refinement with the economic
mechanism'.[4] Articulated by the likes of Adam Smith and Daniel Defoe,
the new interest in profit-seeking was part of a shift towards individualism
and the development of autonomous selfhood that defined eighteenth-
century social identities.[5]

In contrast to theories of rationality, behavioural economists and social
historians of the market have convincingly argued that individuals made
choices for a variety of reasons other than pure profit maximising.
Narratives of trust, emotion and obligation have been integrated into
histories of commerce, showing that economic practices were embedded
in social and emotive relationships. Individuals, from petty tradespeople to
merchants trading internationally, could not act 'merely for money'.[6]
Because credit was based upon reputation, and because it bound households into relationships of functional interdependence, Craig Muldrew
holds it unlikely that contemporaries 'would have used a language which
stressed private desire for profit over mutual interdependence to interpret
the meaning of what they were doing'.[7]

Viewing economic decision-making from the perspective of failed debt
rather than successful credit makes even more apparent the limits of the
eighteenth century's rational economic man by tempering the association
between utilitarian behaviour and masculinity. Debt, like credit, hinged
upon a code of ethics. Prison cases unfolded as part of a moral and
emotional economy of failure, which involved both perceptions of debtors
and the emotional stimulus of creditors, whether that be the desire for
revenge or the fear of their own failure. The networked and entangled
nature of debt could generate anxiety within a precarious economy, causing creditors to make decisions intended to protect their own solvency.
Although fear and emotions are normally associated with femininity, and
are therefore often absent from mainstream economic discourse, the decisions that led to imprisonment by both male and female creditors were

---

[4] Patrick Brantlinger, *Fictions of State: Culture and Credit in Britain, 1694–1994* (Ithaca, NY, 1996), 34;
Jerome Christensen, *Practicing Enlightenment: Hume and the Formation of a Literary Career*
(Madison, WI, 1987), 12.
[5] Michael Mascuch, *Origins of the Individualist Self: Autobiography and Self-Identity in England,
1591–1791* (Stanford, CA, 1996), 19–23.
[6] Muldrew, 'Interpreting the Market'; Finn, *The Character of Credit*; Sheryllynne Haggerty, *'Merely for
Money'? Business Culture in the British Atlantic, 1750–1815* (Liverpool, 2012), 1, 146, 236; Force, *Self-
Interest before Adam Smith*, 1–6.
[7] Muldrew, 'Interpreting the Market', 177.

bound up with relationships of power and social obligation, and motivated by emotion.[8] *Homo economicus* was an emotional actor. However, his social and ethical concerns were not incompatible with his practical self-interest. Behaviour that was not utility maximising was not necessarily irrational. Recent theoretical and historical accounts make clear that even seemingly disinterested and rational acts could have egoist motivations, including self-pride, desire for the approval of others or awareness of the benefits of a good reputation. Avner Offer argues that a desire for regard drives economic decisions. Contemporary political economists recognised that the labouring poor were motivated by pride.[9] Similarly, seemingly social decisions could bring utilitarian benefits. Entangled languages of practical utility, personal reputation and emotional reaction framed middling people's interpretations of default and influenced their treatment of debtors. Rather than seeing profit motives and social motives as mutually exclusive, within the culture of failure, we might conceptualise them as bound together and interrelated.

### Avengers of Their Own Wrongs: The Utility of Imprisonment

Many creditors chose imprisonment because they viewed it as a practical tool offering them their best hope of being repaid. Under such logic, the decision to incarcerate might be interpreted as rational. Creditors who used the legal institution of the prison as a part of an economic calculus for future repayment were supported by prescriptive discourse and by legal theory. British law infused the decision to incarcerate with practical utility. Unlike processes of bankruptcy or small debt, the legal process of insolvency provided few protections to lenders and made them highly competitive. Most debtors owed obligations to multiple people. For example, Archibald How was indebted to 26 people, including four brewers, two writers, a merchant, a journeyman mason, a smith, a glover, a surgeon, a tailor, a tanner, a shoemaker and a miller.[10] One of the advantages of bankruptcy as a legal process was that it ensured the equal treatment of all a bankrupt's creditors. Upon declaring bankruptcy, commissioners were

---

[8] Nelson, 'Fearing Fear', 129.

[9] Finn, *The Character of Credit*; Offer, 'Between the Gift and the Market'; Niall O'Flaherty, 'Malthus and the "End of Poverty"', in *New Perspectives on Malthus*, ed. Robert J. Mayhew (Cambridge, 2016), 88–91.

[10] NRS, Sheriff Court Productions, Papers Relating to How Family, 1708–77, Extract Act of Liberation in Favour of Archibald How, Glover, 11 December 1755, SC39/107/8.

appointed to manage the debtor's estate, and to work directly with creditors to distribute the debtor's assets between creditors according to their
share of interest. One of the main principles of bankruptcy was that from
the moment of failure, an inadequate fund became the common property
of creditors.[11] Unlike bankruptcy, in cases of default in both England and
Scotland, each creditor pursued their debtor independently. The law, as
one Scottish legal theorist explained, sanctioned 'the right of execution by
individuals, rather than equality between all creditors'.[12]

The lack of a legal provision to ensure equality between creditors meant
that they competed for a share of the debtor's dwindling assets. The first
creditor to coerce a debtor into paying could easily walk away with most of
the debtor's wealth. The law encouraged creditors to do whatever was in
their power to squeeze debtors for what they were due, using the social,
economic and institutional resources at their disposal. It was within
a creditor's interest to be the first to imprison a debtor, or to act quickly
if another creditor incarcerated that debtor first. An article in *Scots
Magazine* explained to readers that 'the moveable and personal estate of
the bankrupt comes to be carried off by the favourite creditors of such
bankrupt, and by those creditors who first come to the knowledge of the
circumstances of the bankrupt.'[13] As the shopkeeper Thomas Turner
recounted, he was motivated to pursue a debtor after being informed
that 'it was expected he would soon be sent to gaol', which would alert
others to the debtor's insolvent status.[14] Because of this system, half of
debtors incarcerated in the Fleet and King's Bench prisons between 1728
and 1770 were committed under the actions of more than one creditor.
One quarter of prisoners were incarcerated for obligations to three or more
individuals. Larger creditors often pursued their debts first, followed by
smaller creditors who began to panic as their debtors' defaults became
public. William Poulton was first incarcerated in the Fleet in 1770 for
a debt of £200 to the Earl of Harcourt. The incarceration was followed by
suits from two smaller creditors for £10 each.[15] It was possible for a debtor
to satisfy one creditor, but to remain incarcerated at the suit of another. For
example, George Paul was incarcerated in the Fleet in April 1746 by the

---

[11] Hoppit, *Risk and Failure*, 36–8; Bell, *Commentaries on the Laws of Scotland*, iv.
[12] Bell, *Commentaries on the Laws of Scotland*, ii.
[13] 'Act of Sederunt, Anent Poindings and Arrestments', *The Scots Magazine*, xv (August 1754): 376.
Here 'bankrupt' is used in the general sense to denote a person who failed financially, rather than in
the stricter legal definition. For legal definitions of bankruptcy, see Hoppit, *Risk and Failure*, 32–4.
[14] Vaisey, *The Diary of Thomas Turner, 1754–1765*, 149.
[15] TNA, Fleet Prison Commitment Book, 1770, PRIS 10/21. F. 31.

actions of eight individuals. The following month, seven of the eight creditors agreed to his discharge. Unable to satisfy the eighth, he applied for a writ of habeas corpus to be transferred to the King's Bench, and would eventually be released in 1748 under the Insolvency Act.[16]

As creditors competed for a share of insolvent individuals' limited assets, imprisonment provided a coercive, physical tool that forced debtors to attend to their obligations first, before honouring other debts. The logic of imprisonment, as outlined by legal theorists, was that the suffering experienced during confinement would force debtors to figure out how to pay. The purpose of imprisonment was 'to impose on the debtor, such a hardship as may force him to pay the debt if he can, or to disclose any funds which he may have concealed'.[17] This strategy was pursued with urgency. When deciding whether or not to incarcerate his debtor, Thomas Turner reflected that 'should I neglect this opportunity, it appears as if I should never have such another. Therefore I think if I do not do it now, I am doing a piece of injustice both to myself and creditors. So I am constrained by near necessity.'[18] Where creditors relied on legal counsel, lawyers advocated the use of the prison as a strategy for negotiation. In the commitment records of the Fleet and King's Bench, the presence of attorneys noted in decisions to release debtors indicates that in at least one third of cases, creditors relied on legal counsel to negotiate the prison system.[19] The decision to incarcerate was a carefully crafted legal strategy designed to give creditors the best chance of collecting their debts.

Imprisonment was useful because it encouraged debtors to marshal whatever resources they had access to. The coercive power of the prison gave creditors access to forms of property that were protected in common law debt proceedings, including wages, some forms of paper credit, the tools of one's trade and, perhaps most important, the wealth of others. When faced with incarceration, debtors handed over household goods or other material forms of wealth. In the court cases leading to imprisonment, creditors indicated that they chose to incarcerate those debtors who they knew possessed material assets. Marjory Herriot's creditor 'condescended on her having many valuable objects such as a gold watch and other things of great value'.[20] If debtors lacked goods, they might mobilise their own

---

[16] TNA, Fleet Prison Commitment Book, 1746–8, PRIS1/1.
[17] Bell, *Commentaries on the Laws of Scotland*, 572, 582.
[18] Vaisey, *The Diary of Thomas Turner, 1754–1765*, 252.
[19] TNA, Fleet Prison Commitment Book, 1746–8, PRIS 1/10; King's Bench Prison Commitment Book, 1747–8, PRIS 4/2.
[20] ECA, BCP, 1771, Box 285, Bundle 41.

credit networks or turn to family to pay their debts. In 1729, when the servant Elizabeth Aitcheson was imprisoned for a debt of 18s., her sister and her sister's husband approached the creditor, obtained a loan for 10s. from a third party, laid down 3s. in coin, and pledged a wool blanket as security for the rest.[21] Because contemporaries believed that the debtors' prison endangered the lives of its inhabitants, 'the feelings of the friend were often tortured to administer to the resentment or interest of the creditor.' During a parliamentary debate, it was suggested that 'the creditor often proceeded against the unfortunate debtor to the utmost severity of the law, with a view to torture the compassion of his relations or acquaintances into a subscription for his relief.'[22]

Prisoners called upon their friends and their trade associations to help them to pay their debts. One pamphlet described how a debtor would normally 'send to his Friends, acquaint them with his Misfortune, in hopes of their Assistance'.[23] Collective associations, including trade incorporations and guilds, as well as charitable institutions, provided relief to incarcerated debtors, offered them loans and paid for their discharge. In London, debtors were discharged by the Draper's Company, the Fuller's Charity and the Thatched House Society, who claimed to have discharged 996 individuals from prison in 1774 alone.[24] In Edinburgh, the Incorporation of Wrights and Masons offered similar forms of aid. In 1726, the Incorporation gave £10 to the wright Alexander Anan to liberate him after he had been 'cast in prison about three weeks agoe by a rigid creditor'.[25] Aiding incarcerated debtors like Anan could amount to a significant annual expenditure. In one year alone, the Incorporation spent nearly £30 to relieve members from prison. Expenditures around the debtors' prison were in fact so high that the organisation passed a motion to stop relieving prisoners when it became clear that creditors were using incarceration as leverage to extract the payment of freemen's debts from the Incorporation's stocks.[26]

---

[21] ECA, BCP, 1730, Box 86, Bundle 214; NRS, ETWLB, 1730, HHii/17.

[22] *Cobbett's Parliamentary History of England*, vol. 30, 648, vol. 33, 181.

[23] *The Compulsive Clause in the Present Act of Insolvency, Fully Stated, with Its Good and Bad Consequences Plainly Stated and Clearly Answered: To Which Is Annexed, Proposals for the More Effectual Recovery of Debts, and without Arrests: With the Evils of Goals for Debtors Reasonably Exposed* (London, 1761), 25.

[24] Halifax, *A Sermon Preached at the Parish Church of St. Paul*, 9.

[25] National Library of Scotland (hereafter NLS), Petitions to Marys Chapel 1725–7, Acc. 7332, Box 2.

[26] ECA, Acts and Statutes of Marys Chapel, 4 January 1723, 7 April 1724, 8 February 1725; Peter Clark, *British Clubs and Societies 1580–1800: The Origins of an Associational World* (Oxford, 2000), 107, 337, 378.

Proponents of the debtors' prison both north and south of the border saw the laws of insolvency as commercial in spirit, and read older debt laws through a new economic lens. Credit greased the wheels of commerce and facilitated commercial enterprise. Those who lent needed protection, and imprisonment was an instrumental means of enforcing the payment of outstanding debts. Daniel Defoe defended the rights of tradesmen to imprison their debtors in a 1729 pamphlet, where he wrote about imprisonment as an important tool within an economy where credit depended upon trust. 'The security of the tradesman's trusting his neighbour', he wrote, 'is the power he has by law to *enforce* his payment, and of arresting and imprisoning the debtor if he fails or refuses: The law is the tradesman's *security*'.[27] Without imprisonment, contemporaries feared, credit markets would deteriorate, leading to the stagnation of trade. As Lord Kenyon commented, 'credit would be sparily given, where there were not the means of enforcing payment of the debt.' The power to arrest debtors 'conduced in an essential degree to the increase of commerce and the extension of trade: that if the security it afforded the creditor was weakened, it would produce the most serious consequences'.[28] The law thus shaped the calculus around debt as well as the culture in which failure was negotiated and understood. By failing to regulate the relationship between creditors and debtors who could not pay, British law not only allowed, but even obligated creditors to be their own judges. As one parliamentary debate suggested, creditors were forced into being 'the avengers of their own wrongs'.[29]

## 'A Prison Pays No Debts'?: The Practicalities of Extracting Debtor Wealth

In theory, prisons protected the interests of lenders. However, in practice, creditors had to balance the utility of imprisonment with the knowledge that they might expect no financial reward from incarcerating their debtors. While commentators like Defoe argued that the debtors' prisons made credit more secure, reformers argued that in addition to inflicting undue hardship on debtors, prisons denied creditors their just payment. According to one author, 'the Obstinacy of one Creditor, not only deprives a Man of his Liberty, but also hinders his other Creditors from their just

[27] Daniel Defoe, *Some Objections Humbly Offered to the Consideration of the Hon. House of Commons, Relating to the Present Intended Relief of Prisoners* (London, 1729), 20.
[28] *Cobbett's Parliamentary History of England*, vol. 33, 182.
[29] *Cobbett's Parliamentary History of England*, vol. 30, 648.

Share of his Effects, which the Debtor would be glad to surrender for his Discharge.'[30] A contemporary proverb stated that 'a prison pays no debts.'

Analysis of the mechanisms by which debtors were released from prison, detailed in the extant commitment books of three prisons, suggests that many creditors received at least partial payment of their debts by using incarceration as a tool (Table 3.1), and consented to the discharge of their debtors. Discharge could indicate a number of arrangements, and these changed over time. Acts passed in 1696, 1701, 1704 and 1739–48 facilitated the discharge of debtors if they consented to enlist in the army or the Royal Navy.[31] In the years surveyed, one third of debtors in the Fleet and King's Bench prisons were discharged. In Edinburgh, just over half of incarcerated debtors were released by the pursuer's (plaintiff's) consent, meaning that the incarcerating creditor agreed to the prisoner's release, which was legally possible if the debtor owed less than 200 Merks Scots (£21s. 7s. 8d. Sterling).[32] Creditors might consent to a prisoner's release for a number of reasons. In most cases, presumably they had received some sort of compensation, if not payment of the debt in full.

Discharge could indicate informal arrangements obscured by the formal records of the prisons. Personal papers occasionally provide glimpses of these agreements. In some cases, creditors must have consented to the liberation of their prisoners if it became clear that they had no means to pay. In other cases, creditor consent to discharge was the result of an agreement made between parties outside of the legal system. For example, the Edinburgh prison clerk noted that one prisoner was released by his creditor; 'they have settled matters betwixt themselves.'[33] In 1769, Charles Christison was released by an 'agreement made'.[34] In other cases, agreements might have included arrangements to contract the debtor's future labour. The Lancaster shopkeeper William Stout noted that the insolvent Robert Carter 'by the favour of his creditors had his liberty and got to be land waiter in the Custom House'.[35] In this case, the creditors arranged for Carter's employment in order to secure the repayment of their debts. Occasionally, bailiffs or prison clerks served as intermediaries between

---

[30] *Reasons Humbly Offered for an Act for Relief of Insolvent Debtors, and Fugitives for Debt*, 2.

[31] N. A. M. Rodger, *The Wooden World: An Anatomy of the Georgian Navy* (London, 1986), 156–8; J. Ross Dancy, *The Myth of the Press Gang: Volunteers, Impressment and the Naval Manpower Problem in the Late Eighteenth Century* (Woodbridge, 2015), 114–15.

[32] John Erskine, *An Institute of the Law of Scotland, in Four Books. In the Order of Sir George Mackenzie's Institutions of That Law* (Edinburgh, 1783), 1148.

[33] NRS, ETWLB, 1780, HH11/30.      [34] NRS, ETWLB, 1769, HH11/28.

[35] Marshall, *The Autobiography of William Stout of Lancaster, 1665–1752*, 100.

Table 3.1 *Mechanisms used to release imprisoned debtors, London and Edinburgh*

| London | | | | Edinburgh | | |
|---|---|---|---|---|---|---|
| Release mechanism | $N$ | % | Average no. days incarcerated | Release mechanism | $N$ | % |
| Discharged | 932 | 35.9 | 184 | Pursuer consent | 320 | 50.8 |
| Insolvent Act/Listed in London Gazette | 535 | 20.6 | 632 | Pursuer satisfied | 136 | 21.6 |
| Supersedeas | 474 | 18.3 | 218 | Act of Grace | 96 | 15.2 |
| Died | 184 | 7.1 | 522 | Act of Court | 37 | 5.9 |
| Moved by writ of habeas corpus | 169 | 6.5 | 92 | Cessio bonorum | 18 | 2.9 |
| Court order | 112 | 4.3 | 451 | Released as soldier | 10 | 1.6 |
| Lord's Act | 101 | 3.9 | 304 | Released on bail | 8 | 1.3 |
| Gone/Escaped | 36 | 1.4 | N | Died/Escaped | 5 | 0.8 |
| Certificate of bankruptcy | 28 | 1.1 | 61 | Total | 630 | |
| Other | 26 | 1.0 | N | | | |
| Total | 2,597 | | N | | | |

*Source:* TNA, Fleet Prison Commitment Books, 1736–7, 1745–8, 1770–2, PRIS 1/6, PRIS 1/10, PRIS 10/21; King's Bench Prison Commitment Books, 1747–9, 1772, PRIS 4/2, PRIS 4/4; NRS, ETWLB, 1730, 1750, 1770, HH11/17, 24, 28

creditors and prisoners, and provided opportunities for negotiation. When a creditor initiated the arrest of Margaret Clelland, a widow in Edinburgh, she recounted that David Seedy, the constable, 'hath granted me the faver till his return not to pound nor take me out of my house'. Seedy provided time and space for Clelland to make arrangements before enforcing the arrest.[36] Where payment of the debt was recorded, this was almost always less than the full amount owed. For example, Deborah Melvin, a servant in Edinburgh, was released after paying 5s. Scots of a 13s. debt. In 1760, John Farquhar, a merchant, set his prisoner at liberty after £10 13s. were consigned in the hands of the prison keeper, of a total debt of £13 5s. Creditors in these cases must have felt that partial payment was better than nothing, and consented to release their prisoners with only partial satisfaction of the debt.

[36] NRS, 'Correspondence of George Innes', 1733, GD113/2/42.

Some debtors obtained their discharge by acquiring a loan from a third party to pay off the incarcerating creditor. Moneylending, facilitated by prison keepers and turnkeys, was rife within the debtors' prisons, and appears to have been used both to pay for victuals while in confinement and to secure release.[37] Though moneylending occurred outside of the formal records kept by the prisons, glimpses of the practice emerge in cases where debtors were imprisoned twice, having secured their first release by procuring a loan, then were re-imprisoned when that loan went unpaid. The wright James Wilkinson was imprisoned in the Edinburgh Tolbooth twice in 1780 for debts of the same value. He was first incarcerated by James Hamilton, then released by the creditor's consent. The process of release involved the active participation of a third party, the builder Robert Russel, who seems to have brokered an informal arrangement with the creditor, and placed the loan 'in the hands of the keeper which was paid to the creditors'. There are no further details of the arrangement brokered by Russel, or how the prisoner agreed to repay him. But within one month, Wilkinson again found himself in prison, this time at Russel's mercy.[38] Moneylending also emerges in cases where imprisoned debtors fell prey to predatory lenders. Pamphlets from the early eighteenth century discussed the rise of tallymen around the debtors' prisons.[39] In 1760, the Edinburgh lender James Ross was found guilty of usury and lending several people money and 'taking sometimes at the rate of sixty sometimes at the rate of thirty per annum of interest', which the court noted was 'more than treble the legal interest'. His debtors included Helen Watson, spouse of James Williamson, who was at the time incarcerated in the Edinburgh Tolbooth. Watson had borrowed 40s. at the rate of 6 per cent per month to secure her husband's release.[40]

If one third to one half of creditors in Britain were able to obtain something from their debtors by contracting their labour, forcing them to liquidate assets or encouraging them to make agreements with third parties, many more obtained nothing at all. In Britain, debtors could obtain their release by appealing to various legal technicalities which effectively cleared their obligations. In the King's Bench and the Fleet, 18 per cent of debtors applied successfully for a writ of *supersedeas*. Having been incarcerated on the mesne process, they were released because their cases were never brought to trial. In these instances, frustrated creditors abandoned their suits, leading debtors to be discharged automatically.[41] Six

---

[37] Bodleian Library, John Baptist Grano, 'Journal of My Life inside the Marshalsea', MS. Rawlinson D.34, 30 May 1728, f. 1–2.

[38] NRS, ETWLB, 1780, HH11/30.   [39] White, *Mansions of Misery*, 3.

[40] NRS, ETWLB, 1760, HH11/26.   [41] Innes, 'King's Bench', 255.

per cent of prisoners in Edinburgh and 4 per cent in London were released by acts of court or court orders, usually on the grounds of legal technicalities. Debtors deemed too poor to pay their debts could be released by the Act of Grace in Scotland or by England's Lord's Act. If debtors were found too poor to feed themselves, the court ordered their creditor to provide a weekly allowance for subsistence, and the debtor was freed if the creditor failed to pay. Fifteen per cent of prisoners in Edinburgh and 4 per cent in London were freed by this mechanism, and were not required to hand over any remaining effects to their creditors (nor might creditors expect much given their impoverished condition).[42] Contemporary commentary suggests that there was a certain amount of shame associated with taking the Acts. A German commentator wrote that 'the English do not think it disgraceful to be imprisoned for debt, but they think it exceedingly so to be declared *cleared by the act*,' and further that few debtors chose to take the act because 'the oath that they are obliged to take, hurts their self-love.'[43] Being incarcerated was a signal that a debtor had defaulted, but taking the Act of Grace or the Lord's Act was a sign that they were truly destitute, with little chance of recovering financially.

Legal processes established in the long eighteenth century allowed imprisoned debtors to obtain their release by offering up what they had to their creditors. In 1 per cent of cases in London, debtors were discharged by obtaining a certificate of bankruptcy, essentially shifting their case out of the prison system and into a different legal process. Similarly, in about 3 per cent of cases in Edinburgh, creditors forced their debtors into declaring a process of *cessio bonorum* (essentially the precursor to bankruptcy), and recovered a portion of their debts by sale of the debtors' property. In England, debtors could apply for release under the periodic Insolvency Acts. The Acts were designed to benefit creditors. The application process required debtors to provide an inventory of their wealth. They were allowed to keep property up to a certain amount (normally £10) and to keep their clothes, bedding and tools of their trade. Any property beyond these thresholds had to be itemised, and from 1719, was assigned to the creditors.[44]

---

[42] *Essay on the Forms of Writings, or of Securities and Conveyances, Both of Heritable and Moveable Subjects, as They Are Used in Scotland; and the Law Itself as Applicable to Their Nature, and the Use of Them in General Practice* (Edinburgh, 1786), 166.

[43] Johann Wilhelm von Archenholz, *A View of the British Constitution. And, of the Manners and Customs of the People of England* (Edinburgh, 1794), 285–6.

[44] 'An Act for the Relief of Insolvent Debtors', 1719, 6 George I, c. 21.

Figure 3.1  *Discharge of Insolvent Debtors, Sept. 2, 1743.* London, 1761. © The
Trustees of the British Museum

The Insolvency Acts should have benefitted creditors by forcing debtors
to inventory and ultimately to sell their assets. However in practice,
44 per cent of debtors declared in their schedules that they had no estate
at all. Three per cent listed material goods that could be liquidated, while
half held wealth in the form of debts owing to them, which were often
desperate, difficult to collect and, as discussed in Chapter 2, had most likely
landed them in prison in the first place. Where possible, it seems that
prisoners preferred to obtain other forms of release, and relied upon this
mechanism as a last resort. A 1761 satire of debtors lining up to take the Act,
'Discharge of Insolvent Debtors, Sept. 2, 1743', suggests that contemporaries hardly saw these prisoners as the types with resources to draw upon
(Figure 3.1).[45] Theft, poverty and destitution were represented by
a pickpocket, a distraught man in rags, an old man on crutches,
a woman being seduced by a bawd and a gaoler attempting to extract
fees. These were the desperate whose insecurity had occasioned a sharp
descent into poverty.

---

[45] 'Discharge of Insolvent Debtors, September 2, 1743'. London, 1761, British Museum, 18,680,808.37.

The number of prisoners who relied upon Insolvency Acts for their release varied from year to year: 28 to 40 per cent of those committed during years when Acts were passed turned to this legal mechanism to secure their release, while 8 to 10 per cent of those committed during non-Act years were released in this way. However, during non-Act years, other legal mechanisms became more important means of release. The number of prisoners released by *supersedeas* and the Lord's Acts doubled during non-Act years, then decreased when Insolvency Acts became available. There was therefore a consistent population of one third to one half of prisoners in the Fleet and King's Bench who relied upon different forms of legal relief for release, and whose creditors stood to gain very little by their incarceration.

If mechanisms of release are linked with incarceration time, it becomes clear that there were two classes of prisoners: those who were released very quickly (within a few months if not a few days), who probably found the means to pay and whose creditors used the prison as a short-term means of coercion; and a class of longer-term prisoner who either had no means of payment, or who remained in prison to protect their property. Commitment books show that categories of release that involved paying off at least part of the debt ensured a faster means of liberation. Those prisoners released by Insolvency Acts remained in prison for three times as long as those discharged by their creditors, who were released on average after six months (Table 3.1). Prisoners who were able to obtain certificates of bankruptcy did so fairly quickly, normally within two months.

Those prisoners who did not find a way to obtain their liberty quickly faced a deeper state of ruin. The longer a debtor remained in prison, the more his or her financial situation deteriorated. It was well known that only those with no resources to draw upon ended up in prison for long periods. As one pamphlet explained, gaolers 'keep none confined, but such as have not Money to purchase Liberty'.[46] Incarceration did little to secure payment for creditors because it denied most inmates their labour. Some London prisons enabled prisoners to continue carrying out their trades from within the prison walls. A report made to the parliamentary committee investigating imprisonment for debt suggested that in the King's Bench, as many as one fifth of prisoners worked in their trades. Those with professional occupations who required little space or specialist

---

[46] *The Cries of the Oppressed, Humbly Submitted to the Serious Consideration of the Honourable the House of Commons: Or the Very Hard Case of Insolvent and Other Miserable Debtors Set Forth in Their Proper Colours* (London, 1712).

equipment found it the easiest to continue working, and those on the masters' side had more opportunities than those confined to the common side. The keeper of the Giltspur Compter recorded debtors on the masters' side working as lawyers, carvers, tailors and pattern drawers, while on the common side, 'non[e] work at trades'.[47] Numerous eighteenth-century novels were penned from within prison walls, creating a relationship between the prison and the novel.[48] Prisons provided opportunities for service work, which was taken up especially by women. The incarcerated musician John Baptist Grano's diary recorded examples of women running errands, doing washing, cooking, selling drink and even running a restaurant, although it is not always clear whether these women were incarcerated debtors or women who had crossed the porous boundaries of the prison in search of labour opportunities. Some were certainly the dependents of imprisoned debtors. In a London settlement examination, the widow Ann Jones, who worked as a hired servant to the victualler Thomas Collard, testified having gone to live in the Fleet with her master, where she continued to act as his servant for three years.[49]

Where work opportunities existed in the debtors' prisons, they were often partial. Grano was able to continue teaching music lessons while confined, but he also fretted about the loss of labour occasioned by his incarceration, reflecting in his diary, 'I hope in God I shall not loose all my Labour believing I shall reap some profit and more honour by my Poor Endeavours.'[50] Furthermore, the ability to work seems to have been limited to a few prisons. The facilities at most provincial institutions and the conditions of incarceration prevented debtors from working. Imprisoned debtors claimed that imprisonment denied them their labour, disconnected them from networks of business and credit and caused them lose income. By forcing them to neglect business, the prison ensured that they would never pay their creditors back. The schoolmaster in Edinburgh William Stevenson petitioned the city magistrates that 'had I got time to teach out my scholars and had not been prevented by the creditor's cruelty there would have been owing me . . . seventeen pounds sterling.'[51] Another claimed that his credit had declined since being incarcerated, telling the

---

[47] House of Commons, *Report for the Committee Appointed to Enquire into the Practice and Effects of Imprisonment for Debt* (1792), 69–7, 80–1.
[48] Finn, *The Character of Credit*, 129–30, 52–5; Lucy Powell, 'Doing Time: Temporality and Writing in the Eighteenth-Century British Prison Experience', *Life Writing* 15, no. 1 (2 January 2018): 59–77.
[49] *London Lives, 1690–1880* (www.londonlives.org), St Botolph Aldgate Parish: Pauper Settlement, Vagrancy and Bastardy Exams. 16 July 1795, GLBAEP103030044.
[50] Bodleian Library, Diary of John Baptist Grano, 3 August 1728, f. 57.
[51] ECA, BCPA, 1737, Box 285, Bundle 40.

court that 'he was very much respected by several creditable persons in the city and had considerable business at the time of his being put to for this debt,' but now he was unable to labour and his family was cast into poverty.[52] David Balfour, arrested by his barber for a debt of £25 Scots (£1 18s. 5d. Sterling), complained, 'I have lost all the means and industrie that I could in all possibility use for their satisfactione and payment,' and worried that 'I shall never be capable . . . to get my affairs and bussines put in a regular circumstance no order to the payment of my debts.'[53] The petition of Samuel Fairly from Lancaster told the justices that 'your petitioner is now reduced to the utmost extreamity . . . and cannot this quarter meet with any thing wherewith to employ and subsist himselfe.'[54] A petition for relief from Roger Cropper in Lancaster claimed that he had 'noe effects at all rail or personall whereby he can labour [or] subsist dureing his imprisonment'.[55] The debtors' prisons caused inmates like Balfour, Fairly and Cropper to spiral into downward mobility.

The theme of lost labour was echoed in pamphlet literature. One of the recurring arguments for prison reform in the eighteenth century hinged upon the effect that confining labourers had upon the nation's economic health. As one reform pamphlet argued, 'there are not one hundred persons in the King's Bench, employed in any business.'[56] According to another, imprisoned debtors were 'useless to themselves, and the Publick too, which they are more capable of serving in their several Trades and Professions'.[57] Samuel Johnson estimated in 1759 that the nation lost £300,000 per annum through imprisoned debtors' inability to work.[58] Others worried that skilled tradesmen would flee abroad, contributing their skills to Britain's enemies. One reform pamphlet from 1753 warned that in order to avoid the gaol, indebted manufacturers were fleeing to Spain, Portugal and France, where 'for the Sake of Bread and free Air, they may be induced to enter into Employments detrimental to the Interest of their native Country.'[59] According to another, the relationship between the debtors' prison and labour made the institution 'absurd'. Debtors' prisons

> extracted from the dungeons of distress and the cells of inactivity, to which it doomed the victims of its operation, a something from those very persons,

---

[52] ECA, BCPA, 1721, Box 285, Bundle 40.     [53] ECA, BCPA, 1711, Box 285, Bundle 40.
[54] LRO, Relief for Samuel Faireclough, Debtor Prisoner at Lancaster, 1724–5, QSP/1233/12.
[55] LRO, Relief for Roger Cropper, Debtor-Prisoner, 1722, QSP/1193/10.
[56] Christopher William Johnson, *Considerations on the Case of the Confined Debtors in This Kingdom* (London, 1793), 32.
[57] *The Honour and Advantage of Great Britain*, 8.     [58] Samuel Johnson, *Idler*, no. 38 (1759), 55.
[59] *Reasons Humbly Offered for an Act for Relief of Insolvent Debtors, and Fugitives for Debt*, 2.

which, when free and undisturbed, and in the exercise of all faculties, they could perform, and who were rendered incapable of performing it from the very obstacles thrown in their way by those who exacted that performance.[60]

In addition to denying them their labour, the very process of imprisonment was expensive for debtors and sapped their few remaining financial resources. Debtors often sold what they owned to pay for their maintenance (for which they were responsible while incarcerated), leaving them with little to satisfy their obligations. After several months in prison, the Lancaster debtor John Chetham claimed his 'personal estate is only a few household goods of little value'.[61] George Maychell told the court that he 'is become soe necessitous that he has been forced to sell his bed whereupon he lay for want of maintenance'.[62] Because debtors were expected to assume the costs of their own imprisonment, incarceration caused prisoners to sink further into debt. Britain's eighteenth-century prisons were semi-privatised institutions, run as forms of enterprise. Turnkeys and prison keepers rented lodgings to inmates, sold them ale and food and offered loans. Alexander Allan, a wright in Edinburgh, amassed a debt of 15s. for 13 nights of incarceration. This included arrest fees, prison fees, aliment and 'relief'. At the time of his liberation, William Thompson, a tradesman incarcerated for four months in the Edinburgh Tolbooth in 1773, owed £4 3s. 2d., which included £3 for the price of a bed, 10s. due to the servant of the prison and 5s. 4d. to the prison clerks for drawing up legal papers. He had also taken out loans to maintain himself, and owed £1 3s. for 'relief' from the prison keeper as well as 3s. from a fellow prisoner. These debts could keep prisoners confined even if the obligations that had led to imprisonment had been satisfied. In London, it was reported in the late seventeenth century that 8 per cent of incarcerated debtors were being held for fees only.[63]

Due to the expenses associated with incarceration, it made little sense to imprison a debtor unless a creditor was certain that he or she had assets to hand over. In Scotland, it cost the average creditor 7s. in legal expenses to obtain the right to imprison a debtor, and half of imprisoned debtors owed debts of less than £2. On average, court fees amounted to more than 20 per cent of the total obligation that creditors were owed. Furthermore, these fees did not represent the full costs of pursuing a debtor. In addition to

[60] *Cobbett's Parliamentary History of England*, vol. 30, 647.
[61] LRO, 'Certificate of Poverty of John Chetham', 1725, QSP/1241/8.
[62] LRO, 'Relief for George Maychell', 1722, QSP/1189/2.
[63] NRS, ETWLB, 1773, HH11/29. *Cobbett's Parliamentary History of England*, vol. 30, 647–9; *An Humble Representation upon the Perpetual Imprisonment of Insolvent Debtors* (London, 1687), 25–6.

court fees, payment had to be made to the messenger or bailiff for capturing a debtor, and a nightly fee was due to the gaoler.[64] Given these costs, legal manuals advised their readers that it only made sense to pursue this course of action if the debt was of 'considerable value'. Daniel Defoe warned his readers against 'throwing good money after bad'.[65] The futility of confining debtors was often stated in print, and formed one of the central arguments of reformers who fought to abolish imprisonment for debt. As one pamphlet argued, 'it is needless to imprison the body; for 20 years imprisonment dischargeth not a penny of the debt.'[66] Yet throughout the eighteenth century, creditors found it expedient to imprison individuals who owed the pettiest debts in droves.

As creditors considered the option of incarceration against the possibility of diminishing returns and expenses, their decisions involved a strategic calculation. In pushing for imprisonment, creditors knew that they hampered a debtor's earning potential. When choosing incarceration, they balanced the chance of gaining partial payment with the knowledge that they might receive nothing at all. At the same time, by choosing imprisonment, creditors ensured that any resources leveraged from friends or family would go to them first. If they were not satisfied for the debt in full, the use of imprisonment to squeeze even a fraction of the original obligation could be part of a calculated strategy. Creditors weighed the expected utility of being the first to dun a debtor against holding out and getting paid back in full if the debtor's circumstances improved, balanced with the risk that another creditor might imprison the debtor first and obtain preference for their debt. For many, incarceration was an effective mechanism to pursue their debts, albeit one that was highly coercive and that came with a substantial human cost.

Evidence from diaries lends the impression that this calculus was a relatively normal part of everyday commerce and the negotiation of debts. For example, in attempting to secure a debt of £66 for wool, the young merchant Samuel Jeake of Rye visited his debtor three times 'without more effect then promises', then ordered his lawyer to have the debtor arrested. The act was noted casually in the diary, without any emotion and alongside an account of the weather that day. Within two months, the debtor had paid in full and was released from prison.[67] In another entry, Jeake noted taking out a warrant against Capt. Edwards 'because he refused to let me have the wheat I bought and got

---

[64] ECA, Edinburgh Town Council Minutes, 17 July 1728, SL1/1/51.

[65] Daniel Defoe, *Review of the State of the English Nation*, 1:58, 247–8; Ofspring Blackall, *The Works of Ofspring Blackall*, vol. 1 (London, 1723), 247–8. Quoted in Haagen, 'Imprisonment for Debt', 267.

[66] *The Case of Prisoners for Debt Consider'd* (Dublin, 1727), 4.

[67] William Andrews Clark Library, Samuel Jeake, 'A Diary of the Actions & Accidents of My Life', MS.1959.0006, 8 October 1683, f. 90, 6 December 1683, f. 91.

him arrested same day and he complied'. Jeake had him arrested again 10 days later, 'for after I had paid him for the wheat he did not pay the custome as he was obliged by his bargain.' In these types of cases, debtors had their own negotiating tools. Edwards, 'being a very litigious person', responded to the arrest warrant by going 'all about the towne to get baile which if he could have obtained he would have held me in suite and hindred my sale of the corn'. Finding no one to bail him, Edwards ended up paying the custom fee. Jeake's comments suggest that on the spectrum of legal proceedings, using the prison was a relatively inexpensive and quick tool. He paid fees of 13s. to have Edwards arrested and incarcerated, whereas pursuing a case fully through the courts might have taken much longer and cost much more. As Jeake reflected, by using incarceration as a negotiating tool, he was 'very glad it was ended without more adoe'.[68]

## Deterrence and Coercion

Incarceration had practical applications even if a debtor never saw the inside of a prison. Debtors' prisons gave creditors the power to threaten their debtors in order to coerce payment. Indeed, from creditors' perspective, the threatening power of the prison seems to have been its most useful function. During the period of study, only a fraction of the arrests warranted by the courts were ever actually enforced. Joanna Innes has found that of 12,000 writs issued in 1791 in London, only 1,200 prison commitments ensued.[69] In Edinburgh, only 15 per cent of debt cases pursued before the bailie court resulted in imprisonment. Thus, some 85 to 90 per cent of British debtors who entered the legal system found a way to pay their debts or came to some sort of agreement before incarceration became necessary. Those debtors arrested might never even make it to prison. Thomas Turner had Thomas Darby arrested, but Darby never saw the inside of the gaol. The bailiff first brought him to Turner's house, where they made an agreement that Turner would 'take a bill of sale of Master Darby's goods' in payment of the debt.[70] If many individuals went to prison, many more were threatened by the prospect of incarceration. One parliamentary debate suggested that where creditors had one person in prison, 'they had two or three that were in daily terror of imprisonment.'[71] A reform pamphlet explained how men 'trust Hand

---

[68] Diary of Samuel Jeake, 2 November 1692, f. 156, 12 November 1692, f. 157.
[69] Innes, 'King's Bench', 254.    [70] Vaisey, *The Diary of Thomas Turner, 1754–1765*, 152.
[71] 'Mr Grey's Motion for a Committee on the Effects of Imprisonment for Debt, May 12, 1791', 513–14.

over Head till they have broke, as depending that the Gaol was an infallible Security for their Money'.[72]

The symbolic threat of the prison operated on multiple levels. It could be a catalyst for what Benoît Garnot describes as 'parajustice' or 'infra-justice': the instigation of extralegal arbitration, which could restore neighbourly relations.[73] If a creditor threatened imprisonment, this could force a debtor into informal mechanisms of debt resolution. For example, the debtor might agree to the intervention of a third party to help reach a settlement, mimicking the style of bankruptcy proceedings wherein commissioners were appointed to manage the wealth of the defaulted. John Cannon recounted enlisting the help of a third party, Mr Nicholls, when relations with his creditor, Mr Sutton, broke down. Nicholls was able to 'stop the citation against myself until further orders'. Cannon later reflected that 'this affair was like to have created great trouble but it vanished.'[74]

On a broader ethical level, moralists imagined that the presence of the debtors' prisons acted as a deterrent from taking on unpayable debts by reminding individuals that credit was fragile and discouraging them from spending beyond their means. Debt was discussed as part of the moral rhetoric that informed contemporary attitudes towards consumption. Moral and intellectual debates focused on the distinctions between luxury and necessity.[75] Contemporaries were particularly concerned about the emulation of elite consumption habits by the lower and middling orders, and such emulation was inextricably linked with going into debt.[76] If honesty, frugality and thrift were believed to be the key reasons for success, then individuals and families were believed to decline through imprudent spending.[77] The condition of being in debt was linked to excess, corruption and the consumption of luxuries. In Hogarth's *Gin Lane*, the corruptive effects of consuming gin unfolded in the shadow of the pawn-broker's, while in *The Rake's Progress*, extravagance and immoral behaviour

---

[72] Thomas Baston, *Observations on Trade, and a Publick Spirit...* (London, 1732), 89.
[73] Garnot, 'Justice, infrajustice, parajustice et extra justice dans la France d'Ancien Régime', 109.
[74] Money, *Chronicles of John Cannon*, 403.
[75] Berg, *Luxury and Pleasure in Eighteenth-Century Britain*, 31–7.
[76] For discussion of emulation, see Lemire, *The Business of Everyday Life*, 8; Beverly Lemire, *Fashion's Favourite: The Cotton Trade and the Consumer in Britain, 1660–1800* (Oxford, 1991), 96; McKendrick, Brewer and Plumb, *The Birth of a Consumer Society*; John Styles, *The Dress of the People: Everyday Fashion in Eighteenth-Century England* (New Haven, CT, 2007); John Styles, 'Involuntary Consumers? Servants and Their Clothes in Eighteenth-Century England', *Textile History* 33, no. 1 (1 May 2002): 9–21.
[77] Muldrew, 'Class and Credit', 151, 161; Muldrew, *Economy of Obligation*, 159–65.

landed wealthier individuals in debtors' prison. For both rich and poor, immoral conduct caused the loss of wealth. In this climate of moral and economic degradation, the prison system was deemed effective because it served as a warning against the 'extravagance and folly of incurring debts'.[78] Punishment was a way of curbing bad behaviour, and of helping honest creditors collect their just debts.

## Emotional Strategies and Fear

Though it was envisioned as a practical tool, the prison was also a place where decisions were made based upon emotion. If creditors' economic calculus failed to materialise, if they felt wronged by a debtor's default, or if they feared their own financial vulnerability, imprisonment offered the possibility of emotional fulfilment. At the prison doors, utility overlapped with emotional impulses ranging from anger to vengeance to fear. The place occupied by these motivations, however, sits awkwardly with historiographical accounts of economic practice and gendered selfhood, especially when we consider male behaviour. In early modern domestic advice literature, men were afforded a capacity for rational action that contrasted from the unregulated passions of women, which justified patriarchal authority.[79] Later neoclassical models of the economic man displaced emotions from economic life, suggesting that they negatively influenced or were by nature contradictory to rational thinking, although accounts of female economic practices recognised that commercial activities took place along lines of consumer desire, or along emotional and informal ties of friendship and family.[80] In contrast to established dichotomies of male rational and female emotional decision-making, it seems that emotions formed a constituent part of the cultural and social environments in which everyone's economic practices took place. If the market was conceived of as a place of masculine rationality, it was also a space where cultural meaning and social trust were exchanged. The emotional foundations of the market were especially apparent in the extension of credit. Individuals made decisions about who to trust based upon understandings of ethics, reputation and social obligations. As Craig Muldrew contends, bonds of credit 'were conceived of as both social and emotive relationships'.[81] The act of extending credit involved risk, and taking a risk was an emotional experience.[82]

[78] Bell, *Commentaries on the Laws of Scotland*, 572.
[79] Alexandra Shepard, *Meanings of Manhood in Early Modern England* (Oxford, 2003), 86.
[80] Paul, 'A "Polite and Commercial People"?', 203–4.   [81] Muldrew, *Economy of Obligation*, 152.
[82] Nelson, 'Fearing Fear', 132.

The emotional basis of trust becomes apparent during moments when credit broke down. Emotions were particularly important in shaping how economic conflicts were resolved and how individuals used the law. A range of emotions, from fear to shame to compassion, surfaced when individuals became involved in economic conflicts.[83] In textual sources, legal records and personal papers, creditors incorporated emotional discourse in their descriptions of debtors' failure to pay. The diarist Samuel Jeake wrote of bad debts as causing melancholy. When he learned that a debtor was facing legal action, he wrote of being 'much concerned, fearing [the debtor] would either never be able or willing to pay me'.[84] In legal documents, creditors conceptualised unpaid debts as social transgressions or forms of betrayal, and they used a language of promise and dishonour to describe these failed contracts. Some litigants described having engaged in economic transactions 'on faith'.[85] A model letter from a debtor to his creditor in one epistolary guide begged that the honest debtor who failed through misfortune should 'call for pity instead of resentment'.[86] Emotion, it seemed, was inevitable. The guide therefore advised readers to provoke sympathy rather than anger in their creditors. Yet anger seems to have been a more typical reaction.

The emotional context of broken promises informed the distinction between malfeasant and misfortunate debtors. The anger caused by breaches of trust motivated creditors to take actions intended to make their perceived perpetrators suffer. Prisoners petitioned that their creditors deliberately intended to inflict harm, and, sometimes, that the infliction of harm was more important than repayment. According to one prisoner in the Edinburgh Tolbooth, his creditor intended 'not payment of his sume by this rigorous method, but it seems rather he wants to gratifie his humour'.[87] A debtor imprisoned in Lancaster Castle claimed that he was 'laid here purely out of mallice'.[88] The writer James Leslie claimed to have been confined 'thro the wilfull temper of this creditor who it appears intends to bring your petitioner to the right of misery'.[89] Others testified that their creditors wanted to punish them despite their frequent offers of

---

[83] Merridee L. Bailey, 'Economic Records', in *Early Modern Emotions: An Introduction*, ed. Susan Broomhall (London, 2016), 110.

[84] Diary of Samuel Jeake, 10 September 1681, f. 81, 2 June 1688, f. 122.

[85] NRS, ETWLB, 1773, HH11/29.

[86] *The Accomplish'd Letter-Writer: Or the Young Gentlemen and Ladies' Polite Guide to an Epistolary Correspondence in Business, Friendship, Love, and Marriage* ... (Newcastle upon Tyne, 1787), 44.

[87] ECA, BCP, Petition of James Thorburn, 6 June 1738, Box 285, Bundle 40.

[88] LRO, 'Relief for John Holt, debtor prisoner at Lancaster', QSP/1309/5.

[89] ECA, BCPA, Petition of James Leslie, August 1759, Box 285, Bundle 40.

repayment. As one reform pamphlet argued, 'confinement cannot answer any other Purpose, than only to gratify the Spleen or Resentment of some particular Creditors.'[90] John Ross, incarcerated in 1721, claimed that 'he had offered sixty pounds since he was incarserat' and that 'some friends did offer on the deponents account to engage and give security to the creditor for the said sum, which was refused.'[91]

Stories of wilfully inflicted harm are bolstered by examples of incarceration in which creditors chose imprisonment even though they stood to gain nothing financially by it. If debtors secured the benefit of the Act of Grace in Scotland or the Lord's Act in England, creditors were made responsible for the imprisoned debtors' maintenance. In some cases, creditors chose to continue keeping their debtors incarcerated, deliberately assuming costs equal to or even exceeding the value of the debts owed. John Howard's study of the prisons recounted the story of a debtor in Lostwithiel Gaol in Cornwall, who had obtained the Lord's Act certifying that he was too poor to pay for his own maintenance, and whose creditor continued to pay his groats to keep him incarcerated. The debt amounted to only £6, but the creditor paid groats for two years and left dispensation in his will for their continual payment.[92] In Edinburgh in 1780, John Meldrum, a merchant, paid 10s. to keep his debtor, John Skene, a messenger, incarcerated for six months. Skene's debt amounted to 10s.[93] Incarceration motivated by malice might not have been typical, but these cases suggest that incarceration could serve purposes other than simple repayment of a debt.

Acts of anger and vengeance were in practice not necessarily unmediated expressions of emotion intended to inflict harm as a form of gratification. Comments about wilfully inflicted misery were put forward especially by those advocating reform and by debtors within legal documents as a rhetorical strategy to discredit their opponents' actions as irrational or unmediated displays of emotion, symptomatic of flawed character. But these comments also had to be believable, and they drew upon codes of middling masculine behaviour which problematised passion and idealised men's control over their emotions and impulses.[94] Recent historiography recognises that anger could be deliberate, ritualised and functional rather

---

[90] *Reasons Humbly Offered for an Act for Relief of Insolvent Debtors, and Fugitives for Debt*, 2.

[91] ECA, BCPA, Petition of John Ross, 1721, Box 285, Bundle 40.

[92] Howard, *State of the Prisons*, 355.     [93] NRS, ETWLB, 1780, HH11/30.

[94] Langford, *A Polite and Commercial People*, 316; Elizabeth A. Foyster, 'Boys Will Be Boys? Manhood and Aggression, 1660–1800', in *English Masculinities, 1660–1800*, ed. Tim Hitchcock and Michèle Cohen (London, 1999), 162; John Smail, 'Coming of Age in Trade: Masculinity and Commerce in Eighteenth-Century England', in *The Self Perception of Early Modern Capitalists*, ed. Margaret C. Jacob and Catherine Secretan (New York, 2008), 239; J. G. A. Pocock, *Virtue,*

than uninhibited. Though prescriptive codes framed emotional reactions as impulsive, emotions could in fact be carefully calculated forms of communication, used to claim rights and to serve as a political tools.[95] Between individuals, anger could serve as a strategic sign in a process of symbolic communication and as a means of asserting power.[96] Open displays of anger might emphasise creditors' determination to pursue their debtors, communicating to both the debtor in question and to others within a credit network that a creditor would not hesitate to take away a debtors' liberty if the debt remained unpaid and adding weight to the prison's deterrent effect. Imprisonment might therefore be understood as an action that Gerd Schwerhoff refers to as a form of 'agonal' communication, in which emotive, social and material motives were intertwined under a common language of honour.[97]

While debtors often complained of anger and malice, perhaps the most important emotion that motivated creditors was fear; namely, the fear of their own failure and the anxiety that their own physical liberty might be at risk. In the face of financial instability, fear played a significant role in eighteenth-century economic decision-making and is crucial to understanding why creditors used the prison system. The social and occupational status of creditors and their own positions within credit networks placed them in financially precarious circumstances. Like the debtors they incarcerated, creditors came from the ranks of the commercial middling sort. While petitions for release under England's Insolvency Acts facilitate an assessment of the social composition of prisoners, a comparison of the status of debtors and their incarcerating creditors is made possible by extant commitment books from one prison, the Edinburgh Tolbooth, where the occupations of both were listed. These documents show that both imprisoned debtors and their incarcerating creditors were of broadly lower-middling social status, engaged in various urban commercial occupations (Table 3.2). Petty artisans and tradespeople formed the largest categories of both prisoners and creditors. Those at the lower and upper ends of the social scale, including gentlemen, gentlewomen and labourers,

---

*Commerce and History: Essays on Political Thought and History, Chiefly in the Eighteenth Century* (Cambridge, 1985), 49.

[95] Barbara H. Rosenwein, *Anger's Past: The Social Uses of an Emotion in the Middle Ages* (Ithaca, NY, 1998).

[96] Ute Frevert, *Emotions in History: Lost and Found* (Budapest, 2011), 7; Rosenwein, *Anger's Past*, 59–74.

[97] Gerd Schwerhoff, 'Social Control of Violence, Violence as Social Control: The Case of Early Modern Germany', in *Social Control in Europe. Vol. 1, 1500–1800*, ed. Herman Roodenburg and Pieter Spierenburg (Columbus, OH, 2004), 229–33.

Table 3.2 *Occupational comparison of creditors and debtors in Edinburgh Tolbooth, 1730–1770*

| | Prisoner | | Creditor | |
|---|---|---|---|---|
| Occupation/Status | N | % | N | % |
| Artisan/manufacturer | 210 | 33.5 | 168 | 26.3 |
| Resident (unknown occupation) | 86 | 13.7 | 55 | 8.6 |
| Merchant/shopkeeper | 63 | 10.1 | 133 | 20.8 |
| Agriculture (farmer, drover, gardener) | 34 | 5.4 | 25 | 3.9 |
| Professional | 37 | 5.9 | 61 | 9.6 |
| Transport | 34 | 5.4 | 23 | 3.6 |
| Retail/petty trade | 28 | 4.5 | 12 | 1.9 |
| Lower professional/clerical | 18 | 2.9 | 14 | 2.2 |
| Drinks trade (brewer, victualler, vintner) | 18 | 2.9 | 45 | 7.1 |
| Military/city guard | 16 | 2.6 | 3 | 0.5 |
| Innkeeper | 13 | 2.1 | 14 | 2.2 |
| Servant | 10 | 1.6 | 12 | 1.9 |
| Gentleman/gentlewoman | 6 | 1.0 | 4 | 0.6 |
| Labourer | 5 | 0.8 | 0 | 0.0 |
| Civic or legal official | 5 | 0.8 | 18 | 2.8 |
| Sailor/mariner | 5 | 0.8 | 0 | 0.0 |
| Service (teacher, dancing master) | 5 | 0.8 | 0 | 0.0 |
| Musician | 3 | 0.5 | 1 | 0.2 |
| Wife | 4 | 0.6 | 13 | 2.0 |
| Widow | 17 | 2.7 | 27 | 4.2 |
| Daughter | 3 | 0.5 | 7 | 1.1 |
| Son | 6 | 1.0 | 3 | 0.5 |
| Total | 626 | | 638 | |

*Source:* NRS, ETWLB, 1730, 1740, 1750, 1760, 1769, HH11/17, 20, 24, 26, 28

were notably absent from the prison system as both creditors and debtors. However, merchants (shopkeepers), professionals (especially lawyers) and those in the drink trade (brewers, vintners and victuallers) appeared in noticeably higher numbers as creditors than as debtors.

Though failure is normally understood in terms of a debtor's circumstances, it was equally dependent upon a creditor's own insecurities. The roles of 'creditor' and 'debtor' were indecisive, blurring the distinction between victim and perpetrator in cases of financial distress. Though moral rhetoric drew a clear division between borrower and lender, the extensive and interconnected nature of credit meant that most individuals in a community served in both capacities. Imprisonment could be a response to a shift in roles. In reaction to their own vulnerability, the imprisoned could quickly become debt enforcers. In 1770, for example, the Edinburgh tailor Alexander McInzie was imprisoned as a debtor in February, March and June for debts of 8s., 1s. and 16s. From within the prison walls, he initiated processes against three of his own debtors in April, May and June of the same year. Furthermore, he did so aggressively, paying for the incarceration of the messenger Alexander Fraser for two months after the court declared the prisoner too poor to aliment himself under the Act of Grace.[98]

Reform literature tended to focus on the plight of debtors, but for creditors, unpaid debts could represent a significant loss of savings. Contemporary recognition of the power debtors held over creditors' fortunes elicited cultural sympathy for the character of the creditor as well. The print *First of April*, a satire of a dissolute aristocrat, portrayed creditors as the victims (Figure 3.2). The print depicted a richly dressed young man attempting to beat a creditor who held a lengthy bill with a stick, as other creditors, also holding bills, worriedly looked on. On the wall behind the scene hung six pictures illustrating different forms of self-destruction: a huntsman attacked by his hounds; a fallen rider kicked by his horse; a man pulling his own house down over his head. The message to eighteenth-century viewers was made clear in the date which formed the title. The first of April fell one day after Lady Day, the date when landlords collected rents and when obligations were traditionally attended to. During this period, creditors typically learned if they held bad debts. Thus, while aristocrats and the gentry gambled with debt, causing their own self-destruction, and the poor spent beyond their means, the creditors caught in the middle were the true casualties.

Given their precarious status, middling creditors were in turn relatively aggressive in pursuing their debtors through the prison system. Insecurity ensured that over time, individuals in commercial and manufacturing occupations acquired a greater facility in using the institution of the prison for their own perceived protection. The porous boundary between being a debtor and being a creditor encouraged some individuals to use the prison repeatedly. Recidivism applied to both debtors and creditors, as plaintiffs came to use the prisons multiple times. More than 2 per cent of creditors in the Lancaster sample and nearly 5 per cent of creditors in the Edinburgh sample appeared in more than one case of imprisonment. Sometimes these cases were pursued by professionals tasked with managing the debts of others. For example, in 1780, Patrick Bailie appeared twice as a plaintiff, and in one case as the factor of Mrs Ann Brodie.[99] More often, though, creditors appeared multiple times in quick

[98] NRS, ETWLB, 1780, HH11/30.     [99] NRS, ETWLB, 1780, HH11/30.

Figure 3.2  *The First of April*, c.1780. ©The Trustees of the British Museum

succession when their own debts were called in. Record linkage between prison registers and the litigation records of local civil courts suggests that middlemen tended to incarcerate their debtors as a way of forcing payment when their own credit was put at risk, and they pursued their debtors after being sued themselves. In 1769, the shopkeeper Peter Forrester was taken to the bailie court for a debt by Peter Nimmo and George Innes. In July and October, he incarcerated two of his own debtors.[100] Within a month of being taken to court in December 1750, Andrew Buchanan, a shopkeeper, incarcerated two of his own debtors. Similarly, Mary Wallace was taken to court in August 1750 for a debt of £3 6s. for ale. She incarcerated two of her own debtors in August and December for obligations amounting to £2 15s.[101]

In an economy where the line between being a creditor and being a debtor was thin and porous, where trust was fragile and where individuals were subjected to accident, misfortune and chance, a culture of anxiety prevailed. Middling men and women fretted constantly about paying their debts, and the ability to honour obligations provided a tangible sense of relief. Even when they were profiting, tradespeople feared a quick change of fortunes. The constant threat posed by debt caused the stone cutter Thomas Parsons to reflect that 'anxiety and perpetual uneasiness seem to be my portion in this life.'[102] He wrote in his diary that 'shou'd trouble be shut out there it might rush in at a thousand Avenues.'[103] Samuel Jeake wrote of the experience of negotiating failed debts in terms of 'vexations and pain'.[104] Creditors even feared their own incarceration. William Stout recounted his master's fears of being arrested for debt prior to his death in February 1698. Though once a man of very good credit, the tradesman's circumstances 'became so burdensome to him that he daily expected to be made a prisoner; which, with the shame of forfeiting his former reputation, it drew him into despair and broke his heart, so that he kept to his house for some time and died for grief or shame'.[105]

Recognising economic anxiety has implications for how we view eighteenth-century gender identities. Men's ability to act rationally within the commercial sphere defined the economic man, but early modern manhood has also often been characterised by the trope of anxious patriarchy. Patriarchy, according to some accounts, was dependent upon a man's

[100]  ECA, BCP, 1770, Box 144, Bundle 371; NRS, ETWLB, 1769, HH11/28.
[101]  NRS, ETWLB, 1750, HH11/24; ECA, BCP, 1750, Box 119, Bundle 302, III.
[102]  Parsons, 'Diary, 1769, Jan.–Aug.', 29 July 1769.
[103]  Parsons, 'Diary, 1769, Jan.–Aug.', 6 May 1769.
[104]  Diary of Samuel Jeake, 29 April 1689, f. 126.
[105]  Marshall, *The Autobiography of William Stout of Lancaster, 1665–1752*, 121.

ability to control the sexual behaviour of his wife and dependents. The impossible demand of maintaining authority over disorderly women created 'anxious patriarchs'.[106] But if men in the eighteenth century were anxious, evidence from the debtors' prisons suggests that their anxieties stemmed from fears of insolvency and economic loss rather than the behaviour of their wives. Furthermore, while tropes of anxious patriarchy suggest that men lost by female gains, men were in fact more likely to express anxiety when their wives *lost* economic agency, rather than when they gained it. Numerous studies have disputed the ideal of masculine economic autonomy and make clear that household maintenance was dependent upon the contributions of all members. By extension, the incapacitation of wives could cause male financial anxiety. The wigmaker Edmund Harrold expressed deep financial worries when his wife fell ill. Without the benefit of her work in managing the household and the income that she gained by washing clothes and boarding lodgers, he described himself as being 'in great straite what to do' and fretted extensively about the household's maintenance.[107] Furthermore, men were not the only ones to worry about financial status and to use incarceration as a tool. Women also dealt with the emotional consequences of debt, and as creditors, they used incarceration strategically as a tool in debt negotiations.

For men and women, specific concerns over debt were exacerbated by a broader climate of financial anxiety. Though the eighteenth century was a period of economic growth and expansion, it has also been described as an 'anxious age'.[108] This was the age of the moral panic, driven by a new broad-circulation press, the anxiety-driven middling public and regular parliamentary sessions. The public read reports about forgery and fraud and watched catastrophes, including the South Sea Bubble in 1720 and the crash of the York Buildings Company during the same year, envelope private credit. Reports generated fear over gambling, fraud, dishonesty and deception in Britain's financial system.[109] These generalised fears had specific implications for interpersonal economic relationships. Financial

---

[106] Anthony Fletcher, *Gender, Sex, and Subordination in England, 1500–1800* (New Haven, CT, 1995), part 2; Elizabeth A. Foyster, *Manhood in Early Modern England: Honour, Sex and Marriage* (London, 1999), 4; David E. Underdown, 'The Taming of the Scold: The Enforcement of Patriarchal Authority in Early Modern England', in *Order and Disorder in Early Modern England*, ed. Anthony Fletcher and John Stevenson (Cambridge, 1985), 116–36.

[107] Horner, *Diary of Edmund Harrold*, 6 January 1713.      [108] Hoppit, *A Land of Liberty?*, 4–5.

[109] David Lemmings, 'Law and Order, Moral Panics and Early Modern England', in *Moral Panics, the Media and the Law in Early Modern England*, ed. David Lemmings and Claire Walker (Basingstoke, 2009), 2; Jack Lynch, *Deception and Detection in Eighteenth-Century Britain* (Aldershot, 2008).

crimes like forgery usually involved the discovery of betrayal on the part of someone the victim of the crime had trusted.[110] Hoodwinking and stock-jobbery became perceived tools of the financial trade, creating sustained fears of vulnerability that were then applied to individual credit relationships. The underbelly of trust was a fear of deceit, and this fear helped to shape how debtors were perceived and how creditors treated their debtors. As Julian Hoppit suggests, 'Even if some of these anxieties were imagined rather than real, self-interested rather than general, because they were felt in so many different ways they had a pervasive influence. In particular, pessimism was a breeding ground for the fractious and factious.'[111]

Fear, based upon perceptions of debtors and fuelled by a broader climate of anxiety, motivated the decisions creditors made. Credit relationships were dependent upon trust. But when faced with the perpetual threat of failure, this trust was rendered fragile. In diaries, creditors described the process of imprisonment using a language that conveyed both their fears of deception and their fears of losing their own status. Thomas Turner, the Sussex shopkeeper, 'fearing a delay in the affair might prove of a dangerous consequence (I mean as to my getting of the debt)', made the decision to 'send for a writ this day and to arrest [his debtor] a-Saturday next'. Motivated by anxieties over their own credit, creditors expressed ambivalence towards the process of imprisonment. They were clearly aware of the hardships they inflicted, but at the same time, they were driven by their own sense of self-preservation. As Turner reflected,

> Oh, what confusion and tumult there is in my breast about this affair! To think what a terrible thing it is to arrest a person, for by this means he may be entirely torn to pieces, who might otherwise recover himself and pay everyone their own. But then on the other hand let me consider some of this debt hath been standing above 4 years . . . and [I] cannot get one farthing . . . And I have just reason to suspect they must be deep in debt at other places, for undoubtedly no people of £200 a year go gayer than Mrs Darby and her two daughters . . . I really and sincerely have no other motive in doing this but to secure my just due, and I think there is no probability of ever getting it but by doing this.[112]

---

[110] Randall McGowen, 'Forgers and Forgery: Severity and Social Identity in Eighteenth-Century England', in *Moral Panics, the Media and the Law in Early Modern England*, ed. David Lemmings and Claire Walker (Basingstoke, 2009), 157; Donna T. Andrew and Randall McGowen, *The Perreaus and Mrs. Rudd: Forgery and Betrayal in Eighteenth-Century London* (Berkeley, CA, 2001).

[111] Hoppit, *A Land of Liberty?*, 5.

[112] Vaisey, *The Diary of Thomas Turner, 1754–1765*, 149–50. Quoted in Muldrew, *Economy of Obligation*, 280.

Turner's logic in arresting Darby began with emotion and ended with a practical decision based upon a calculation of probability that the prison was his best tool. His choices combined practical utility and fear.

## Perceptions of Failure

Turner's decision to incarcerate Darby was not based upon thresholds such as the quantity of debt that he was willing to tolerate, or the length of time that the debt remained outstanding. Rather, his thinking was based upon perceptions of the debtors' behaviour and circumstances, namely his knowledge that Darby must have been indebted to others and his observations of the public behaviour of Darby's wife and daughter. Creditors like Turner might have acknowledged the structural problems that shaped their own insecurity, but when dealing with debtors, they saw failure as occasioned by poor choices and character. Default was not interpreted as merely a financial circumstance, but rather as an outcome of a person's behaviour. When faced with a world where failure was just around the corner, creditors constructed stories to justify their actions. These stories emerge both in diaries, where creditors reflected upon their choices, and in legal petitions for release under England's Lord's Act and Scotland's Act of Grace. The two acts, which allowed prisoners to secure their release by proving that they were too poor to pay their debts, involved a process of petitioning. Creditors had the opportunity reply to debtors' pleas for liberation, and the documents generated provide insight into why they deemed it just and necessary to restrict their debtors' liberty, and why, when creditors were normally owed debts from numerous people, and when desperate debts were so common, they singled out certain individuals for incarceration. The coordinates debtors used to claim their own sense of worth and character are described in more detail in Chapters 4 and 5.

Documents generated by the petition process reinforce the notion that the decision to incarcerate was closely linked with assessments of a debtor's character. Contemporaries made sense of insecurity by conceptualising the failure to pay in terms of the moral judgement of individuals, in which failure was cast in binary terms as malfeasance or misfortune. When creditors were asked to justify to the courts why their debtors should remain imprisoned, debtor behaviour was paramount. In the face of declining wealth, creditors drew upon a moral language of social judgement. These judgements and perceptions were crucial to the experience of indebted people, because they gave creditors power where the law made no

intervention. Insolvency did not distinguish between the different underlying causes of debt. Contemporaries understood that there were varying
shades of indebtedness and that debtors failed for different reasons, but the
law failed to distinguish between honest and dishonest debt. It defined
debtors in black-and-white terms as defaulting or not, and offered protection to neither creditor nor debtor. As one pamphlet explained, 'no legal
means can be used to oblige the Debtor to part with the property he has got
to satisfy the just claim of his Creditors.'[113] Another explained the lack of
security available to the honest debtor. After the estate was divided, 'and
the honest Debtor has resign'd up all, and given a fair Account, there not
being enough to satisfy every Body's Demands, he is committed a Prisoner
for Life, to starve, or beg the Remainder of his Days, for his open Sincerity
and plain Dealing'.[114] While bankruptcy reform introduced the concept of
'discharge', allowing the debtor to walk away essentially debt-free if he
cooperated, laws of insolvency offered no similar protections.[115] Even when
released under Insolvency Acts, debtors could be imprisoned again for
different debts.

The narratives in legal documents ascribed failure to character flaws and
immoral conduct. Stories of fraud, cheating and dishonesty were common
in creditors' statements. Creditors claimed that they chose imprisonment
after their debtors violated ethical and moral codes of conduct. The candle-
maker John Johnston was imprisoned because he had acted 'contrary to all
faith and just dealing'. His creditor, Elizabeth Baxter, claimed that they
mutually agreed that a debt for candles would stand as partial payment for
a larger debt that Johnston owed her. But Johnston later took 'a most
manifest and unjust advantage' of her by assigning the debt to someone
else, who then pressed for payment before the justices of the peace.
According to Baxter, Johnston's dishonesty was further proven by her
understanding that he had the means to pay her, but had concealed his
goods so that he would appear poor before the city magistrates. Here,
ethical and utilitarian motivations overlapped. Baxter's justification for
incarcerating Johnston, like so many others, was not only that he deserved

---

[113] *Considerations on the Laws between Debtors and Creditors; and an Abstract of the Insolvent Acts. With
Thoughts on a Bill to Enable Creditors to Recover the Effects of Their Debtors, And to Abolish
Imprisonment for Debt* (London, 1779), 4.
[114] *The Honour and Advantage of Great Britain*, 7.
[115] For a fuller account of the legal concept of 'discharge', see Emily Kadens, 'The Last Bankrupt
Hanged: Balancing Incentives in the Development of Bankruptcy Law', *Duke Law Journal* 59, no. 7
(2010): 1229–1319.

to be punished, but that the unpleasant nature of the experience would force him to reveal hidden assets.[116]

Creditors argued that those they incarcerated had the means to satisfy them, but refused to own up to their obligations. Those involved in lending had a keen awareness of what their debtors owned and what they were worth. So as Baxter claimed, Johnston had not given a 'full condescendence of all his effects, but has concealed the same he being possest of materials and utensils for making candels in or suburbs of Edinburgh under a borrowed name'.[117] Similarly, James Thorburn's creditor, the merchant Archibald Laing, claimed that Thorburn and his wife were 'in a good way of living' from the income they derived, 'he by his business and she by keeping entertaining borders'. Though his debt amounted to 'a very small soume', he refused to pay it.[118] The merchant John Aitken told the court that his debtor, Marjory Herriot, had 'many valuable objects such as a gold watch and other things of great value' that would allow her to pay off the debt.[119] William Foulis claimed that his debtor had a 'stock of moveables and household plenishings'.[120] Creditors even knew how much specie their debtors possessed. William Stevenson's creditor knew that he had 'a well furnished house in town and money resting to him, and further that his wife acknowledged to severall persons that she had 12 guineas lying by her'.[121]

Drawing on contemporary fears about luxury, the type of debts that individuals contracted shaped impressions of their insolvency.[122] Different kinds of debts were considered less moral than others. In practice, tradespeople used the legal system to pursue a variety of debts, including consumer necessaries. However, narratives of failure tended to focus on imprudent spending. Thomas Turner's impression that Darby's wife and daughter lived too extravagantly for people who had £200 per year fuelled his perception that they were going into debt for the sake of luxury, and that 'instead of getting out of debt, [they] go farther in.'[123] Debts taken on as part of speculative activity were eyed with similar contempt. For example, building projects in provincial towns drew criticism. Upon seeing an

---

[116] ECA, BCPA, Petition of John Johnston, 8 December 1750, Box 285, Bundle 40.

[117] ECA, BCPA, Petition of John Johnston, 8 December 1750, Box 285, Bundle 40.

[118] ECA, BCPA, Petition of James Thorburn, 6 June 1738, Box 285, Bundle 40.

[119] ECA, BCP, *Heriot v Aitken*, 1770, Box 285, Bundle 41.

[120] ECA, BCP, *Scott v Foulis*, 1730, Box 285, Bundle 40.

[121] ECA, BCP, *Stevenson v Montgomery*, 1730, Box 285, Bundle 40.

[122] For contemporary debates about luxury, see Berg, *Luxury and Pleasure in Eighteenth-Century Britain*, 31–7.

[123] Vaisey, *The Diary of Thomas Turner, 1754–1765*, 149.

acquaintance's new house in Bath, the stonecutter Thomas Parsons
reflected that there were 'more than several who build themselves into
Gaol'. Parsons considered building to be 'like a lottery – some thrive by it –
this incourages others to venture and one who has success influences
[others] ... how anxious are people, yeah how infatuated, to exhaust
their time their all in building habitations'.[124]

Perhaps the most important personal ethic in considering the character
of those who failed was honesty. Contemporaries believed that it was
possible to fail honestly or dishonestly. Just as honesty sat at the basis of
trust, so it framed perceptions of decline.[125] Honest failure could be proven
in different ways, first by openness. As they failed, debtors were expected to
be willing to submit accounts for the scrutiny of creditors. One epistolary
guide suggested that the insolvent offer his creditors the opportunity to
examine his books in order to convince them that his conduct had been
'consistent with the strictest rules of honesty'.[126] Visible account keeping
was essential to perceptions of honest business. The moral failure of James
Wanchope, an imprisoned shopkeeper, was framed by his creditor in
relation to how he managed his accounts as his circumstances declined.
After his business in London became insolvent, which obliged him to 'fly
from the law of England' to Scotland, Wanchope had apparently
attempted to 'farce his creditors to a shameful composition'.[127]

Perceptions of a debtor's honesty as he or she sank into insolvency were
closely linked to the management of wealth. Within Britain's early modern
culture of valuation, individuals had a clear idea of what others were worth
and what kinds of goods and property they possessed. Good use of moveable property was imperative to notions of fair dealing and the management of wealth was a point of honesty.[128] Perceptions of failure, in turn,
depended upon creditors' knowledge (or perceived knowledge) of how
individuals administered their material wealth as their circumstances
declined. Their management was normally framed as dishonest or fraudulent. At the time James Walker had George Stinson arrested for a debt of
£25 Scots, Walker testified that his debtor possessed valuable goods, but
'refused to give the goods for payment of what he was owing to his said
creditor'. Walked testified that Stinson also possessed 'bills to
a considerable value of his own, and being desired before he was incarcerat
to indorse to his creditor some of said bills, he refused likewise to doe this,

---

[124] Parsons, 'Diary, 1769, Jan.–Aug.', 3 February 1769.
[125] Muldrew, *Economy of Obligation*, 127; Defoe, *The Compleat English Tradesman*, 226–40.
[126] *The Accomplish'd Letter-Writer*, 44.    [127] NRS, ETWLB, 1756, HH11/25.
[128] Shepard, *Accounting for Oneself*, 44.

but said he would goe to prison and would come out upon the Act of Grace'.[129] Creditors like Walker conveyed an attitude that debtors deliberately mismanaged their wealth and used the legal system to facilitate their actions.

Creditors often claimed that debtors had more effects than they admitted to, and believed that they wilfully and deliberately concealed their wealth. In one typical case, the creditor claimed that his debtor, John McConnachie, 'has a great deal more effects' than what was contained in the debtor's inventory, which the creditor believed 'he had industriously concealed'. In addition to 'several goods and effects', McConnachie's creditor believed that 'there is owing him mony to the extent of the sum for which he is incarcerat.'[130] Similarly, the baker James Dundas was imprisoned in 1760 because his creditor believed that his wife had sold a calf that should have been under sequestration.[131] Thomas Langwell, a surgeon, imprisoned his debtor John Tait, a gentleman's servant, for a debt for house rent 'until he replace the whole goods carried off by him and Helen Tait his spouse which had been sequestrated for payment of the rent'.[132] Such arguments echoed pamphlet literature, wherein debtors were described as 'very ill Men, and have effects to Answer in part their Creditors Demands, which no doubt is what the Debtors, when first in trouble, design secure to their own use and behoof'.[133] The failure to pay had broad consequences beyond disadvantaging creditors. The mismanagement of wealth harmed the very fabric of society. Due to the entangled nature of the credit system, debt bound households together, and failures implicated entire communities. Those who mismanaged their money gambled with the wealth and security of others. As one description of the failed man contended, 'They steal under the appearance of an honourable man. They cut a figure with other people's money.'[134]

This emphasis on social behaviour and on the moral and ethical perceptions of debtors is supported by broader quantitative patterns in prison registers. An analysis of how long the debts of the incarcerated remained outstanding and how large their debts became suggests that creditors lacked consistent economic and temporal thresholds determining when a debt became intolerable. Where prison registers recorded the date that a debt was due, a wide variation in tolerance for debt is clear (Table 3.3).

[129] ECA, BCPA, Petition of George Stinson, 30 April 1730, Box 285, Bundle 40.
[130] ECA, BCPA, Petition of John McConnachie, 1759, Box 285, Bundle 40.
[131] NRS, ETWLB, 1760, HH11/26.   [132] NRS, ETWLB, 1773, HH11/29.
[133] *The Cries of the Oppressed*, 3.   [134] Safley, *The History of Bankruptcy*, 2.

Table 3.3 *Time elapsed between due
date of a debt and date of imprisonment,
Edinburgh Tolbooth, 1730–1770*

| Time elapsed | N | % |
|---|---|---|
| < 1 year | 29 | 53.70 |
| 1–2 years | 6 | 11.11 |
| 2–3 years | 8 | 14.81 |
| > 3 years | 11 | 20.37 |
| Total | 54 | 100.00 |

*Source:* As Table 3.2

Some debtors were imprisoned within a few days of a debt being due, while a substantial portion of creditors (more than 20 per cent) waited more than three years before using the prison as a tool. In Edinburgh, creditors waited an average of 29 months after a debt was due before resorting to imprisonment. Similarly, there appears to have been little in the way of a debt threshold. The debts pursued through imprisonment varied considerably, from a few shillings to upwards of £100 (Table 3.4). Incarcerated debtors were not people who waited too long to pay, or whose debts became too large, but were rather people perceived to have lost their credit by failing to observe the ethics of the market.

Creditors' claims that their debtors possessed valuable assets seem at odds with the very small sums pursued through the prison system (Table 3.4). Debtors with relatively small obligations occupied the majority of prison populations throughout Britain. More than one third of debtors in London owed less than £5, and more than half owed less than £10. In Edinburgh, nearly half of debtors were incarcerated for obligations of under £2, and more than 80 per cent owed less than £10. The differences between the two cities reflected the fact that London, as the capital and centre of trade, was a much wealthier city, but were also a consequence of differences in the legal system. After 1726, debtors owing less than £2 could not be incarcerated under English common law, whereas Scotland had no such thresholds. The legal system thus facilitated the incarceration of a population of pettier debtors in Edinburgh.

The debts owed by prisoners became even smaller over time. In Edinburgh, debtors before 1750 owed an average of £8.5, and a median

Table 3.4 *Value of debts due by prisoners
incarcerated in Edinburgh and London, 1730–1770*

| Debt owed | Edinburgh | | London | |
|---|---|---|---|---|
| | N | % | N | % |
| < £2 | 336 | 49.05 | 69 | 7.6 |
| £2–5 | 135 | 19.71 | 243 | 26.7 |
| £5–10 | 96 | 14.01 | 165 | 18.1 |
| £10–20 | 61 | 8.91 | 158 | 17.3 |
| £20–100 | 50 | 7.30 | 217 | 23.8 |
| > £100 | 7 | 1.02 | 59 | 6.5 |
| Total | 685 | | 911 | 100.0 |

*Source:* LMA, 'Lists from the Several Prisons of Insolvent
Debtors in the Prisons on Certain Dates, Sworn to at the
Sessions, for the Debtors to Take Benefit of the Insolvent
Acts', 1719–72, CLA/047/LJ/17/001–002; NRS, ETWLB,
1730, 1750, 1770, HH11/17, 24, 28

debt of £3.4. After 1750, they owed an average of £6.5 and a median debt of
£1.7. These figures roughly echo the trends in England. In London before
1750, the median debt of prisoners was £10, but after 1750, it fell to £8,
while the average debt fell from £35 to £30. During the second half of the
eighteenth century, small debts were enforced in increasing numbers. One
might conclude that imprisonment was used against poorer debtors,
punishing them for spending above their means. Margot Finn argued
that during the second half of the eighteenth century, the use of confinement was part of a broader effort to 'demarcate the experience of imprisonment for debt along socioeconomic lines'. Petty debtors were associated
with petty criminals, and there was a general mistrust of debtors from the
lower ranks of society.[135] But though most prisoners' debts were small, the
occupational profile of the prison population shows that their owners were
not from the lowest ranks of society. Rather than reflecting a shift in the
rank of prisoners, the decreasing debts of the prison population reflected
the increasing difficulty of collecting debts. As consumption increased, so
too did credit, and book debts were the hardest to collect. When one
considers that most of these small debts belonged to middle-ranking
people, the tenor of indebtedness changes. Contemporaries considered

[135] Finn, *The Character of Credit*, 209.

lingering small debts to be the most dishonest because they were the easiest to pay. Creditors felt strongly that the debtors they incarcerated were not unable, but rather unwilling to honour their obligations. Debts were frequently described as 'small' or 'triffling'. According to Marjory Herriot's creditor, Herriot was imprisoned for 'just' and 'very small' debt, but refused to pay it 'tho posest of upwards of £30 sterling in cash'.[136] Creditors imprisoned debtors precisely because they were not poor. Instead, they targeted those with credit, those they had trusted because they understood them to be worth something in both social and physical terms, and whom they believed had the wealth to meet their obligations.

The moral and ethical behaviour creditors cited as evidence of poor character or dishonour did not even have to be economic or commercial in nature. Because a person's credibility rested upon both social and economic assessment, social transgressions could also result in a loss of trust.[137] Failure was entangled with personal reputation. People regarded as having lost their reputation through social, sexual or criminal behaviour also lost their financial power. Public cases of scandal show how quickly social and financial credit could unravel. Non-economic forms of litigation might be quickly followed by cases of imprisonment for debt as creditors feared the loss of their debtors' public credit. For example, John Watson, a printer, was held in the Edinburgh Tolbooth on 9 March 1780 for an assault on Isobella Watson. The next week, two suits for debt were brought against him by James Pyet, an engraver, for 4s., and James Ogilvie, a barber, for 3s.[138] As Watson's household life and personal reputation unravelled, so did his financial credit.

## Conclusion

In a period often characterised by a rise in economic rationality and impersonal market transactions, the decision to incarcerate a debtor involved a tangled web of practical, emotional and social considerations. Depending upon what kind of debtor a creditor was dealing with, incarceration could provide the best way of enforcing a debt. Because British law failed to protect the interests of creditors and to ensure equality between them when a debtor failed financially, the coercive apparatus of the prison provided their best tool to obtain payment. At the same time, failed debts and broken bonds of trust

---

[136] ECA, BCPA, Petition of Marjory Herriot, 19 July 1771, Box 285, Bundle 41.
[137] Muldrew, *Economy of Obligation*, 152.      [138] NRS, ETWLB, 1780, HH11/30.

often caused emotional reactions. It is clear that anger, a desire for revenge and a desire to punish motivated some creditors. For many more, financial anxiety provided the impetus to incarcerate. Creditors made clear that a debtor's failure to pay harmed their own financial solvency.

Debtors and creditors were the same kinds of people. Occupational designations in prison commitment books show that both creditors and debtors inhabited the ranks of urban tradespeople and manufacturers. They were subjected to the same kinds of structural insecurities through their positions within credit networks. Creditors and debtors were very literally the same people. If the Dickensian image of the debtors' prison envisions a separate class of borrowers and lenders, in the eighteenth-century credit economy, the categories of 'debtor' and 'creditor' were indecisive and could quickly change. Once a creditor, if an individual's own debts were suddenly called in, he or she could quickly become a debtor. Although prison reform literature focused on the plight of debtors, creditors, who held seemingly limitless power, were in fact equally as vulnerable.

Insecurity was the result of structures of credit, and these structures shaped the economic lives of debtors and creditors alike. Imprisonment was one of the outcomes of financial insecurity, but it was also the consequence of circumstances and perceptions. As a civil process, imprisonment was the result of the decisions and actions of individual creditors and their legal counsel. Failure depended upon the narratives that people could tell, both about their debtors and about themselves. Failure in the courtroom was cast by deploying stereotypes, and these stereotypes were confirmed by the cultural and literary world in which contemporary actors lived. In Tobias Smollett's novel *Sir Launcelot Greaves* (1762), the hero visits a London debtors' prison. Two chapters provide comic and sentimental accounts of debtors. The same stereotypes that emerged from the court narratives appear in the novel: the woman in debt for extravagant spending whose honour was described as 'bankrupt', the honest tradesman held in confinement by a single uncharitable creditor who was seeking revenge, and the morally corrupt bankrupt living out his life in gaol. Just like the stories that emerged from the prisons of London, Lancaster and Edinburgh, Smollett's text makes no attempt to reconcile conflicting perceptions. The reader is left with two internally coherent stereotypes.[139] Depending upon which stereotype was invoked, the behaviour of debtors and the practices of creditors could be represented as defensible or not.

---

[139] Tobias Smollett, *The Adventures of Sir Launcelot Greaves* (London, 1762). Thank you to Joanna Innes for this reference.

PART II

*The Insecure Self*

CHAPTER 4

# Keeping in Credit
## Reputation and Gender

Gaining and losing credit were profoundly social processes. In a cash-scarce economy, credit-based economic transactions were conducted on trust. When extending credit, a tradesperson made the decision to trust a customer with credit based upon the belief that he or she had the disposition and the ability to repay the debt. Credibility was dependent upon perceptions of an individual's worth. Similarly, understandings of indebtedness depended upon estimations of individual worth. A creditor's decision to incarcerate a debtor depended upon his or her judgement of what kind of person the debtor was as well as how he or she had failed. Perceptions of debtors were informed by contemporary stereotypes, by how individuals presented themselves and by how their worth was framed by others. While creditors characterised their debtors through the institution of the prison, the following two chapters attend to how debtors represented their own sense of worth. In the experiences of the middling people, the coordinates of selfhood were forged in relation to class, gender and seemingly uncontrollable financial fortunes.

In the eighteenth century, reputation was increasingly important to financial status. This period has long been framed as a time when estimations of credit changed.[1] Once considered an era of depersonalisation and institutionalisation, the early decades of the century are now understood to be a moment when the importance of reputation in fact intensified. Margot Finn has argued for the 'persistently social character of modern economic relations' and the 'protracted nature and partial effects of the eighteenth century's modernising impulses'.[2] Credit did not become abstracted and depersonalised. Rather, it continued to be socially embedded and constructed in personal terms. Alexandra Shepard's account of individual

[1] Karl Polanyi's 'great transformation' from socially embedded reciprocity to impersonal price-driven market exchange culminated in late eighteenth-century Britain. Polanyi, *Great Transformation*.
[2] Finn, *The Character of Credit*, 10, 327.

worth in early modern England charted a profound shift in estimations of credit from the late seventeenth century. As credit relations expanded and the economy quickened, credit came to be anchored less to material forms of wealth. Social estimations of reputation and character formed the foundations of financial worth, rather than a household's stock and flow of goods. As Shepard posited, credit 'became *more heavily reliant* on judgements about reputation and character ... reputation *grew* in importance as judgements about credit became reconfigured in relation to material markers.'[3] The eighteenth-century credit economy was therefore an economy of circulating selves. A reputation for fair and honest dealing became the currency for lending and borrowing, making a good name a kind of portable coin.[4]

If reputation was central to credit in the eighteenth century, it was forged in an increasingly insecure economic environment. Precarious balance sheets created precarious identities. Credit and debt shaped middling selfhood. As Scott Sandage writes, 'buying and selling, borrowing and lending, acquiring and forfeiting were not simply economic behaviours; they were liberal virtues that remade daily life, individual selfhood, and national culture ... the talents of good businessmen – investment, management, innovation – became hallmarks of personal autonomy and growth.'[5] Illiquidity and downward mobility made wealth unstable, and middling people judged themselves and others according to their financial predicaments and their changing levels of wealth. Diarists recorded the fortunes and failures of others in their communities. As Craig Muldrew suggests, 'change in fortune and the moral and uncontrollable causes of such change, was probably the most important lens through which society was seen.'[6]

Because credit was built upon social reputation, it had the potential to liberate individuals from the inequalities of property and the uncertainties of the market. Theoretically, through behaviour and the establishment of a good name, people with few material resources but with good reputations could gain access to financial credit, increasing their wealth. However, built upon the slippery and ever-changing perceptions of reputation, credit seemed to lack solid foundations. It was fickle and changeable and it involved a process of constant achievement. The language and concepts of reputation and selfhood had fluid meanings.[7] The components of credit, and the ways in which these components were shaped and claimed by men

---

[3] Shepard, *Accounting for Oneself*, 64.    [4] Muldrew, *Economy of Obligation*, 148.
[5] Sandage, *Born Losers*, 27.    [6] Muldrew, 'Class and Credit', 154.
[7] Faramerz Dabhoiwala, 'The Construction of Honour, Reputation and Status in Late Seventeenth- and Early Eighteenth-Century England', *Transactions of the Royal Historical Society* 6 (1996): 201.

and women of different social ranks, remain open to debate. Credit, used interchangeably by contemporaries with the words 'honour', 'reputation', 'worth' and, in the eighteenth century, 'character', was made up of a confluence of social and economic factors ranging from honesty to chastity to moveable property to income.[8] It was forged both individually and collaboratively within the context of the household.

## Public Insult and Credit

This chapter draws upon cases of 'scandal' or public insult to explore the coordinates of social credit. It draws upon a collection of 158 cases raised between 1700 and 1770 before the consistory court of Edinburgh, and uses the unique evidence generated by Scotland's legal context to reflect upon wider constructions of honour, reputation and credit amongst individuals in urban, commercial settings. During the long eighteenth century, hundreds of men and women in Edinburgh brought cases to the court because they felt that through insulting words, their credit or 'good name and reputation' had been ruined. Because reputation circulated by word of mouth and because the loss of credit had the very real ability to ruin a person's livelihood, public insults were taken very seriously. As Daniel Defoe wrote,

> Nothing can support credit, be it public or private, but honesty; a punctual dealing, a general probity in every transaction. He that once breaks through his honesty violates his credit – once denominate a man a knave, and you need not forbid any man to trust him.[9]

Litigants in court were often able to mark out the effects of insult in explicit financial terms. The servant Janet Cowan claimed that after being called a 'cheating bitch' by a local shopkeeper, she was 'disregarded by every person as one not to be credited or imployed and so rendered destitute of bread'.[10] The wigmaker Alexander Campbell claimed that a public allegation of dishonest business had caused him to lose 'upwards of fiftie pounds sterling'.[11] When James Somerville spread a rumour that the brewer James Flemming was involved in debt litigation, Flemming claimed that the act 'made [his] credite greatly suspected' and 'made those

---

[8] Muldrew, *Economy of Obligation*, 121–57. For the shift to character, see Finn, *The Character of Credit*, 18–20.

[9] Defoe, *The Compleat English Tradesman*, 226–40.

[10] NRS, Consistorial Processes, *Janet Cowan v Archibald Sheills*, 1749, CC8/6/328.

[11] NRS, *Campbell v Campbell*, 1711, CC8/6/224.

who dealt with him insist immediately for their money and resolve to trust him no more and even not to deliver the bear which he had formerly contracted for and part of which he hade got so that in effect he was looked upon as bankrupt'.[12]

Honour and reputation are subjects that have been widely studied in the early modern period, and litigation for verbal injury, drawn especially from church courts, has proven an ample source from which to study them. The language used to insult and ruin individuals provides insights into the attributes that made up a good reputation.[13] But while recent research on credit and worth emphasises the increasing reliance on reputation in eighteenth-century credit markets, most case studies of public insult focus on the period before 1730. England seems to have witnessed a sharp decline in defamation litigation, alongside a more general decline of business before the central courts, so that by the mid-eighteenth century, the willingness to defend one's honour by resorting to the courts was a rare phenomenon.[14]

Nearly everyone participated in the credit economy, but the reputation of different actors was drawn according to different coordinates. The bulk of recent research on honour and defamation has focused on gender difference, and particularly on the sexual language of insult waged against women. Drawing on church court records, historians have found remarkably high numbers of women acting as plaintiffs in defamation cases.[15] It has been asserted that for women, honour depended primarily upon sexual

---

[12] NRS, *Fleming v Sommerville*, 1743, CC8/6/306.

[13] Some seminal works on honour and reputation include Fay Bound, '"An Angry and Malicious Mind"? Narratives of Slander at the Church Courts of York, c.1660–c.1760', *History Workshop Journal*, no. 56 (2003): 59–77; Laura Gowing, 'Gender and the Language of Insult in Early Modern London', *History Workshop Journal*, no. 35 (1993): 1–21; Laura Gowing, 'Language, Power and the Law: Women's Slander Litigation in Early Modern London', in *Women, Crime and the Courts in Early Modern England*, ed. Jenny Kermode and Garthine Walker (London, 1994), 26–47; Laura Gowing, *Domestic Dangers: Women, Words, and Sex in Early Modern London* (Oxford, 2005); Steve Hindle, 'The Shaming of Margaret Knowsley: Gossip, Gender and the Experience of Authority in Early Modern England', *Continuity and Change* 9, no. 3 (1994): 391–419; Ingram, *Church Courts, Sex and Marriage in England, 1570–1640*; Tim Meldrum, 'A Women's Court in London: Defamation at the Bishop of London's Consistory Court, 1700–1745', *The London Journal* 19, no. 1 (1994): 1–20; Leah Leneman, 'Defamation in Scotland, 1750–1800', *Continuity and Change* 15, no. 2 (2000): 209–34; J. A. Sharpe, *Defamation and Sexual Slander in Early Modern England: The Church Courts at York* (York, 1980); Robert B. Shoemaker, 'The Decline of Public Insult in London, 1660–1800', *Past & Present* 169, no. 1 (2000): 97–131. For an account of the increasing reliance on reputation in the eighteenth century, see Shepard, *Accounting for Oneself*, 302.

[14] Sharpe, *Defamation and Sexual Slander in Early Modern England*, 9; Shoemaker, 'The Decline of Public Insult in London, 1660–1800', 100; Brooks, *Lawyers, Litigation, and English Society*.

[15] Shoemaker, 'The Decline of Public Insult in London, 1660–1800', 114; Gowing, *Domestic Dangers*, 33.

morality, while for men, issues of honesty and trust within business were more important.[16] Further studies challenged these simplistic gender boundaries by suggesting that men were also vulnerable to accusations of sexual misconduct and that women's reputations did not rely solely upon chastity.[17] But in making these assertions, scholars have not always been careful to heed the limitations of the court's evidence. Gender disparities in the court records do not allow for sustained comparison of male and female reputations. Furthermore, English church courts were restricted to cases of a moral or spiritual nature and these seem to have been confined primarily to sexual offences. For example, if a woman was called a thief and a whore, only the word 'whore' was actionable.[18] Additionally, gender has often been discussed in isolation from other categories of analysis such as rank and occupation, when in fact an individual's honour related to both.

Defamation cases drawn from Scotland offer a ripe opportunity to reconsider some of these historiographical conclusions, and to compare the reputation and credit of middling men and women in the eighteenth century during a period when litigation had declined south of the border. The eighteenth century represented a period of relative stability in the number of defamation cases raised, and in two periods of crisis, 1700–9 and 1780–1800, business before the court even doubled.[19] Public insult as a form of community censure and the use of the courts in regulating interpersonal disputes may have remained more important in Scotland than they did south of the border. Here, defamation emerged within a broader culture of financial insecurity, and many disputes can be linked to cases of debt. The consistory court provided men and women with a forum for defending their honesty. Defamation cases can therefore be used to investigate reputation in a period when comparable evidence in England is unavailable.

As litigants wove narratives about their reputations, they generated evidence that reveals both how and by whom reputation was established and maintained, as well as what made a credible character. The insults

---

[16] Susan Dwyer Amussen, *An Ordered Society: Gender and Class in Early Modern England* (New York, 1993), 98–104; Gowing, 'Gender and the Language of Insult in Early Modern London'; Sharpe, *Defamation and Sexual Slander in Early Modern England*, 28–9.

[17] Bernard Capp, 'The Double Standard Revisited: Plebeian Women and Male Sexual Reputation in Early Modern England', *Past & Present* 162, no. 1 (1999): 70–100; Dabhoiwala, 'The Construction of Honour, Reputation and Status in Late Seventeenth- and Early Eighteenth-Century England', 208; Shepard, *Meanings of Manhood in Early Modern England*, 154.

[18] Bernard Capp, *When Gossips Meet: Women, Family, and Neighbourhood in Early Modern England* (Oxford, 2004), 252, 96–7.

[19] Paul, 'Credit, Reputation, and Masculinity in British Urban Commerce', 228–9.

brought to court were considered sufficiently damaging and believable to merit litigation, and they provide an indirect guide to the components of credit that men and women negotiated in their daily lives, while also demonstrating that arrest for debt could be enmeshed in wider conflicts not normally visible in the historical record. Scottish cases provide an opportunity to compare the components of male and female credit and the intersections between gender and social rank. Unlike in London, the majority of litigants who came before the Edinburgh consistory court were male.[20] Women were involved in about one third of cases, either as individual parties or acting jointly with their husbands (Table 4.1). The court material therefore offers an opportunity to explore gendered constructions of reputation in comparative detail. Joint cases of slander, together with evidence of collaboratively forged reputation, point towards forging credit as a cooperative endeavour, rather than something that only converged or diverged along gendered lines.

Of course, litigation does not offer unmediated or unprejudiced access to the social behaviour of the individuals who came to court. Litigants described their actions carefully in ways that would make them appear most favourable to the court, probably making serious omissions, exaggerations and distortions. Depositions must therefore be read as examples of how litigants framed their behaviour according to dominant ideals rather than as descriptions of social life. Men framed their selfhood in relation to the eighteenth century's new economic man, with its emphasis on rationality and self-interest. Even if this trope constituted little more

Table 4.1 *Gender composition of litigants in defamation cases, Edinburgh consistory court, 1700–1770*

|                          | Pursuers | | Defenders | |
| ------------------------ | --- | ----- | --- | ----- |
|                          | N   | %     | N   | %     |
| Men                      | 107 | 67.7  | 105 | 66.5  |
| Women                    | 38  | 24.1  | 37  | 23.4  |
| Joint (husband and wife) | 13  | 8.2   | 16  | 10.1  |
| Total                    | 158 | 100.0 | 158 | 100.0 |

*Source:* NRS, consistorial processes, 1700–70, CC8/6/86–482

[20] Leneman, 'Defamation in Scotland, 1750–1800'.

than a contemporary fiction, cases suggest that men were attuned to and used to positioning their behaviour within these coordinates.

## The Legal Contexts of Defamation

The evidence that emerges from defamation cases was shaped by two legal contexts. The first was the jurisdiction of the consistory court, which shaped the nature of the cases that appeared before it and privileged certain forms of evidence. The second was the broader environment of financial insecurity, borne out through debt litigation, which encouraged middling people to pursue defamation cases in order to protect their credibility. Cases of public insult often emerged as part of broader disputes between parties, and cases can be linked with litigation in other courts.

Defamation could be defined as a criminal or a civil affront, and like Londoners, the residents of Edinburgh had a choice of courts to go to if they felt damaged by insulting words. The kirk sessions (church courts) dealt with slander of a moral or spiritual nature. Cases involving physical as well as verbal injury could be taken to the justices of the peace or the burgh courts. The sheriff courts were also willing to hear cases of defamation. The consistory courts, a division of the commissary courts created after the Reformation to replace the civil jurisdiction exercised by bishops, were supposedly confined to dealing with cases and disputes of an ecclesiastical nature. But when compared to the English church courts, they seem to have had a much wider scope.[21] While they were technically church courts, the consistories functioned much like secular courts in terms of legal procedure. Unlike spiritual courts, they heard evidence presented by both sides and made decisions based upon legal precedent.[22] The consistory court claimed its power to rule in slander cases from the Christian law that one should 'love thy neighbour', and almost any insult could be considered a breach of this law. A variety of slanderous expressions, such as 'cheat', 'knave', 'villain' or 'liar', were equally as actionable as moral insults and appeared more commonly than sexual insults. The presence of other courts in both Scotland and England also contributed to the difference in apparent consistorial jurisdiction. English secular courts required

---

[21] Leah Leneman, *Alienated Affections: The Scottish Experience of Divorce and Separation, 1684–1830* (Edinburgh, 1998), 6.

[22] *An Introduction to Scottish Legal History / by Various Authors; with an Introduction by Lord Normand* (Edinburgh, 1958), 369; Leneman, *Alienated Affections*, 6; George Joseph Bell, *A Dictionary and Digest of the Law of Scotland: With Short Explanations of the Most Ordinary English Law Terms* (Edinburgh, 1838), 179.

individuals to prove that they had sustained actual material loss from the words spoken, making cases problematic. Because the ecclesiastical courts had no such rule, most individuals chose to take their slander cases there. In Scotland, kirk sessions were primarily concerned with church discipline and drained off the cases of a more moral or spiritual nature.[23] Both men and women were able to raise cases before the consistory court, but married women were required to have the concurrence of their husbands, thus significant numbers of cases involved married couples.[24]

Two essential ingredients made slander actionable in the consistory courts: the affront and malicious intent.[25] Court cases were structured around proving these two points. The affront referred to the occasion and nature of the insult. In order to be actionable, it had to be public. In intent, slanderous words had to be spoken not just in passion or in passing, but with the design of causing real damage to the recipient. Whether the slanderous expressions spoken were true seemed to have made little difference to the court. They needed only to be damaging and specific in their charge. As James Fergusson, a contemporary legal commentator described,

> Such reproaches are deemed actionable, not when they consist in general expressions, but in as far as they charge particular crimes, faults, or blemishes, which bring a man's life, his fortune, or moral character into question, to the effect of harassing his mind, or of subjecting him to patrimonial loss or damage.[26]

The continuing emphasis on malicious intent probably contributed to the popularity of defamation litigation in Scotland through the eighteenth century. Because most parties were engaged in long-term disputes, proving malice was never difficult, and initiating a case nearly always resulted in a positive outcome for the pursuer (plaintiff).[27] The numbers of defamation cases fell in the early nineteenth century, when the shift to strict liability required pursuers to prove detailed financial loss.[28]

Initiating a case before the consistories was a significant financial investment. The expenses associated with pursuing a case were at least partially

[23] Stair Society, *An Introduction to Scottish Legal History*, 369.
[24] Leneman, 'Defamation in Scotland, 1750–1800', 214.
[25] James Fergusson, *Treatise on the Present State of the Consistorial Law in Scotland, with Reports of Decided Cases* (Edinburgh, 1829), 229.
[26] Fergusson, *Treatise on the Present State of the Consistorial Law in Scotland*, 234.
[27] This chapter employs the terms 'pursuer' and 'defender', the Scots words for plaintiff and defendant, in order to preserve the original language of the documents.
[28] John Blackie, 'Defamation', in *A History of Private Law in Scotland. Volume 2: Obligations*, ed. Kenneth Reid and Reinhard Zimmermann (Oxford, 2000), 656–62.

responsible for limiting the court's business to middling tradespeople and craftspeople. The dues of posting a libel (the first and only necessary step in a case) cost 7s., the equivalent of one half day's wages for a wright or a mason, or one day's wages for a labourer.[29] In reality, expenses of plea ranged from £1 to £41, with an average of around £3. This included court charges and fees due to the lawyers who helped litigants to shape their stories into believable and strategic narratives. The cost of coming to court varied depending upon the duration and complexity of a case. In Edinburgh, about half of all cases reached a verdict, meaning that they were lengthy and fought until the end. This figure also stands in contrast to London, where 14 per cent of cases from 1700 to 1710 and 7 per cent from 1735 to 1745 went to sentence.[30] Litigants coming to the Edinburgh court had to be prepared to spend tens of pounds on a case.

The cost of pursuing a case limited the types of people who had access to the court. In terms of rank and occupation, the court attracted most of its business from a narrowly defined group of tradespeople. The self-defined occupations and designations of those who appeared in court can be divided into roughly nine categories ranging from common labourer to gentleman (Table 4.2). The extremes of the social scale – gentlemen, labourers and sailors – held only a minor presence in the court. Like the incarcerated debtor population, most litigants came from the ranks of small traders and craftspeople, who made up about 30 per cent of Edinburgh's middle ranks.[31] In contrast to London, where the middling sorts came to court to defend their reputations in lesser numbers over the course of the eighteenth century, choosing not to 'air their dirty laundry in public', in Edinburgh, these ranks continued to patronise the court, while the lower orders never assumed a significant presence.[32] Though its patrons were not rich, defending their reputations was a financial investment worth making. The great expense that litigants sustained in clearing their good names could be crucial to re-establishing their honesty. As one pursuer declared, 'it is with very great reluctance that the respondent raised his summons of scandal against the defender as, by the great losses he has sustained, he is very unable to bear the expence of a prosecution of this kind.'[33] Furthermore, fighting a case until the end usually guaranteed a positive outcome for the pursuer. In

---

[29] NRS, *Cuthbertson v Thomson*, 1766, CC8/6/432; A. J. S. Gibson and T. C. Smout, *Prices, Food and Wages in Scotland, 1550–1780* (Cambridge, 1995), 298–9.

[30] Leneman, 'Defamation in Scotland, 1750–1800', 216.

[31] T. C. Smout, *A History of the Scottish People 1560–1830* (London, 1969), 357.

[32] Shoemaker, 'The Decline of Public Insult in London, 1660–1800', 116–17.

[33] NRS, *Fleming v Sommerville*, 1743, CC8/6/306.

Table 4.2  *Occupational status of litigants in defamation cases, Edinburgh consistory court, 1700–1770*

| Occupation/status | Number of Pursuers | Number of Defenders |
|---|---|---|
| Professional | 25 | 20 |
| Craftsperson | 46 | 61 |
| Servant/apprentice | 17 | 13 |
| Labourer | 3 | 4 |
| Gentleman | 4 | 2 |
| Merchant/shopkeeper | 17 | 18 |
| Food/drink service | 2 | 2 |
| Soldier/sailor | 2 | 1 |
| Government official | 3 | 3 |
| Widow (occupation unknown) | 16 | 7 |
| Daughter (occupation unknown) | 8 | 1 |
| Wife (occupation unknown) | 15 | 20 |
| Unknown occupation | 0 | 6 |
| Total | 158 | 158 |

*Source:* As Table 4.1

nearly all cases reaching a final verdict, the libel was declared proven and the defender was obliged to read a 'palinode' or public recantation before the kirk. Thus, until the 1790s (when the palinode was replaced with a fine), court cases triggered a public, ritualistic restoration of the honour of the injured party as well as the public shaming of the defamer.[34]

The tendency of middling individuals to rely upon the courtroom reflects the urban uncertainties faced by middling tradespeople, which Edinburgh shared with other provincial capitals. During the eighteenth century, the city's population doubled. As migration from the countryside increased, Edinburgh became home to increasing numbers of transients and outsiders, making anonymity in social and commercial life a real possibility.[35] Like other growing cities, Edinburgh became a legal, administrative and consumer centre, bringing affluence to many of its citizens. The service and trading industries expanded, catering to the demands of the city's growing numbers of professionals and gentry.[36] But while

---

[34] Leneman, 'Defamation in Scotland, 1750–1800', 229.
[35] Houston, *Social Change in the Age of Enlightenment*, 18.
[36] Nenadic, 'Middle-Rank Consumers and Domestic Culture in Edinburgh and Glasgow 1720–1840', 117–18, 125–7; Stana Nenadic, *Lairds and Luxury: The Highland Gentry in Eighteenth-Century Scotland* (Edinburgh, 2007), 49–52, 109, 199–203.

Edinburgh offered opportunities for success, tradespeople were also vulnerable to market fluctuations and periods of economic crisis that punctuated the period.[37] Periodic political conflicts arose as artisans became increasingly dissatisfied with the powerful oligarchy of merchants who continued to control trade and city politics.[38] The loosening of guild regulation resulted in demarcation disputes and conflicts between free and unfree traders.[39] In this environment, the consistory court provided lower-middling commercial people a forum for addressing the interpersonal conflicts that inevitably resulted from these economic and social tensions, as well as to represent their own sense of worth, which was essential to gaining financial credit.[40]

Not only were reputations forged in an insecure commercial environment, but cases of public insult can be directly linked to the broader legal context of indebtedness and incarceration. Historians have often noted that defamation emerged as part of broader conflicts, and that the insults deployed rarely related to the substance of those disputes. Debt disputes constituted one of these contexts. Financial failure rarely emerged directly as a theme in defamation cases: only four cases of the total studied involved plaintiffs insulted as 'bankrupts', and one case alleged that the pursuer had been imprisoned. However, record linkage reveals a direct relationship between public insult, commercial dispute and the negotiation of failure. Failure and the unravelling of financial credit lurked in the background of defamation.

Public insult was often bound up with multiple suits. For example, in 1766, the printer John Reid was called a 'thief and a villain' who 'had not sixpence'.[41] Reid's case emerged as part of a wider dispute involving his financial failure and the breakdown of a printing partnership between himself and the alleged insulter, Alexander Donaldson. By the time the insult was pursued in court, their dispute had generated a case in the sheriff court relating to books belonging to Donaldson which had been taken by

---

[37] R. A. Houston, 'Economy of Edinburgh, 1694–1763', in *Conflict and Identity in the Economic and Social History of Ireland and Scotland since the 17th Century*, ed. S. J. Connolly, R. J. Morris and R. A. Houston (Edinburgh, 1992), 45–63.

[38] Alexander Murdoch, 'The Importance of Being Edinburgh: Management and Opposition in Edinburgh Politics, 1746–1784', *Scottish Historical Review* 62, no. 173 (1983): 1–16; R. A. Houston, 'Popular Politics in the Reign of George II: The Edinburgh Cordiners', *Scottish Historical Review* 72 (1993): 167–89.

[39] Smout, *History of the Scottish People 1560–1830*, 348–9; Houston, *Social Change in the Age of Enlightenment*, 366–71.

[40] Smout, *History of the Scottish People 1560–1830*, 349; Houston, *Social Change in the Age of Enlightenment*, 6.

[41] NRS, *Reid v Donaldson*, 1766, CC8/6/430.

Reid's creditors. Within these broader disputes, the courtroom served as a public forum to repair reputations injured by allegations of dishonest failure and to discredit the behaviour of creditors. Reid represented himself as an 'unfortunate person, in a languishing state of health, who has nothing but a poor subsistence'. He also claimed that Donaldson looked upon his dwindling estate 'with a greedy devouring eye, and wants to grasp at, that he may have the pleasure of seeing the respondent reduced to beggary'. Eventually, Reid would declare bankruptcy.

The cases of public insult that were bound up with debt cases were normally brought by those facing debt charges as a way of attempting to restore their reputations. For example, David Rennie, a brewer, brought a case against James Mylne after Mylne 'delt with the pursuer for the payment of a just debt'.[42] Occasionally, such cases can be linked to the prison. A case of public insult brought by the writer Hector McLean was claimed by the defender (Neal Beatton) to have been raised by 'resentment harboured in the breast of Mr McLean against the defender for his having turned out from the possession of his lands at the defender's instance'. Beatton had later 'committed [McLean] to prison where he remained for nine or ten days'.[43] Cases of public insult could also link to cases where the pursuers had acted as creditors. As Chapter 3 made clear, creditors reacted to their insecurity and anxiety by pursuing their debtors in the legal system. This act could be harmful to the financial reputations of creditors, as it was to the debtors pursued. A creditor pursuing multiple debtors in court could signal that that individual was in financial trouble and was desperate to collect on his or her own debts. For example, the 1790 case of scandal between the merchant Robert Scott and the carrier John Waldie emerged in relation to a case of debt that was being pursued before the Edinburgh magistrates over contents lost by Waldie during transport.[44] A case of scandal brought by the merchant John Murray against the glazier Mungo Scott emerged as part of a longer dispute about reciprocal debts contracted between their households. The case can be linked with a formal sentence against Scott, and with a public insult by Scott claiming that Murray was 'four times the sum in the defenders debt'.[45]

[42] NRS, *Rennie v Mylne*, 1700, CC8/6/86.     [43] NRS, *McClean v Beatton*, 1764, CC8/6/413.
[44] NRS, *Scott v Waldie*, 1790, CC8/6/858.     [45] NRS, *Murray v Scott*, 1760, CC8/6/380.

## Collaborative Credit

Cases of defamation were linked to other court cases, but they were also linked to other people. While most studies discuss reputation as something that belonged to individuals, the construction of a credible character in Scottish cases, both within the courtroom and beyond, emerges as a collaborative process. The tendency of litigants to appear in court alone can give the false impression that reputations were constructed and defended alone. However, in an environment where autonomous individualism had not yet taken hold, it would be inconsistent to see reputation as a concept constructed purely around individual selves.

Perhaps the most overt and visible locus of collaboration was the courtroom. As Frances Dolan argues, though social historians use court records to seek historical presence or individual voice, 'they always stood in its place'. Legal statements were not composed as first-person voices, but were collaboratively composed, third-person texts, reflecting the nature of trials as documentary, rather than as dramatised spaces involving oral testimony.[46] Framing a reputation was a cooperative process between litigants and the lawyers who represented them. Before they reached the court, reputations were both interdependent and spun collectively within households and families. The presence of clerks and lawyers in helping to frame character is never explicit in the court documents, but their influence is visible in the formulaic nature of libels (the charge or first step in litigation) and in the repetition of key phrases and tropes across different cases. Libels spun convincing stories that attested to the harm pursuers had suffered by the insult and that portrayed them as credible characters by ordering narratives around ideals of polite, commercial masculinity. These codes were especially important to men engaged in business because they 'encouraged and regulated public conversation in order to make commercial transactions easier, resolve disputes, and facilitate economic and social exchanges between men of varying levels of status and wealth'.[47] The court became a space to discuss appropriate conduct within public commercial settings and for individuals to position their own behaviour around coordinates of economic manhood, and in contrast to fictions of femininity. Given the consistency within which these narratives were deployed, we might see the litigant as 'transistor or

---

[46] Frances E. Dolan, *True Relations: Reading, Literature, and Evidence in Seventeenth-Century England* (Philadelphia, PA, 2013), 24, 114–20.

[47] Robert B. Shoemaker, 'Reforming Male Manners: Public Insult and the Decline of Violence in London, 1660–1740', in *English Masculinities, 1660–1800*, ed. Tim Hitchcock and Michèle Cohen (London, 1999), 137–8.

a discourse jockey, choosing from a limited menu of storylines, calculating what will persuade, and combining available materials in creative ways'.[48]

Outside of the courtroom, the second visible space where reputations were collaboratively constructed was within and in relation to the household. It is important that we recognise reputations as interdependent within the broader context of household economies. If, as Muldrew suggests, the household was the unit of credit, then it should also be considered the unit of reputation.[49] Litigants testified that the insults waged against them had consequences for their families. When Marion Denune was accused of fornication, the insult resulted in the 'discredit and injury of her mother and other relations'.[50] James Watt claimed that an insult waged against him 'is enough to ruin the complainer and his family'.[51] In several cases, the insults pursued in court had been waged against families rather than individuals. Drawing on the ties of family honour, other defamers insulted parents and children alike. Alexander Johnston called Helen Anderson a witch and 'her sons the sons of a witch'.[52] In 1742, Robert Wilson said the writer David Fall was dishonest and called his daughters 'two light tailed bitches'.[53]

The collaborative nature of reputation challenges gendered approaches to reputation by showing that male and female honour was not merely overlapping or divergent, but intertwined. Reflecting this, just under 10 per cent of public insult cases before the consistory court were brought jointly by husbands and wives (Figure 4.1). While it was a legal requirement for a married woman to bring her husband to court 'for his interest' in a defamation case, in most of these cases, both husband and wife were actively engaged in the dispute.[54] In these instances, the credibility of husband and wife were explicitly tied, and they were insulted as a unit. For example, Christine Crawford and her husband, James Rennie, came to court after being accused publicly and jointly by William Dobbie of stealing meal from his barn.[55] Men and women also participated in the act of insult as couples, a phenomenon reflected by the 11 per cent of cases involving joint defenders. In 1712, Martha Bannerman and John Lock said in the public market that James Watt, a meal-maker, 'was a thief and had stolen peese and put them in his pocket and taken them to his house'.[56]

[48] Dolan, *True Relations*, 143.    [49] Muldrew, *Economy of Obligation*, 157.
[50] NRS, *Denune v Walker*, 1734, CC8/6/263.    [51] NRS, *Watt v Bannerman*, 1712, CC8/6/165.
[52] NRS, *Anderson v Johnston*, 1720, CC8/6/194.    [53] NRS, *Fall v Wilson*, 1742, CC8/6/300.
[54] Leneman, 'Defamation in Scotland, 1750–1800', 214.
[55] NRS, *Rennie and another v Dobbie and others*, 1700, CC8/6/87.
[56] NRS, *Watt v Bannerman*, 1712, CC8/6/165.

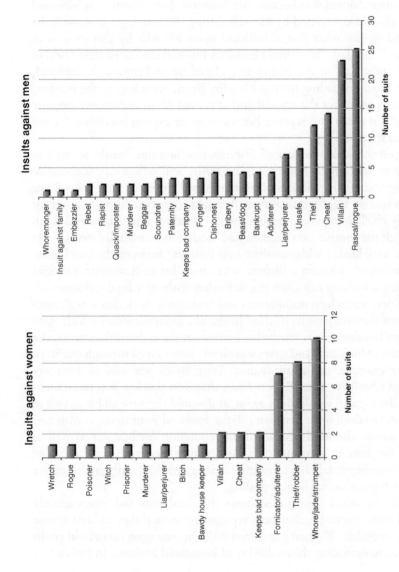

Figure 4.1   Public insults waged against men and women in Edinburgh
Source: As Table 4.1

Other litigants argued that the credit of husbands and wives was legally bound in such a way that husbands should be held responsible for insults waged by their wives. When Isobel Livingston was accused of public insult, the pursuer claimed that because her husband, John Nairn, was 'ablidged to pay all debt contracted by his wife during the marriage, so must he be ablidged to pay what fine is inflicted upon his wife by this process of scandle'.[57] Similarly, after Mrs Fergusson insulted the sexual reputation of Janet Lamb, part of the blame was placed upon Fergusson's husband, Robert Boyd, for failing to stop his wife. Boyd, according to the pursuer, had been present for the scandal and approved of the expressions because 'He did not check and reprove her therefore or express his dislike for her criminal speeches.'[58]

Taking the wider context of disputes into account, insults seemed to emerge in relation to household enterprise, and reflect the cooperative working and credit practices of husbands and wives. In 1719, John Rawe and his spouse, Euphraim Falconer, brought John Hutchison to court for publicly challenging and accusing them of stealing a brass candlestick, an act which the complainers claimed had 'loaded them with dishonestie'. As the case unfolded, a wider conflict over property between the two households emerged, wherein a dispute over credit led to Rawe and Falconer detaining a bathing tub from the defenders without a legal judgement.[59] Even where wives held occupations and undertook work that was distinctive from the occupations of their husbands, a phenomenon which Amy Erickson has shown was relatively common in the eighteenth century, the enterprise of husbands and wives was clearly intertwined through credit. In 1711 for example, an insult against Anny Byres was said to hurt her husband's business. After Robert MacLellan said that she 'was twice mensworn already and would do it again, and would she have all his as well as her own, the devil be in her then', Byres' husband went to court with her. In his words, the insult impacted his reputation for business as well as calling her honour into question. As a young merchant, accusations of falsely swearing or falsely promising made against his family could impact his own reputation for honest dealing.[60]

Incidental detail from cases shows that husbands and wives actively upheld and defended each other's reputations, even if they did not appear in court together. Women's responsibilities in managing household credit extended to defending the credibility of household business. In 1718, a case

[57]  NRS, *Livingston v Livingston*, 1707, CC8/6/45.    [58]  NRS, *Lamb v Ferguson*, 1719, CC8/6/188.
[59]  NRS, *Rawe v Hutchison*, 1719, CC8/6/191.    [60]  NRS, *Byres v Ogilvie*, 1717, CC8/6/176.

was taken to court by Andrew Thomson, a founder, against David Darling, a smith, disputing an unpaid balance due to Thomson by Darling. The wives of both parties were involved in the dispute, Thomson's wife declaring in the high street and in the public market in Edinburgh that Darling had 'mansworn' (falsely promised) them certain sums of money, and Darling's wife responded by defending her husband's honesty.[61] The active role that women played in their husbands' honour might support Garthine Walker's assertion that though women lacked 'the occupational and institutional identity that provided the highly visible locus for male honour', their roles within household economies 'gave them a sense of social identity, self-worth, and neighbourhood status', all of which had a relation to honour.[62]

The intertwined nature of credit was visible not only between husbands and wives, but also between heads of household and their dependents. Though contemporary codes of masculinity emphasised men's economic autonomy, male honour and reputation clearly depended not only upon a man's own actions, but also upon the behaviour of other members of his household. Naomi Tadmor has shown that servants, apprentices and lodgers were considered 'family' and that their behaviour was interpreted as 'familial actions'.[63] Men responded to the dishonourable behaviour of dependents by dismissing them, distancing them or even prosecuting them at court. Several actions of scandal were brought against men in positions of patriarchal authority who had attempted to distance themselves publicly from dishonourable dependants through gossip or insult. Some masters dismissed servants upon finding them engaged in theft or sexual misbehaviour. In 1720, when the servant Helen Whyte was found to be pregnant, her master turned her out and scandalised her by making the event public.[64] In 1716, the lawyer Thomas Russell made public that his servant had stolen a shovel and corn from another man's barn and dismissed him from service. The servant later sued Russell for ruining his credit.[65]

Family credit spread beyond members of a household to span generations. Because both honour and dishonour could be inherited, the families of Scottish middling men continued to manage their reputations posthumously, by publishing written accounts and building tombstones and

[61] NRS, *Darling v Thomson*, 1718, CC8/6/184.
[62] Garthine Walker, 'Expanding the Boundaries of Female Honour in Early Modern England', *Transactions of the Royal Historical Society* 6 (1996): 236.
[63] Foyster, *Manhood in Early Modern England*, 87; Naomi Tadmor, 'The Concept of the Household-Family in Eighteenth-Century England', *Past & Present* 151, no. 1 (1996): 111–40.
[64] NRS, *Sheriff v Rolland*, 1720, CC8/6/196.   [65] NRS, *Steill v Russell*, 1716, CC8/6/174.

monuments.[66] They also defended posthumous reputations in the court-room. In one case, two sons fought a defamation case to recover the honour of their deceased father, George Fall. Fall, a lawyer, had raised a case in 1742 against a merchant for saying that 'there was not an honest drop of blood or an honest inch in all his body.' Fall died before the proceedings came to an end. A year later, his children picked up the case. In so doing, they felt that they were 'acting a right part in supporting and maintaining the reputation of their deceast father, for surely if to honour our parents be a command to suffer them to be dishonoured must be criminal'.[67]

### Gender and the Language of Insult

Men and women came to the court jointly and independently to defend themselves against a variety of insults and verbal injuries. By attending to the substance of slanderous words, the components of what made a credible person emerge. Public insults suggest that credit was composed of a combination of assessments of social, economic and moral factors, which were in some ways deeply gendered, but in others remarkably consistent for men and women. Contemporaries used a variety of terms when speaking about their reputations. 'Virtue', 'honesty' and 'character' referred to moral standing, while 'rank' and 'quality' referred to a person's worldly position. 'Credit', meaning a person's reputation for financial solvency, conflated these moral, social and economic assessments.[68]

Credit was achieved through behaviour and actions in public and in business as well as in the home. Narratives of failure emerging from the prisons emphasised prudent spending, honesty and the appropriate man-agement of wealth as the components of good character. Similarly, the credible, middling male tradesman, read through the inverse of public insult, was honest, fair dealing and sociable, provided for his family and adhered to codes of appropriate sexual behaviour. Female credibility was assessed according to similar coordinates, including fair dealing, appro-priate household management and chastity. The frequency with which different insults were brought to court according to gender (Figure 4.1) shows variation between the insults waged against women and men, though overlap between them suggests that male and female honour was

[66] Stana Nenadic, 'Writing Medical Lives, Creating Posthumous Reputations: Dr Matthew Baillie and His Family in the Nineteenth Century', *Social History of Medicine* 23, no. 3 (2010): 519–22.
[67] NRS, *Fall v Wilson*, 1742, CC8/6/300.
[68] Dabhoiwala, 'The Construction of Honour, Reputation and Status in Late Seventeenth- and Early Eighteenth-Century England', 204.

not 'wholly incommensurable', as Laura Gowing has suggested.[69] Men were slandered with a greater range of insults than women. At least 23 different categories of insult were waged against men, while only 15 were waged against women. However, business acumen and honesty were important to both, as were insults related to both their public behaviour and their management of the domestic sphere.

The most common terms of insult waged against men alleged 'theft', 'villainy', 'cheating', 'knavery' and 'dishonesty'. While these were all generic terms of abuse, they also related directly to the attributes of good business. The most important attribute for a person engaged in commerce was honesty. Notions of honesty underpinned about half of the slanderous words brought to court by men, and they were often invoked if a customer felt that the quality of a tradesman's products was inferior or his prices too high. In 1711, George Campbell declared at the market cross of Edinburgh that Alexander Campbell, a wigmaker, was a 'damned cheat and a common cheat'. George Campbell claimed that he had purchased a wig for £3 'entirely upon the pursuer's word' that it was a 'good and sufficient and marketable ware worth that price', but it turned out to be of poor quality. When Alexander Campbell refused to make a 'just reparation for the fault done him', his customer retaliated with the most effective weapon in his arsenal, words ruining the wigmaker's reputation for just dealing.[70]

Cases of insult related to debt and business were more commonly waged against men than women; however, the minority of professionally based insults against women show that the virtues of honesty, good business and financial management were not unique to men.[71] Indeed, women were slandered with professional insults in only slightly lower numbers than they were sexually insulted. Thievery ranked in the top four most common insults used against both men and women. When the widow Grizel Blaickie was accused of selling stolen goods, she claimed that the insult was particularly injurious because it was expressed in the public market.[72] Female servants were especially vulnerable to accusations of theft, especially by their masters, and they claimed that these insults had an adverse effect on their livelihoods. Accusations of cheating were also common. Helen Livingston, the widow of a solicitor, was defamed as a 'covetous cheat' by her sister in law, who also told Livingston that 'she would rather

---

[69] Gowing, 'Gender and the Language of Insult in Early Modern London', 19.
[70] NRS, *Hill v Syme*, 1710, CC8/6/154.
[71] Christine Wiskin, 'Businesswomen and Financial Management: Three Eighteenth Century Case Studies', *Accounting, Business and Financial History* 16, no. 2 (2006): 143–61.
[72] NRS, *Blaikie v Goudy*, 1713, CC8/6/171.

take her by the nose than by the hand.'[73] Given women's extensive roles as credit brokers, lenders and tradespeople in the eighteenth-century economy, the relationship between reputation, credit and business asserted by litigants should not be surprising.

While women assumed reputations related to public market activity, so male credit was established not only through public business, but also through appropriate patriarchal engagement with family and home. Prescriptive texts of the period articulated men's relationships with the home through a model of economic management which emphasised authority and economic provision.[74] Though recent studies have suggested that prescriptions of patriarchy were unattainable for most men and that they were contested by counter-codes of conduct, these ideals formed potent categories for evaluating men's credit both in the courtroom and in the marketplace.[75] Several men prosecuted insults insinuating that they were unable to provide for their families through good business. Business failure and bankruptcy were framed in gendered terms that linked failure in trade with failure at home. In 1760, Mungo Scott accused John Murray, a widower, of having caused the death of his late wife 'by keeping from her the real necessaries of life'.[76] Murray was involved in several disputes over debt and eventually failed in business. In his insult, Scott linked Murray's business failures with the inability to provide adequately for his family. In a similar case, Roderick Pedison's servant took him to court for defamation after he accused her of stealing gold from his house. The servant claimed that the gold was taken and sold as part of her household duties, in order to defray the cost of liquors and cordials purchased by her for Pedison's dying wife. Pedison took offence to the notion that his late wife would have depended upon her servant for provision, calling the statement 'ane absurd reflection on the defender, seeing it is well known, his deceased spouse was sufficiently provided by him, of what was necessary for her, under her sickness, and was under no necessity of being supplied by the pursuer'.[77]

A patriarch was expected to exert control over his dependents and to act as the moral authority of the household.[78] Some men prosecuted insults suggesting that they used their power to coerce dependents into

[73] NRS, *Livingston v Livingston*, 1707, CC8/6/141.

[74] Foyster, *Manhood in Early Modern England*, 65; Karen Harvey, *The Little Republic: Masculinity and Domestic Authority in Eighteenth-Century Britain* (Oxford, 2012); Shepard, 'Manhood, Credit and Patriarchy', 75–7.

[75] Shepard, 'Manhood, Credit and Patriarchy', 98–9, 102–3.

[76] NRS, *Dickson v Webster*, 1750, CC8/6/380.    [77] NRS, *Lochead v Pedeson*, 1711, CC8/6/158.

[78] Foyster, *Manhood in Early Modern England*, 4–5; John Tosh, *A Man's Place: Masculinity and the Middle-Class Home in Victorian England* (New Haven, CT, 1999), 3.

dishonourable or even criminal behaviour. In 1764, Neil Beatton said that Hector McLean, a writer (solicitor) 'was a forgerer, villain, cheat and rascal and taught his own servant to be so'.[79] In another case, the smith Robert Anderson was accused of reselling stolen goods and of going to a workhouse 'under cloud of night and seducing and inticing his servant to steal goods'.[80] Insults such as these ran deeper than calling a man a forger or a thief. These insults questioned men's patriarchal status, suggesting that they were unfit to wield the power, influence and honour they had gained as independent heads of household.

Insults based upon household behaviour and honest business suggested that the spheres in which men and women established credit, and types of behaviour deemed creditworthy, were similar. But turning to insults based upon status, a point of divergence becomes clear. For commercial men, occupation and rank formed an important component of honour and credit. Insults debasing status were waged primarily against men and not women.[81] Terms of insult might include 'rascal', 'knave' and 'rogue', which insinuated lowly birth, rootlessness, menial employment or marginal status. Insults degrading male status were even more powerful if they were not waged as generic terms of abuse, but referred specifically to an individual's actions or circumstances. Status-based insults could deprive men of the credit associated with economic autonomy. In 1755, Elizabeth Gifford said that her neighbour George Hog, a brewer, was of lowly status because he engaged in manual labour by carrying stones.[82] The cause of the insult remains unclear, but to portray a middling man such as Hog as a manual labourer deprived him of the social standing derived from his occupational title. For men, as the following chapter discusses in more detail, identities depended heavily upon occupational status. Work was not only a means of earning a living, but also a form of social relation essential to establishing independence. To call a man a labourer insinuated dependent status.

The biggest point of divergence between male and female honour was sexual. Only about 5 per cent of insults waged against men as opposed to half of insults waged against women were sexual in nature. However, this figure stands in stark contrast to English case studies, where insults waged against women were almost exclusively sexual.[83] There is not necessarily a correlation between the number of cases and concern for sexual reputation. While sexual insults were not normally waged against men, their

---

[79] NRS, *McLean v Beatton*, 1764, CC8/6/413.    [80] NRS, *Anderson v Bull*, 1767, CC8/6/441.
[81] For comparison with early modern England, see Shepard, *Meanings of Manhood in Early Modern England*, chapter 6.
[82] NRS, *Gifford v Hogg*, 1755, CC8/6/354.    [83] Gowing, *Domestic Dangers*, 62–3.

reputations depended upon all aspects of their character, including sexual honesty.[84] Sexual looseness was equated with looseness in lending and borrowing, and 'whoring' was believed to lead to extravagance and non-payment of debts.[85] Men in the consistory court claimed that accusations of sexual misbehaviour had economic consequences. When John Ivie, a weaver, was accused of letting another man lie with his wife, he claimed to have been 'exposed to the contempt of the neighbourhood' and to have had his credit ruined.[86] For some men, sexual insults could reflect directly upon their business practices. When Catherine Watson slandered the innkeeper James Douglas by saying that 'he brought in whores and whoremongers to his house and that he kept a house only for such persons', the insult reflected badly on the morality of his business transactions.[87] Credit depended upon a combination of social, moral and financial assessments, and as Muldrew has convincingly argued, there was no distinction between 'economically rational transactions and other social transactions, such as courtship, sex and patronage. What we choose to call "economic" must be treated carefully'.[88]

Both men and women experienced sexual insult, but they experienced it in different ways. For women, chastity was the primary component of reputation. Women's virtue, honour and reputation were perceived through their sexuality. Playing to contemporary perceptions of gender divergence, one litigant claimed that 'virtue is to a young woman what honesty is to a man.'[89] Once lost, it was not recoverable.[90] As Marion Denune told the court, when James Walker spread a rumour that she gave birth out of wedlock, he destroyed her 'character of virtue and chastity, a thing of the most permenent and dangerous consequence'.[91] In contrast, male sexual misconduct carried varied and contradictory meanings. Men had more power to manipulate the meanings of their sexual misconduct according to circumstance.[92]

For men, unlike women, appropriate sexual behaviour was tied to their place in the life cycle. For young men, sexual mastery was a point of manhood. In early modern England, some felt it necessary to engage in a 'youth culture where manhood was learnt by drinking, fighting and

---

[84] Foyster, *Manhood in Early Modern England*, 86–7, 121.    [85] Hunt, *The Middling Sort*, 50, 68.

[86] NRS, *Ivie v Roxburgh*, 1710, CC8/6/131.

[87] NRS, *Douglas v Watson and another*, 1711, CC8/6/74.

[88] Muldrew, *Economy of Obligation*, 148.    [89] NRS, *Fall v Wilson*, 1742, CC8/6/300.

[90] Dabhoiwala, 'The Construction of Honour, Reputation and Status in Late Seventeenth- and Early Eighteenth-Century England', 207; Gowing, *Domestic Dangers*, 2.

[91] NRS, *Denune v Walker*, 1734, CC8/6/263.    [92] Gowing, *Domestic Dangers*, 113.

sex'.[93] Young men might respond to these sexual pressures by bragging about their conquests in public in order to assert their maturity.[94] Behaviour in Edinburgh appears to have followed these patterns. Sexual appetite was a fundamental part of James Boswell's concept of 'masculine virtu', and his sexual activities, as described in his diaries and letters, are well known to historians.[95] Men sometimes deployed sexual insults against women as a way of bragging to peers. Thus in 1766, Robert Thomson boasted to his friends in an Edinburgh alehouse that 'he was taken in when drunk by Mrs Murray and laid her down and played with her on the floor of her own house.'[96] If sexual misbehaviour was tolerated amongst young men, marriage and maturity, especially in terms of heading households, brought new codes of sexual behaviour. Boswell wrote that in order to become more 'manly', he sought to rise above the temptations of city life and to 'achieve the steadiness of a man of dignity'.[97] Once they married and became heads of household, men were expected to control their sexual appetites. When Beatrice Wood publicly accused her master, John Caddell, of sexual abuse, she testified that 'it would not have surprised her to have mett with such treatment from a young vigorous unmarried man ... but she could not have expected such usage from the pursuer a grave married man and of character.' Caddell brought a case of defamation against Wood. Due to expectations of patriarchal behaviour, he told the court that the accusations were particularly damaging and called the insult 'highly aggravated in respect of his having a wife and children'.[98]

Unlike the cases involving women who experienced sexual insult, cases alleging sexual insult against house-holding men suggest that morality was not always the main issue at stake. It did not cause the kind of ruin women experienced. Neither did extramarital sex bring the kind of shame described in an earlier period, which was bound with humiliation and which called into question a man's sexual honesty, causing men to flee or to pay off their accusers.[99] Rather, married male sexual misconduct in eighteenth-century Edinburgh was looked down upon because it could destabilise the family economy. Debates before the consistory court reflected middling fears that the birth of an illegitimate child could drain a family's resources and lead to

[93] Fletcher, *Gender, Sex, and Subordination in England, 1500–1800*, 92–3.

[94] Capp, 'Double Standard', 72–4; Foyster, *Manhood in Early Modern England*, 43.

[95] Philip Carter, 'James Boswell's Manliness', in *English Masculinities, 1660–1800*, ed. Tim Hitchcock and Michèle Cohen (London, 1999), 114.

[96] NRS, *Cuthbertson v Thomson*, 1766, CC8/6/432.    [97] Carter, 'James Boswell's Manliness', 116.

[98] NRS, *Caddell v Wood*, 1743, CC8/6/304.

[99] Capp, 'Double Standard', 70–2; Foyster, *Manhood in Early Modern England*, 80–2.

ruin, and bastards were viewed as threats to the inheritance of legitimate children.[100] These issues were especially problematic in Scotland, where canon law dictated that children of 'irregular' marriages had the same inheritance rights as legitimate children, and where legitimation by marriage was allowed after birth.[101] The early modern Scottish legal system did not have mechanisms in place to enforce child support; however, if a mother sought poor relief, the kirk might pursue the father for payment. Men were expected to provide for their dependents, and their honesty depended upon fulfilling this obligation.[102] In 1740, James Dalrymple, a married man, brought a suit against Mary Gainer for spreading a rumour that she had been his lawful wife. According to Gainer, after having taken her on as his housekeeper in London, Dalrymple took her to Edinburgh, where they cohabitated and she bore a child.[103] The depositions taken during the case focused not on his moral actions of sleeping with two women, but on his honesty and willingness to provide for dependents. Sexual misbehaviour was linked to avoiding the financial responsibilities associated with patriarchy. By speaking publicly about their relationship, Gainer was perhaps trying to force financial support for her child by threatening Dalrymple's honour. She might also have been attempting to establish an irregular marriage by 'habit and repute', giving her a legal claim to Dalrymple's support.

In cases involving insults of adultery, illegitimacy and sexual misbehaviour, the differences between male and female honour did not seem as stark as historians have often made out. Men were not alone in facing economic consequences to adultery. For most women, sexual misbehaviour brought shame. But for some, the consequences of sexual misbehaviour were framed in economic terms. In 1719, Mrs Fergusson, the spouse of a wigmaker, insulted the widow Janet Lamb by saying that she had brought forth two bastard children. In the insulting words, Fergusson linked the act of adultery with Lamb's poverty, claiming that had she 'not had the charge and burden of maintaining these children', Lamb 'might certainly have had a considerable deall of money scrapt

---

[100] Hunt, *The Middling Sort*, 67–8; Susan Staves, 'Resentment or Resignation? Dividing the Spoils among Daughters and Younger Sons', in *Early Modern Conceptions of Property*, ed. Susan Staves and John Brewer (London, 1995), 209–14.

[101] Leah Leneman, 'Legitimacy and Bastardy in Scotland, 1694–1830', *Scottish Historical Review* 80 (2001): 45–6.

[102] See Leneman, *Alienated Affections*, 180–1, 192; Rosalind Mitchison, *The Old Poor Law in Scotland: The Experience of Poverty, 1574–1845* (Edinburgh, 2000), 23–44; Margo Todd, *The Culture of Protestantism in Early Modern Scotland* (New Haven, CT, 2002), 306–8; Shepard, *Meanings of Manhood in Early Modern England*, 188.

[103] NRS, *Dalrymple v Cunningham*, 1740, CC8/6/288.

together'.[104] Many women told the court that sexual insults ruined their occupational identities rather than complaining that they had been shamed, suggesting that women's sexual behaviour had direct implications for their reputations for honesty and credit in the marketplace.

For men, reputation was claimed through adherence to codes of appropriate behaviour and manners. One of the most common characteristics of commercial manhood deployed by litigants and their collaborators was the use of reason and self-control.[105] This was reflected in the speech that pursuers were said to have used, in comparison with the defamers. Men contrasted their speech to that of women, who were prone to 'meer scolding or flyting'.[106] Men hoping to discredit the words of others described their speech as feminine, calling it 'scolding, 'coeing' and 'gosoping'.[107] In contrast, words uttered by reasonable men had more meaning. As James Tweedie testified, his opponent's slanderous expression was especially harmful 'by its being often repeated and in the most voluntary, deliberate, obstinate manner; not merely in a *mad rage or passion*, but, as is expressly deponed to by all the witnesses, repeatedly after the defender had returned to a *cool and dispassionate* mood' (emphasis added).[108]

The words 'passion' and 'passionate' appeared frequently in libels to describe and discredit opponents. Third-person narratives emphasised pursuers' use of reason in contrast to the passionate outbursts of those who insulted them. In one case relating to a larger conflict over the payment of debts, it was said that when the merchant John Murray tried to take the matter to reconciliation, 'the defender in place of accepting the friendly offer answered the same only with rage and passion.'[109] Honest men reacted calmly to passionate outbursts. The surgeon-apothecary James Smith was walking on the high street when a fellow surgeon, John Clerk, 'called out aloud to him – hear you – are you ready to acknowledge this day before the persons I shall name that you gave Mrs Addison poison and murdered her'. The complainer 'calmly answered that he fancied he had not forgot the nature of opium'.[110] Examples of violent conduct were also consistently used to discredit adversaries in court narratives, especially women. Thus, William Christie, a stabler who stood accused of calling

---

[104] NRS, *Lamb v Ferguson*, 1719, CC8/6/188.
[105] Foyster, *Manhood in Early Modern England*, 29.
[106] NRS, *Duncan v Anderson*, 1732, CC8/6/248.
[107] NRS, *Thomson v Dickson*, 1710, CC8/6/155; *Fall v Wilson*, 1742, CC8/6/300.
[108] NRS, *Tweedie v Wood*, 1769, CC8/6/463.     [109] NRS, *Murray v Scott*, 1760, CC8/6/380.
[110] NRS, *Smyth v Clark*, 1757, CC8/6/370.

Margaret Watt a common whore, emphasised his own reason in the face of her violent behaviour as a way to claim credit. William 'speaked civilly' to her, but she 'in a rude and passionate manner not only scandalised and defamed . . . but likeways fell upon him beat him made a great noise and tumult in his house'.[111] The statement of Christian Gray, a dyer accused of insulting Mary Watson, claimed that Watson had beaten him and torn the clothes off his head.[112]

Comments about behaviour reflected the changing spaces and methods of constructing and disputing character. Case studies drawing on defamation in seventeenth-century England described public insult as a form of street theatre. Incidents were dramatic, direct confrontations. Slanderers often clapped their hands or cried out to draw attention to the scene, attracting crowds of people around them.[113] Defamations rarely took place in private company and within private spaces.[114] By the eighteenth century, as Gowing and Shoemaker note, insults had moved indoors. This shift happened earlier in London than in Edinburgh, but the trend in Scotland's capital is clear. In Edinburgh, there was a significant shift in the public nature of the insult. Until 1730, most insults involved a direct confrontation between parties. These confrontations fit within what contemporaries called 'passionate outbursts'. They often involved crying out, yelling and physical gestures. After 1730, public insult began to occur more within the bounds of polite conversation. Most slander took place not through a direct confrontation, but through gossip behind a pursuer's back. Techniques to draw attention such as clapping and shouting were no longer used. Instead of a large crowd, pursuers described the presence of only a few people, and they were generally friends and acquaintances of the parties involved. Insults became public when servants or acquaintances overheard conversations or became aware of tarnished reputations through gossip. Pursuers were able to name exactly who had heard the insulting words, and with whom their credit had been ruined. James Smith claimed that insulting words uttered by a fellow surgeon had an impact on his credit with particular patients, causing them 'injustly to refuse payment' as well as threatening his standing within the incorporation of surgeons.[115] In cases after 1730, what was at stake was more likely to be a pursuer's reputation with a select group of people who mattered to his business, not the community at large.[116]

---

[111] NRS, *Watt v Chrystie*, 1739, CC8/6/284.    [112] NRS, *Watson v Gray*, 1718, CC8/6/182.
[113] Capp, *When Gossips Meet*, 198.    [114] Gowing, *Domestic Dangers*, 98–9.
[115] NRS, *Smith v Clark*, 1757, CC8/6/370.
[116] Shoemaker, 'The Decline of Public Insult in London, 1660–1800', 113.

## Conclusion

Credit in the eighteenth century was constructed and negotiated in social terms that were both deeply personal and, at times, deeply gendered. Selfhood and financial credit were intimately tied and were shaped by opinion and perception. The experience of gaining and losing credit was framed by perceptions of morality and social behaviour. When negotiating a precarious economic environment, people represented themselves as socially and financially honest individuals tied to stable households. The evidence makes clear how dependent financial credit was upon self-presentation. If the debtors' prisons provided a space for creditors to frame the character of their debtors, then the defamation courtroom constituted a place where debtors defined their own sense of worth.

For middling men and women in the eighteenth century, honour and reputation depended upon a relatively consistent set of factors. A man's sexual behaviour, his honesty and fairness in business, his occupation and rank, his ability to provide for and control his household, the way he socialised with other men in public, and the behaviour of his family members all contributed to his financial credibility. For women, household management, honesty in business and sexual honour were the primary components of reputation. In constructions of credit, gender and occupation or rank intersected, so that men and women of similar rank and occupational positions derived their credit by similar coordinates. The professional insults made against both sexes overlapped. For both men and women in business, reputations for honesty and fairness were essential. Both men and women were slandered as cheats and dishonest business-people. Both were also slandered with sexual insult, though they experienced these insults in different ways. Furthermore, men framed their credit and negotiated it in different ways, often in relation to women and to perceptions of female behaviour. Men in the consistory court sought constantly to augment their credit by setting their behaviour apart from the behaviour of women. This involved both framing the behaviour of adversaries in feminine terms and emphasising their own manliness as not feminine.

Perhaps the greatest point of divergence in male and female negotiation of credit was in the use of the court itself as a space to claim reputation. Both men and women had access to the court, but men chose to use it in much greater numbers. For men in eighteenth-century Edinburgh, the courtroom was a space of masculine competition and arbitration. Men used the court to compete in the marketplace. Initiating a case was a way of claiming respectability and of shaping and publishing a credible character, especially when engaged in broader disputes and multiple suits, which might include debt or even imprisonment. Unlike in London, where the middling sorts ceased to use the court system during the eighteenth century, defending one's self through legal means remained an honourable act in Edinburgh. As one litigant in 1760 claimed, 'no man will sit in a publick company and hear himself reproached with the odious names of villain and damned villain, without sueing for a proper vindication of his character, otherwise the world might very justly conclude that from his silence he deserved these epithets.'[117]

Most importantly, male and female credit did not simply converge or diverge, but was interdependent. Credit was forged cooperatively. The credit of different household members was closely intertwined. Though historians have tended to consider reputation as tied to autonomous individuals, the continuing sociability of credit was reflected in reputation's embeddedness in the collective unit of the household. The credit of householders was upheld by their dependents. Men and women defended and upheld each other's credit in their everyday business and social activities. In disputes over reputation, husbands and wives went to court together. When reputation made it to the courtroom, collaboration expanded to include the input of lawyers and clerks. They guided litigants with the questions they asked, and with their knowledge of what made believable and strategic cases, organising narratives around tropes of commercial masculinity and middling respectability.

[117]  NRS, *Laing v Robieson*, 1760, CC8/6/379.

# CHAPTER 5

# Occupational Identities and the Precariousness of Work

Financial credit depended upon reputation, character and status.[1] Occupational identity was an important part of how middling people thought about themselves. By the eighteenth century, assessments of worth depended increasingly upon what people did and how they made their living.[2] Work was an important component of selfhood. It is what middling people spent most of their lives doing. The middling sorts were relatively independent and they were skilled, but they depended upon their productive activities to make a living. Occupational identities also conferred civic and social status. Apprenticeship in a trade was a means of social mobility.[3] Membership in a collective association such as a livery company, guild or trade incorporation was a marker of civic status. Men identified themselves in legal and administrative records by stating their occupations. Claiming an occupation was an important feature of social distinction, used by middling people to distinguish themselves from those who lived merely by their labour.[4] Work was also part of a person's calling. According to Keith Thomas, work was 'not a means to an end, but an end in itself; not a job, but a vocation'.[5] In contemporary literature, character attributes, bodily characteristics and physical deformities were linked with particular trades, suggesting that occupational identity was

---

[1] An earlier version of this chapter appeared in publication as K. Tawny Paul, 'Accounting for Men's Work: Multiple Employments and Occupational Identities in Early Modern England', *History Workshop Journal* 85 (2018): 26–46.

[2] Shepard, *Accounting for Oneself*, chapters 7–8.

[3] Christopher Brooks, 'Apprenticeship, Social Mobility and the Middling Sort, 1550–1800', in *The Middling Sort of People: Culture, Society, and Politics in England, 1550–1800*, ed. Jonathan Barry and Christopher Brooks (Basingstoke, 1994), 52–83.

[4] Malcolm Chase, *Early Trade Unionism: Fraternity, Skill, and the Politics of Labour* (Aldershot, 2000); Shepard, *Accounting for Oneself*, 268; Keith Thomas, *The Ends of Life: Roads to Fulfilment in Early Modern England* (Oxford; New York, 2009), 106–7; Waddell, *God, Duty and Community in English Economic Life, 1660–1720*, 205.

[5] Thomas, *The Ends of Life*, 100–1; Mark Hailwood, '"The Honest Tradesman's Honour": Occupational and Social Identity in Seventeenth-Century England', *Transactions of the Royal Historical Society (Sixth Series)* 24 (2014): 79–103.

written on the person. In assessing how individuals communicated their worth, it is thus crucial to take account of occupation. Work supported both security and selfhood.

If claims to an occupational identity formed part of the basis of credit, they were also far from stable. Working life was part of the experience of insecurity. By the eighteenth century, the career progression from apprentice to master was not guaranteed. Apprenticeship no longer provided a direct route to upward social mobility, and increasing numbers of apprentices were failing to achieve the status of freemen.[6] Individuals also could not rely on a single occupation to support themselves. Seasonal and irregular work opportunities and changing occupational landscapes meant that people tended to combine multiple forms of work and to move during their lives from one form of employment to another.[7] Edmund Harrold, a barber in Manchester who kept a diary between 1712 and 1715, was a typical example. A barber by training and title, he rented a small shop where he shaved customers' heads, bought and sold hair and crafted wigs. In the hours unfilled by shaving, cutting and weaving, he also performed 'cupping', a medical service offered to lactating women. In addition to these principal employments, Harrold undertook other temporary income-generating activities or by-employments. He worked as a book dealer, and eventually as an auctioneer, selling various items in alehouses within Manchester and in outlying towns. In 1713, when times got hard, Harrold took on paid employment offered by civic authorities and worked as a dog muzzler. He lent out money, when he had it, earning 10 per cent interest on his holdings. Harrold's household also depended upon the productive activities undertaken by his wife and dependents. His wife, Sarah, managed the rental of a room in their house to lodgers, retailed second-hand clothing, and operated a business washing clothes. In addition to these income-generating activities, Sarah contributed to the household's maintenance by producing foodstuffs, including bread, which were consumed at home.[8] The occupational plurality that characterised the Harrold household was a feature of achieving what he described as a 'computency of living' in a precarious economic environment.[9]

[6] Ben-Amos, 'Failure to Become Freemen'.
[7] Thomas, *The Ends of Life*, 106; Overton, *Production and Consumption*, 74, 76; Shepard, *Accounting for Oneself*, 149–90. For an argument against the prevalence of by-employments, see Keibek and Shaw-Taylor, 'Early Modern Rural By-Employments'.
[8] Horner, *Diary of Edmund Harrold*, 30 September 1713, 3 October 1712, 11 September 1712, 27 April 1713, 5 May 1713, 23–24 November 1714, 20–23 October 1713.
[9] Horner, *Diary of Edmund Harrold*, 15 October 1713.

The work-based insecurities faced by people like Edmund Harrold were not new to the eighteenth century. However, with the shift from having to getting, individuals increasingly defined their worth and established their financial status according to what they did.[10] But establishing a stable occupational identity could be a challenge when a person undertook multiple forms of work. What happened to the sense of occupational status when, by necessity, people undertook multiple jobs; when, as in Harrold's case, a wigmaker was in practice not a wigmaker, but a wigmaker, bookseller, medical practitioner and landlord? When men identified themselves by a single occupation (which was typical in legal and administrative records), which occupation did they choose? Working multiple jobs made developing a stable sense of work-based identity a precarious process.

Because of the relationship between work and selfhood, the insecurity of work contributed to a second form of insecurity: that of status or identity. Sociologists have found that those engaged in modern gig economies might piece together a decent living, but they experience 'failed occupationality'. In other words, they are unable to assume stable occupational identities. This can have consequences for an individual's sense of fulfilment and selfhood.[11] In an era when individuals defined their worth according to what they did, the experience of constantly shifting from one form of work to another could render it difficult to establish a stable sense of identity, which provided the foundations for credit. As Harrold reflected in his diary, 'I think well of my bargain in general, but for the wanderings and settleness of human nature that's never satisfied, I find it hardest to please self.'[12] Clearly, Harrold's sense of self and his feeling of being satisfied with his work were about more than being supported by his earnings or, as he put it, his 'bargains'. When individuals accounted for their own sense of worth within the credit economy, they did so against a background of multiple employments.

This chapter considers how men defined and made sense of their work as part of the process of claiming credit. In so doing, it takes a unique approach to the study of labour and multiple employment. Previous studies of by-employment tend to focus on the prevalence and nature of supplementary work, and on the amount of income generated by a person's different productive activities.[13] While these are important issues, there is much more to say about by-employment in terms of

---

[10] Shepard, *Accounting for Oneself*, 232.
[11] Guy Standing, *The Precariat: The New Dangerous Class* (London, 2011), 32.
[12] Horner, *Diary of Edmund Harrold*, 21 October 1712.
[13] Keibek and Shaw-Taylor, 'Early Modern Rural By-Employments'.

identity. Work was about much more than getting by, and lists of what people did do not tell us what work meant to them.[14] Considering the meanings and status of different forms of work contributes to our understandings of men's working identities in two key ways. First, it reorients the relationship between different kinds of productive activities. Though by-employments are normally considered to provide supplementary income while a person's primary occupation provided his or her principal means of maintenance, we might position the status of different working activities differently if we consider them in terms of worth, skill and reputation rather than just income. When we think broadly about the different kinds of benefits that working activities could confer, we gain insights into productive activities that were not paid. Second, it considers the meanings and identity implications of different forms of multiple-employment. By-employment can include forms of work undertaken by men at one point in time, the multiple and changing activities that individuals undertook across their lives, and the multiple productive activities undertaken by dependents within a household.[15] Recognising different forms of occupational plurality is useful to reconstructing male occupational identities because it encourages us to attend to life cycle issues, and because it allows us to consider work as a cooperative endeavour performed in relation to other people, especially within the household.

In order to consider the relationship between identity and occupational plurality, this chapter draws upon autobiographical material, a source that has proven fruitful for investigating female and child labour.[16] In addition to the diary of Edmund Harrold (1712–15), the Manchester barber and wigmaker, I draw upon the diaries of two other lower-middling tradesmen: Thomas Parsons (1769), a stone carver working in Bath who was also an amateur scientist, and John Cannon (1735–43), an agricultural labourer, exciseman, failed maltster and teacher in the West Country, and of course Edmund Harrold.[17] The diaries provide glimpses of men at different points in the life cycle, and with different experiences of occupational fluidity. Parsons was 25 years old when he penned his diary. Cannon's memoir reflected over several decades of working life, and Harrold was in mid-life,

---

[14] Jonas Lindström, Rosemarie Fiebranz and Göran Rydén, 'The Diversity of Work', in *Making a Living, Making a Difference: Gender and Work in Early Modern European Society*, ed. Maria Ågren (Oxford, 2016), 24–56.

[15] Keibek and Shaw-Taylor, 'Early Modern Rural By-Employments', 250.

[16] Jane Humphries, *Childhood and Child Labour in the British Industrial Revolution* (Cambridge, 2010).

[17] Money, *Chronicles of John Cannon*; Horner, *Diary of Edmund Harrold*; Parsons, 'Diary, 1769, Jan.–Aug.'

married with children, and served as the head of his household. All three men experienced financial precariousness. Cannon described himself as the 'tennis-ball of fortune', and Parsons and Harrold struggled constantly with debt.

The three tradesmen did not pen their diaries with the intention of keeping account of their work, per se, however, all three wrote extensively about their working lives, positioning labour within social and religious practices, and within the financially precarious world of maintenance. Parsons, a devout Baptist, and Harrold, a devout Anglican, both wrote with a religious impetus. By contrast, Cannon's writing practices were more secular. He wrote as a form of participation in the eighteenth-century world of letters. However, though written with different motivations, the diaries intersect within the project of self-fashioning, which brought together religious and secular interests.[18] When confronted with the uncertainties associated with working life, diaries provided all three men with spaces to 'account' for themselves within their communities. They served as spaces for what Jason Scott-Warren calls 'makinge up', or what Matthew Kadane refers to as 'watchfulness', an examination of the self which was conceptualised both as a spiritual process meant to cultivate personal piety and as a form of more secular constructions of industriousness.[19] Writing was a form of self-examination that involved recounting one's actions as a means of securing creditworthiness with the community, a task important enough that we might even consider diary keeping a form of work itself.[20] As Edmund Harrold described it, 'it is every mans duty to examin and communicate.' He went on to explain, 'from this way of living springs al[l] our comforts of long life riches and honours, a good name, and peace of conscience.'[21]

In their diaries, all three men reflected upon their employment both in terms of the income and the competency of living which their work

[18] For diaries as spaces for self-fashioning, see Felicity Nussbaum, *The Autobiographical Subject: Gender and Ideology in Eighteenth-Century England* (Baltimore, MD, 1989); Patricia Meyer Spacks, *Imagining a Self: Autobiography and Novel in Eighteenth-Century England* (Cambridge, MA, 1976); Barker, 'Soul, Purse and Family'; Elaine Mckay, 'English Diarists: Gender, Geography and Occupation, 1500–1700', *History* 90, no. 298 (1 April 2005): 191–212.

[19] Jason Scott-Warren, 'Books in the Bedchamber: Religion, Accounting the Library of Richard Stonely', in *Tudor Books and Readers: Materiality and the Construction of Meaning*, ed. John N. King (Cambridge, 2010), 247–9; Matthew Kadane, 'Self-Discipline and the Struggle for the Middle in Eighteenth-Century Britain', in *In Praise of Ordinary People: Early Modern Britain and the Dutch Republic*, ed. Margaret C. Jacob and Catherine Secretan (Basingstoke, 2013), 267–9.

[20] Scott-Warren, 'Books in the Bedchamber', 247–9; Muldrew, 'Class and Credit', 172; Kadane, 'Self-Discipline', 267–9.

[21] Horner, *Diary of Edmund Harrold*, 5 October 1713.

afforded (a form of financial security), and in terms of the sense of self and status that they derived from these activities (social security). They also reflected upon the spiritual concerns that shaped their management of wealth. Diaries combined narrative entries and social accounts with descriptions of items purchased and sold, goods lent and borrowed, work and services contracted and performed and sermons heard and read. They accounted for their work, not just in terms of the pounds, shillings and pence that they earned, but also in terms of the status, knowledge and the relationships with others that work afforded.

### Defining Work

Data drawn from diaries contribute to the project of defining work. The narrow definition of work as 'income-generating activity' is now largely considered inadequate because it is limited to monetised labour and it excludes both the numerous forms of unpaid work that took place within early modern households, as well as non-monetised forms of trade. Alternatively, broader verb-oriented or time-use approaches have defined work as the 'use of time with the goal of making a living'. This methodology emphasises what people *did* rather than what they *were*, and it has the capacity to include both monetised and non-monetised labour. The 'third party criterion', related to the verb-oriented approach, posits that anything that could be substituted with paid services or purchased should be considered work.[22] However, these expansive definitions of work, which provide inclusive understandings of production, have been more readily applied to women than to men in the early modern context.

The diaries of the three tradesmen build upon historical definitions of work by providing insights into how individuals classified their *own* activities. These contemporary categorisations suggest that in accounting for men's labour, like women's, we must move beyond the definitions of work implied in studies of by-employment that prioritise monetary remuneration. Just as definitions of capital delineate between economic, social and cultural forms, so work had economic, social and cultural benefits.[23]

---

[22] Rosemarie Fiebranz, Erik Lindberg, Jonas Lindström and Maria Ågren, 'Making Verbs Count: The Research Project "Gender and Work" and Its Methodology', *Scandinavian Economic History Review* 59, no. 3 (1 November 2011): 273–93. For a critique of these definitions, see Cynthia Wood, 'The First World/Third Party Criterion: A Feminist Critique of Production Boundaries in Economics', *Feminist Economics* 3, no. 3 (1997): 47–68.

[23] Pierre Bourdieu, 'Forms of Capital', in *Handbook of Theory and Research for the Sociology of Education*, ed. John G. Richardson (New York, 1986), 47–58. For a discussion of the different

While historians normally use 'work' as a label for the variety of things that individuals did to make a living, contemporaries had a diverse lexicon that sorted work into different categories according to function and fulfilment, and in which different tasks were afforded different forms of status.

The three diarists described their work using primarily three different words: 'business', 'work' and 'living'. Thomas Parsons used the word 'business' when describing the management of his stonecutting work. He described his daily activities as 'Business which comprehends writing drawing, giving directions to others – working myself – and a great variety of articles that must constantly be remember'd to prevent confusion'.[24] Similarly, Edmund Harrold used the word 'business' when referring to his capacity to earn an income and to remain solvent. He frequently thanked God for 'good business'. In 1713, he recounted purchasing hair on credit 'upon necessity to put on business if I can'.[25] 'Business', therefore, was the process by which individuals converted their labour and their credit into a living.

For both Parsons and Harrold, business had strong connotations of management. Their uses of the word reflected contemporary definitions of business as a pursuit demanding time and attention, distinctive from a pastime. 'Business' bore a strong relationship with the notion of 'oeconomy', a term understood to mean the management of resources according to an ordered system, and which came to define male governance over the household. Within the home, oeconomy constituted one of the important routes to patriarchal status and honour.[26] While it anchored men to the domestic sphere, oeconomy was a crucial feature of work. Successful business was not just about deriving an income, but also about the appropriate management of resources, people, relationships, credits and debts. Harrold, for example, described the business of managing a bargain, recounting 'I swapt Spark for 19 pampheletts and books with John Brook. And so Im for turning about the business if I can.'[27] The management activity associated with business was often a source of anxiety. Parsons noted at one point that 'Business increases my perplexity and confusion.'[28]

---

forms of capital in an early modern British context, see Keith Wrightson, *Earthly Necessities: Economic Lives in Early Modern Britain* (New Haven, CT, 2000), 290–6.

[24] Parsons, 'Diary, 1769, Jan.–Aug.', 27 January 1769.

[25] Horner, *Diary of Edmund Harrold*, 13 March 1713.

[26] Harvey, *The Little Republic*, 33–43, 64–6.

[27] Horner, *Diary of Edmund Harrold*, 30 November 1713.

[28] Parsons, 'Diary, 1769, Jan.–Aug.', 18 July 1769.

The undertaking of 'business' was at least partly conceptualised in religious terms, tempering Margaret Hunt's assertions that middling businesspeople understood their wealth and their work in increasingly more secular terms rather than in terms of divine providence.[29] For the diarists, appropriate management was not signalled by maximising profits, but rather by arranging resources according to a code of Christian ethics. Harrold and Parsons considered the possession of resources and the availability of work a feature of divine providence, and management of those resources a matter of religious duty. Harrold frequently thanked God for the provision of work. In 1712, he wrote, 'I had a good business to day, blessed be God for't.' When work and resources were bestowed, wealth was not a reward, but rather an obligation. Parsons reflected that when entrusted with goods from God, 'we must soon give an account of our management.'[30] As part of their religious and ethical conceptualisations of work, diarists used a group of terms, including 'calling', 'vocation' and 'station', to discuss their labour. These words referred to work less as a task undertaken, and more as a form of duty, obligation or station to be fulfilled.[31] As Parsons wrote, 'Providence seems to increase my business and I must certainly pursue it – it is my duty.'[32] Appropriately carrying out one's work as a 'duty' could bring material reward, while similarly, vice or failure to fulfil duty could result in wealth lost. As Harrold wrote, 'nothing more common than vice, yet nothing so much debases a mans courage, whereas virtue brings with it both pleasure and profit and easiness of mind and conscience.'[33] Even the more secularly minded John Cannon understood work and wealth according to Christian ethics. Reflecting upon the working practices of a broker, who spent money as if it were his own, Cannon wrote that 'a secret curse goes with goods ill-gotten . . . But goods and wealth honestly gotten will endure to all posterity according to the words of Solomon.'[34]

While the diarists wrote of 'business' or 'duty' to refer to the broader ethics and management of labour, they had other vocabularies with which to describe more specific responsibilities. 'Work' was a word used broadly to describe the specific tasks performed either by the diarists themselves or by others, and which seemed to lack connotations of management. Work had clear undertones of manual labour. In Harrold's text, work was often associated with physical effort. He often wrote of 'working hard' or

---

[29] Hunt, *The Middling Sort*, 34–40.　　[30] Parsons, 'Diary, 1769, Jan.–Aug.', 15 January 1769.
[31] Waddell, *God, Duty and Community in English Economic Life, 1660–1720*, 98.
[32] Parsons, 'Diary, 1769, Jan.–Aug.', 16 January 1769, 13 February 1769.
[33] Horner, *Diary of Edmund Harrold*, 31 August 1712.　　[34] Money, *Chronicles of John Cannon*, 8.

'working close'. In 1712, he recounted, 'I worked close a reversion' and later, 'Worked till 8 at night hard'. Here, work was used to describe tasks associated with some sort of material gain or remuneration. Parsons used another related word, 'living', to describe activity undertaken for material gain, probably a derivative of the common contemporary phrase 'living by one's labour'. Harrold prayed to God to 'get into a method of living well and comfortably', and thanked heaven for being out of debt.[35]

While the three diarists used a clutch of terms to refer to the business of making a living, including 'work', 'business' or 'living', and the obligations of duty or calling, they employed yet different vocabularies when writing about more social or intellectual forms of work, namely their participation in intellectual or scientific activity and the pursuit of knowledge. Like many men of their generation, Parsons, Harrold and Cannon participated in a public and increasingly available world of science and letters. Parsons was an avid reader and noted purchasing and reading a variety of Enlightenment texts, including Newton's *Optics* and Burnet's *Theory of the Earth*, a book on the origin of the cosmos. He also conducted amateur experiments. In one entry, Parsons noted having 'spent a good part of this day in filling thermometers to a proper height and sealing them'.[36] Cannon and Harrold shared a similar interest in learning and books. To describe this intellectual or scientific labour, diarists used the word 'imploy' or 'employment'. John Cannon, who stole time away from his agricultural labour to read in the hedgerows, counted reading as one of his many 'employments'.[37] Parsons described being 'imploy'd as usual in drawing' and later being occupied by 'my own private imploy – reading (just now) Newton's *Optics* – copying some of Wordlidge's Etchings'.[38]

It might be tempting to classify reading and amateur science as forms of leisure, distinctive from making a living. However, if the ability to make a living depended not only upon the act of production, but also upon the cultivation of an environment and a social status in which such production would be possible, then the definition of 'work' might be expanded to include not only forms of labour that were not paid, but also forms of leisure that were not merely pleasure. It is possible that the stress on scientific and intellectual pursuits by the three diarists was not shared more widely in middling communities, representing a clash of values. However, the diaries seem to have fit within a broader culture of work in

[35] Horner, *Diary of Edmund Harrold*, 15 August 1712, 14 May 1713.
[36] Parsons, 'Diary, 1769, Jan.–Aug.', 30 January 1769.
[37] Money, *Chronicles of John Cannon*, 36.
[38] Parsons, 'Diary, 1769, Jan.–Aug.', 30 January 1769, 27 January 1769.

which labour was understood not only as an income-generating activity, but also as a social practice that generated status. The different vocabularies and languages the diarists used to describe how they spent their days complicate historical definitions of 'work'. Rather than distinguishing between work and leisure, paid and unpaid work or work that took place domestically or was external to the home, the diarists described their tasks in terms of a more diffuse understanding of reward that took issues of fulfilment and status into account alongside material gain.

From one perspective, books served important economic functions as material assets and forms of investment or savings. Collecting books might be conceptualised as a financial strategy. As repositories of value, books, like other material objects, could be exchanged and sold at crucial moments in the credit cycle. During moments of financial crisis, Cannon noted making arrangements to have books appraised and sold.[39] Harrold borrowed, loaned, read and reflected upon his printed material, but he also conceptualised his book trading in terms of profits and losses. He used his diary as a space both to copy out passages from historical and religious texts and to carefully account for what he purchased and sold, noting profits and losses. In one entry, reflecting upon a recent purchase and upon the state of his library, Harrold wrote that he 'Bought 16 books for self and more. Bought 8 for others [including] Samuel Oakes and John Whitworth. Sold 2 for good profit again to WD and Laurence'.[40] From a different perspective, as important as their concrete value, books provided the diarists with a means of acquiring knowledge. By the late eighteenth century, as John Rule asserts, men saw skill as a possession. However, much earlier in the century, the three diarists seemed to commodify their knowledge in similar terms as did Rule's labourers. The property of knowledge was essential to credit and could be commodified, sold or marshalled into forms of work. As John Money has suggested, knowledge and the ability to talk, listen and remember 'amounted to an exchangeable fund which served as the specie of a commercial sociability . . . knowledge ceased to be simply a medium of exchange to be used for temporal advantage and became a very personal possession'.[41] John Cannon was introduced to

[39]  Money, *Chronicles of John Cannon*, 500–1.
[40]  Horner, *Diary of Edmund Harrold*, 31 December 1713.
[41]  John Rule, 'The Property of Skill in the Period of Manufacture', in *The Historical Meanings of Work*, ed. Patrick Joyce (Cambridge, 1989), 99–118; John Money, 'Teaching in the Marketplace, or "Caesar Adsum Jam Forte: Pompey Aderat": The Retailing of Knowledge in Provincial England during the Eighteenth Century', in *Consumption and the World of Goods*, ed. John Brewer and Roy Porter (London, 1993), 353.

knowledge as a saleable commodity early in life. While visiting an alehouse, his friend Stephen Bush asked an excise officer, Mr Bosley, 'if he would sell his trade for he would buy it', in response to which Bosley agreed to teach them his trade for 40s. each.[42] Cannon clearly saw the acquisition of knowledge as a form of investment that would help him on a path towards upward mobility. Later in life, knowledge became a primary source of credit and employment. He survived through what he called 'employment at intervals', which consisted of charging fees for 'forms of writing and accounting'.[43]

## Knowledge, Status and Title

Thinking about reading and intellectual pursuits as a form of work disrupts the status load held by occupational title. Though titles are acknowledged as having little relationship to everyday working practices, they are often afforded meanings as indicative of status and lineage.[44] However, diaries suggest that in the eyes of middling people, a title was not necessarily the most elevated form of social standing that a man could claim. The three diarists derived status from work separate from their occupational titles. For an upwardly aspiring middling sort, a title could be seen as limiting and inflexible, while other forms of work and the possession of knowledge as a form of property provided better opportunities for self-fashioning. Thomas Parsons had a particularly ambiguous relationship with his occupational title. As Parsons was a guild-trained carver and the master of his workshop, his occupation theoretically ought to have provided him a positive source of local, civic status. However, Parsons wrote of his title as a burden and as a detriment to financial gain. In one entry, he even fantasised of casting his title off, reflecting 'I find myself in a business that is not so well as to profit, as I think I cou'd get with the same attention by working as a journeyman.'[45] In a later entry, he wrote of resenting the responsibility for management that came with being a master, implying that business prevented mobility by denying him time to acquire knowledge: 'I starve my mind in the attainment of 40 or 50 pounds a year! And spend my thoughts and time about this little Business as if it was ten times as much'.[46] Not only did Parsons gain more status from his intellectual endeavours, but in surmising that he might make more money as

---

[42] Money, *Chronicles of John Cannon*, 57–8.    [43] Money, *Chronicles of John Cannon*, 180.
[44] Shepard, *Accounting for Oneself*, 232.    [45] Parsons, 'Diary, 1769, Jan.–Aug.', 13 April 1769.
[46] Parsons, 'Diary, 1769, Jan.–Aug.', 13 March 1769.

a journeyman, his comments suggest a feeling that in the rapidly changing building industry, his occupational title and position limited his ability to make a living.

Both Parsons and Cannon expressed their own worth and judged the worth of others according to the demonstration of knowledge and skill rather than the claim to a title or the possession of wealth. Parsons took great pride in possessing a mind 'superior to the crowd', and he assessed other artisans' worth according to the degrees to which they possessed knowledge, at one point criticising 'illiterate tradesmen'. His capacity for intellectual pursuits allowed him to distinguish himself from his workmen. Parsons wrote of one of his apprentices that he had 'the Mind of a country fellow who has never perhaps thought of reading etc but plods on in one contracted sphere, [and] will with great difficulty make any considerable attainment'.[47] Cannon judged himself and others according to similar coordinates, noting especially the possession of knowledge and literacy. He wrote disparagingly of 'Mechanicks such as Black Smiths, Tanners, Taylors, Chandlers, Woolcombers etc. whose learning is so rife that they could as well distinguish the wrong end of a Warrant uppermost as the right way'.[48]

Participation in scientific inquiry was an important means of claiming status. As Henry French suggests, the qualities of science overlapped with the qualities of genteel status, reinforcing one another. Establishing reputations as thinkers allowed middling men to step out of local and competitive estimations between craftsmen, based upon financial ability, business volume or civic responsibility.[49] For Parsons, Cannon and Harrold, though, I would argue that learning did even more. A reputation for knowledge provided a stable sense of self and credit that transcended the precariousness of work, which included not only multiple employments, but also financial insecurity and a changing occupational landscape. Cannon understood the condition of moving from job to job as being insecure. Later, reflecting on his career trajectory in 1734, he wrote that 'from a schoolboy I became a plowboy, from a plowboy an Exciseman from an Exciseman a Maltster from a Maltster to an almost nothing except a Schoolmaster.'[50] Within this insecure world, reading provided a point of continuity. As he reflected, 'for all these my hard and laborious

[47] Parsons, 'Diary, 1769, Jan.–Aug.', 26 January 1769.
[48] John Cannon, quoted in Muldrew, 'Class and Credit', 166–7.
[49] Henry French, '"Ingenious & Learned Gentlemen": Social Perceptions and Self-Fashioning among Parish Elites in Essex, 1680–1740', *Social History* 25, no. 1 (2000): 60.
[50] Money, *Chronicles of John Cannon*, 174.

employments I never slighted or disregarded my books, the study of which augmented and much increased my understanding.' As John Money suggests, as a self-described 'tennis-ball of fortune', Cannon found in reading and writing a way of convincing himself that he was not an 'almost nothing'.[51] Rather than looking upwards and aspiring towards gentility, the pursuit of knowledge was part of a descendant gaze and an effort to avoid downward social mobility.

For Parsons, the pursuit of knowledge was a means of coping with a changing artisanal landscape. During his coming of age as a stonecutter, the professional status of artisans was placed under threat by a newly professionalised artistic culture that depended upon drawing status distinctions between the artist and the craftsman. British artists attempted to carve out a new identity for themselves, refuting the notion that they were little better than ordinary mechanics.[52] Emergent British theories of painting defined painting as a liberal art and an intellectual activity, which sat in distinct contrast to the craftsman's manual labour. This idea was reflected in texts like Sir Joshua Reynolds' *Discourses on Art*, where he distinguished between the 'liberal professional' who 'works under the direction of principle', and the 'mechanical trade', which was carried out by men of 'narrow comprehension and mechanical performance' in obedience to 'vulgar and trite rules'.[53] The capacity for judgement, or taste, set the artist and the craftsman apart. These theories both created professional distinctions and had social and civic consequences, denigrating the craftsman in particularly gendered ways. While the artist was cast as the enfranchised citizen or the independent man, the craftsman-mechanic was depicted as servile.

Parsons penned his diary in 1769, the same year that the Royal Academy was founded: an institution that was central to the professionalisation of the arts.[54] Parsons' diary provided a space for him to engage with these discourses and to position and account for his labour against the central features of artistry versus craft that formed the intellectual and cultural context for his work. He went to great lengths to claim an aptitude for judgement and taste. Self-instruction through reading and amateur experimentation took him beyond the 'narrow interests' of mechanics. He wrote

---

[51] Money, *Chronicles of John Cannon*, cxxviii.

[52] John Barrell, *The Political Theory of Painting from Reynolds to Hazlitt: 'The Body of the Public'* (New Haven, CT, 1986), 16–17.

[53] Joshua Reynolds, *Discourses on Art*, ed. Robert R. Wark (New Haven, CT, 1975), 93, 97, 117. Quoted in Barrell, *The Political Theory of Painting*, 15.

[54] Holger Hoock, *The King's Artists: The Royal Academy of Arts and the Politics of British Culture, 1760–1840* (Oxford, 2003). See especially chapters 1–3.

of experimenting with materials, for example melting glass and bringing it into a paste. Gaining a deeper understanding of the scientific qualities of his materials differentiated his labour from that of the humble craftsman below him. This self-fashioning through intellectual pursuits went hand in hand with his attitudes towards manual labour. He wrote of disliking manual labour, and though his work was very often manual, he rarely emphasised his physical attributes, such as bodily strength, when discussing his work. Only when recounting an accident wherein his hand was injured while he was moving a statue did Parsons acknowledge the importance of his material body to his working identity. Recounting the incident, he wrote of being 'very much vexed because I know 'twou'd hinder my working a long time'.[55]

Alongside reading and intellectual pursuits, one of the forms of unpaid work that is crucial to account for in terms of male status and identity is office holding. As householders, Harrold, Cannon and Parsons were 3 of the some 400,000 individuals in eighteenth-century England who were expected to assume civic responsibilities, and who made up the pool from which parish officers were drawn.[56] All three diarists were designated as 'inhabitants', a status signifying that an individual was a ratepayer, which carried connotations that he or she possessed a material stake in the parish community.[57] Harrold was elected as a muzzler 'of mastiff dogs and bitches' in 1713. Cannon referred periodically to his duties as 'officer' and parish accountant. Henry French has argued that assuming these civic roles at the parish level was one of the defining elements of middling social identity, which distinguished individuals as 'chief inhabitants'.[58] The experiences of undertaking civic responsibilities, as described by the three diarists, suggest that they could indeed be important sources of status. Harrold noted when others had been elected for Leet Court, as well as the occasions when he attended and who else was there.[59] But just as occupational title had a limited bearing on status, so the impact of office holding was partial. The diaries suggest a slightly different urban middling relationship with the state than the rural world of the parish described by French. First, relying on parish office as the main indicator of status leaves out

---

[55] Parsons, 'Diary, 1769, Jan.–Aug.', 21 February 1769.

[56] David Eastwood, *Government and Community in the English Provinces, 1700–1870* (Basingstoke, 1997), 48.

[57] French, *The Middle Sort of People*, 27. Edmund Harrold's father, Thomas, was a tobacconist and served on the Manchester Court Leet. Edmund seems to have achieved less civic status than his father. Parish entries list him as a 'barber' and a ratepayer. Horner, *Diary of Edmund Harrold*, xi–xii.

[58] French, *The Middle Sort of People*, 94–120.

[59] Horner, *Diary of Edmund Harrold*, 24 October 1712, 6 October 1712.

middling dissenters, who were increasingly numerous in the eighteenth century. Thomas Parsons, a Baptist dissenter, recounted undertaking civic responsibilities within the national dissenting community rather than the parish, including visiting, caring for the ill, moneylending and welcoming travelling ministers.[60] Second, office holding and the tasks associated with this role competed with other forms of work as indicators of status. In Harrold's diary, one gets the distinct impression that civic tasks were something that he was co-opted into and which called him away from more fulfilling or profitable work. As Craig Horner suggests, civic posts had different levels of status. Being conferred a civic title could reflect or imply low standing in town society. Thus, when he was elected 'dog musiller', Harrold missed the swearing-in ceremony, for which he was fined.[61]

## Masculine Independence and the Life Cycle

Work had a crucial relationship to one of the central features of eighteenth-century masculine identity: independence.[62] However, a man's capacity for independence depended upon his life cycle position. While historians have long recognised the importance of marital status to women's employment opportunities, the importance of life cycle to male labour is less well conceptualised. In its simplest form, work created the income that allowed men to claim a reputation for self-sufficiency, which was understood in terms of being able to maintain oneself without relying on others. By the eighteenth century, maintenance in terms of income came to constitute one of the primary means by which many people claimed their status.[63] Income and self-sufficiency also supported male gender identities within the household, allowing men to claim the ideal of provisioning, and in turn, to benefit from the dividends of patriarchy. All three diarists earned a comfortable though modest subsistence for tradesmen of the time, earning between £50 and £70 per year, which placed them squarely within the lower bounds of the 'middling' in terms of income.

If income provided the basis for independence, this independence was fragile. All three diarists fretted frequently about paying their debts and feared the potential for failure. Harrold often had difficulty paying rent,

---

[60] Parsons, 'Diary, 1769, Jan.–Aug.', 5 January 1769, 23 May 1769, 8 June 1769.
[61] Horner, *Diary of Edmund Harrold*, xxvi, 20–23 October 1714.
[62] Matthew McCormack, *The Independent Man: Citizenship and Gender Politics in Georgian England* (Manchester, 2005).
[63] Shepard, *Accounting for Oneself*, 191, 274.

noting in one entry that he was forced to sell his grey mare in order to satisfy his landlord.[64] Parsons agonised about his financial obligations, noting in one entry 'am in debt and know not how to pay. This gives me great uneasiness – what a multiplicity of concerns have I to employ my thoughts!'[65] Just as divine providence could bestow wealth, so it could take riches away. Debt combined temporal and religious anxieties. As Harrold reflected, 'the world and the things of the world are mutable.'[66] In October 1713, he thanked God for 'tolerable business' and noted 'I live very comfortablay'. By the next month, he would write that he was 'ill set for money. Very dull business . . . A great rent and little trade, so that I'm in great straite what to do'.[67] Given the fragility of financial self-sufficiency, work's contribution to an independent status was conceptualised less in terms of material gain, and more by the relationships that working life conferred. Work was a social practice, and the social relations structuring and structured by eighteenth-century working lives were as important to a reputation for independent status as the tasks that individuals undertook or the material benefits that they derived from productive activity. Working life placed lower-middling men into relationships with family, apprentices and other craftsmen that were based upon dependence, status and hierarchy. Thinking about work in terms broader than monetised labour allows us to probe the limitations of the eighteenth century's independent economic man.

Just as life cycle position had a bearing on women's work, the kinds of relationships that men established through work, and the degree to which these supported claims to independence, depended upon their place in the life cycle. Thomas Parsons devoted many lines in his diary to hierarchical relationships of work with his father. A 25-year-old at the time he wrote the diary, Parsons served nominally as the 'master' of his workshop, but found himself in a transitional life cycle stage, in the process of taking over the business from his father. Parsons therefore occupied a liminal space between independence and dependence, between patriarchy and subordination. He recounted his father's criticisms over the management of his business and the ways he spent his time. Fashioning an independent working self-proved a constant source of anxiety for Parsons, who often wrote about the desire for a different means of making a living. 'I have

---

[64] Horner, *Diary of Edmund Harrold*, 30 August 1714.
[65] Parsons, 'Diary, 1769, Jan.–Aug.', 27 January 1769.
[66] Horner, *Diary of Edmund Harrold*, 30 August 1712.
[67] Horner, *Diary of Edmund Harrold*, 15 October 1713, 9 October 1713, 28 November 1713, 27–30 December 1713.

often thought of, and wish'd for some other way of getting my bread, so as to be detach'd from my Father.'[68] Similarly, Cannon complained of his parents' meddling in his employment opportunities. He believed that parents should allow their children to 'seek honourable employments and honest callings' suitable to their skills, and resolved in 1720 'to get in some employ that should separate me from them a good distance'.[69] Parsons' and Cannon's experiences make clear that while the household family provided a source of security and the means to achieve a patriarchal status, the collusion of work and family also posed challenges for men in subordinate positions as they sought to establish independent working identities.

Against the grain at parental critique, diaries served young men as space in which to fashion an independent self by deploying a language of paternalist discourse. Through work, Parsons claimed independence by placing himself within a hierarchal working relationship above journeymen, apprentices and other dependents, which gave him a partial claim to patriarchal dividends. For example, as a nominal patriarch, he expected to 'gain credit' from his journeymen. As studies of credit and reputation have made clear, male reputation was derived from men's own actions as well as the positive and negative reputations of dependents and family.[70] He reflected upon hiring a journeyman that this individual would 'prove a workman and a credit to his Master who intends also to be his instructor'.[71]

## Cooperative Maintenance

As men transitioned from positions of dependence and youth to potential positions of patriarchy, the complex relationship between work, family and independence changed. Male working identities came to be constructed in relation to the work of their dependents. Though conduct literature placed a heavy emphasis on the ideals of patriarchal provision, we know that household economies did not in reality rely solely on the capacity of a patriarchal 'breadwinner'. The extent, however, to which men recognised the contributions of dependents and how they made sense of them in the formulation of their own occupational identities is more opaque. On the one hand, marriage in the early modern period was seen by contemporaries

[68] Parsons, 'Diary, 1769, Jan.–Aug.', 13 April 1769.
[69] Money, *Chronicles of John Cannon*, 57; Muldrew, 'Class and Credit', 163.
[70] Paul, 'Credit, Reputation, and Masculinity in British Urban Commerce', 240.
[71] Parsons, 'Diary, 1769, Jan.–Aug.', 14 February 1769.

as an economic partnership in terms of financial assets, and household management was a cooperative endeavour.[72] On the other hand, the roles of women as central to household earnings would seem to betray the ideal of the independent, autonomous man. As Joanne Bailey suggests, 'co-dependency worked against male autonomy.'[73]

While legal and institutional records tend to hide women's work, diaries suggest that in non-institutional sources, men recognised and even expected women to contribute household labour. The expectation that a wife's work should contribute to the financial well-being of the household started at courtship. For the young Thomas Parsons, anxieties about finding a suitable marriage partner were bound up with concerns over solvency and financial competency. He judged the women he met according to their skill. Similarly, the widowed wigmaker Edmund Harrold wrote about his decision to remarry after his first wife's death as being bound up not only in loneliness, but also in the need for a new wife to contribute to household provisioning. Fretting over the decision of whether to marry, he wrote, 'I'm much concerned about my affairs.' He described one potential courtship partner using a language of management: 'she [is] a maneger, but is manag'd. She wants to be satisfied.'[74]

Within lower-middling households, business decision-making and economic management were joint endeavours. Harrold's economic relationship with his wife might be described as cooperative. In his diary, he referred to Sarah as his 'assistant'. He read his business letters to her before sending them. Decisions related to renting lodgings in their household were made jointly or deferred to his wife. Sarah was intimately involved in debt collection and the decision to 'dun' those who were obligated to the Harrold household. She also had input into his exchange decisions. In 1712, Harrold 'swapt 1 wig with Rob Parley of Whitehaven for 1 wig and 2 boxes, long ones, of wood'. Apparently responding to Sarah's discontent with the bargain, Harrold later noted having 'swapt and unswapt with Robert Parley to please wife'.[75]

If men like Harrold shared household provisioning and decision-making with their wives, and though we might describe their relationships as

---

[72] Amy Louise Erickson, 'The Marital Economy in Perspective', in *The Marital Economy in Scandinavia and Britain, 1400–1900*, ed. Amy Louise Erickson and Maria Ågren (Aldershot, 2005), 3–20; Harvey, *The Little Republic*.

[73] Joanne Bailey, *Unquiet Lives: Marriage and Marriage Breakdown in England, 1660–1800* (Cambridge, 2003), 199.

[74] Horner, *Diary of Edmund Harrold*, 25 May 1713, 5 March 1713.

[75] Horner, *Diary of Edmund Harrold*, 17 December 1712, 29 June 1712, 16 June 1712.

cooperative, the task of managing and keeping track of household production seemed to be their endeavour alone. Accounting linked men's everyday practices to notions of masculine household management.[76] In the pages of his diary, Harrold accounted for his wife's labour alongside his own, keeping track of how 'busie' she was, and what kinds of work she completed during the day, even where this work was independent of his wig-making business. On 25 July, he noted, 'about ¼ past my wife was kneading and she had teemed the barm [yeast] of oth 2 bulled pot', aspects of the bread-making process. He noted how productive she was, writing in one entry that 'My wife made all her mak,' and in another that she cleaned out stock while he worked.[77]

Harrold clearly benefitted from this task of economic management, which gave him power over the household. However, diaries suggest that household management roles did not come easily. Accounting was negotiated between husband and wife, and men were judged according to the skill and success with which accounting was performed. Wives expected their husbands to manage effectively and questioned their abilities to do so. Harrold wrote that Sarah 'asked questions about books'.[78] In the Cannon household, management was not John's sole prerogative. He wrote that his wife 'consented' to his selling property in order to pay off their debts, and she criticised his ability to effectively manage their household resources. In 1728, when the family was in particularly bad straits, Susanna told him 'that she and the children must spin only to support such a lazy, indolent fellow as I was . . . who had for a great many times past had a very fair opportunity to have made a sufficient provision for himself and his family but took no further care than for the present time, and that I riotously wasted that which might have been treasured up for future support'.[79]

Spouses adopted joint strategies to mitigate against the risks and uncertainties of employment. One of these strategies was to diversify or to engage in distinctive forms of employment that could be relied on if work in one field dried up. As Amy Erickson has shown, married women in eighteenth-century London tended to work in occupations distinctive of their husbands. In cases of indisposition, the diarists recognised that household maintenance depended upon female contributions and, more specifically, upon their wives' distinctive occupations. In Cannon's case, his wife's contributions became apparent when he fell ill and was unable to provision the household.

---

[76] Harvey, *The Little Republic*, 65–98.
[77] Horner, *Diary of Edmund Harrold*, 25 July 1712, 22 November 1712, 23 February 1714.
[78] Horner, *Diary of Edmund Harrold*, 27 September 1712.
[79] Money, *Chronicles of John Cannon*, 172–3, 189.

While he was in 'a low condition', his family depended upon his wife's labour, who 'took up the trade of selling bread for the bakers and butter for the dairy folks, in which she continued about two years'.[80] While Harrold accounted for his wife's activities frequently in his diary, the full extent of her financial contributions and the household's dependence upon them was acknowledged only after her death, when he was forced to assume tasks that she once carried out, or to hire help to perform them. He wrote of being 'busie in the house', and later of having 'both shops to tend now, all by plunges. I had 4 customers at once and 3 went away'.[81] Five days after his wife's burial, Harrold hired a housekeeper. He was forced to take on new by-employments and to manage the lodgers. Eventually he began selling off household goods. As time progressed, Harrold fought to single-handedly support his household, and he spiralled into debt.[82]

Over the course of the life cycle, working identity continued to change. Just as working identity shifted in the transition from youth to middle age, and as men assumed positions as heads of household, their occupational identities shifted again in old age as their ability to work declined. Because work was so important to male selfhood, this transition into old age poses conceptual problems. When men stopped working, how did their occupational identities change? Some men were able to maintain their occupational identities after retirement. Keith Thomas suggests that unlike today, retirement in the early modern period did not require a complete disengagement from occupational life.[83] However, by the eighteenth century, it came to be expected that older men would withdraw from their professions, or at least hire additional help.[84] Susannah Ottaway has argued that in eighteenth-century England, self-sufficiency and autonomy were the central ideals of old age, shaping attitudes about whether the aged should labour. The view that individuals should continue working until they reached decrepitude was matched by a developing attitude that it was acceptable, or even desirable, for those of middling status who had achieved independence to retire from work.[85]

[80] Money, *Chronicles of John Cannon*, 189.
[81] Horner, *Diary of Edmund Harrold*, 27 September 1712. 'In plunges' means in a hurry and with difficulty.
[82] Horner, *Diary of Edmund Harrold*, 25 November 1712, 29 November 1712, 22 December 1712, 30 December 1712, 14 January 1713, 6 January 1713.
[83] Keith Thomas, 'Age and Authority in Early Modern England', *Proceedings of the British Academy* 62 (1978): 236–7.
[84] Susannah R. Ottaway, *The Decline of Life: Old Age in Eighteenth-Century England* (Cambridge, 2007), 68.
[85] Ottaway, *The Decline of Life*, 66–8.

Occupational plurality facilitated the transition into different occupations later in life. Men might take up work that relied less on physical strength and agility. Thus, Thomas Parsons' ageing father, Robert, once the master of the stonecutting workshop, followed spiritual aspirations and began lecturing as a Baptist minister. Diaries suggest that for middle-rank men who possessed independent businesses, old age seemed to involve less of a complete stepping away from work and more of a long period of semi-independence as they handed over some tasks and responsibilities to younger family members. Parsons' diary recounts father and son working together. In January, he described being 'employed myself with my Father in getting the pieces of timber from the top of the orchard to the pit'. Later that month, he showed his father a copy of one of Worlidge's prints, a gesture that led to an argument about taste. Thomas Parsons' father continued to maintain oversight of the stonecutting workshop, a position that prevented his son from claiming full independence. They constantly disputed tasks and working methods, as Thomas attempted to assert his independence. In one typical entry, he noted that 'Father seem'd chagrin'd at [my] refusing to comply with his proposal – telling me that was but one among many instances in which his mentioning a thing was a sufficient reason for my objecting to it.'[86] Other diaries suggest similar practices of partial retirement. When the grocer William Stout of Lancaster handed over his shop to his apprentice, John Troughton, he maintained oversight of the business from a distance and returned to manage affairs when Troughton fell into bankruptcy. Older men like Stout felt that maintaining partial control was a responsibility towards the interpersonal obligations that they built over their career. As Stout reflected, as former owner of the business and the person who secured Troughton's credit, 'I thought my selfe obliged to use my endevors to make the most for the crediters.'[87]

### Conclusion: Work and Identity

Work was part and parcel of the experience of insecurity in the eighteenth century. Maintaining regular employment and managing household contributions to maintenance were essential to ensuring financial solvency. But negotiating changing occupational landscapes and shifting and seasonal work opportunities also exposed individuals to insecurities associated with identity. This is not to dispute the importance of occupational

[86] Parsons, 'Diary, 1769, Jan.–Aug.', 23 January 1769, 30 January 1769, 15 January 1769.
[87] Marshall, *The Autobiography of William Stout of Lancaster, 1665–1752*, 148–9.

identities for women, but rather to note that while the nuances with which women engaged with work have been widely recognised, historians have assumed that men achieved stable occupational identities. Establishing occupational status was a much more precarious process than we have recognised, and it exposes the ways in which for men, the achievement of modern economic identities was partial at best. If autonomy was an ideal for eighteenth-century men, patterns of household maintenance show just how fictitious this ideal was in practice. From young to old age, working practices were integrated with others and maintenance was dependent upon other household members.

Work was, for lower-middling men, a central feature of identity and of status. However, this status depended neither solely or even principally upon occupational title, nor upon the income derived from productive activities. In order to truly understand what work meant to the people who performed it, we have to start in a different place than occupational titles or incomes.[88] Working identities were derived from a more complex accounting for the different activities that men undertook during their working lives as well as the productive activities undertaken by other members of the household. In order to understand the functions that work played in constructions of masculine selfhood, we require a broader definition of what constituted 'work'. This definition must take into account activities that did not generate income and that might not even be considered straightforwardly 'productive', but that provided men with a means of developing and asserting skill and status. In a credit economy, cultivating a reputation for skill and status was inseparable from 'making a living'.

'Work' could include activities that were not paid, but also leisure that was not pleasure. Men like Parsons, Harrold and Cannon clearly understood their work as encompassing a broad range of activities, and they employed complex vocabularies, using the words 'work', 'business' and 'employment' to describe the different but interrelated benefits conferred by their various forms of work. The benefits of work, forged in a precarious environment, could be financial, but they could also be social, related to public reputation and to relationships of power forged especially within the household. In effect, the value of work in terms of status and income could have an inverse relationship. Thomas Parsons made most of his money from his stonecutting business rather than from his intellectual pursuits, but it was from his participation in an intellectual world of scientific experimentation that he derived the most status. Furthermore, work did

---

[88] Lindström, Fiebranz and Rydén, 'The Diversity of Work', 26.

not only confer 'benefits'. Given the precariousness of working lives, work was not necessarily a positive source of identity for lower-middling men. For upwardly aspirational men in different places in the life cycle, occupational title and position could be limiting. While work could contribute to independence, it could equally challenge male autonomy. Work was a social practice performed in cooperation with or in relation to other people. It was not only a productive activity to provide maintenance or to generate income, but was rather an undertaking that established skill, status and self-worth. It was performed in relation to people outside of the household, as well as in relation to people within the household. Relational meanings of work changed over the source of the life cycle. For younger or subordinate men, working practices confirmed dependent status. As men transitioned into positions of patriarchy, managing other people's work within the household became an important feature of independence. But equally, they recognised the importance of spousal interdependence in maintaining the household's livelihood and negotiating the world of risk and uncertainty. As revealed in diaries, status, selfhood and credit were integral to the world of work, and the world of work was integral to the experience of insecurity.

# PART III

## *The Debtor's Body*

CHAPTER 6

# Punishing the Body
## Harm and the Coercive Nature of Credit

In his 1701 *History of Myddle*, Richard Gough recounted the arrest of William Tyler, a baker in the village of Balderton. Tyler was indebted to a local resident, Thomas Bradocke. When the debt became long overdue, Bradocke sent a special bailiff named Reece Wenlocke to serve Tyler with a writ to arrest him. Tyler first assaulted the bailiff, then, like many debtors, he resisted his arrest, forcing Wenlocke to beat him into submission before he could be transported to the debtors' prison. As Gough recalled, after being served with the warrant,

> Tyler, by faire words persuaded Reece to come to Thomas Pickering's house; and Tyler stepping into the house, shut the doore, butt Reece had got his legge in, and Tyler with his knive, stroke Reece in the legge; but Reece beeing a strong man, burst open the doore, broake the knife ... hee got Tyler downe on the floore, and fell to beateing of him.[1]

The violent assault on a debtor that took place in Balderton that night, which involved the use of the debtor's body as a site to negotiate credit and coerce payment, might seem surprising in a world where credit and reputation seemed like relatively abstract social concepts. When it came to debt, however, these concepts were anchored to a physical self. Failure to pay was dealt with through physical treatment of the body. The eighteenth-century debtors' prison was not, as Foucault has suggested of incarceration, primarily a response to disquiet about public punishment.[2] Rather, it was a form of economic sanction. It was a space where debtors were punished by their creditors for failing to abide by the ethics of the marketplace. As one creditor in Edinburgh suggested, two of his debtors should be 'punished in their bodys to the terror of others to commit the like practices'.[3]

---

[1] Richard Gough, *The History of Myddle* (Firle, 1979), 103.   [2] Foucault, *Discipline and Punish*.
[3] NRS, ETWLB, 16 December 1746, HH11/23.

Violent assaults, like that Wenlock experienced, also seem unusual in the world of polite and commercial people. Both rate-paying tradesmen, Wenlocke and Tyler were the types of middling men who embodied the decline of public violence in eighteenth-century Britain proposed by Norbert Elias and confirmed by subsequent social histories. These were the middling men who sat at the centre of Langford's polite economy.[4] One of the ideological threads of eighteenth-century capitalism was a belief in 'doux commerce': that by pursuing material interests, men's passions would be calmed. Commerce conveyed 'sweetness, softness, calm and gentleness', and contemporaries saw it as the 'antonym of violence'.[5] In the new civilised, commercial world, open displays of rage and harm stood at odds with eighteenth-century dictates of polite and prudential masculinity. New forms of behaviour, which emphasised dexterity and a mildness of manners, were seen as crucial to the smooth functioning of the economy.[6]

As part of Tyler's descent into debt and his eventual incarceration, the physical altercation in Balderton was probably not his last experience of violence. Imprisonment for debt was a coercive act. Previous accounts of the debtors' prisons, which present them as microcosms of the outside world and as spaces where inmates could continue to work and socialise, have obscured the punitive nature of these institutions and the experiences of harm that unfolded within them.[7] While it is certainly true that porosity characterised the prison in some cases, for most inmates prior to the prison reforms of the 1770s, poor conditions, mental and physical hardship and deliberately imposed hunger were the norm. Some debtors were subjected to corporeal punishments, while others were denied light and fresh air.[8] Legally, the debtors' prison was not considered a form of punishment. Rather, it was a space of safe custody for debtors' bodies.[9] The law assumed that the debtors had the ability to pay, and the purpose of incarceration was to confine them until they met their financial

---

[4] Norbert Elias, *The Civilizing Process: Sociogenetic and Psychogenetic Investigations*, rev. edn, trans. Edmund Jephcott, ed. Eric Dunning, Johan Goudsblom and Stephen Mennell (Oxford; Malden, MA, 2000); Robert Shoemaker, 'Male Honour and the Decline of Public Violence in Eighteenth-Century London', *Social History* 26, no. 2 (2001): 190–208; Langford, *A Polite and Commercial People*.

[5] Hirschman, *The Passions and the Interests*, 57–61.

[6] Pocock, *Virtue, Commerce and History*, 49; Smail, 'Coming of Age in Trade: Masculinity and Commerce in Eighteenth-Century England', 229–52; Langford, *A Polite and Commercial People*, 316.

[7] Innes, 'King's Bench', 275; Finn, *The Character of Credit*.

[8] White, *Mansions of Misery*; White, 'Pain and Degradation in Georgian London'.

[9] Finn, *The Character of Credit*, 110.

obligations. In practice, however, imprisonment could be a punitive act. As contemporaries understood it, the conditions within the prisons made incarceration 'a punishment of no light degree'.[10] Interpretations of failure as a form of malfeasance justified the violent treatment of debtors. Imprisonment was conceptualised as a form of punishment waged by creditors against those who they understood to have wilfully failed to pay, or whose immoral conduct occasioned their financial decline.

The social dynamics that emerged from around Britain's debtors' prisons facilitate a recasting of how we might conceptualise the eighteenth century's culture of credit, as one that could be coercive rather than consensual. Previous accounts of the social nature of credit, both literary and historical, tend to represent credit as positive, emphasising relationships of trust and neighbourliness. Interpersonal credit was built upon neighbourly and familial relations. Craig Muldrew's depictions of credit relationships in early modern England suggest that credit solidified bonds of mutual obligation. Contemporaries understood trade through a language that stressed social relations and trust.[11] Middling tradespeople structured business around kinship obligations, and risk entrenched even these bonds.[12] Yet the social consequences of a system of credit and capital grounded in moral standing were not always positive. The nature of the relationships visible through the lens of prison shows that credit had a hard edge. The world of credit included vindictive attempts to punish enemies and opportunities for individuals to justify sublimated violence and the infliction of harm upon one another that would otherwise be impermissible. As Laurence Fontaine suggests, the same networks of obligation that bound communities together could also force individuals into poverty.[13]

Attending to the treatment of debtors' bodies provides a glimpse into an economy tinged with violence, coercion and aggression. The world of polite and commercial people had a dark underbelly. The infliction of harm in various forms was a constituent part of the culture of credit, and it did not necessarily sit at odds with new eighteenth-century dictates of politeness. While polite dictates against aggression would seem to problematise the use of the prison, the use of this legal mechanism accorded with rhetorical codes of restraint, control and emotional mastery. As acts of public violence were increasingly viewed as intolerable, they were superseded by more acceptable forms of harm that could be concealed by the

---

[10] Bell, *Commentaries on the Laws of Scotland*, 582.
[11] Muldrew, 'Interpreting the Market', 163, 181.    [12] Hunt, *The Middling Sort*, 23–9.
[13] Laurence Fontaine, *The Moral Economy: Poverty, Credit, and Trust in Early Modern Europe* (New York, 2014).

aggressor. Use of the law itself could constitute a form of harm. Legal verdicts can be understood as forms of 'restraint or violation imposed by somebody on somebody against their will'.[14] The law sublimated violence.

## Forms of Harm

Different varieties of harm were waged within relationships of debt, ranging from verbal aggression to damaged reputation to violent physical assault, and these were arranged around a dynamic of power established at the moment that credit was contracted. Bourdieu's theory of gentle violence suggests that we might consider the very contracting of credit as an 'attack' on the freedom of debtors because it established control and created the obligation to reciprocate, much like a gift.[15] The extension of credit involved expectations of reciprocity which combined social gifts and financial obligations. Thomas Turner described these entangled forms of obligation in his diary. A local gardener gifted Turner's wife 'a present of some grapes in gratuity for my trusting him sometimes' (with financial loans). Meanwhile, a local man who had been in Turner's debt was described as unreasonable and unjust for having called in a debt owed by Turner.[16] Credit created an imbalance of power between individuals who otherwise stood as relative equals, opening up legitimate roads to harm. People could establish power over one another by buying up coercive debts. In one case before the Edinburgh consistory court, a litigant complained that his opponents 'dayly used their utmost to ruin his credit by purchasing and buying up his debts, torturing and tormenting him with groundless lawsutes, by all which the defenders are guilty of abuse against the complainer'.[17] In 1716, after William Nost angered his fellow printers by leaking information to the Secretary of State, they exacted revenge by burying him beneath an avalanche of actions for debt.[18] Though credit could form the basis for community bonds, people could also manipulate a system based upon trust and social networks, coupling debt with legal force. Instead of building trust and wealth, the credit market could be used as a means to conspire against individuals, causing poverty.

---

[14] Christoph Menke, 'Law and Violence', *Law and Literature* 22, no. 1 (2010): 2.

[15] Walter Benjamin, 'Critique of Violence', in *Reflections: Essays, Aphorisms, Autobiographical Writings*, ed. Peter Demelz (New York, 1978), 294–5; Pierre Bourdieu, *Outline of a Theory of Practice* (Cambridge, 1977), 193; Finn, *The Character of Credit*, 10; Mauss, *The Gift*.

[16] Vaisey, *The Diary of Thomas Turner, 1754–1765*, 68.

[17] NRS, Consistorial Processes, *Thompson v Guild*, 1738, CC8/6/276.

[18] McKendrick, Brewer and Plumb, *The Birth of a Consumer Society*, 211.

When credit broke down, the most common form of harm was reputational and verbally inflicted. Because credit was based upon reputation, aggressive verbal threats to harm men and women's social standing could become tools waged within commercial relationships. For example, in a dispute between the mason Thomas Smith and Robert Lauder in Edinburgh, Smith used his possession of Lauder's financial debt as a point of coercion, and threatened that if the debt remained unpaid, he 'would do all he could to stop and hinder masons and other tradesmen from working to him' and furthermore that 'no person should possess his houses and that he would endeavour to keep them from tennents'.[19] Others threatened to ruin their opponents' honour or fortune. In 1738, John Mitchell, a merchant, in an altercation over the payment of customs duties with a sailor, 'threatened to send letters to every port he knew the complainer went and inform his acquaintances what kind of a man he was'.[20] The efficacy of verbal harm was what prompted so many men and women to take cases of slander to court.[21] As Gerd Schwerhoff suggests, honour and reputation were at least as important as the integrity of the physical body. Honour can be viewed almost like a '"second skin", which had to be defended against violent attacks just like one's physical skin'.[22]

Verbal harm could transition into violent physical assault at the moment of dunning, when violence was a tool creditors used to coerce their debtors to repay. In his diary, the wigmaker Edmund Harrold recounted a violent altercation with two men, Thomas Chandler and Robert Bradshaw, who owed the Harrold household money. After being ordered by his wife to dunn them, Harrold followed Chandler to a local Manchester alehouse, the Golden Keys. There, Harrold and Chandler had 'a sad tug' over the debt. After the violence had settled and 'passion ceased', Harrold noted that 'we brought Thomas Chandler to do fair things and order a note of particulars to be drawn and he would pay in time by 12 d a time'. For Harrold, a physical fight was an effective tool to bring about order, and it was central to the process of justice. By harming a debtor who failed to pay, the act of violence towards Chandler restored a social balance previously broken by his transgression, and restored peace between the two households.[23]

[19] NRS, *Lauder v Traill*, 1758, CC8/6/374.  [20] NRS, *Jameson v Mitchell*, 1738, CC8/6/278.
[21] See Chapter 4.
[22] Gerd Schwerhoff, 'Early Modern Violence and the Honour Code: From Social Integration to Social Distinction ?', *Crime, Histoire & Sociétés / Crime, History & Societies* 17, no. 2 (2013): 36.
[23] Horner, *Diary of Edmund Harrold*, 1 Sept 1712; Garnot, 'Justice, infrajustice, parajustice et extra justice dans la France d'Ancien Régime', 113.

While physical harm, or the threat of physical harm, was used as a tool to informally resolve debts, it also occurred at the moment of formal arrest, when the body of the debtor had to be seized. Physical altercations were common enough during arrest for Gough to write that 'it was usual to put some stout strong person the sheriff's warrant' to serve the writ.[24] Not only were debtors forced into submission by acts of violence, but they might resist arrest by attacking bailiffs. Quarter sessions records from Essex and Lancashire contained two to four cases each year involving bailiffs being assaulted while attempting to perform their duties.[25] Gough told the story of how when Sir Edward Kinaston sent his servant and a bailiff to arrest a tenant for arrears of rent, the tenant's son attacked the bailiff, at which his servant 'came with his sword drawn, and swore he would make hay with them. But one of Clarke's sons, with a turf spade ... struck sir Edward's man on the head, and cloave out his brains'.[26] In Edinburgh in 1746, when John Gant, a soldier, came to the house of a local stabler with a court officer to seize a horse, he was 'most barberously attacked' by the stabler and 'beat to the effusion of [his] Blood and [his] cloth Gore and Hatt interely lost in the scuffell'.[27]

Once imprisoned, debtors experienced harm in the form of restrictions to their liberty. In a period when the liberty of Englishmen was said to define the nation, and when liberty held a central position in political debates, the denial of agency was a highly symbolic act and a serious concern to reformers. As one reform pamphlet argued, 'What a Banter is our talk of Liberty and Property in a Kingdom, where Liberty is so necessary to its Trade ... People that lived handsomely, are plagued with the Loss of their Liberty, Penury, Stench, Dirtiness, Vermin of divers Sorts.'[28] Incarceration, especially on the mesne process (before trial), was particularly problematic by contemporary understandings of the writ of habeas corpus, which protected individuals' bodies from wrongful impri-sonment without trial.[29] The pamphlet *Imprisonment of Men's Bodyes* described imprisonment as a form of 'corporall punishment, a griefe and torture of the mind'. By giving the creditor complete control over the debtor's body, imprisonment 'betrayed the liberty of the subject' and 'was against Magna Carta'.[30]

---

[24] Gough, *The History of Myddle*, 103.    [25] Muldrew, *Economy of Obligation*, 402.
[26] Gough, *The History of Myddle*, 22.    [27] NRS, ETWLB, 31 January 1746, HH11/22.
[28] *The Attempt: Or, An Essay towards the Retrieving Lost Liberty ... By a Prisoner in the Poultry-Compter* (London, 1751), 8, 21.
[29] Paul D. Halliday, *Habeas Corpus: From England to Empire* (Cambridge, MA, 2010).
[30] *Imprisonment of Mens Bodyes for Debt, as the Practise of England Now Stands ...* (London, 1641).

The experience of incarceration could involve physical hardship and hunger. Some inmates were able to rent superior accommodation on the 'masters' side' of London prisons, but others were consigned to dangerous and life-threatening spaces. Institutional records suggest that 6 to 7 per cent of prisoners died while confined (table 3.1) and reform texts represented overcrowding as a serious threat to health. Commentators complained of these threats even during a period when cities themselves were coming to be recognised as spaces with serious problems related to pollution and sanitation, prompting the major urban improvements of the eighteenth century.[31] A 1729 parliamentary committee found that most of the 330 prisoners in the common side of the Marshalsea were 'in the utmost necessity' and that 'great Numbers ... appeared to have perished for Want'. James Ogelthorpe described prisoners 'nearly starved to death' and prisons so overcrowded that inmates were forced to sleep in rows on top of one another.[32] Petitions from prisoners complained frequently of inadequate food resources.[33] Poor sanitation and inadequate ventilation made the prisons both unpleasant spaces and ripe breeding grounds for contagious disease. The Recorder of York complained that 'when the turnkey opens the cells in the morning, the steam and stench is intolerable and scarce credible.' Bouts of typhus, which contemporaries referred to as 'gaol fever', swept through the prisons across the country. Samuel Johnson's description of imprisonment in *The Idler* in 1759 suggested that one quarter of imprisoned debtors died every year from disease, which, if true, meant that imprisonment led to more deaths than did war.[34]

Reformers and prisoners had political reasons to emphasise poor sanitary conditions, but prison conditions also became broader public health concerns when they threatened the population outside. After a particularly bad outbreak of gaol distemper in London, the debtors' prisons became a case study for doctors interested in the spread of communicable disease. The dense, vapid airs of the prisons were identified as a cause of infection. In

---

[31] William M. Cavert, *Smoke of London: Energy and Environment in the Early Modern City* (Cambridge, 2017); Michael Reed, 'The Transformation of Urban Space 1700–1840', in *The Cambridge Urban History of Britain*, ed. Peter Clark, vol. 2 (Cambridge, 2000), 615–40.

[32] Quoted in Hitchcock and Shoemaker, *London Lives*, 103; House of Commons, *A Report from the Committee Appointed to Enquire into the State of the Goals of This Kingdom: Relating to the Marshalsea Prison; and Farther Relating to the Fleet Prison. With the Resolution of the House of Commons Thereupon* (London, 1729), 8–9.

[33] Margaret Dorey, 'Reckliss Endangerment? Feeding the Poor Prisoners of London in the Early Eighteenth Century', in *Experiences of Poverty in Late Medieval and Early Modern England and France*, ed. Anne M. Scott (London, 2016), 183–98.

[34] Quoted in William Holdsworth, *A History of English Law* (London, 1938), vol. 10, 182, n. 7; *The Idler*, 6 January 1759, no. 38.

1750, the physician and president of the Royal Society John Pringle identified the prisons as 'insidious sources of slow and malignant fever'.[35] Health reformers worried that 'poisenous effluvia' wafting over the prison walls would infect London's population. Local shopkeepers around Newgate even feared that the stench from the gaol was driving away customers.[36]

Prison conditions north of the border were notoriously bad. Scotland's law of *squalor carceris* stipulated that debtors be deliberately denied fresh air and freedom of movement as a way of coercing them to pay their debts. As the law stated, 'after a debtor is imprisoned, he ought not to be indulged with the benefit of the air, nor even under a guard; for Creditors have an interest, that their debtors be kept under close confinement, that by squalor carceris they may be brought to pay their debt.'[37] Prison keepers had a vested interest in keeping debtors closely confined because by a 1671 statute, if a prisoner escaped, the gaoler would become liable for the prisoner's debt.[38] John Howard described the Tolbooth in the 1770s as 'dirty and offensive, without court-yards, and also generally without water'. It lacked proper city control and oversight, and was instead left to the authority of gaol keepers, who used it to make a profit. City magistrates never visited the institution, and inside, gaolers 'allowed the free sale of the most pernicious liquors'.[39] In Scotland, the debtor was 'consigned to the closest and most severe confinement. He has no yard to walk in ... he is kept like the vilest criminal, often crowded together in a close and fetid room which he is never allowed to quit'.[40]

Petitions from prisoners on both sides of the border confirmed the poor conditions that reformers described. In the Tolbooth, where there were only two open rooms to confine the male debtors, there was no possibility for debtors to rent their own rooms. Those incarcerated were furnished

[35] R. Brookes, *The General Practice of Physic; Extracted Chiefly from the Writings of the Most Celebrated Practical Physicians, and The Medical Essays, Transactions, Journals, and Literary Correspondence Of the Learned Societies in Europe ...*, The second edition with improvements, 2 vols (London, 1754), 155; *Six Discourses, Delivered by Sir John Pringle, Bart. When President of the Royal Society; On Occasion of Six Annual Assignments of Sir Godfrey Copley's Medal ...* (London, 1783), 29; John Pringle, *Observations on the Nature and Cure of Hospital and Jayl-Fevers* (London, 1750), 2.
[36] Haagen, 'Imprisonment for Debt', 47.
[37] Act of Session 14, June 1771, in Erskine, *Institute of the Law of Scotland.*
[38] *Essay on the Forms of Writings*, 381.    [39] Howard, *State of the Prisons*, 103.
[40] Joseph John Gurney and Elizabeth Gurney Fry, *Notes on a Visit Made to Some of the Prisons in Scotland, and the North of England ... in Company with E. Fry. With Some General Observations on the Subject of Prison Discipline* (London, 1819), 107–8. Quoted in Lorna Ewen, 'Debtors, Imprisonment and the Privilege of Girth', in *Perspectives in Scottish Social History: Essays in Honour of Rosalind Mitchison*, ed. Leah Leneman (Aberdeen, 1988), 58–9.

only with a blanket, a straw mattress, and two rugs. Debtor petitions frequently complained of ill health and poor conditions. David Balfour complained, 'I being now ane old weak man and ever since the tyme of my imprisonment hath had no bed to be upon but the stones of the floor which is like to put ane end to my old dayes in misery.'[41] Others framed their experiences in terms of hunger. David Henderson, a messenger in Edinburgh, petitioned the bailies in 1738 that 'I have been thrie or four days that I have never tasted meett.'[42] Alexander Goldie, a writer, described the prison conditions as 'small incommodious and unholsome', and claimed that by being denied exercise and fresh air, he had 'declined fast in his health'.[43] At Lancaster, prisoners complained of being 'in want of common necessarys and in close confinement'. One petition wrote of 'starveing and miserable conditions', the petitioner being 'almost ready to starve for want of relief'.[44]

In some cases, imprisonment for debt could be considered an act of violence. In addition to hunger and physical hardship, some debtors were subjected to corporeal punishment, and this became a common theme of prints and reform pamphlets. The engraving 'A Debtor Thumscru'd' depicted a male figure fastened by the neck to a fireplace with iron pot-hooks, feet barely grazing the floor, and thumbscrews attached to his hands. Two figures, presumably his creditors or their agents, looked on.[45] Ogelthorpe's 1729 report depicted a variety of instruments of torture used against prisoners, including the collar, skullcap, shears and fetters. During his investigation, prisoners testified that the instruments were used in the violent punishment of debtors when they escaped, as a means of extorting confessions and, according to one prisoner, to inflict harm by the keepers 'for their Diversion' and to solidify 'their pretended Authority'. While Ogelthorpe focused on the London prisons, it seems that these instruments were transferred and traded between gaol keepers across the country. William Acton, the keeper of the Marshalsea, told the committee that he had given thumb screws to the gaoler at York.[46]

If the experience of incarceration did not include physical violence, it caused social harm. Imprisonment could be both the consequence and the

[41] ECA, BCP, Petition of David Balfour, 17 July 1711.
[42] ECA, BCP, Petition of David Henderson, September 1738.
[43] NRS, ETWLB, 14 December 1764, HH11/27.
[44] *Essay on the Forms of Writings*, 381. LRO, Quarter Sessions Petitions, QSP/1189/4.
[45] 'A Debtor Thumscru'd and Iron Pothooks about His Neck', c. 1680–1730. British Museum, 18,530,112.22.
[46] House of Commons, *A Report from the Committee Appointed to Enquire into the State of the Goals of This Kingdom*, 8–9; White, 'Pain and Degradation in Georgian London', 69–73.

cause of downward mobility. Prison signalled to a community that an individual had lost his or her moral and social position, causing financial harm. As one reform pamphlet stated, imprisonment had the power to 'overthrow a man's reputation and destroy all that is good and dear unto him. His kindred grow strange, his friends forsake him, his wife and children suffer with him, or leave him'.[47] Imprisonment not only harmed a person's finances; it ruined his or her status. Debtors framed this loss of status in gendered ways.[48] Incarceration took away autonomy and independence, features which (though often fictional) were deemed central to middling masculine status.[49] The imprisoned debtor lost control over the management of his household, both symbolically and very literally by being denied access to his account books. Prison denied men access to the physical documents that were part of their household management practices. Account books, bills and other financial records did not normally come to prison along- side men's bodies. Karen Harvey suggests that men accrued authority from these domestic writings. Activities such as accounting were part of men's economic duties of property management and were a means by which men attempted to impose order on household life.[50] With some notable exceptions, the debtor's ability to continue trading, to manage affairs and to communicate with the outside world was limited. When he entered the prison, control over a debtor's assets was normally handed to others to manage or forcibly taken by creditors, effectively placing prison- ers in a state of dependency. When Thomas Holme, a surgeon from Lancaster, was arrested, he 'assigned over all my goods and personal estate and all the monies which I was intitled unto' to John Styth 'to be sold for the use of my creditors'.[51] Richard Stanley of Liverpool placed his goods in the hands of Thomas Toran in the Isle of Mann.[52] John Rothwell testified to having £9 in the possession of Henry Whittaker, composed of 'money in his hands' given to be kept while Rothwell went to prison.[53]

In debtors' schedules, prisoners referenced losing control of their estates and being unaware of the quantity and whereabouts of their goods. One prison in Lancaster Castle described how his household goods, valued at £7, were 'gathered in' and disposed of 'without my order or consent'.[54]

[47] *The Case of Prisoners for Debt Consider'd*, 6.
[48] For American comparative perspectives, see Ditz, 'Shipwrecked; or, Masculinity Imperiled'; Sandage, *Born Losers*.
[49] McCormack, *The Independent Man*.     [50] Harvey, *The Little Republic*, 99–133.
[51] LRO, Insolvent Debtor Papers, QJB/31/23.     [52] LRO, Insolvent Debtor Papers, QJB/10/48.
[53] LRO, Insolvent Debtor Papers, QJB/31/12.     [54] LRO, Insolvent Debtor Papers, QJB/10/72.

Another debtor testified in 1722 that he handed over his goods to trustees but that they 'never gave me any account what they made on the goods and debts as yet'.[55] Timothy Jackson, a yeoman, told the court that his household goods, husbandry, stock on hand and other things had been 'sold and disposed of . . . for such sume and sumes of money as are altogether unknown to me'.[56] Yet another claimed to have 'assigned over all my goods and personal estate and all the monies which I was entitled ... in trust to be sold for the use of my creditors'. But the people he trusted had 'rendered no account of their transactions'.[57] As prisoners accounted for their worth, the loss of knowledge and control over estates and assets was a consistent theme. By denying prisoners access to physical documents and processes of wealth management, creditors prevented them from accounting for their own worth in a financial sense, and from participating in the household practices that were so crucial to masculine selfhood. Thomas Dicey, a dealer in wines, wrote that after being incarcerated by William Tash, a wine merchant, Tash entered upon his premises and seized his goods and effects, 'together with bills, notes, receipts, and other securities for debts due, and oweing to me, and did also possess himself of all my books of accounts, private papers, writings and memorandums of debts due, and oweing to me'.[58] Tash effectively left Dicey without knowledge of his wealth and without the means to manage his own estate.

Symbols of masculine social debasement were prominent in visual representations of debtors, and they communicated debasement through the self-presentation of indebted bodies. Popular prints illustrating moments of arrest depicted male debtors with their wigs dishevelled or falling off. In *The Distrest Poet*, a poet sits at a table writing a poem entitled 'poverty', as a milkmaid presents a tally to his wife. The poet's hair is dishevelled and his hair grows out beneath his wig. Similarly, in *A Noted Bard*, a writer is approached from behind by two bailiffs who present a writ for his arrest.[59] The poet's wig is falling off, and the dishevelled appearance adds to a sense of hopelessness and despair. Once imprisoned, prisoners' coiffure continued to deteriorate. In plate seven of Hogarth's *Rake's Progress*, which depicts Rakewell in the cellar of the Fleet Prison, the prisoner helping Sarah has a curl-less wig and his hair has grown underneath it. In addition to tattered clothing, the unkempt wig was part of

---

[55] LRO, Insolvent Debtor Papers, QJB/10/20.     [56] LRO, Quarter Sessions Petitions, QJB/10/71.
[57] LRO, Insolvent Debtor Papers, QJB/31/23.
[58] LMA, Schedule of Thomas Dicey, 1748, CLA/047/LJ/17/024/008
[59] William Hogarth, *The Distrest Poet*, 1737, British Museum, 1868,0822.1541; 'A Noted Bard. Writing a Poem in Blank Verse to Lay before Sr R – on the Great Necessity at This Time for an Act of Insolvency', 1737, British Museum, 1874, 0808. 202.

a general letting go of appearances, in which the descent into poverty was physically rendered. Just as contemporaries saw poverty as embodied, causing the poor to be recognisable by physical marks or deportment, so the poverty of disaster involved physical deterioration.[60] For middling men, the tattered wig was an obvious symbol of financial distress. Wigs dominated male fashion in the eighteenth century. They were often the most expensive article of clothing that a man owned, and they were central to communicating identity and status.[61] Thus, when faced with financial economic decline, not only would a man lose his ability to coif his wig, but the tattered wig had particular social significance.

The deterioration of a man's wig symbolised his debased status and made clear that the act of imprisonment was a form of dishonour. When depicted as part of the moment of arrest, the tattered wig represented the debtor's humiliation, echoing a popular form of public insult. In early modern Britain, physical gestures aimed at the head or face were interpreted as denying a man his autonomy. Knocking a man's hat off or tearing off his wig were amongst the most serious affronts and acts of dishonour that one man could wage against another.[62] But pulling off a wig was also a form of exposure, and it hit at some of the central concerns surrounding middling failure. As Marcia Pointon describes, wigs were an important part of social performance and it was expected that a man's wig would be dressed appropriately according to his rank. The wig, in other words, was a sort of costume that men put on to display their status. It was associated especially with the rising middling sorts and with the communication of middling identity. But within this performative context, a wig was not always a sign of respectability. It could be a badge of artifice, deceptiveness and corruption. Wigs came to represent anxieties about being duped, and about the challenges of knowing the 'true' character of men as opposed to their outward appearance.[63] These anxieties had particularly economic manifestations. Tradespeople extended consumer credit

---

[60] For depictions of poor people's bodies, see Simon P. Newman, *Embodied History: The Lives of the Poor in Early Philadelphia* (Philadelphia, PA, 2013); Tim Hitchcock, *Down and Out in Eighteenth-Century London* (London, 2004), 97–123; Styles, *The Dress of the People*, chapter 2.

[61] Susan Vincent, 'Men's Hair: Managing Appearances in the Long Eighteenth Century', in *Gender and Material Culture in Britain since 1600*, ed. Hannah Greig, Jane Hamlett and Leonie Hannan (London, 2016), 61.

[62] Rosalind Carr, *Gender and Enlightenment Culture in Eighteenth-Century Scotland* (Edinburgh, 2014), 162–74.

[63] Marcia Pointon, *Hanging the Head: Portraiture and Social Formation in Eighteenth-Century England* (New Haven, CT; London, 1997), 114–23; Amelia Rauser, 'Hair, Authenticity, and the Self-Made Macaroni', *Eighteenth-Century Studies* 38, no. 1 (2004): 102–3; Vincent, 'Men's Hair: Managing Appearances in the Long Eighteenth Century', 49–67.

based upon evaluations of character. But in an era when character was seen as increasingly difficult to assess, this was risky business. Thus, while the dishevelled wig was a visual representation of distress that might evoke sympathy on the part of the viewer, it also indicated the exposure of a debtor who had ventured too far with his credit.

Women experienced harm in ways different than men. Though the debts that led to imprisonment belonged to and were contracted by households, men were more likely to experience indebtedness in terms of the denial of liberty. Women, by contrast, tended to be placed in positions of material want outside of the prison walls and were more often cast as dependents upon prisoners than prisoners themselves. Petitions for relief by both men and women framed women as the victims of incarceration. In a petition to the Lancaster justices of the peace, William Etherington claimed to have 'a wife and three small children and no estate either real or personall except a few household goods for the support and maintenance of himself and family'.[64] Similarly, John Scotson wrote in 1726 for aid on the basis that he had 'a wife and one little child at home who are unable to maintain themselves'.[65] While depictions of male harm emphasised the loss of autonomy and control over property, women were more likely to reference the material harm inflicted on the collective unit of the household rather than their own independent status. In prisoner petitions, women complained of their inability to maintain themselves and household dependents. When Elizabeth, the wife of John Grimshaw, incarcerated in 1727, sent a petition to the magistrates begging for relief, she claimed that 'your poor petitioner's husband and his mother whom is near 80 years of adge being cast into prison for debt and in danger to starve for want Your petitioner unable to relieve them being left with six smale children and nothing to support them with but hard labour'.[66]

Even if they were not imprisoned as frequently as men, women were not protected from physical harm outside the prison walls. Altercations over credit and reputation could involve physical threats and violent assault. For example, in 1699 in Edinburgh, in a dispute over debt and the ownership of goods between the servant Isobell Williamson and the householder James Steil, Williamson was attacked. Steil sent his servant to Williamson's house, where she 'Violently lay hands on the said Isobell Williamson' and 'carried her out of her said house to her great shame and disgrace, to an cellar', where she was kept against her will until she signed a bond.[67]

---

[64] LRO, Quarter Sessions Petitions, QSP/1237/10.
[65] LRO, Quarter Sessions Petitions, QSP/1261/3.
[66] LRO, Quarter Sessions Petitions, QSP/1267/10.
[67] NRS, *Williamson v Steill*, 1699, CC8/6/84.

Williamson was physically coerced into signing her name to a legal contract. Even if such acts were not routine, the incident reveals the functional
role assumed by physical harm, and is suggestive of the ways in which
debtors' bodies could become sites for the negotiation of debt. If the sense
of reciprocity and obligation between neighbours broke down, the debtor's
body became a tool to resolve conflict by using the coercive mechanism of
the prison. For example, Thomas Turner's decision to incarcerate his
debtor, Thomas Darby, hinged in part upon his perception that the
family's sense of obligation and custom towards him had been cast aside.
He reflected in his diary that 'they have almost quite forsaken my shop,
buying nothing of me that amounts to any value, but every time they want
anything of value, they go to Lewes.'[68] Turner expected custom. He was
angered by Darby's decision to take his business elsewhere, while letting
the debt with Turner linger. From someone like Darby's perspective,
however, credit bound individuals into relationships and expectations
from which they could not escape, shaping their day-to-day economic
practices and experiences. Debt could haunt day-to-day life, shaping where
individuals went and who they socialised with. As John Cannon recalled,
'the butcher, maltster, grocer, chandler and workmen ... daily followed
me with a detail of their wants.'[69]

## Harm and Social Distinction

Inflicting or threatening harm upon debtors had potential consequences
for creditors. Aggression sat at odds with eighteenth-century constructions
of politeness, and in an economic culture framed by neighbourliness and
doux commerce, it was difficult to justify. Market ethics applied to creditors as well as debtors, and creditors risked harming their own reputations
when they failed to adhere to moral standards. While the stereotype of the
dishonest, fraudulent debtor who deserved to be punished was a powerful
trope, the behaviour of creditors was understood in equally moral terms.
Perceptions of failure therefore hinged not only on attitudes towards
debtors, but also on cultural views of lenders as well. Just as dishonest
debtors could be vilified, so creditors could be popularly characterised as
vindictive and miserly. Because credit was so ubiquitous and extensive,
creditors who pressed their debtors too hard were seen to threaten society's
economic and social fabric. The cruel creditor therefore became a frequent

---

[68] Vaisey, *The Diary of Thomas Turner, 1754–1765*, 149.
[69] Money, *Chronicles of John Cannon*, 184.

trope of early modern popular literature.[70] One pamphlet described creditors as 'the Locusts that visited the Land of *Egypt* and eat up every green Thing',[71] Religious tracts reminded creditors that by pursuing their debtors, they endangered their souls. A sermon preached in 1709 described in grim detail the fate and damnation that awaited creditors who threw 'unfortunate Debtors … into Prison till they have paid the utmost Farthing'.[72] Those who lent money were expected to treat their borrowers with a degree of charitability, and creditors who pursued their debts too aggressively risked gaining reputations for being litigious, uncharitable or unpredictable. One litigant in Edinburgh, James Grant, told the court that he refused to do business with a particular creditor whom he found 'indistinct and uneasie in his demands' and who he feared 'would have wanted his payment of the defender'.[73]

In the fictions of the courtroom, debtors picked up on these tropes and waged a language of morality, appealing to notions of honour to discredit their incarcerators. Debtors described creditors as uncompromising and unwilling to resolve their disputes. One prisoner in Lancaster told the court that his creditor, Thomas Birch of Manchester, kept him in prison indefinitely despite 'your said petitioner having delivered up all his estate reall and personall and all other effects whatsoever unto your petitioner assignees'.[74] Social descriptions of debtors who failed contrasted with social descriptions of creditors who pressed too hard. Alexander Anan, a wright in Edinburgh, described his creditor as 'rigid'.[75] William Burne, imprisoned in Lancaster Castle, was 'unable to make any satisfaction that will be accepted by his cruell creditors'.[76] Creditors were said to conspire with gaolers, those 'merciless extractors' who would 'glean and cull' from the debtor 'all he had thoughts of saving from his obdurate Creditors'.[77]

Despite the risks associated with harm, creditors used this tool against debtors because it was functional. When waged between equals, imprisonment served creditors' claims to status by acting as a form of social control intended to enforce market ethics, and it provided a means for creditors to

---

[70] For images of the creditor in popular print, see Waddell, *God, Duty and Community in English Economic Life, 1660–1720*, 49–50.

[71] *The Case of Insolvent Debtors, Now in Prison* (London, 1725), 1.

[72] Luke Mulbourne, *Debtor and Creditor Made Easy: or, The Judgment of the Unmerciful Demonstrated, in a Sermon* (1709), 3. Quoted in Waddell, *God, Duty and Community in English Economic Life, 1660–1720*, 49; Haagen, 'Imprisonment for Debt', 267.

[73] ECA, *Grant v Moncurr*, 1730, Box 86, Bundle 213.

[74] Waddell, *God, Duty and Community in English Economic Life, 1660–1720*, 49.

[75] NLS, Petitions to Marys Chapel, 1725–7, Acc. 7332, Box 2.

[76] LRO, Insolvent Debtor Papers, QSP/1226/26.      [77] *The Cries of the Oppressed*, 4.

assert their own status and authority within trading communities. This was partly a function of the relative social status of creditors and debtors. When waged between people of equal standing, harm contributed to the creation of social status and distinction within an economic culture of honour. For middling people, wealth and taste were crucial to creating status.[78] However, the mutability of wealth also meant that individuals needed to look to other forms in which they could assert status. Anger directed towards the physical body was a strategic sign in a process of symbolic communication. Imprisonment gave individuals a form of power over those of similar status. The power to deny another person his or her liberty was the most extreme form of distinction, and it reflected broader shifts in how honour was established and maintained. As Schwerhoff argues, there was a shift in the eighteenth century from violence as a tool of social integration to violence as a tool of distinction. Violence did not disappear, but its forms and settings changed so that 'interpersonal violence referring to honour concepts was only to be practiced among social equals.'[79] As Rosalind Carr suggests, violence could be polite. Physical autonomy was an important component of masculine public honour, and rituals of social distinction, such as duelling, hinged around playing with this sense of autonomy.[80]

In England, where creditors theoretically had the power to keep their debtors in prison indefinitely, the length of imprisonment contributed to its function as a form of power and coercion. The threat of perpetual confinement, balanced by pardoning debts, echoed the system of terror and mercy within England's penal code.[81] This threat of unending imprisonment enforced by creditors terrified contemporaries. According to one pamphlet, 'When a Tradesman fails, by unavailable Misfortunes, his Creditor shall have more Power over him than his Prince, or as much as the most absolute Tyrant, to take all he has, and then punish his Body with the worst of Deaths: perpetual Imprisonment.'[82] By giving creditors discretion over their debtors' fates, the law enabled them to use debt as a means of claiming power. Like the duel, imprisonment served as a means of conferring horizontal honour, or asserting power between relative social equals.[83]

---

[78] Bourdieu, *Distinction*.    [79] Schwerhoff, 'Early Modern Violence and the Honour Code', 42.

[80] Carr, *Gender and Enlightenment*, 151–74.

[81] Douglas Hay, 'Property, Authority and the Criminal Law', in *Albion's Fatal Tree: Crime and Society in Eighteenth-Century England*, ed. Douglas Hay, Peter Linebaugh and John G. Rule (London, 1975), 17–64.

[82] *The Attempt*, 8.

[83] Markku Peltonen, *The Duel in Early Modern England: Civility, Politeness and Honour* (Cambridge, 2006), 286.

As a site for punishment, the debtor's body, like the penal body, was an object for acting out relations of power.[84] Though the prosecution and punishment of crime and the treatment of debtors normally receives separate treatment, we might see debtor incarceration and the infliction of harm upon the body as part of a spectrum of violence used by social groups, individuals and the state in the eighteenth century to protect economic interests. New laws known as the Bloody Codes sanctioned the use of violent punishment against individuals convicted of harming private property. It was a capital crime to steal a horse, and after 1741, a sheep, to pickpocket more than a shilling, to steal more than 40s. in a dwelling place, and to take linen from a bleaching ground. New laws focused especially on protecting new forms of commercial property, including commercial paper and capital investments. As Carl Wennerlind has argued, the imposition of the death penalty for crimes of forgery and counterfeiting should be considered a form of monetary policy intended to restore confidence in Britain's system of credit.[85] Considered within this broader context of violence waged against economic deviants, the harm inflicted by the debtors' prison might not seem so unusual.

In Scotland, the creditor's ability to inflict imprisonment was less about the dynamics of terror and mercy, and more about the power to dishonour a debtor. Imprisonment was understood as a form of shame. Alexander Goldie, a Writer to the Signet, wrote that incarceration 'occasion[ed] him much shame and distress'.[86] Unlike in London prisons, debtors in Scotland were incarcerated with limited consideration of their rank or station. In June 1726, James the Second Earl of Rosebury wrote that he was confined in the Edinburgh Tolbooth 'without any respect or regard to my quality'.[87] The prison's distinctly public nature reinforced its role as a tool of social power. Imprisonment for debt sent a public signal that a debtor was either in serious financial trouble or recalcitrant.[88] In Edinburgh, the Tolbooth stood adjacent to the most important commercial spaces in town, reminding passers-by of the importance of honour within economic life. Through the prison windows, prisoners could interact with the population outside, making the urban population aware of who was confined.[89] The status of

---

[84] Foucault, *Discipline and Punish*.
[85] Hay, 'Property, Authority and the Criminal Law'; McGowen, 'Making the "Bloody Code"?'; Frank McLynn, *Crime and Punishment in Eighteenth-Century England* (London, 1989), xii; Wennerlind, 'The Death Penalty as Monetary Policy'.
[86] NRS, ETWLB, 14 December 1764, HH11/27.
[87] NRS, Seafield Correspondence, 1726, GD248/564/72.
[88] Muldrew, *Economy of Obligation*, 274–9.
[89] Michael F. Graham, *The Blasphemies of Thomas Aikenhead: Boundaries of Belief on the Eve of the Enlightenment* (Edinburgh, 2008), 95.

shame within the debtors' prison echoed its function in other spheres of social life and forms of judicial sanction. Mechanisms of social control in early modern Scotland, imposed especially by kirk sessions and drawing upon Calvinist theology, often involved shaming punishments. While these kinds of judicial punishments faded in England, they remained in force until at least the mid-eighteenth century in Scotland.[90] Unlike the dynamics of terror and mercy, where the creditor's ability to keep a person incarcerated indefinitely formed the basis of imprisonment's power, shame could be inflicted by incarcerating an individual for only a few days. Once a debtor was incarcerated, the prison served its function. Unlike in England, there was little advantage to the creditor in keeping the individual in prison for a long period of time. Reformers believed the threat of shame resulted in lower numbers of prisoners for debt in Scotland. As John Howard explained, 'There are in Scotland but few prisoners; this is partly owing to the shame and disgrace annexed to imprisonment.'[91]

Throughout Britain, shame and terror constituted forms of social control that served the interests of creditors. Social control, defined as 'social interaction and communication in which persons or groups define deviant behaviour and react by taking measures against it', could involve a range of sanctions, including verbal stigmatisation, exclusion from social circles or material or bodily punishments.[92] Creditors could achieve social status by enforcing ethical norms upon individuals understood to have acted against community interests. Many of the people imprisoned were incarcerated several times. James Somervaile, goldsmith, was incarcerated twice in the same month, first by Charles Bruce, a glazier, for a debt of £4 that had been outstanding for several years, then later by Antony Murray, his former servant, for wages. Some of those who were imprisoned were widely understood to be fraudulent, and were already being actively ostracised by the community. For example, the financial demise of Charles Cock, the box master of the Edinburgh Incorporation of Hammermen, began with the accusation in 1768 that he had broken into the incorporation's box, forged its minute book in order to manipulate the results of an election, and stolen money. By the time Cock was incarcerated by a brewer three years later in 1771, his reputation lay in ruins and he had lost his position in the incorporation. Creditors therefore did not always act independently, but in cooperation with others and in the apparent interests of a wider

[90] Leneman, 'Defamation in Scotland, 1750–1800', 229; Paul, 'Credit, Reputation, and Masculinity in British Urban Commerce', 246; Leah Leneman and Rosalind Mitchison, *Sin in the City: Sexuality and Social Control in Urban Scotland 1660–1780* (Edinburgh, 1998), 31–5.
[91] Howard, *State of the Prisons*, 163.     [92] Schwerhoff, 'Social Control of Violence', 223.

community. By punishing transgressors through imprisonment, creditors could establish a claim as stakeholders in the maintenance of the commercial order. Disciplinary violence had a functional role in confirming social hierarchies.[93] As Shepard suggests, 'in devaluing the status of offenders through physical correction, regulatory officials and household heads reiterated their own power and authority.'[94] If debtors were deemed to have acted immorally by defrauding their creditors, it makes sense that they would have been subjected to shame by their social equals. As Margaret Hunt has suggested, the interdependencies created by the credit economy made middling people 'more concerned about the morals of people who were their equals, at least in contractual terms, than they were with the morals of their social inferiors'.[95]

In a credit economy in which social standing determined financial opportunities and access to credit, punishing moral transgressions and protecting or harming reputation was at once an economic, social, emotional and ethical strategy. Inflicting vengeful and unnecessary harm on a debtor could injure a creditor's own reputation, but aggression towards those who had acted unethically was deemed reputable. As Pierre Bourdieu suggested, it was only honourable to challenge someone who could face the challenge, not a social inferior.[96] Thus, though the prison system was characterised by an imbalance of power and agency, its use by and against relative equals may have contributed to its societal acceptance, where other forms of aggression towards those considered 'vulnerable' were not tolerated. For creditors, use of this institution could even provide a means of asserting status. In an environment where distinctions of status were insecure, individuals responded by asserting their own power and status through processes of social distinction. The assertion of social difference between people of like status made sense given the amorphous quality of the middling sort, which constituted both its greatest power and its greatest weakness. Languages of middling identity were broadly applicable, and could be adopted by seemingly anyone below the gentry and above the poor. While this flexibility was politically expedient, it also created insecurities as individuals attempted to place themselves within a flexible social category. Equality can create inherent disquiet. In his conceptualisation of a 'society of equals', Pierre Rosanvallon depicts a middle class fuelled by

---

[93] NRS, Court of Session, Charles Cock v Hammermen of Kinghorn, 1771, CS271/14459; Susan Broomhall and Jacqueline van Gent, 'Policing Bodies in Urban Scotland, 1780–1850', in *Governing Masculinities in the Early Modern Period: Regulating Selves and Others*, ed. Susan Broomhall and Jacqueline van Gent (Aldershot, 2011), 263.

[94] Shepard, *Meanings of Manhood in Early Modern England*, 139.

[95] Hunt, *The Middling Sort*, 40–1.     [96] Bourdieu, *Outline of a Theory of Practice*, 11.

insecurities about its own position.[97] Contemporaries in the long eighteenth century noted similar dynamics. Alexis de Tocqueville remarked that happy men could be made restless 'in the midst of abundance' that was created by a perceived impermanence of condition. Relative equality opened the door to universal competition, encouraging competition for power. As de Tocqueville explained, 'when men are nearly alike, and all follow the same track, it is very difficult for any one individual to walk quick and cleave a way through the dense throng which surrounds and presses him.'[98] By looking sideways, middling men and women targeted others whom they could judge using familiar categories. In so doing, they ensured that the lines demarcating status passed below themselves.

For others, the prison functioned as a means of maintaining the social order. The creditor's interest, especially where it overlapped with socio-economic status, was seen as a crucial mechanism for restoring a perceived decaying social order and upholding the common good. According to James Boswell, Britain had witnessed an increase in both 'riches' and 'barbarity', and a developing culture of 'upstarts', who, as he asserted, 'picked up fortunes as they best know how'. The commercial revolution and the availability of credit enabled men of low rank to accumulate wealth and to ape their betters through luxury, extravagance and negligence, creating 'an abominable spirit of levelling all those distinctions which ages of civilized society have, through all the gradations of politeness introduced amongst mankind'. For Boswell, financial failure was useful because it 'winnowed our traders, and separated the wheat from the chaff'. Failure, properly regulated and properly enforced, provided a means of 'restoring just notions of subordination, frugality, and every other principle by which the good order of society is maintained'. Within this context, the power of tradesmen to enforce prison upon one another, and upon individuals who had ventured with the money and credit of their neighbours, was an act of upholding the common good.[99]

For middling individuals, the types of harm inflicted by the prison were, furthermore, acceptable as part of an economic culture in which self-restraint and civility were increasingly valued ways of behaving. The law legitimised and sublimated violence. Violence did not decline, but was rather displaced and changed in its forms and settings. Laws of credit and debt helped to facilitate this transition.[100] Middling people wrote and

---

[97] Pierre Rosanvallon, *The Society of Equals*, trans. Arthur Goldhammer (Cambridge, MA, 2013).
[98] Alexis de Tocqueville, *Democracy in America* (New York, 1945), book 2, chapter 13.
[99] James Boswell, *Reflections on the Late Alarming Bankruptcies in Scotland: Addressed to All Ranks: . . . With Advice to Such, How to Conduct Themselves at This Crisis* (Edinburgh, 1772), 7, 10, 23.
[100] Schwerhoff, 'Early Modern Violence and the Honour Code', 41.

spoke about the law using a language of harm. One English pamphlet warned readers against doing business in Scotland because 'there a spirit of litigation frequently operates with such violence that expense is disregarded when victory is the consequence'.[101] In 1742, the merchant Robert Wilson described himself as 'being attacked' by litigation carried out against him.[102] The legal system legitimised the use of aggression by imbuing it with signs of acceptability: process, procedure, paperwork and careful and deliberate calculation. Though debtors attempted to discredit their creditors by describing their actions as motivated by emotional impulses such as passion or rage, controlled and legitimate forms of violence, committed through the legal system, could appear civilised. The Scottish legal theorist George Joseph Bell could even describe imprisonment for debt as 'a measure of constraint' legitimised by the law.[103] During a period when acts of public violence declined, the legal institution of the prison allowed individuals to maintain respectability while perpetrating acts that would never have been acceptable in public social settings.[104]

The sublimated violence of the law allowed individuals to use credit coercively to further disputes that were not essentially about debt. Cases of debt, by far the most common type of court case and a form of litigation that was relatively easy and inexpensive to instigate, provided a means for parties to further a variety of economic and non-economic disputes. Because interpersonal credit was so ubiquitous, litigants could establish debts that allowed them to seize the bodies of others in the service of a range of disputes. Using the institution of law, imprisonment for debt therefore served as a weapon for revenge. For example, in cases of marital dispute, writs of trespass popularly known as 'criminal conversation' or 'crim con' actions were used by husbands in the eighteenth century to punish men believed to have had intimate relations with their wives. The principle of the action was that the husband could sue the wife's lover for damages for using the body of his wife, which was his property.[105] When damages remained unpaid, the plaintiff could incarcerate the defendant. As one litigant in a crim con case stated, 'he who cannot pay with his purse must pay with his person.'[106]

---

[101] A. Grant, *The Progress and Practice of a Modern Attorney; Exhibiting the Conduct of Thousands towards Millions! To Which Are Added, the Different Stages of a Law Suit, and Attendant Costs . . .* (London, 1795), 78.

[102] NRS, *Fall v Wilson*, 1742, CC8/6/300.      [103] Bell, *Commentaries on the Laws of Scotland*, 578.

[104] Shoemaker, 'Male Violence'.

[105] Lawrence Stone, *Broken Lives: Separation and Divorce in England, 1660–1857* (Oxford, 1993), 23–4.

[106] Quoted in Stone, *Broken Lives*, 231.

Neighbourly disputes and transgressions resulting in a fine could be transmuted into debts and enforced using the debtors' prison. In the eighteenth century, church and civil courts gradually replaced a number of traditional shaming punishments, including whipping and public recantation, with the imposition of fines due to victims as a form of reparation.[107] Victims could then use unpaid fines, as form of debt, to inflict imprisonment upon their adversaries. For example, in 1734, William Watson had his fellow mason John Overwhyte imprisoned for non-payment of a fine that was awarded after Overwhyte publicly called Watson a villain and 'beggarly dog'.[108] In 1736, James Shearer, a wigmaker who was engaged in a trade demarcation dispute with his former servant Alexander Finney, accused Finney of stealing his customers, shaving their heads and selling wigs. After pursuing a case before the Dean of Guild, in which Finney was fined, Shearer was able to have the servant imprisoned for non-payment of the debt.[109] Thus, while punishments appear to have been 'modernised' and 'economised' by authorities in some legal settings, individuals found ways to use the legal system to impose punishments of their own. Here, the law emerged as a form of sublimated rage, 'indistinguishable from revenge', as indebtedness was manipulated to pursue broader disputes.[110]

## Conclusion: Coercion and the Credit Economy

In contrast to previous accounts of credit, which emphasise its socially positive nature and liberating tendencies, routine practices of imprisonment reveal an economy in which credit was coercive. Creditors threatened and inflicted a variety of forms of harm on their debtors in order to coerce them into paying. Harm ranged from verbal abuse and damage to reputation to the denial of liberty and to physical assault and violence. Imprisonment for debt could in itself be a form of violence. A minority of prisoners were able to maintain a relative degree of freedom, but most experienced material hardship, and some were exposed to forms of corporeal punishment. This violence was consistent with a commercial sphere characterised as civilised and polite. As part of the civilising process, violence did not disappear, but was rather sublimated and legitimised by

[107] Leneman, 'Defamation in Scotland, 1750–1800', 229. For the continuing importance of shaming, see David Nash and Anne-Marie Kilday, *Cultures of Shame: Exploring Crime and Morality in Britain 1600–1900* (Basingstoke, 2010); David G. Barrie and Susan Broomhall, *Police Courts in Nineteenth-Century Scotland* (Farnham, 2014), 458–72.
[108] NRS, ETWLB, 18 October 1734, HH11/18.
[109] ECA, Dean of Guild Extracted Processes, 1736, Box 49.    [110] Menke, 'Law and Violence', 12.

law. Harm and punishment were justified because debtors were framed as having behaved immorally or unethically, and they even served creditors by providing a means to assert social distinction.

Harm waged between commercial people was normalised by ambivalence. Some creditors clearly intended to inflict physical or social harm on debtors. But for others, the hardships of the debtors' prisons were the unintended consequences of overcrowding, the result of the power placed in the hands of gaolers or a strategy pursued at the behest of legal advice. Even if it was not their intent, it was a consequence that they were willing to accept because it served their functional interest. So, while Thomas Turner fretted about putting his debtor in prison because he feared that it would make him guilty of 'harsh or inhuman usage', he also considered his actions consistent with the dictates of 'self-preservation and the laws of equity'.[111] The ambivalent harm imposed upon debtors was ultimately justified because falling into debt was understood within a code of ethics.

---

[111] Vaisey, *The Diary of Thomas Turner, 1754–1765*, 152.

# CHAPTER 7

# The Worth of Bodies
## Debt Bondage, Value and Selfhood

In August 1689, in the parish of Fawley, Berkshire, the corpse of John Matthews was arrested for debt. As his family carried his coffin towards the churchyard to be buried, they were stopped by one of Matthews' creditors, who seized the body. After four days, the local justices of the peace intervened, and issued a warrant for the body to be 'buried in the place to prevent annoyances'. A full six weeks later, the local Sessions returned Matthews' body to his wife, who buried him in the churchyard.[1] Nearly 40 years later, a similar event was recorded outside of the Fleet Prison. As the body of Captain Christopher Billup, who died insolvent, was being carried out the front gates by his family, his corpse was arrested by the prison keeper for prison dues and debts for ale and food. As a pamphlet recounted, the corpse was detained for two hours, until the relations of the deceased man 'were forced, at last to comply with the said Warden's demands, and to give him Ten Guineas, or Ten Pounds, for the purchase of the said dead Body, and to procure the Liberty to bury it themselves'.[2]

The cases of Matthews and Billup suggest that value was embodied, and further, that the body's value persisted even after debtors were no longer alive.[3] The treatment of corpses was described by onlookers using explicitly economic language. The body outside the Fleet was described as having been 'purchased', while in Fawley, the creditor had 'seized' the body like an object. In the eighteenth century, the bodies of debtors, dead and alive, were taken, held and exchanged for money, blurring the distinctions between bodies and things. In an economy of circulating selves, where a

---

[1] F. G. Emmison, *Elizabethan Life*, vol. 2 (Chelmsford, 1973), 174; quoted in Clare Gittings, *Death, Burial and the Individual in Early Modern England* (London, 1984), 66–7.

[2] John Mackay, *A True State of the Proceedings of the Prisoners in the Fleet-Prison …* (Westminster, 1729). Quoted in Haagen, 'Imprisonment for Debt', 5.

[3] For the commodification of death and the dead, see Thomas W. Laqueur, *The Work of the Dead: A Cultural History of Mortal Remains* (Princeton, NJ, 2015); Jeremy Boulton, 'Traffic in Corpses and the Commodification of Burial in Georgian London', *Continuity and Change* 29, no. 2 (2014): 181–208.

person's financial credibility depended upon estimations of their worth, these examples suggest that we might think more broadly about the diverse forms that 'worth' could assume within a developing commercial economy. In histories of credit, the worth of people is normally anchored to reputation, physical property or labour capacity. The shifting between these forms is understood as a consequence of change over time. In the seventeenth century, as Alexandra Shepard has shown, a household's stock of goods formed the basis of credit. Early modern people operated in a 'culture of appraisal' in which individuals had a keen sense of what others were worth in material terms. The late seventeenth and early eighteenth centuries witnessed a shift in estimations of credit. Worth came to be assessed through notions of character and reputation.[4] In the later eighteenth century, constructions of credit again changed. The value of people became a function of their labour capacity and their possession of skill. The fledgling life insurance industry applied actuarial techniques to assign specific monetary values to persons according to their capacity for labour, balanced with probable life expectancy. Similarly, Adam Smith's labour theories of value, drawing on his famous example of pin-makers, envisioned people as 'hands'. The value of the person in this account was a function of the labour that he or she performed. By the early nineteenth century, workers came to see their skills as forms of property, subject to ownership and protection.[5]

Individual worth was anchored to a complex arrangement of different forms, but in historical accounts, the material body is largely absent from these constellations.[6] From early modern credit to nineteenth-century skill, worth appears to be disembodied. The value of a person, expressed in terms of credit, was a function of his or her bodily performance. Yet men and women in eighteenth-century Britain had another way of viewing their bodies: as flesh and blood with intrinsic economic value. This value could be owned, transferred and mobilised. The value of the body, living or dead, came into particular prominence in the eighteenth century as status and worth were detached from material wealth. Credit's increasing attachment to the self, in terms of character and reputation, provided a context in

---

[4] Shepard, *Accounting for Oneself*, 232, 274, 303–5.
[5] Geoffrey Wilson Clark, *Betting on Lives: The Culture of Life Insurance in England, 1695–1775* (Manchester; New York, 1999); Smith, *An Inquiry into the Nature and Causes of the Wealth of Nations*, I.i; Rule, 'The Property of Skill in the Period of Manufacture'.
[6] An exception is studies of the medical trade, where bodies were directly implicated in market transactions. See Lisa Forman Cody, '"No Cure, No Money," or the Invisible Hand of Quackery: The Language of Commerce, Credit, and Cash in Eighteenth-Century British Medical Advertisements', *Studies in Eighteenth-Century Culture* 28, no. 1 (2010): 103–30.

which value could be more easily attached to the borrower's body. Bodies were targeted more frequently during a period when, due to changes in structures of wealth, middling households had comparatively little material wealth to sequestrate in cases of default, and when, due to legal practices, creditors found it difficult to access that wealth. Debtors' bodies were therefore incarcerated under a logic that roughly paralleled the pawnshop. When debtors turned to the pawnshop, they secured loans by offering up their material possessions. Pawnbrokers would hold these valuables until loans were repaid. Similarly, under a system of reputational credit, people contracted and secured loans on their personhood. If a debtor failed to pay back their obligation, their person stood in for the debt. The creditor could seize their body and hold it in prison until the debt was repaid. Thus, while the social value of persons provided the foundations of financial credit, the body offered a physical anchor to the more ephemeral selves that formed the eighteenth century's main source of currency.

Bodies were part of the process of transmuting one form of value into another, and they were implicated in emergent notions of capital and property in the eighteenth century. The body offered a partial solution to problems of liquidity, which shaped the deep-seated insecurities faced by middling households. During the eighteenth century, understandings of value were in flux. The expanding commercial economy required wealth to be portable, and this portability depended upon its fungibility. Different forms of capital needed to be transformed from one form to another, so that reputation, status, material wealth and labour could be combined and exchanged.[7] The Financial Revolution from the late seventeenth century expanded the means by which value was made fungible, and the eighteenth-century market has been recognised for its fluid and representational forms.[8] As Carl Wennerlind has argued, the emergence of new technologies of money facilitated new ways of seeing and understanding credit. The links between credit and belief facilitated comparison between credit and alchemy as technologies of money turned worthless objects into value.[9]

In order to support the need for fungible value, during the eighteenth century, a new onus was placed on the medieval practice of imprisoning the body. The body assumed an important position as a locus of transferable value. The body's capacity to serve as an enduring notion of value allowed for the arrest of debtors like John Matthews, long after his corpse had

---

[7] For theories of fungibility, see Bourdieu, 'Forms of Capital'.

[8] Cody, '"No Cure, No Money"', 119–22; Jean-Christophe Agnew, *Worlds Apart: The Market and the Theater in Anglo-American Thought, 1550–1750* (Cambridge, 1986), 124–8.

[9] Wennerlind, *Casualties of Credit*, 7, 44–80.

grown cold. As a mobile repository of value, positioned within a network of social relations, the body could be even more 'valuable' to some creditors than the monetary payment of the debt. If a debt was secured on a bond, it could be financially advantageous for the creditor to take the body of the debtor rather than his or her things. Bonds gave the body strategic value because they allowed creditors to take double the debt as penalty, which gave creditors a clear avenue towards profit. In Tim Stretton's account, the risk many creditors faced was not that debtors would not repay, but that they *would*, leaving creditors with no profit.[10] By the late seventeenth century, most actions for debt were taken against the debtor's body rather than his or her property.[11] One debtor in Edinburgh claimed that his creditor had indicated 'it was not money he wanted but only my person and that he would rather give twenty shillings out of his own pocket than that anybody should offer to pay the money for me'.[12] As another contemporary commentator wrote, '*bona corporis* are better than *bona fortuna*, a man's body is of more value than his estate.'[13]

The anchoring of unpaid debts to the physical body complicated developing notions of selfhood in the eighteenth century. Scholars argue for the development of a liberal, autonomous self during this period, which became increasingly embodied.[14] But if this was a period of developing autonomous selfhood, debt law also incorporated a contradictory logic that a body could be owned by another. The blurring of bodies and things made possible by the process of incarceration had significant implications for middling lives. The embodiment of value created a distinctive form of precariousness that threatened not only a person's financial security, but also his or her physical liberty. It also had substantial implications for mobility, both limiting individual capacity for movement and forcing migration as individuals fled their debts, were transferred to debtors' prisons many miles from home or sold their own bodies into servitude in order to satisfy their financial obligations. Attending to the embodiment of debt, as borne out through imprisonment, provides new insights into contemporary understandings of worth and selfhood during a period that was pivotal to the development of both commercial networks and

---

[10] Stretton, 'Written Obligations', 203–4.    [11] Muldrew, *Economy of Obligation*, 275.

[12] ECA, BCP, Petition of William Stevenson, 20 May 1737, Box 285, Bundle 40.

[13] Thomas Grantham, *A Motion against Imprisonment, Wherein Is Proved That Imprisonment for Debt Is against the Gospel, against the Good Church, and Commonwealth* … (London, 1642), 8. Quoted in Bailey, Of Bondage, 7.

[14] Dror Wahrman, *The Making of the Modern Self: Identity and Culture in Eighteenth-Century England* (New Haven, CT, 2004); Mascuch, *Origins of the Individualist Self*.

notions of individualism. The assignment of imaginary and temporary monetary values to people had significant consequences for individual mobility, autonomy and developing notions of middling selfhood.

## Changing Legal Contexts and the Body's Value

The commodification of bodies was a function of credit, but the process was animated by debt and financial failure. The notion that the body constituted a form of transferable value was not new to the eighteenth century. Indeed, Shakespeare's powerful image of the pound of flesh in *The Merchant of Venice* communicated the potential of the loan contract to commodify the person. Amanda Bailey's literary analysis of debt bondage locates the establishment of the debtor's body as a form of value with the introduction of the penal bond. Also known as a bill obligatory or a conditional bond, this was a transferable instrument in which one party agreed with another to repay a sum or to take some specified action. Bonds were the most common legal device used in the central common courts in the sixteenth and seventeenth centuries.[15] If a person failed to pay, the creditor was given power over his or her body. The English legal system therefore recognised the body as a form of collateral. In the event that a debtor forfeited on a loan, their body stepped in to satisfy the unpaid creditor. Bonds therefore construed the human body 'not as something to be used or exchanged, but as a vehicle of promise'. While coins and paper money represented value, the primary function of the bond was to incarnate value. Human flesh 'became a redeemable form of property, the worth of which was determined by the creditor's interest and affirmed by the law's mandates'.[16]

English law gave creditors their principal legal remedy against debtors' bodies rather than their property. In Bailey's account, bonds provided the primary form of litigation brought before central courts in the early modern period, but by the eighteenth century, bond litigation had virtually disappeared. The acceleration of commercial transactions involved informal agreements (including scores, tallies and verbal agreements) and prioritised new forms of proceeding, and a variety of financial instruments led to incarceration.[17] While taking a debtor's good and chattels would

---

[15] Brooks, *Law, Politics and Society*, 310, 317.

[16] Bailey, *Of Bondage*, 7, 17. For the frequency with which bonds appeared in central court litigation, see Stretton, 'Written Obligations', 193–4; C. W. Brooks, *Pettyfoggers and Vipers of the Commonwealth: The 'Lower Branch' of the Legal Profession in Early Modern England* (Cambridge, 1986), 67, 69.

[17] Brooks, *Law, Politics and Society*, 317; Brooks, *Lawyers, Litigation, and English Society*, 58; Champion, 'Recourse to the Law', 180.

seem to provide the most logical solution to collecting an unpaid debt, creditors in fact had limited access to their debtors' property. As Chapter 1 outlined more fully, creditors instead possessed broad powers of arrest.[18] The mesne process allowed creditors to demand the arrest of their debtors before trial and to hold the body as a form of surety until the debtor paid (or triggered a legal mechanism for release).[19] If the creditor chose to imprison a debtor after judgement, using a writ of elegit, they lost the right to seek any other form of relief.[20] In other words, a creditor could not proceed against both a debtor's person and their property at the same time, but had to choose one or the other. In practice, this meant that when choosing imprisonment, the creditor was deliberately taking a person's body *rather* than his or her goods. Thus, as Margot Finn suggests, the legal system allowed the debtor's body to be substituted for payment, transforming the person into a form of collateral for goods or services received on credit.[21] The debtor's body therefore assumed a temporary cash value.

The conceptual positioning of the body as a form of value was not experienced equally by all individuals, and Britain's two national legal systems construed the value of the debtor's body in different ways. While the English legal system allowed the body to be transformed into a form of collateral, in the Scottish system, the body was positioned as a resource. There, the body was not a repository *of value*, but was rather *valuable* as a form that could be used to mobilise other forms of worth. In Scotland, imprisonment did not legally constitute substitution or collateral for a debt. Rather, it was a means of punishing a debtor for failing to honour a contract. Under the notion of 'specific implement', imprisonment was intended to be recuperative, in other words, to enforce the 'actual performance of the defender's contractual obligations'.[22] This legal definition of obligation gave the creditor the power of exaction, whereby he or she could 'exact, obtain, or compel the debtor to pay or perform what is due'.[23] Imprisonment was therefore a form of compulsion intended to force the debtor to pay, rather than a process wherein the debtor's body was substituted for a different form of property. As a means of coercion,

---

[18] Haagen, 'Eighteenth Century English Society and the Debt Law', 225.

[19] Innes, 'King's Bench', 253–7.    [20] Haagen, 'Imprisonment for Debt', 11, 30.

[21] Finn, *The Character of Credit*, 10.

[22] Kenneth Reid and Reinhard Zimmermann, *A History of Private Law in Scotland. Volume 2* (Oxford, 2004), 196.

[23] James Dalrymple Stair, *The Institutions of the Law of Scotland, Deduced from Its Originals, and Collated from the Civil, and Feudal Laws, and with the Customs of Neighbouring Nations. In Four Books* (Edinburgh, 1759), Book I, 1.22.

debtors in Scotland were subjected to deliberate hardship, regardless of their social status.[24] Because of the legal basis of imprisonment, creditors did not have to choose between pursuing assets and pursuing the body as they did in England, but could proceed against both debtors' persons and their things 'without prejudice' (though in practice, due to legal expenses, they tended to choose one process or the other).[25]

Despite legal differences, creditors used the English and Scottish legal systems in similar social and strategic ways. Even in England, where the prisoner's body functioned as collateral, the deployment and conversion of that value into a form that was useful to the creditor depended upon the debtor's coercion. Furthermore, the form of value accorded to the body by both legal systems was distinct from labour value. As Chapter 3 detailed, prisons actively prevented most individuals from working and denied prisoners their labour value. Indeed, one of the narratives that emerged in protesting incarceration during the eighteenth century was that it rendered the debtor's body useless. As reform pamphlets consistently argued, the prison denied the nation the productive labour of skilled tradespeople.[26] Finally, in the cases of most middle-rank prisoners in both countries, the body's value was closely related to notions of social worth, particularly their capacity to mobilise social networks of credit and other forms of wealth.

Britain's two legal systems, while blurring the distinctions between bodies and things, encouraged the bodies of different people to be valued in different ways and facilitated different means for that value to be mobilised. In domestic Britain, the worth of women and the poor was explicitly tied to their bodies. Commodification was arguably a more common experience for women than it was for men, and it took more varied forms. Feminist readings of the early modern marriage market envision matrimony as involving the exchange of female bodies. The early modern gift economy, which confused objects and people, provided a framework for female bodies to circulate as objects. Through marriage, the movement of women sealed kinship bonds, as one family 'gave' to another.[27] Furthermore, women's economic status as creditworthy depended upon their bodily performance, namely their sexual honesty and chastity.[28] As Chapter 4 revealed, public insults waged against

---

[24] Act of Session, 14 June 1771, in Erskine, *The Principles of the Law of Scotland*.

[25] Bell, *Commentaries on the Laws of Scotland*, 572.    [26] See for example, *The Attempt*, 21.

[27] Felicity Heal, *The Power of Gifts: Gift-Exchange in Early Modern England* (Oxford, 2014), 57; For a sociological perspective, see Marilyn Strathern, *The Gender of the Gift: Problems with Women and Problems with Society in Melanesia* (Berkeley, CA, 1988).

[28] Gowing, *Domestic Dangers*.

women, ruining their credit, were more readily based upon sexual behaviour than the insults used against men, meaning that credit was much more a function of the performances and perceptions of their bodies. As an extension of bodily performance, a married woman's worth was often dependent upon her ability to bear children, meaning that her value was very explicitly anchored to her physical self. As one of the religious and household duties expected of women, bearing children was even construed to have a direct relationship with financial credit. In one Edinburgh defamation case between two women, the defendant had apparently claimed that 'she was ane honest Kitty for that she had kittled [borne] so many children', and asserted that the plaintiff 'had not the credite to kittle any'.[29]

The institutionalised poor constituted another group whose selfhood was explicitly tied to the corporeal self. As Sarah Lloyd has demonstrated, an enduring eighteenth-century commonplace was that the poor's only asset was the physical body.[30] It was by their bodies that they laboured and made shift. But poverty also occasioned a loss of control over their own bodies. Institutions like workhouses were established to discipline and regulate them by committing their bodies to confinement and labour. It was also understood that the bodies of the poor could be appropriated. Though political theorists believed that enslavement could not exist in domestic Britain, Rozbicki has shown that proposals to seize the labour services of the poor through enslavement remained part of the English discourse on vagrancy until at least the eighteenth century.[31] Representations of the poor also focused significantly on their bodies. Simon Newman envisions impoverished bodies as a kind of 'text' upon which social status, identity and ideas about power and deference were written.[32]

## Selfhood and the Economic Man

If the embodiment of value is a recognised phenomenon affecting women, the poor and unfree labourers, the commodification of debtors' bodies through processes of incarceration exposes the extension of this logic to a broader and more unlikely group of individuals normally characterised by

[29] NRS, *Campbell v Campbell*, 1751, CC8/6/318.
[30] Sarah Lloyd, 'Cottage Conversations: Poverty and Manly Independence in Eighteenth-Century England', *Past & Present*, no. 184 (2004): 98.
[31] Michal J. Rozbicki, 'To Save Them from Themselves: Proposals to Enslave the British Poor, 1698–1755', *Slavery & Abolition* 22, no. 2 (2001): 29–50.
[32] Newman, *Embodied History*.

their independent status. Given the profile of the debtors' prison population outlined in Chapter 1, the bodies of middling, married men and
widowed women formed the most common, and hence most valuable,
kind of debt collateral. The idea that the body served as a repository of
value that could, in practice, be taken and mobilised came into conflict
with new eighteenth-century ideals of selfhood, which formed an important component of middle-rank identity. Literary and economic histories
both point to the eighteenth century as a time when a new kind of
individualism and sense of personal identity emerged that was built upon
the notion of the self. These constructions of selfhood were often gendered
and related to notions of male autonomy. Michael Mascuch describes the
development of an 'essentially masculine and middle-class paradigm' of the
'upwardly mobile, self-made subject', while Dror Wahrman suggests an
eighteenth-century shift towards interiority, wherein 'identity became
personal, interiorized, essential, event innate'.[33] New individualist identities, emphasising autonomy, agency and sovereignty, extended to the
market. Control over this emergent 'self' was a point of middling masculine credit.[34] Notions of male autonomy have not gone uncontested. The
idea of masculine independent selfhood has been complicated by studies of
the household, which erode notions of autonomy by making clear that
men depended upon the household and its members to provision the
family and to establish their sense of gender identity and personhood.[35]
The imprisoned debtor and the notion of the body as a form of value add
further nuance to the ideal of masculine independence. If a man's body had
been taken as collateral for a debt, and he did not own his own body, did he
therefore own himself?

Political and legal theories of property emergent in the long eighteenth
century anchored the self to a physical body. John Locke posited that 'every
man has a property in his own person.'[36] Man, according to Locke, was the
'master of himself, and proprietor of his own person, and the actions or
labour of it'.[37] Thus, in the realm of interpersonal dealings, every person

---

[33] McCormack, *The Independent Man*; Mascuch, *Origins of the Individualist Self*, 6; Wahrman, *The Making of the Modern Self*, 276.

[34] Paul, 'Credit, Reputation, and Masculinity in British Urban Commerce', 241–3.

[35] Hunt, *The Middling Sort*; Harvey, *The Little Republic*, 167.

[36] John Locke, *Two Treatises of Government*, ed. Peter Laslett (Cambridge, 1988), book 2, chapter 5, section 27, p. 287; Gerald Allan Cohen, *Self-Ownership, Freedom, and Equality* (Cambridge, 2010); Kiyoshi Shimokawa, 'The Origin and Development of Property: Conventionalism, Unilateralism, and Colonialism', in *The Oxford Handbook of British Philosophy in the Seventeenth Century*, ed. Peter R. Anstey, 2013, 563–86.

[37] Locke, *Two Treatises*, book 2, chapter 5, section 44, p. 298.

had a right in his or her body. Ownership applied to persons as well as goods.[38] But if debt animated the body as a kind of property, by extension, it could also be sold or owned by another. Through laws of property and debt, one person could acquire the rights over another person's body. Lord Stair's theories of Scottish law posited that though liberty was a 'Natural Power which Man hath of his own person', this liberty was complicated by the laws of obligation.[39] As he explained,

> our *Ingagements* do commonly import a *Diminution* of our personal Liberty, but much more, of that Natural Liberty of things without us, whence it is, that the Law alloweth personal Execution or restraint, and Incarceration of the debtor's person, until he do all the deeds which are in his power for the satisfaction of his Creditor.[40]

The idea of autonomy and propriety over one's own body was clearly undercut by systems of debt, which even shaped understandings of the relationship of different parts of the body to selfhood. One Edinburgh court case addressed which part of the body had to be over the boundary of the local debtors' sanctuary in order for a person to claim protection. The court determined that if the debtor's head fell over the line, he would be safe, 'for the *head* is the noblest part of the *body*'.[41]

Imprisonment for debt further betrayed the ideal of the independent economic man because the debts that led to imprisonment were often not his own. Incarceration was an outcome of the contingencies inherent in credit networks and the social system that underpinned the exchange of debt. Some prisoners found themselves in debt not through their own spending, but by acting as security for others. James Braidwood, a burgess and candle-maker petitioning for release from the Edinburgh Tolbooth, claimed that his financial misfortunes were 'in no ways owing to any prodigality, but by being unluckily Engaged as Cautioner for other people'.[42] Acting as a cautioner or guarantor to secure a loan for someone else was considered an act of hospitality and neighbourliness, and was often entered into as a form of social obligation or charity. However, when debts remained unpaid, guarantors became vulnerable for debts that were not contracted directly by them. For example, in 1769, the chapman Edward Turner 'having

---

[38] Matthew H. Kramer, *John Locke and the Origins of Private Property: Philosophical Explorations of Individualism, Community, and Equality* (Cambridge, 2004), 133–5.

[39] Stair, *Institutions of the Law of Scotland*, I.2.1.

[40] Stair, *Institutions of the Law of Scotland*, I.2.7.

[41] Duncan Anderson, *History of the Abbey and Palace of Holyrood* (Edinburgh, 1849), 154.

[42] NRS, James Braidwood vs Parties unstated: Act and Warrant in favours of, 1746, CS177/14; CS233/C/1/123.

occasion for some small money', borrowed two pounds two shillings sterling from Elizabeth Rogers through an intermediary, William Corbett, who was known to Rogers. When the debt remained unpaid by Turner, Corbett ended up in prison.[43] Similarly, Thomas Mashiter, imprisoned in Lancaster Castle, claimed that he was 'imprisoned at the suit of Henry Brackan doctor of physick for a debt unknown and not contracted by your petitioner'.[44] William Burrel, a sailor in Edinburgh, incarcerated for one year in November 1720, was in debt for a bill 'accepted by the said William Burrell payable to Alex Williamsone dated the 6 Sept 1715 and by him indorsed to the said David Tod'.[45] The turner Nehemiah Wallington recounted the distress caused in his household when two bailiffs arrived to collect on the bond of a deceased debtor which Wallington had signed as surety.[46] Because suretyship could be risky and even disastrous for households, this practice elicited a certain amount of contemporary sympathy. Charity bequests for imprisoned debtors even specifically targeted those imprisoned by virtue of being bound to others.[47]

Imprisonment was also a result of men's legal responsibilities for household spending, wherein male bodies could be taken as collateral for debts contracted by dependants. For example, Samuel Levy, a chapman in London, was imprisoned for debts that included two debts 'to his wife' and one 'to his servant'.[48] Contemporary legal writers made clear that while a married woman's person was 'free from all execution upon debts contracted by herself', at the same time, 'the husband, who is not the proper debtor, is liable to personal diligence at the suit of her creditors.'[49] This meant that a man's bodily autonomy was not only a function of his own actions, but tied into familial and household networks. As Margot Finn has shown, the bodies of children, servants and wives who purchased goods on credit for the household were exempt by law from imprisonment for these debts. Male contractual autonomy could therefore be limited rather than bolstered by their status as heads of households.[50] Imprisonment exposed a significant paradox in men's control over property: on one hand, legal control over financial resources was a crucial source of patriarchal power.

---

[43] Muldrew, *Economy of Obligation*, 160; NRS, ETWLB, 1769, HH11/28.
[44] LRO, Quarter Sessions Petitions, 1725, QSP/1235/2.    [45] NRS, ETWLB, 1720, HH11/13.
[46] Paul S. Seaver, *Wallington's World: A Puritan Artisan in Seventeenth-Century London* (Stanford, CA, 1989), 80.
[47] Finn, *The Character of Credit*, 127.    [48] LMA, CLA/047/LJ/17/028.
[49] Erskine, *Institute of the Law of Scotland*, 92.    [50] Finn, *The Character of Credit*, 264.

On the other hand, this source of responsibility could become a point of masculine corporeal vulnerability.

The role that female dependents played in men's embodied experiences of debt might account for some of the cultural anxieties over female spending that were so prevalent in the eighteenth century. Women were often identified as consumers and accused of vanity, avarice and extravagance, and descriptions of women spending their money on goods catching their 'idle fancy' are all too familiar.[51] Narratives from the debtors' prisons suggest that female consumption was feared not only because it threatened codes of domesticity and household financial status, but also because the ability to spend household credit gave women power over male bodies. In cases of separation or marital breakdown, fears over the power that credit gave to women over their husbands' bodies prompted some men to place newspaper ads warning creditors that they would not be responsible for their wives' spending. In 1731, Edward Finch, a shopkeeper in Westminster whose wife had apparently eloped, placed an advertisement in the *Daily Advertiser* to 'forewarn all Persons at their Peril to give her any credit or Entertainment'.[52] In 1743, William Whelpley, an innholder in Middlesex, placed an advertisement stating that his wife, Mary, had 'frequently declared that she would utterly ruin him' and cautioned 'all Persons from giving the said Mary any Credit'. Because it was normal practice for wives to collect household debts, Whelpley further requested that any people indebted to him not pay Mary on his account and instead directed them to his attorney.[53] Lawrence Stone's account of martial separation has highlighted a system of litigation in the eighteenth century intended to protect husbands from their wives' debts, and suggests that the problem of indemnifying husbands from this financial responsibility was an area of contemporary legal concern.[54] The vulnerability of the male body caused by imprisonment exposed cracks in the fictions of masculine control.

If the power afforded to wives to contract credit was negatively portrayed in court cases and newspapers, in practice, female agency was more often a source of strength and relief for male debtors than a cause of vulnerability. Through their ability to contract credit and to manage household assets, women purchased prisoners' liberty and ensured their subsistence. Wives were, as Chapter 1 described, integral to keeping the

[51] Maxine Berg, *The Age of Manufactures: 1700–1820: Industry, Innovation and Work in Britain* (London, 2005), 160.
[52] *London Daily Advertiser*, 11 March 1731, issue 32.
[53] *London Daily Advertiser*, 26 May 1743, issue 3854.
[54] Lawrence Stone, *Road to Divorce: England 1530–1987* (Oxford, 1990), 150–61.

indebted household afloat. We gain a sense of what this work was worth in cases where male prisoners' wives did not manage the dispersal of household wealth, but where this task was instead carried out by hired help. Women worked with prisoners professionally as pawnbrokers or auctioneers, or in Scotland, wadsetters or roup women, helping debtors to dispose of their goods in order to pay off creditors. In London, the prisoner Adam Shakell hired Mrs Eden, a widow, to sell off some of his household goods in order to pay his landlord. Her fee amounted to £4 10s.[55] While imprisoned in 1748, the merchant Robert McCulloch had his household and mercantile goods sold to pay off his debts, including cloth, molasses and rum, to the value of £315 16s. He paid a factor, Benjamin Cook, to undertake the sale.[56] Samuel Jacomb, a wine merchant in London, paid an attorney to sell his household goods and to collect his debts. The sale generated £150, of which Jacomb received £137 'after a deduction of his fees', which amounted to some 8 per cent of the value of the household goods.[57] Female management of loss had significant financial value that is demonstrated when it was contracted outside of the household.

The ideal of masculine autonomy was further betrayed by discussions over the efficacy of imprisonment, in which the interests of individual autonomy were clearly subordinate to the body politic. In early eighteenth-century reform pamphlets, the plight of the imprisoned debtor was considered in terms of his relationship to the community rather than in terms of his selfhood. This relationship drew heavily upon metaphors of the body. In arguing against imprisonment for debt, one pamphlet published in 1707 blamed Britain's decaying trade on the numbers of individuals confined in prison. 'The Life's Blood of the Nation', the author opined, 'appears now to flow, almost all of it, in one Channel, the little Streams that seem so necessary to support the Heart, and convey Nourishment to the Body Politick, are, as it were, diverted from bringing their usual supplies'.[58] Like the human body, the economy required all the individual parts to work together. Confining men prevented them from working, creating a kind of blockage. Debt reinforced a connection between the well-being of the individual body and the national body. However, the physical bodies of economic individuals were seen as serving the interests of the body politic. Debates over the efficacy of imprisoned debtors thus focused on how debtors should be treated to best benefit society. From one perspective,

---

[55] LMA, Schedule of Adam Shakell, 1761, CLA/047/LJ/17/043/137.
[56] LMA, Schedule of Robert McCulloch, 1748, CLA/047/LJ/17/024/015.
[57] LMA, Schedule of Samuel Jacomb, 1748, CLA/047/LJ/17/024/014.
[58] *The Honour and Advantage of Great Britain*, 12.

the body of the debtor should not be confined, but rather should labour in the service of the common good. From another, echoing contemporary debates over execution, removing a recalcitrant debtor from the credit market, like the amputation of a diseased part from the body, would restore the health of the whole organism.[59]

## Agency and Mobility

The transformation of the body into a form of value, animated by the process of incarceration for debt, was often described as an experience of restricted liberty, coercion and the denial of selfhood. But as a form of value, the body could also be a resource used by debtors to claim agency. While creditors used incarceration as a means of leveraging payment, debtors could use the incarceration of their own bodies strategically as well. Because creditors could not distrain goods and pursue bodies under common law at the same time, going to prison in England protected assets. Some debtors exploited the legal system and initiated processes called 'friendly actions', in which they deliberately had themselves imprisoned in order to protect their property.[60] In other words, debtors could take advantage of the blurring of persons and goods, strategically substituting their bodies for their things in order to prevent creditors from accessing their wealth.

In Scotland, where creditors did not have to choose between pursuing person and property, the body could not be substituted to protect property. However, debtors used their bodies as resources in petitions seeking their freedom. They invoked a language of bodily suffering, drawing upon images of ill health, old age, illness and pain to elicit sympathy. A prisoner in Edinburgh obtained a certificate by a local surgeon stating that the debtor, 'in a bad state of health, complains of rheumatic pains in his legs and arms, likewise a severe pain in his breast all which complaints I think have arisen from his confinement in prison, the continuance of which may prove very dangerous'. Proving bad health had a legal basis and was a means of obtaining release from prison under Scottish law, but claiming physical pain was also a strategy by which debtors could position themselves as victims and their creditors as irrational and vindictive.[61] Another prisoner noted his creditor's 'satisfaction' in observing his declining

---

[59] Randall McGowen, 'The Body and Punishment in Eighteenth-Century England', *The Journal of Modern History* 59, no. 4 (1987): 673.
[60] Innes, 'King's Bench', 256.
[61] NRS, Court of Session, Charles Cock v Hammermen of Kinghorn, 1771, CS271/14459; Bell, *Book V, Imprisonment for Debt*, 584–6.

health.[62] Appealing to notions of character through a language of the body was strategic in a legal system increasingly concerned with distinguishing between honest and fraudulent debtors, and between reasonable and persecuting creditors.[63]

Prisoners could also use their bodies strategically via their access to the writ of habeas corpus, a legal instrument intended to prevent wrongful imprisonment, which they could invoke to move themselves between different prisons. Even if the legal costs and associated expenses of moving were significant investments, ensuring that this option was available only to debtors with means, the writ did provide imprisoned debtors with recognised agency to position their bodies to their legal advantage.[64] Most debtors used writs to transfer themselves from provincial prisons to the Fleet or King's Bench, where they had access to masters' side accommodation and to the Rules, where they could live in a state of partial freedom. Long-term incarcerated debtors also used writs to move seasonally, opting for the more spacious and safer location of the King's Bench in Southwark during the hot summer months, and the Fleet's urban location during the winter.[65] But moving to these prisons was not only a means of achieving better conditions. Obtaining a writ to transfer could also be a legal strategy, and was pursued by significant numbers of debtors who moved back and forth between the King's Bench and the Fleet and therefore between different court jurisdictions. In sample years 1746–8, more than 6 per cent of Fleet prisoners moved to the King's Bench, and 9 per cent of King's Bench prisoners moved to the Fleet.[66]

Outside of the prisons, the nature of the body's value encouraged debtors to pursue migration and movement to protect their freedom and their interests. Debts travelled with the bodies of their owners, which had significant implications for the mobility of people within eighteenth-century Britain. As anthropological accounts have made clear, debt can be used to both generate and constrict the body's movement through space-time.[67] Pursuing a debt required locating a debtor's person. Just as a debtor might hide material wealth in order to prevent it from being sequestrated, so relocating the body could be a form of protection (pursued both legally and illegally). In a world of

[62] ECA, BCP, Petition of David Henderson, September 1738, Box 285, Bundle 40.
[63] Hoppit, Risk and Failure, 20–4.
[64] Haagen, 'Imprisonment for Debt', 65, 161–3, 222; Halliday, Habeas Corpus.
[65] House of Commons, A Report from the Committee Appointed to Enquire into the State of the Goals of This Kingdom, 36.
[66] TNA, Fleet Prison Commitment Books, 1746–8, PRIS1/10; King Bench Prison Commitment Books, 1747–9, PRIS4/2.
[67] Peebles, 'The Anthropology of Credit and Debt', 227.

urbanisation and increased migration, moving away was relatively easy and made pursuing debts much more difficult for creditors. For this reason, debts noted in accounts as 'uncollectable' were often the debts of individuals who fled. Eight pounds (or 15 per cent) of the innkeeper Richard Wilson's credits were due by five individuals described as 'late' of the county, having relocated.[68] Relocating across the border placed a debtor within a different legal jurisdiction, complicating a creditor's efforts to pursue them. The pot painter Edward Cranage of Lancaster noted the residence of Isaac Harrison, who owed him £1 10s., as 'late of Lancaster now of Glasgow'.[69] Not only had Harrison moved more than 150 miles away, he was now living under Scottish law, a system with which Cranage was unlikely to be familiar.

Because their bodies were possibly their most valuable assets, when faced with the threat of confinement, debtors chose flight as a common strategy. Daniel Defoe estimated in 1710 that 5,000 people were abroad (about the same number as in prison). By 1729, Parliament became worried about the 'great numbers of workmen, skillfull in the several trades and manufactures of this kingdom, and also many able seamen and mariners' who fled abroad because of their debts. Fears of losing skilled labour to British enemies, especially France, inspired efforts to repatriate refugee debtors. As one reform pamphlet argued, 'Many of our best Artificers, tradesmen, Merchants, and Gentlemen of Sense and Learning, to avoid it, have undergone a voluntary Banishment from their Native Soil, to foreign Countries; where they daily encourage them to engross all our Manufactories and trade; nay, to fight against their own natural Countrymen and Relations.'[70] Responding to these fears, temporary Insolvency Acts from 1729 included provisions to 'induce and enable' debt fugitives to return home. Their numbers were not insignificant. Thousands applied for relief during the first five acts. Until 1772, the courts relieved at least one refugee debtor for every two imprisoned debtors.[71] Their flight from debt had taken them throughout the British Isles, Continental Europe and the Atlantic world.

## Markets for Bodies

Once debt animated the body's value, it was a small step to commodify and sell that body as part of a market. During the long eighteenth century, the

---

[68] LRO, LCQS, Insolvent Debtor Papers, 1755–6, QJB/31/8.
[69] LRO, LCQS, Insolvent Debtor Papers, 1755–6, QJB/31/28.    [70] *The Attempt*, 21.
[71] Haagen, 'Imprisonment for Debt', 325–6.

expanding British Empire required bodies to populate and to labour. Debtors' prisons provided a direct pipeline into colonial indentured servitude, which was one of the primary ways that white British men and women migrated to the American colonies.[72] Under this system, individuals who were either unable or unwilling to pay the costs of passage sold their own bodies by becoming bondservants to colonial masters. In compensation, servants received passage, keep and occasionally a specified reward at the end of service. The indenture was often organised by a third-party agent, who procured the servant, arranged his or her passage and was paid a bounty by the merchant who ultimately transported and sold the individual to a colonial master. During this period of temporary unfreedom, servants were bound to masters who enjoyed legally sanctioned power over their bodies.[73] As a market developed to satisfy the logistics of moving debtors around Britain and into Atlantic labour markets, the bodies of debtors, already commodified by the legal framework of insolvency, were bought and sold, blurring the distinctions between people and things.

For many indentured servants, the path to Atlantic labour passed directly through the debtors' prison doors. Prisons provided a ready population of individuals whose bodies had already been substituted for a debt, who were likely to be desperate, and who might be willing or coerced into commodifying their bodies as a strategy for removing themselves from the cycle of perpetual incarceration. The relationship between the population of recently released debtors and indenture is hinted at by comparing extant indenture contracts from London with the names of debtors listed in the *London Gazette* who applied for relief from London prisons.[74] Comparing these populations for a single year, 1729, when both sets of records survive, shows that just over 7 per cent of those signing indentures took a direct route from the prison to indentured migration. This figure is almost certainly a low estimate. While many indentured servants departed from London, not all came from London prisons.[75] For example, John Phelps, a baker in Bristol, petitioned for release from the Bristol Newgate prison in May 1729 and was then bound to Joseph

[72] Sharon V. Salinger, *'To Serve Well and Faithfully': Labour and Indentured Servants in Pennsylvania, 1682–1800* (Cambridge, 1987), 8.

[73] Simon P. Newman, *A New World of Labor: The Development of Plantation Slavery in the British Atlantic* (Philadelphia, PA, 2016), 20, 29.

[74] Peter Wilson Coldham, *The Complete Book of Emigrants. Volume 3: 1700–1750* (Baltimore, MD, 1987), 397–433.

[75] John Wareing, *Indentured Migration and the Servant Trade from London to America, 1618–1718: 'There Is Great Want of Servants'* (Oxford, 2017), 60, 100–30.

Whilton in London in October, heading for Antigua.[76] Furthermore, the path from prison to servitude was not always so direct, and may have involved a longer descent into poverty that led to indenture several years after release from prison.

Most free British servants were procured by an agent who facilitated the signing of their contract and arranged for their transportation.[77] Once in the colonies, the servant would either go to work for a master who had used the agent to procure labour, or they would be sold at auction. There was a significant profit to be made for the middlemen involved in transferring bodies around the Atlantic world. It cost £4–10 to transport a servant to the American colonies and to pay for their keep. At auction in America, a servant sold for between £6 and £30, depending on the colony, the need for labour and the servant's age and skills.[78] The servant trade was populated by a range of people who saw human cargo as a form of investment. This included ship captains who transported servants to the colonies, intermediaries and agents who procured servants and arranged their contracts, and individuals who bought into the servant market as investors. While the trade in servants was dominated by a few key individuals who famously amassed fortunes by the purchase and sale of servant contracts, ordinary people in London also recognised British human bodies as forms of investment. John Wareing's analysis of the servant trade in the late seventeenth century found that 70 per cent of traders owned only one or two contracts.[79] Analysis of the agents who organised indenture contracts in London in 1729 from the indentures reveals 15 men active in the trade that year. The majority of servants were bound to large traders who mobilised 20 or more individuals in one year. But 19 per cent of servants were bound to much humbler individuals who invested in the trade in small numbers. Alexander Cash, a weaver in London, invested in three servants in January and another three in June, bound for Nevis and Maryland. Samuel Gloynes, a chapman, invested in two servants in January and another in February, all destined for Maryland. The population of those who purchased bound labour swelled with shoemakers, shopkeepers and victuallers who owned three indentures or less.[80] People with a modest amount of surplus wealth could invest their money in newly formulated bonds or stocks generated during the Financial Revolution. They could also invest in local forms of Atlantic human cargo.

[76] *London Gazette*, 27 May 1729, no. 6782, p. 12.
[77] For description of the different legal forms of servitude, see Wareing, *Indentured Migration*, 46.
[78] Smith, *Colonists in Bondage*, 86; Galenson, *White Servitude*, 99.
[79] Wareing, *Indentured Migration*, 100–1.   [80] Coldham, *Complete Book of Emigrants*, 397–433.

Indenture owners, both in Britain and in America, did not see themselves as having contracted servants' labour, but as owning their bodies as forms of property.[81] In the 1740s, a petition was heard in the Pennsylvania assembly that working people struggled to purchase servants 'only to have their investment vanish'. While relying upon their labour, artisans and lower- or middle-status owners in America also traded servants as their financial status changed.[82] Hilary Beckles has uncovered how the trading of servants amongst planters in the English West Indies was a strategy pursued in order to pool capital.[83] In a cash-poor credit economy, servants' bodies functioned as fungible repositories of value that could be mobilised according to a family's financial needs. Investing in servants could even serve as a means of transferring assets across the Atlantic, even facilitating their owners' own migration. Thus, the American merchant Robert Parke advised an acquaintance in Ireland to 'Procure three of four lusty Servants and agree to pay their passage on this Side'. Once in America, Parke explained, he could 'sell two and pay the others passage with the money'.[84] John Taylor, who was similarly advised to invest in human cargo in order to fund his own travels to Jamaica, recounted having 'the opportunity to dispose of his three servants' for $145. After accounting for the costs of purchase and passage, he 'got clear 45 dollars or £9–15-00 sterling'.[85]

Debt's ability to transform the body into a form of collateral made it a useful tool for agents and procurers. The agent who indentured one servant, William Moraley, purchased ale for him, paid to have him shaved and gave him clothing, binding him into a relationship of legal and social obligation that locked him into the servant contract.[86] Timothy Shannon has recently uncovered the practices of the merchant William Smith in Aberdeen, who hired agents to bring him pauper children, then racked up charges for their maintenance that parents would be unable to pay, ensnaring their families into a relationship of debt and eventually bound labour.[87] In these cases, the legal system of imprisonment for debt allowed creditors to coerce debtors by threatening control over their bodies.

---

[81]  Wareing, *Indentured Migration*, 97–8.      [82]  Salinger, *To Serve Well and Faithfully*, 66, 74.

[83]  Hilary McD. Beckles, 'Plantation Production and White "Proto-Slavery": White Indentured Servants and the Colonisation of the English West Indies, 1624–1645', *The Americas* 41, no. 3 (January 1985): 21–45.

[84]  Quoted in Meyers, *Quaker Immigration*, 99.

[85]  David Buisseret, ed., *Jamaica in 1687: The Taylor Manuscript at the National Library of Jamaica* (Kingston, Jamaica, 2008), 28–9.

[86]  William Moraley, *The Infortunate: The Voyage and Adventures of William Moraley, an Indentured Servant*, ed. Susan E. Klepp and Billy G. Smith (University Park, PA, 1992), 48–52.

[87]  Timothy Shannon, 'A "Wicked Commerce": Consent, Coercion, and Kidnapping in Aberdeen's Servant Trade', *The William and Mary Quarterly* 74, no. 3 (2017): 461.

In the most visible cases, debtors sold their bodies into indenture after being released from prison, or were coerced into indenture through established relationships of indebtedness. But there is also evidence to suggest that servants and labourers were procured directly from the prisons, and that the indentured labour contract could form part of the negotiation for release. In 1776, while trying the case of a girl who had been kidnapped and sold into servitude, the Old Bailey heard evidence to suggest that confined debtors were being actively recruited into the ranks of indentured servants from London's sponging houses. One agent, Henry Quirforth, procured upwards of 100 servants from a lock-up house run by John and Jane Dennison, for which he had been paid £9 7s. 6d.[88] Similarly, a prison reform pamphlet published in 1757 told of how a ship captain trading to the American colonies had enticed prisoners to go abroad with him by paying their fees.[89] Given that more than one third of incarcerated debtors in England owed less than £5 (table 3.4), purchasing a prisoner's debts and selling his or her body as a servant could be a sound investment strategy for a merchant. If the cost of paying the servant's transport and keep was up to £10, and a servant could fetch as much as £30 in a colonial labour market, then an agent could easily afford to pay a prisoner's debts, negotiate their release and bind them into servitude while still making a substantial profit. The grey areas and opportunities for extra-legal negotiation which are obscured by notations of 'discharge' in prison commitment books leave open the possibility of these kinds of arrangements. Being bound into servitude might have looked like an appealing prospect for the confined. Promotional literature portrayed the American colonies as places of abundance, where individuals might make a new start and live better lives as Britons. Workers were told that they could earn wages double what they were paid in London.[90] For the facilitators of the trade, the debtors' prisons provided a ready population of skilled labour, badly needed in the colonies, whose bodies had already been commodified.

For imprisoned debtors who joined the ranks of indentured servants, the line between coercion and consent was thin. Debt could be used as a tool to

---

[88] *Old Bailey Proceedings Online* (www.oldbaileyonline.org), April 1776, trial of John Quirford, John Dennison, Jane Dennison (t17760417-96).

[89] Jacob Ilive, *Reasons Offered for the Reformation of the House of Correction in Clerkenwell* (London, 1757), 26.

[90] Howard Mumford Jones, 'The Colonial Impulse: An Analysis of the "Promotion" Literature of Colonization', *Proceedings of the American Philosophical Society* 90 (1946): 131–61; Hope Frances Kane, *Colonial Promotion and Promotional Literature of Carolina, Pennsylvania, and New Jersey, 1660–1700* (Ann Arbor, MI, 1948); Bernard Bailyn, *Voyagers to the West: Emigration from Britain to America on the Eve of Revolution* (London, 1987), 285, 391, 560–1.

commodify, but at the same time, we can see glimpses of debtors claiming agency as they negotiated the commodification of their own bodies. The account books of the merchant William Fordyce, analysed by Timothy Shannon, show not only payments to tradesmen and procurers, but also bounty payments (cash rewards) to the servants themselves.[91] Without downplaying the pain of separation that was thrust upon migrants, servitude might be recognised as one of a range of options which, like institutional forms of relief, were used and negotiated by poor households according to their own needs as part of an economy of makeshifts.[92] The ability to commodify one's own body and to mobilise its value through the process of debt bondage allowed some prisoners to escape cycles of poverty. For the downwardly mobile, the body became a person's last resource, which could be commodified and sold according to need.

## Conclusion

Male, female, rich and poor bodies were all incorporated by credit networks, where they became forms of value. However, they were incorporated in different ways. The bodies of Africans were sold, against their will, into commercial markets in highly racialised terms. The linking of credit to women's bodies was explicit. Women's bodies could be and were sexually commodified through prostitution. The very notion of a marriage 'market' and the onus to bear children placed quantifiable value on the early modern woman's body. Furthermore, assessments of female credibility and reputation depended upon sexual behaviour and upon how a woman had used her body (although we see that, in practice, female reputation depended upon much more). For the indebted male body, value took physical form as well. Debt was embodied. Not only did this involve the use of imprisonment as a punishment for those who failed to use their credit in ways that accorded with notions of honest indebtedness, but through the institution of the debtors' prison, the body took on concrete value. Imprisoned debtors' bodies were substituted for goods and services obtained on credit.

Imprisonment was part of a much wider cultural transition in which selfhood and objecthood became confused in the eighteenth century, reflected in the economies, literatures and legal practices of the British

---

[91]   Shannon, 'A "Wicked Commerce"', 457.
[92]   Hindle, *On the Parish?*; Steven King and Alannah Tomkins, eds., *The Poor in England, 1700–1850: An Economy of Makeshifts* (Manchester, 2010).

Atlantic world.[93] The interrelationship between people and things occurred within British households and domestic practices. The worth of households was made up of a combination of moveable property and people, in ways that shaped the relationships between people and their things. The practice of valuing persons as forms of concrete worth, though exercised throughout the early modern period, reached a crucial point in the eighteenth century. Problems with the structures of credit, which made it difficult for people to mobilise the wealth that they owned, alongside the changing bases of worth from goods to reputation, created the conditions for bodies to become uniquely flexible and transferrable forms of capital. Looking forward, nineteenth-century prison reform would associate the conflation of money and the body with 'barbarism', insisting on a stark distinction between the body and money. The debtors' prison and its legal infrastructure would come to be seen as 'the barbarous expedients of a rude age, repugnant to justice as well as to humanity', and threatening to capitalist and civilised life.[94] But in the eighteenth century, the assessment of worth and the experience of debt were more than financial and social things: they implicated the experiences, definitions and capacity for mobility that was accorded to the middle-rank embodied self.

---

[93] Julie Park, *The Self and It: Novel Objects and Mimetic Subjects in Eighteenth-Century England* (Stanford, CA, 2009).
[94] John Stuart Mill, *Principles of Political Economy* (1848). Quoted in Gustav Peebles, 'Washing away the Sins of Debt: The Nineteenth-Century Eradication of the Debtors' Prison', *Comparative Studies in Society and History* 55, no. 3 (2013): 704.

# Conclusion

How prevalent was financial failure in eighteenth-century Britain? Who experienced debt insecurity, and how did it shape the ways in which they saw themselves and expressed their own sense of worth? How did individuals cope with and respond to the uncertainties they faced? And finally, how should paying attention to insecurity shape the ways in which historians describe the developing class structures and economy of eighteenth-century Britain?

This book has argued that insecurity was one of the unintended side effects of the transition to capitalism. It was an especially common condition amongst the middling sorts of people. During a period of commercial development and market expansion, their lives were shaped by the potential for success and the prospect of independence and upward mobility, but they were equally shaped by the potential for failure. Insecurity had a profound effect on their day-to-day lives. It affected their standards of living, their status, their sense of selfhood, their bodily autonomy and their relationships with others. Precariousness created a psychosocial context in which daily economic activities were carried out. It created deep-seated anxieties, causing many middling people to live in fear of hitting the bottom. Given the prevalence of middling sort insecurity, two of the grand frames that structure the social and economic history of eighteenth-century Britain – economic success and proletarianisation – begin to look less plausible.

The standard narrative of Britain's economy during the eighteenth century is a story of spectacular economic growth and success which made England (and later Britain) unique in comparison to the rest of Western Europe, enabling it eventually to become the richest and most powerful nation on earth.[1] This success story is bolstered by accounts of

---

[1] This trajectory is summarised by Wrigley, *The Path to Sustained Growth*; Broadberry et al., *British Economic Growth, 1270–1870*.

236

increasing GDP, of commercial expansion and of proto-industrial development. Between the last quarter of the seventeenth century and 1800, GDP per head nearly doubled, and economic growth outstripped population growth. Improvements in agriculture facilitated more output with less labour, allowing the bulk of the nation's growing population to work in the manufacturing and service sectors rather than in the fields. By 1759, only 37 per cent of the English labour force was employed in agriculture, while industry had expanded to 34 per cent.[2] Subsequently, urbanisation and industrialisation in England outpaced that in the rest of Europe.[3]

The extent to which the fruits of economic growth were shared throughout society is contested. It is often assumed that a rising tide lifts all boats, but economists also recognise that growth, especially in its early stages, tends to generate inequality. Even if average wealth increases, expansion provides opportunities for the rich to become richer.[4] However, by several measurements, during the first half of the long eighteenth century, national economic growth improved living standards for the majority of the population. As national wealth advanced, the purchasing power of the majority of the population, as measured by wages and prices, steadily improved.[5] There were gradual gains in life expectancy.[6] Famine was eradicated.[7] Diets became more diverse and caloric intake higher.[8] The Consumer Revolution saw the widespread availability of consumer products, from clothing to durables, and an increase in the per capita consumption of non-essential foodstuffs like tea and sugar.[9] At the same time, increasing consumption has had to be reconciled against a backdrop of falling real wages. This phenomenon is partially explained by De Vries' notion of an 'industrious revolution', in which households reallocated their resources and labour in order to support consumer habits.[10] The number of

[2] Broadberry et al., *British Economic Growth, 1270–1870*, 205, 211–12, 2, 203.
[3] E. A. Wrigley, 'The Divergence of England: The Growth of the English Economy in the Seventeenth and Eighteenth Centuries', *Transactions of the Royal Historical Society* 10 (December 2000): 118–23.
[4] Simon Kuznets, 'Economic Growth and Income Inequality', *The American Economic Review* 45, no. 1 (1955): 1–28; Branko Milanovic, Peter H. Lindert and Jeffrey G. Williamson, 'Measuring Ancient Inequality', Working Paper (National Bureau of Economic Research, October 2007), www.nber.org/papers/w13550.
[5] Broadberry et al.; For an alternative vision of wage stagnation, see Clark, *A Farewell to Alms*, 43. *British Economic Growth, 1270–1870*, 331.
[6] E. A. Wrigley and Roger Schofield, *The Population History of England, 1541–1871: A Reconstruction* (Cambridge, 1981), 528–9.
[7] Gráda, 'Neither Feast nor Famine', 17.
[8] Muldrew, *Food, Energy and the Creation of Industriousness*; Kelly and Gráda, 'Numerare Est Errare'.
[9] McKendrick, Brewer and Plumb, *The Birth of a Consumer Society*; Weatherill, *Consumer Behaviour*; Lemire, *Fashion's Favourite*; Shammas, *The Pre-industrial Consumer*.
[10] De Vries, *The Industrious Revolution*.

individuals living in poverty seems to have declined, as measured by the proportion of families able to afford a basket of consumables.[11] By one account, between 1688 and 1756, the number of households living in poverty reduced from one quarter to 14 per cent of the population.[12]

Narratives of eighteenth-century economic progress have never taken account of the fact that during this period of growth and rising living standards, increasing numbers of the middling sorts, as defined by their occupational status in skilled trades, commerce, service and manufacturing, were also incarcerated for failing to pay their debts. One in four middling men experienced the debtors' prison during their lifetimes. Nearly half of middling households in England would experience the incarceration of a household member every generation. In urban Scotland, at least 2 per cent of the male population was incarcerated annually, and in every generation, at least one third of households would experience the prison. Some found ways to pay their creditors and were released within a few days, but others remained incarcerated for more than one year. Everyone in urban commercial communities would have known someone who had gone to prison for debt because, by the eighteenth century, incarceration was a routine practice. It was one of the most common ways of enforcing debt in an economy built upon credit. Yet narratives of shared prosperity and class formation fail to acknowledge how widespread the insecurity represented by incarceration was, and they fail to account for it in their explanatory frameworks.

## Reconciling Insecurity and Economic Growth

In many ways, the prevalence of insecurity in the eighteenth century is unsurprising, because risk was built into the capitalist model. Credit, the ability to create imaginary value, was a tool that allowed for innovation and entrepreneurship, but it also brought people down. New commercial ventures, innovations in manufacturing and the expansion of markets required risk-taking. These ventures could fail as easily as they could succeed. As Michael Zakim argues, 'The risk economy proves to be the least protective of all built environments. It offers no safeguards from its incessant agitations and uncertainties, not even to those who stand to gain the most from it since their gains are, of course, derived from those same

---

[11] Robert C Allen, *The British Industrial Revolution in Global Perspective* (Cambridge, 2009), 25–56.

[12] Broadberry et al., *British Economic Growth, 1270–1870*, 332. This estimate contrasts with Floud et al., who argue that in 1759, 21.4 per cent of households lived in poverty. See Floud, *The Changing Body*, 91.

agitations.'[13] The relationship between risk, failure and growth has rarely been part of the standard debates in classical economics. Ricardo, Smith and Malthus were more interested in the economy's capacity for unlimited growth and expansion, and the tensions between economic and biological reproduction, and their questions continue to infuse investigations of the historical economy today. Yet failure and crisis were recognised and discussed by other contemporary economic thinkers, who did not necessarily view the changes taking place around them as progressive.[14] Lord Kaims noted that 'when activity increases and people are roused to adventure, there must be larger losses as well as larger gains.'[15] Henry George later wrote in *Progress and Poverty* that 'the phenomena we class together and speak of as industrial depression are but intensifications of phenomena which always accompany material progress.'[16]

The experience of risk was common amongst a broader population than those who ventured. The uncertainty of debt affected everyone who traded in credit, and what made credit so precarious was its combined ubiquity and volatility. Most people depended upon credit, and nearly everyone served as both a creditor and a debtor. These roles were easily and unpredictably interchangeable. A small shift in a creditor's circumstances, such as a changing balance of payments, the demand of an obligation or the failure of a debtor several times removed within a network of credit, could trigger a crisis and a switch in roles, forcing the creditor suddenly into the role of the debtor. As Daniel Defoe explained, 'uncertainty in human affairs, and especially in trade' could cause 'the furious and outrageous creditor [to] become bankrupt himself in a few years, or perhaps months after, and begging the same mercy of others'.[17] But the uncertainties of the credit market are best understood as forms of insecurity rather than as risks, because they were unchosen and unexpected. Insecurity was defined by environmental uncertainty rather than objective risk. Its defining characteristic was unpredictability, rather than scarcity.[18] The middling sorts who fell into debt did not necessarily suffer from the worst material consequences of insecurity, such as hunger. Rather, they suffered from the inability to *control* the events which impacted their life experiences.

---

[13] Michael Zakim, 'The Best of Times and the Worst of Times', *Common-Place* 10, no. 3 (2010).
[14] Hoppit, 'Attitudes to Credit in Britain, 1680–1790', 305, 322.
[15] Quoted in Ashton, *Economic Fluctuations in England, 1700–1800*, 114.
[16] Henry George, *Progress and Poverty: An Inquiry into the Cause of Industrial Depressions and of Increase of Want with Increase of Wealth: The Remedy* (London, 1881).
[17] Defoe, *The Compleat English Tradesman*, 198.
[18] Barbara Adam, Ulrich Beck and Joost van Loon, eds., *The Risk Society and Beyond: Critical Issues for Social Theory* (London, 2000), 35–6.

The eighteenth-century experience calls into question the deeply held assumption that economic growth is good for society. Eighteenth-century debt insecurity supports the notion that the growth of an economy does not necessarily lead to increasing prosperity, and furthermore, that prosperity is not synonymous with well-being. Histories that calculate prosperity by dividing up total gains amongst the population can provide important indications of long-term change. But they do not give us a complete picture of people's feelings of economic well-being during periods of growth because they overlook the small fluctuations which might have little material impact on an economy at large, but which can cause deep-seated anxiety within a populous. T. S. Ashton argued many years ago that the short-term fluctuations in an economy are worth attending to. He discovered that the upward slope of economic growth 'was not continuous but was broken throughout by declivities' and that 'it was at these points that most of the instances of misery were concentrated'.[19] Against a backdrop of unbridled success, small fluctuations based upon seasonality, life cycle and unpredictable life events had a decisive impact on people's lives, livelihoods and well-being. Because of the interconnected nature of debt, one individual's fluctuating circumstances could implicate a broader network.

Insecurity provides an important but underutilised measure by which we might assess living standards and well-being during periods of relative prosperity. It acts as a counterpoint to rising living stands, and it provides particular insights into the experiences of individuals with middle-rank wages, who fell above the poverty line and whose living standards, by most measures, were adequate. A class of households emerged in the eighteenth century which might have looked prosperous by most measures. Their occupations provided them wages well above the poverty line. Their consumption habits indicated that they could afford the plethora of newly available consumer goods. But they lived on the edge. These material measures of household prosperity were built on borrowed money. The fragility of the credit economy meant that these types of households could easily fall under. Debtors' prisons provide a measurement of downward mobility, even if that mobility was not permanent. Middling people *looked* materially prosperous, but they did not enjoy the benefits of material security.

---

[19] Ashton, *Economic Fluctuations in England, 1700–1800*, 177, 29–30.

## Placing the Middling Sort

By attending to *who* was made insecure by proto-industrialisation, we come up against another grand narrative of the eighteenth century: that of class formation. Changes in land tenure, technological developments in industry and the organisational restructuring of manufacturing contributed to the growth of a wage-dependent labour force and to the rise of the middling sorts. These changes were social and political as much as they were economic. Proletarianisation involved a separation of interest between labour and capital, as an early modern patriarchal relationship between master and worker gave way to a cash relationship. Capital exploited labour. Though the factory system of the nineteenth century remained in the distant future, and manual modes of production and small workshops persisted, workers experienced profound changes in the possibility of taking pride in their craft, in control over the labour process and in the intensity and remuneration of labour.[20] All of these changes contributed to the rise of a working class. Between 1780 and 1832, English working people began to feel an 'identity of interests' between themselves and against their employers.[21] Within the narrative of labour exploitation, the middle classes were thoroughly on the side of industrialisation as the possessors of capital and the employers of the proletariat. The labour of exploited workers contributed to their newfound affluence. Wealth and cultural power concentrated in the middle sections of society. Studies of the burgeoning middling sort, while noting some underlying insecurities, have largely bolstered this narrative by emphasising their penchant for upward mobility, their aspirational character, their increasing power and the extent to which their cultural lives were built on new wealth.[22]

The story of middling insecurity during a period of economic growth is missing from both neoclassical economic models and social histories of class formation. The economic growth story which assumes that expansion helps everyone, alongside histories of labour exploitation, has given us permission to forget the experiences of some people.[23] There was a much broader segment of society than the proletariat who were precarious, but they were precarious in very different ways. Middling precariousness was not built around the middling sorts' relationship to the means of

---

[20] Rule, *The Labouring Classes in Early Industrial England, 1750–1850*, 13.
[21] Thompson, *The Making of the English Working Class*, 11.
[22] Langford, *A Polite and Commercial People*; Hunt, *The Middling Sort*; French, *The Middle Sort of People*.
[23] Standing, *The Precariat*.

production, their relationship to land tenure or their need to sell their labour. Instead, their insecurities were a result of their relationship to debt. Middling people may have owned the means of production, but the nature of that ownership, which was built on borrowed money, made their status and power profoundly insecure.

Given the instability of middling wealth and status, a new vision of class formation is necessary, one which positions insecurity as part of its central framework. Insecurity had a significant influence on class consciousness, in other words, how middling people described their condition and positioned themselves within the social order. They are often characterised as ascendant, and within the social order, they are positioned in relation to an upper boundary that separated them from ranks of elites. Middling people achieved status by adopting markers of gentility.[24] But they might be more accurately positioned against a lower boundary of poverty. Living in the shadow of the debtors' prisons, the ambition of most middling people was not to be upwardly mobile, but rather to *not* be downwardly mobile. The mutability of wealth shaped how individuals viewed their own positions within the eighteenth century's social hierarchy, and how they judged others.[25] Diarists like Cannon, Parsons and Harrold fretted constantly about paying their debts, and about the insecurity of their financial status. They watched as their neighbours marked their place in society with material and social displays, and they noted the changing fortunes of the households around them.

Even the consumption habits which have so defined the ways in which middling people projected their power and status can be understood within a framework of insecurity. Historians of material culture have long argued that the consumption of goods was a crucial aspect of status and display. Goods were 'indispensable props'. Status, particularly gentility, was judged by 'whether you owned the right items, whether they were sufficiently genteel in their design, and whether you were capable of using them in the right way'.[26] When one considers both how uncertain the financial and social world of the middling sorts was, and how crucial forms of status and reputation were to financial credibility and solvency, the impetus to consume becomes more understandable. Projecting status through the ownership and use of material objects was a practical form of communicating financial status. Consumption was a means of

---

[24] French, *The Middle Sort of People*.    [25] Muldrew, 'Class and Credit'.

[26] Michael Snodin and John Styles, *Design and the Decorative Arts: Britain 1500–1900* (London, 2001), 184; Berg, *Luxury and Pleasure in Eighteenth-Century Britain*, 6–7.

projecting security in an insecure world, and it served as a critical indicator of both current status and confidence in one's future. Sustaining an impression of prosperity could be a crucial means of securing credit in a world where financial credit depended upon reputation and character. But contemporaries were perhaps correct to be suspicious of such projections. George Berkeley described luxury in 1721 as something which generated a false, insubstantial sort of prosperity. Luxury, according to Berkeley, was in fact 'only debt disguised as wealth'.[27] In this context, consumption was intended less to signal upward mobility and more to mitigate the potential for downward mobility. The impetus was not to get ahead, but rather not to fall or be left behind.

Insecure identities manifested themselves in different ways. The broad social, psychological and physical consequences of insecurity are what make this condition so worth attending to. Debt insecurity took different forms and had far-reaching consequences for middling lives. When threatened with incarceration, middling people had more to lose than their financial assets. Incarceration threatened and shaped notions of selfhood. Credit in the eighteenth century was increasingly anchored to reputation, rather than to the possession of a moveable estate.[28] Because the moveable, material wealth holdings of the middling sort were relatively small and credit was insecure, individuals focused upon the moral and social components of credit. Negotiations around incarceration therefore cut to the heart of who a person was. Reputation, character and occupational identity, informed by gender expectations, became the stuff of credit within an economy of circulating selves. Going to prison could involve gaining a reputation for having failed, and a reputation for failing could lead to a loss of credit. When they were incarcerated, middling people risked losing their independent status. So while the loss of reputation could cause the loss of credit, so the loss of financial credit could result in the loss of social status.

Financial security was closely tied to the world of work. Seasonal fluctuations, uncertain career progression and periodic unemployment meant that most people organised their working lives around a system of by-employments. They undertook multiple jobs in order to sustain themselves and their households. Fluctuations in working life impacted a household's wages, but these fluctuations also created insecure identities because men and women derived status and worth from their occupational

---

[27] George Berkeley, *An Essay towards Preventing the Ruine of Great Britain* (London, 1727), 92.
[28] Shepard, *Accounting for Oneself*, 279.

identities. A person's occupation brought a number of reputational attributes, from skill to industriousness to lineage. Insecurity therefore involved the negotiation of a broad range of activities in their working lives, which conferred different forms of benefit, and which individuals discussed using complex vocabularies.

Insecurity was also physical. In the eighteenth century, selfhood was increasingly attached to the body. Legal and philosophical codes emphasised the idea that every man had property in his own person.[29] But the system of debt incarceration betrayed these ideals, as a person's body could be taken by another. Incarceration threatened bodily autonomy and liberty, central features of British masculine identities. Debtors' prisons functioned like pawnshops, where people obtained credit on their selfhood, and submitted their bodies when they failed to pay their debts. Prisons transformed the body into a form of collateral for goods and services received on credit.[30] Debt insecurity thus encouraged people to think about their bodies as repositories of value. The nature of this value was different than forms of worth and credit that were derived from a person's reputation or labour capacity. In contrast to these other forms, the body served as a concrete form of value that could be moved, transferred and owned. Debt was therefore a cause of mobility in the eighteenth century. For those who lived in the countryside, this mobility began with the transportation of debtors to county prisons, which were often tens of miles away from their homes. From there, many were transferred to London prisons. Fearing the threat of incarceration, some fled their debts abroad to Europe or the American colonies. Others entered states of partial commodification by selling their bodies into indentured labour bound for the New World. When the middling sort experienced the poverty of disaster, their bodies became resources in ways that intersected with Atlantic regimes of migration and labour. A form of unfreedom, within a broad spectrum of Atlantic unfreedom, was therefore familiar to middle-class life.

## Eighteenth-Century Economic Culture

Individuals' coping mechanisms and responses to insecurity, with its financial, social, emotional and physical forms, had profound consequences for the nature of economic relationships in the eighteenth century. Insecurity fostered

[29] Locke, *Two Treatises of Government*, book 2, chapter 5, section 27, p. 287.
[30] Finn, *The Character of Credit*, 10.

an economic culture that was less about accumulating capital and competing for the spoils of growth, and more about avoiding loss. People competed over the disadvantages of insecurity. As Ulrich Beck describes, in a society coping with high levels of risk, people respond to threats by attempting to shift the burdens of insecurity onto others. Individuals seek to create a situation of relative security by shifting their burdens sideways.[31] Thus, when individuals in the eighteenth century faced solvency crises, they attempted as creditors to shift the burdens of insolvency onto their own debtors, using the coercive apparatus of the prison. This created a dynamic of exploitation and accumulation, but one that looked very different than the processes described by models of proletarianisation. In a negative zero-sum game that Beck refers to as 'collective self-injury', those accumulating damages (in this case illiquid debts) were marginalised within the credit economy by losing their reputations for solvency and their physical autonomy. However, they were not exploited in the usual sense because their marginalisation did not lead to others' gain. Instead of becoming rich, winners in this scenario shifted their disadvantage onto another group, so that their 'advantage' was in fact their reduced disadvantage, reduced by the amount of risk they could alleviate by shifting it onto others. By choosing incarceration, a creditor did not get 'ahead' in terms of accumulating wealth, but rather reduced his or her chances of falling behind.

The act of shifting risk could lead to actions that appeared brutal and violent in an economy normally defined as 'polite'. The middling sorts have been characterised as a 'polite and commercial people', yet in the fight to maintain their own security, it was acceptable to inflict harm on others and to use coercion as a mechanism for negotiation. The positive values that we associate with commercial society have obscured the social violence that adheres to those values. In the eighteenth century, people facing default pursued their own debtors aggressively, using the full weight of the law to protect their own liberties. The potential for coercion was an important feature of the culture of credit. Numerous scholars have emphasised that credit was built upon trust. As credit became less stable, creditors may have been willing to extend loans because they trusted the system of debt enforcement rather than because they trusted the reputation of the borrower. In contractual systems of early modern justice, coercion could serve as the basis of promise rather than trust.[32] The infliction of harm, or

---

[31] Ulrich Beck and Mark Ritter, *Risk Society: Towards a New Modernity* (London, 1992).

[32] Lynn Johnson, 'Friendship, Coercion and Interest: Debating the Foundations of Justice in Early Modern England', *Journal of Early Modern History* 8 (2004): 46–64.

the threat to inflict harm, was an acceptable and functional tool within the culture of debt. Harm took different forms. It could be social, it could be reputational or it could target a person's physical autonomy. Incarceration was a form of violence. Yet it was one which accorded with the dictates of politeness. As an action that required restraint, calculation and deliberation, incarceration made use of the sublimated violence of the law.

Acts of coercion were justified by assigning blame to individuals for their financial failure. Failure was the result of belief and perception. Creditors' decisions to treat debtors as insolvent were based upon many factors, including perceptions of debtor character and the circumstances under which they broke. Indebtedness was understood as the consequence of overspending, unethical behaviour and dishonesty. Creditors drew upon an arsenal of stereotypes to justify their actions. But assigning blame to moral or behavioural failures distracted from broader sources of crisis, which were imbedded in the very structures of an economy built systematically upon borrowed money. Middling households were insecure because of the architecture of the credit economy. Probate inventories and debtors' schedules show that households held their wealth in the form of credit, or debts owing to the household, rather than in the form of moveable wealth.[33] Insecurity was exacerbated by the positions that middling people occupied within credit networks. As shopkeepers, manufacturers and distributors, they sat at the centre of long chains of credit, which were becoming increasingly complex and distant. The delayed payments of workers' wages and the illiquidity of elite finances found their way into middling account books. Debtors could move, pass away or default, leaving middling people with bad debts and with a loss of savings. The accumulation of credit left middling households with illiquid assets. Households threatened with incarceration often had assets exceeding their obligations, but it was not possible to transfer those assets to creditors. Debt accumulated in the middle ranks of society.

The legal system did little to help middling creditors who faced illiquidity and the loss of savings. Despite the recent emphasis on institutional economics, the experience of tradespeople was characterised by a lack of institutional regulation. If this was the bourgeoisie accumulating capital, then they did so with little to no legal protection. In England, the law did not provide an expedient means of collecting debts of between £2 and £100. Bankruptcy and small claims courts were available only for very small

---

[33] Shammas, *The Pre-industrial Consumer*; Overton, *Production and Consumption*.

and very large debts. Processes of debt litigation at common law, which were so popular in the sixteenth and seventeenth centuries, had become slow and expensive, and much of the wealth owned by households was legally protected and inaccessible for lenders to distrain.[34] By the eighteenth century, arrest was the cheapest, quickest and most comprehensive means of pursuing middle-sized debts. By threatening incarceration, creditors could coerce debtors into handing over two forms of property against which they had no claim: protected forms of property and assets belonging to other people. If debtors had truly gone broke, incarceration might force them to draw upon their own networks of credit and support.

In negotiating insecurity by transferring risk, using coercive mechanisms and attempting to protect reputation and selfhood, middling people behaved in ways that are poorly explained by models of the economic man. *Homo economicus* does little to explain the feelings, choices and actions of people who lived in a precarious world. The threat of the prison, or the perceived threat of the prison, encouraged middling people to think about their positions in the world in ways that were shaped by the economy's insecurities rather than its potential rewards. As debt collected in the middle ranks of society, individuals made choices and interacted with one another in ways that combined utility, emotion and social concern. Men and women of the eighteenth century were far from autonomous subjects. They were acutely aware that their solvency and their livelihoods were intimately tied into networks of credit and debt, which could help their fortunes to rise but also cause them to fall. Middling failure, as borne out through incarceration, was a consequence of the fragility of credit which underpinned livelihood, status and commercial activity in the eighteenth century. The labouring poor experienced a poverty of inheritance, but middling people were subjected to the poverty of disaster.

---

[34] Brooks, *Lawyers, Litigation, and English Society*; Brooks, *Law, Politics and Society*; Champion, 'Recourse to the Law'.

# Bibliography

## Manuscripts

### Bodleian Library, University of Oxford

John Baptist Grano. 'Journal of My Life inside the Marshalsea', 1728. MS. Rawlinson D.34.

### Edinburgh City Archives

Acts and Statutes of Marys Chapel
Dean of Guild Extracted Processes.
Edinburgh Bailie Court Processes, 1707–80. HH11/11–28.

### Henry E. Huntington Library, San Marino, CA

Parsons, Thomas. 'Diary, 1769 Jan.–Aug.', 1769. HM 62593.
Stutterd Family Papers, 1768–1823. SFP 1–857.

### Lancashire Record Office, Preston

Lancashire Court of Quarter Sessions
  'An Alphabetical List' of Debtors, 1712–19. QJB/8.
  Certificates of Discharge, 1725, 1755–6. QJB/16, 33.
  Debtors' Insolvency Papers, 1725–61. QJB/10-36.
  Lists of Prisoners, 1725, 1736, 1742/3, 1748, 1755–6. QJB/13/1, QJB/26/1 QJB/30/1-3, QJB, 31/1.
  Quarter Sessions Petitions, 1722–30, 1748–50. QSP/1189–1327, 1599–1642.

### London Metropolitan Archives

City of London, Courts of Law, Petition by 33 poor debtors, 1742–3. CLA/040/08/009.

City of London Sessions, Debtors' Schedules: Fleet Prison, Ludgate Prison, Newgate Prison, Poultry Compter, Wood Street Compter, 1725–65. CLA/047/LJ/17/020-053.

City of London Sessions, Lists from the Several Prisons of Insolvent Debtors in the Prisons on Certain Dates, Sworn to at the Sessions, for the Debtors to Take Benefit of the Insolvent Acts, 1719–55. CLA/047/LJ/17/001–002.

Ludgate Prison, Lists of prisoners, 19 Jan. 1724/5, CLA/033/01/09.

Ludgate Prison, 'Rough Minutes and Papers of the Committee Appointed to Consider Legal and Proper Methods for Removing Prisoners from Ludgate to the London Workhouse', May–July 1731. CLA/033/01/014.

Poultry Compter, Lists of prisoners. CLA/030/02.

Middlesex Sessions of the Peace. Debt Cases. MJ/SD.

Woodstreet Compter, List of prisoners. CLA/028/01.

### The National Archives, London

Condensed Version of Fleet Commitment Book, 1769–72, PRIS 10/21.

Entry Book for Discharges, Fleet, 1734–40, PRIS 10/49.

Fleet Prison Commitment Books, 1708–13, 1719–21, 1725–48, 1770–2, PRIS 1/2–10, PRIS 4/1.

Habeas Corpus Book: Fleet Prison, 1739–58, PRIS 10/89.

King's Bench Commitment Books, 1748–78, PRIS 4/2–6.

### National Library of Scotland

Petitions to Marys Chapel, 1725–7. Acc. 7332.

### National Records of Scotland, Edinburgh

Edinburgh Commissary Court, Consistorial Processes. CC8/6.

Edinburgh Court of Session: Bill Chamber Processes, Old Series, CS271.

Edinburgh Tolbooth, Warding and Liberation Books. HH11.

Papers of the Innes Family of Stow, Peeblesshire. GD113.

Seafield Correspondence, 1726. GD248.

Sheriff Court Productions. 'Miscellaneous Legal Papers and Correspondence Relating to How Family', 1708–77, SC39/107/8.

### Surrey History Centre

Debtor Appearance Books, 1696–1704. QS3/2/12.

## William Andrews Clark Library, Los Angeles, CA

Jeake, Samuel. 'A Diary of the Actions & Accidents of My Life: Tending Partly to Observe & Memorize ye Providences Therein Manifested, & Partly to Investigate ye Measure of Time in Astronomical Directions and to Determine the Astrall Causes &c', 1694. MS.1959.006.

## Printed Primary Sources

### Images

*The Bubblers Mirrour: or England's Folly*. London: Bowles and Carver, 1720. British Museum, 1935,0522.1.4.
*Discharge of Insolvent Debtors, Sept. 2, 1743*. London, 1761. British Museum, 18680808.37.
*The First of April*, c.1780. British Museum, 18,680,808.13.
Hogarth, William. *The Distrest Poet*, 1737. British Museum, S,2.54.
Vanderbank, Moses. *A Noted Bard. Writing a Poem in Blank Verse to Lay before Sr R – on the Great Necessity at This Time for an Act of Insolvency*, 1737. British Museum, 1874,0808.202.

### Periodicals

*Cobbett's Parliamentary History of England*
*The Idler*
*Journals of the House of Commons*
*The London Gazette*
*Scots Magazine*

### Edited Primary Source Collections

Boswell, James. *Boswell's London Journal, 1762–1763*. Edited by Frederick A. Pottle. New Haven, CT, 1992.
Buisseret, David, ed. *Jamaica in 1687: The Taylor Manuscript at the National Library of Jamaica*. Kingston, Jamaica, 2008.
Coldham, Peter Wilson. *The Complete Book of Emigrants. Volume 3: 1700–1750*. Baltimore, MD, 1987.
de Tocqueville, Alexis. *Democracy in America*. New York, 1945.
Gough, Richard. *The History of Myddle*. Introduction with bibliographical notes by Peter Razzell. Firle, 1979.
Grano, John Baptist. *Handel's Trumpeter: The Diary of John Grano*. Edited by John Ginger. Stuyvesant, NY, 1998.
Horner, Craig, ed. *The Diary of Edmund Harrold, Wigmaker of Manchester 1712–15*. Aldershot, 2008.

Johnson, Christopher William. *Considerations on the Case of the Confined Debtors in This Kingdom*. London, 1793.

Johnston, J. A. 'Worcester Probate Inventories 1699–1716'. *Midland History* 4, no. 3 (1978): 191–211.

King, Gregory. 'A Scheme of the Income and Expense of the Several Families of England Calculated for the Year 1688'. In *Seventeenth-Century Economic Documents*. Edited by Joan Thirsk and John Phillips Cooper, 780–1. Oxford, 1974.

Kyd, James Gray and Alexander Webster. *Scottish Population Statistics, Including Webster's Analysis of Population, 1755*. Edinburgh, 1952.

Locke, John. *The Second Treatise of Civil Government, and A Letter Concerning Toleration*. Edited by Peter Laslett. Cambridge, 1988.

Marshall, J. D., ed. *The Autobiography of William Stout of Lancaster, 1665–1752*. Manchester, 1967.

Miller, Robert. *The Municipal Buildings of Edinburgh. A Sketch of Their History for Seven Hundred Years Written Mainly from the Original Records ... With an Appendix Suggesting Improvements and Extensions to the Present Buildings in the Royal Exchange*. Edinburgh, 1895.

Money, John, ed. *The Chronicles of John Cannon, Excise Officer and Writing Master*. Oxford, 2010.

Moraley, William. *The Infortunate: The Voyage and Adventures of William Moraley, an Indentured Servant*. Edited by Susan E. Klepp and Billy G. Smith. University Park, PA, 1992.

Reynolds, Joshua. *Discourses on Art*. Edited by Robert R. Wark. New Haven, CT, 1975.

Smith, Adam. *An Inquiry into the Nature and Causes of the Wealth of Nations*. Edited by R. H. Campbell, Andrew S. Skinner and William B. Todd. Oxford, 1976.
   *Lectures on Jurisprudence*. Edited by Ronald L. Meek, D. D. Raphael, Peter Stein and Edwin Cannan. Oxford, 1978.

Thirsk, Joan and John Phillips Cooper, eds., *Seventeenth-Century Economic Documents*. Oxford, 1974.

Vaisey, David, ed. *The Diary of Thomas Turner, 1754–1765*. Oxford; New York, 1984.

Willan, Thomas Stuart and John Waller, eds. *An Eighteenth-Century Shopkeeper: Abraham Dent of Kirkby Stephen*. Manchester, 1970.

## Printed Materials

*An Abridgment of the Public Statutes in Force and Use Relative to Scotland, from the Union, ... to the Twenty-Seventh ... George II. ... In Two Volumes*. Edinburgh, 1755.

*The Accomplish'd Letter-Writer: Or the Young Gentlemen and Ladies' Polite Guide to an Epistolary Correspondence in Business, Friendship, Love, and Marriage ...* Newcastle upon Tyne, 1787.

'Act of Sederunt, Anent Poindings and Arrestments'. *Scots Magazine* xv (August 1754): 375–7.

Aikin, John. *A Description of the Country from Thirty to Forty Miles Round Manchester; The Materials Arranged, and the Work Composed by J. Aikin, M. D. Embellished and Illustrated with Seventy-Three Plates.* London, 1795.

Anderson, Duncan. *History of the Abbey and Palace of Holyrood.* Edinburgh, 1849.

von Archenholz, Johann Wilhelm. *A View of the British Constitution. And, of the Manners and Customs of the People of England.* Edinburgh, 1794.

*The Attempt: Or, An Essay towards the Retrieving Lost Liberty, Reforming the Corrupt and Pernicious Laws of This Nation, and Rendering the Recovery of Debts Easy and Effectual. Fairly Stated between Debtor and Creditor; Being the Natural Interest of Every Man in Trade. Humbly Addressed to the Consideration of Both Houses of Parliament. By a Prisoner in the Poultry-Compter.* London, 1751.

Bankton, Andrew MacDowall. *An Institute of the Laws of Scotland in Civil Rights: With Observations upon the Agreement or Diversity between Them and the Laws of England,* vol. 2. Stair Society 42. Edinburgh, 1994.

Baston, Thomas. *The Debtors Glory; And the Gaolers Lamentation, for His Majesties Act, Concerning the Imprisonment of Insolvent Debtors . . .* London, 1727.

*Observations on Trade, and a Publick Spirit. Shewing, I. That All Trade Ought to Be in Common, and the Danger of Monopolies. II. That the Abuse of It, by Publick Companies, Was the Origin of Stock-Jobbing. III. Of the Deceits Arising from the Encouragement of Projectors, Lotteries, and Other Cheats. IV. Of the General Benefit of Trade. V. Of the Selling of Places, Corruptions in Elections of Members, in the Law, in the Commission of the Peace, and Select Vestries. VI. The Advantages of a Publick Spirit, and Wherein It Consists.* London, 1732.

Bell, George Joseph. *Commentaries on the Laws of Scotland, and on the Principles of Mercantile Jurisprudence. Considered in Relation to Bankruptcy; Competition of Creditors; and Imprisonment for Debt.* Edinburgh, 1810.

*A Dictionary and Digest of the Law of Scotland: With Short Explanations of the Most Ordinary English Law Terms.* Edinburgh,1838.

Berkeley, George. *An Essay towards Preventing the Ruine of Great Britain.* London, 1721.

Bickham, George. *The Universal Penman.* London, 1743.

Blackall, Ofspring. *The Works of Ofspring Blackall,* vol. 1. London, 1723.

Blackstone, William. *Commentaries on the Laws of England,* Oxford, 1765.

Blackwell, Elizabeth. *A Curious Herbal, Containing Five Hundred Cuts, of the Most Useful Plants, Which Are Now Used in the Practice of Physick. Engraved on Folio Copper Plates, after Drawings, Taken from the Life.* London, 1739.

Boswell, James. *Reflections on the Late Alarming Bankruptcies in Scotland: Addressed to All Ranks: . . . With Advice to Such, How to Conduct Themselves at This Crisis.* Edinburgh, 1772.

Boyer, Abel. 'On Conversation, Society, Civility, and Politeness'. In *The English Theophrastus; or, Manners of the Age.* London, 1702.

Brookes, R. *The General Practice of Physic; Extracted Chiefly from the Writings of the Most Celebrated Practical Physicians, and The Medical Essays, Transactions,*

*Journals, and Literary Correspondence of the Learned Societies in Europe* ... The second edition with improvements. 2 vols. London, 1754.

Burke, Edmund. *A Philosophical Enquiry into the Origin of Our Ideas of the Sublime and Beautiful.* The eighth edition. With an introductory discourse concerning taste, and several other additions. London, 1776.

*The Case of Insolvent Debtors, Now in Prison.* London, 1725.

*The Case of Prisoners for Debt Consider'd.* Dublin, 1727.

*A Collection of the Yearly Bills of Mortality, from 1657 to 1758 Inclusive. Together with Several Other Bills of an Earlier Date.* London,1759.

*The Compulsive Clause in the Present Act of Insolvency, Fully Stated, with Its Good and Bad Consequences Plainly Stated and Clearly Answered: To Which Is Annexed, Proposals for the More Effectual Recovery of Debts, and without Arrests: With the Evils of Goals for Debtors Reasonably Exposed.* London, 1761.

*Considerations on the Laws between Debtors and Creditors; and an Abstract of the Insolvent Acts. With Thoughts on a Bill to Enable Creditors to Recover the Effects of Their Debtors, And to Abolish Imprisonment for Debt.* London, 1779.

*The Cries of the Oppressed, Humbly Submitted to the Serious Consideration of the Honourable the House of Commons: Or the Very Hard Case of Insolvent and Other Miserable Debtors Set Forth in Their Proper Colours.* London, 1712.

*The Debtors Glory; And the Gaolers Lamentation, for His Majesties Act, Concerning the Imprisonment of Insolvent Debtors* ... London, 1727.

Defoe, Daniel. *The Compleat English Tradesman, in Familiar Letters: Directing Him in All the Several Parts and Progressions of Trade* ... London, 1726.

*An Essay upon Loans: Or, an Argument Proving That Substantial Funds Settled by Parliament,* ... *Will Bring Inloans of Money to the Exchequer, in Spight of All the Conspiracies of Parties to the Contrary;* ... *By the Author of the Essay upon Credit.* London, 1710.

*The Life and Strange Surprizing Adventures of Robinson Crusoe, Etc.* London, 1719.

*Review of the State of the English Nation.*

*Some Objections Humbly Offered to the Consideration of the Hon. House of Commons, Relating to the Present Intended Relief of Prisoners.* London, 1729.

Dickens, Charles. *Little Dorrit.* Edited by Hablot Knight Browne. 1st edn. London, 1857.

Ellis, Charles. *A Treatise on the Law of Debtor and Creditor.* London, 1822.

Erskine, John. *An Institute of the Law of Scotland, in Four Books. In the Order of Sir George Mackenzie's Institutions of That Law.* Edinburgh, 1783.

*Essay on the Forms of Writings, or of Securities and Conveyances, Both of Heritable and Moveable Subjects, as They Are Used in Scotland; and the Law Itself as Applicable to Their Nature, and the Use of Them in General Practice.* Edinburgh, 1786.

Fergusson, James. *Treatise on the Present State of the Consistorial Law in Scotland, with Reports of Decided Cases.* Edinburgh, 1829.

George, Henry. *Progress and Poverty: An Inquiry into the Cause of Industrial Depressions and of Increase of Want with Increase of Wealth: The Remedy.* London, 1881.

Granger, James. *A Biographical History of England, from Egbert the Great to the Revolution: . . . With a Preface, Shewing the Utility of a Collection of Engraved Portraits . . . By the Rev. J. Granger.* 4 vols., vol. 1. London, 1769.

Grant, A. *The Progress and Practice of a Modern Attorney; Exhibiting the Conduct of Thousands towards Millions! To Which Are Added, the Different Stages of a Law Suit, and Attendant Costs . . .* London, 1795.

Grantham, Thomas. *A Motion against Imprisonment, Wherein Is Proved That Imprisonment for Debt Is against the Gospel, against the Good Church, and Commonwealth . . .* London, 1642.

Grosley, Pierre Jean. *A Tour to London; Or, New Observations on England, and Its Inhabitants. By M. Grosley, . . . Translated from the French by Thomas Nugent, . . . in Two Volumes.* London, 1772.

Gurney, Joseph John and Elizabeth Gurney Fry. *Notes on a Visit Made to Some of the Prisons in Scotland, and the North of England . . . in Company with E. Fry. With Some General Observations on the Subject of Prison Discipline.* London, 1819.

Great Britain Parliament, House of Commons. *A Report from the Committee Appointed to Enquire into the State of the Goals of This Kingdom: Relating to the Marshalsea Prison; and Farther Relating to the Fleet Prison. With the Resolution of the House of Commons Thereupon.* London, 1729.

Haines, Richard. *A Model of Government for the Good of the Poor and the Wealth of the Nation . . . the Stock Rais'd and Presented, All Poor People and Their Children for Ever Comfortable Provided for, All Idle Hands Employed . . . all Beggars and Vagrants for the Future Restrained, Poor Prisoners for Debt Relieved, and Malefactors Reclaimed.* London, 1678.

Halifax, James. *A Sermon Preached at the Parish Church of St. Paul, Covent-Garden, on Thursday, May 18, 1775, for the Benefit of Unfortunate Persons Confined for Small Debts.* Published by Request of the Society. London, 1775.

Halkerston, Peter. *A Treatise on the History, Law, and Privileges of the Palace and Sanctuary of Holyroodhouse.* Edinburgh, 1831.

*The Honour and Advantage of Great Britain, in a General Act of Redemption for Insolvent Debtors.* London, 1707.

Howard, John. *The State of the Prisons in England and Wales, with Preliminary Observations, and an Account of Some Foreign Prisons and Hospitals.* 2nd edn. Warrington, 1780.

   *Appendix to the State of the Prisons in England and Wales, Containing a Farther Account of Foreign Prisons and Hospitals, with Additional Remarks on the Prisons of This Country.* Warrington, 1780.

*An Humble Representation upon the Perpetual Imprisonment of Insolvent Debtors.* London, 1687

Ilive, Jacob. *Reasons Offered for the Reformation of the House of Correction in Clerkenwell.* London, 1757.

*Imprisonment of Mens Bodyes for Debt, as the Practise of England Now Stands . . .* London, 1641.

*An Introduction to Scottish Legal History / by Various Authors; with an Introduction by Lord Normand.* Edinburgh, 1958.

Johnson, Christopher William. *Considerations on the Case of the Confined Debtors in This Kingdom.* London, 1793.

Mackay, John. *A True State of the Proceedings of the Prisoners in the Fleet-Prison: In Order to the Redressing Their Grievances before the Court of Common-Pleas: Impartially Collected and Publish'd as a Key for the More Clear Apprehension of Some Part of the Late Glorious and Memorable Report in Parliament.* Westminster, 1729.

Mackie, Charles. *The History of the Abbey, Palace, and Chapel-Royal of Holyroodhouse.* Edinburgh, 1825.

Macky, John. *A Journey through England: In Familiar Letters from a Gentleman Here, to His Friend Abroad.* London, 1722.

Macmillan, Anthony. *Forms of Writings Used in Scotland, in the Most Common Cases.* The second edition, with considerable additions. Edinburgh, 1786.

North, Roger. *The Gentleman Accomptant: Or, an Essay to Unfold the Mystery of Accompts. By Way of Debtor and Creditor, Commonly Called Merchants Accompts, . . . Done by a Person of Honour.* London, 1714.

Pringle, John. *Observations on the Nature and Cure of Hospital and Jayl-Fevers.* London, 1750.

*Reasons Humbly Offered for an Act for Relief of Insolvent Debtors, and Fugitives for Debt.* London, 1753.

*Six Discourses, Delivered by Sir John Pringle, Bart. When President of the Royal Society; On Occasion of Six Annual Assignments of Sir Godfrey Copley's Medal . . .* London, 1783.

Smith, William. *Mild Punishments Sound Policy: Or Observations on the Laws Relative to Debtors and Felons, With an Account of the Frauds Practised by Swindlers, Sharpers and Others. Also, Some Clauses Necessary in Any Future Insolvent Act; and a Plan for the Relief of Poor Distressed Families and Others, The Second Edition, with an Appendix, Wherein Hard Labour, Substituted in Place of Transportation, Is Elucidated and Proved to Be Sound Policy, and Profitable to the State.* London, 1778.

Smollett, Tobias. *The Adventures of Sir Launcelot Greaves.* London, 1762.

Society for the Discharge and Relief of Persons Imprisoned for Small Debts, *An Account of the Rise, Progress and Present State of the Society for the Discharge and Relief of Persons Imprisoned for Small Debts throughout England and Wales.* London, 1774.

*Some Thoughts Concerning Government in General: And Our Present Circumstances in Great Britain and Ireland.* Dublin, 1731.

Stair, James Dalrymple. *The Institutions of the Law of Scotland, Deduced from Its Originals, and Collated from the Civil, and Feudal Laws, and with the Customs of Neighbouring Nations. In Four Books.* Edinburgh, 1759.

Townshend, Charles *National thoughts, recommended to the serious attention of the public. With an appendix, shewing the damages arising from a bounty on corn. By a Land-owner.* London, 1751.

*A True Description of the Mint: Giving an Account of Its First Becoming a Place of Refuge for Debtors.* 1710.

## Secondary Sources

Adam, Barbara, Ulrich Beck and Joost van Loon, eds. *The Risk Society and Beyond: Critical Issues for Social Theory*. London, 2000.

Allen, Robert C. *The British Industrial Revolution in Global Perspective*. Cambridge, 2009.

Agnew, Jean-Christophe. *Worlds Apart: The Market and the Theater in Anglo-American Thought, 1550–1750*. Cambridge, 1986.

Ågren, Maria, ed. *Making a Living, Making a Difference: Gender and Work in Early Modern European Society*. Oxford, 2016.

Amussen, Susan Dwyer. *An Ordered Society: Gender and Class in Early Modern England*. New York, 1993.

Anderson, B. L. 'Money and the Structure of Credit in the Eighteenth Century'. *Business History* 12, no. 2 (1 July 1970): 85–101.

Andrew, Donna T. and Randall McGowen. *The Perreaus and Mrs. Rudd: Forgery and Betrayal in Eighteenth-Century London*. Berkeley, CA, 2001.

Arkell, Tom, Nesta Evans and Nigel Goose, eds. *When Death Do Us Part: Understanding and Interpreting the Probate Records of Early Modern England*. Oxford, 2000.

Ascott, Diana E., Fiona Lewis and Michael Power. *Liverpool 1660–1750: People, Prosperity and Power*. Liverpool, 2006.

Ashton, T. S. *Economic Fluctuations in England, 1700–1800*. Oxford, 1959.

Aston, Jennifer and Paolo Di Martino. 'Risk, Success, and Failure: Female Entrepreneurship in Late Victorian and Edwardian England'. *The Economic History Review* 70, no. 3 (2017): 837–58.

Bailey, Amanda. *Of Bondage: Debt, Property, and Personhood in Early Modern England*. 1st edn. Philadelphia, PA, 2013.

Bailey, Joanne. *Unquiet Lives: Marriage and Marriage Breakdown in England, 1660–1800*. Cambridge, 2003.

Bailey, Merridee L. 'Economic Records'. In *Early Modern Emotions: An Introduction*. Edited by Susan Broomhall, 108–11. London, 2016.

Bailyn, Bernard. *Voyagers to the West: Emigration from Britain to America on the Eve of Revolution*. London, 1987.

Balleisen, Edward J. *Navigating Failure: Bankruptcy and Commercial Society in Antebellum America*. Chapel Hill, NC, 2001.

Barker, Hannah. *The Business of Women: Female Enterprise and Urban Development in Northern England 1760–1830*. Oxford, 2006.

 *Family and Business during the Industrial Revolution*. Oxford, 2016.

 'Soul, Purse and Family: Middling and Lower-Class Masculinity in Eighteenth-Century Manchester'. *Social History* 33, no. 1 (2008): 12–35.

Barrell, John. *The Political Theory of Painting from Reynolds to Hazlitt: 'The Body of the Public'*. New Haven, CT, 1986.

Barrie, David G. and Susan Broomhall. *Police Courts in Nineteenth-Century Scotland*. Farnham, 2014.

Barry, Jonathan. 'Bourgeois Collectivism? Urban Association and the Middling Sort'. In *The Middling Sort of People: Culture, Society and Politics in England: 1550–1800*. Edited by Jonathan Barry and Christopher Brooks, 84–112. Basingstoke, 1994.

Barry, Jonathan and Christopher Brooks, eds. *The Middling Sort of People: Culture, Society and Politics in England, 1550–1800*. Basingstoke, 1994.

Beattie, J. M. 'London Crime and the Making of the "Bloody Code" 1689–1718'. In *Stilling the Grumbling Hive: The Response to Social and Economic Problems in England, 1689–1750*. Edited by Lee Davison, Robert B. Shoemaker, Tim Keirn and Tim Hitchcock, 49–76. Stroud, 1992.

*Policing and Punishment in London 1660–1750: Urban Crime and the Limits of Terror*. Oxford, 2001.

Beck, Ulrich and Mark Ritter. *Risk Society: Towards a New Modernity*. London, 1992.

Beckles, Hilary McD. 'Plantation Production and White "Proto-Slavery": White Indentured Servants and the Colonisation of the English West Indies, 1624–1645'. *The Americas* 41, no. 3 (January 1985): 21–45.

Ben-Amos, Ilana Krausman. 'Failure to Become Freemen: Urban Apprentices in Early Modern England'. *Social History* 16, no. 2 (1991): 155–72.

Benjamin, Walter. 'Critique of Violence'. In *Reflections: Essays, Aphorisms, Autobiographical Writings*. Edited by Peter Demelz, 277–300. New York, 1978.

Berg, Maxine. *The Age of Manufactures: 1700–1820: Industry, Innovation and Work in Britain*. London, 2005.

*Luxury and Pleasure in Eighteenth-Century Britain*. Oxford, 2005.

Small Producer Capitalism in Eighteenth-Century England'. *Business History* 35, no. 1 (1993): 17–39.

Berry, Daina Ramey. *The Price for Their Pound of Flesh: The Value of the Enslaved, from Womb to Grave, in the Building of a Nation*. Boston, MA, 2017.

Berry, Helen. 'Polite Consumption: Shopping in Eighteenth-Century England'. *Transactions of the Royal Historical Society* 12 (2002): 375–94.

'Rethinking Politeness in Eighteenth-Century England: Moll King's Coffee House and the Significance of "Flash Talk"'. *Transactions of the Royal Historical Society* 11 (2001): 65–81.

Blackie, John 'Defamation'. In *A History of Private Law in Scotland. Volume 2: Obligations*. Edited by Kenneth Reid and Reinhard Zimmermann, 633–708. Oxford, 2000.

Borsay, Peter. *The English Urban Renaissance: Culture and Society in the Provincial Town, 1660–1770*. Oxford, 1989.

Boulton, Jeremy. 'Microhistory in Early Modern London: John Bedford (1601–1667)'. *Continuity and Change* 22, no. 1 (2007): 113–41.

*Neighbourhood and Society: A London Suburb in the Seventeenth Century*. Cambridge, 2005.

'Traffic in Corpses and the Commodification of Burial in Georgian London'. *Continuity and Change* 29, no. 2 (2014): 181–208.

Bound, Fay. '"An Angry and Malicious Mind"? Narratives of Slander at the Church Courts of York, c.1660–c.1760'. *History Workshop Journal*, no. 56 (2003): 59–77.

Bourdieu, Pierre. *Distinction: A Social Critique of the Judgement of Taste*. London, 1979.

'Forms of Capital'. In *Handbook of Theory and Research for the Sociology of Education*. Edited by J. G. Richardson, 47–58. New York, 1986.

*Outline of a Theory of Practice*. Cambridge, 1977.

Brantlinger, Patrick. *Fictions of State: Culture and Credit in Britain, 1694–1994*. Ithaca, NY, 1996.

Brewer, John and Roy Porter, eds. *Consumption and the World of Goods*. London; New York, 1993.

Briggs, Chris. *Credit and Village Society in Fourteenth-Century England*. Oxford, 2009.

Broadberry, Stephen, Bruce M. S. Campbell, Mark Overton, Alexander Klein and Bas van Leeuwen. *British Economic Growth, 1270–1870*. Cambridge, 2015.

Brooks, Christopher. 'Apprenticeship, Social Mobility and the Middling Sort, 1550–1800'. In *The Middling Sort of People: Culture, Society, and Politics in England, 1550–1800*. Edited by Jonathan Barry and Christopher Brooks, 52–83. Basingstoke, 1994.

*Law, Politics and Society in Early Modern England*. Cambridge, 2008.

*Lawyers, Litigation and English Society since 1450*. London, 1998.

*Pettyfoggers and Vipers of the Commonwealth: The 'Lower Branch' of the Legal Profession in Early Modern England*. Cambridge, 1986.

Broomhall, Susan and Jacqueline van Gent. 'Policing Bodies in Urban Scotland, 1780–1850'. In *Governing Masculinities in the Early Modern Period: Regulating Selves and Others*. Edited by Susan Broomhall and Jacqueline van Gent, 263–82. Aldershot, 2011.

Capp, Bernard. 'The Double Standard Revisited: Plebeian Women and Male Sexual Reputation in Early Modern England'. *Past & Present* 162, no. 1 (1999): 70–100.

*When Gossips Meet: Women, Family, and Neighbourhood in Early Modern England*. Oxford, 2004.

Carr, Rosalind. *Gender and Enlightenment Culture in Eighteenth-Century Scotland*. Edinburgh, 2014.

Carter, Philip. 'James Boswell's Manliness'. In *English Masculinities, 1660–1800*. Edited by Tim Hitchcock and Michèle Cohen, 111–30. London, 1999.

*Men and the Emergence of Polite Society, Britain, 1660–1800*. Abingdon, 2001.

Cavert, William M. *Smoke of London: Energy and Environment in the Early Modern City*. Cambridge, 2017.

Champion, W. A. 'Recourse to the Law and the Meaning of the Great Litigation Decline, 1650–1750: Some Clues from the Shrewsbury Local Courts'. In *Communities and Courts in Britain, 1150–1900*. Edited by Christopher Brooks and Michael Lobban, 179–98. London, 1997.

Chase, Malcolm. *Early Trade Unionism: Fraternity, Skill, and the Politics of Labour.* Aldershot, 2000.

Christensen, Jerome. *Practicing Enlightenment: Hume and the Formation of a Literary Career.* Madison, WI, 1987.

Clark, Geoffrey Wilson. *Betting on Lives: The Culture of Life Insurance in England, 1695–1775.* Manchester; New York, 1999.

Clark, Peter. *British Clubs and Societies 1580–1800: The Origins of an Associational World.* Oxford, 2000.

Cody, Lisa Forman. '"No Cure, No Money," or the Invisible Hand of Quackery: The Language of Commerce, Credit, and Cash in Eighteenth-Century British Medical Advertisements'. *Studies in Eighteenth-Century Culture* 28, no. 1 (2010): 103–30.

Cohen, Gerald Allan. *Self-Ownership, Freedom, and Equality.* Cambridge, 2010.

Cohen, Stanley and Andrew T. Scull, eds. *Social Control and the State: Historical and Comparative Essays.* Oxford, 1983.

Coquery, Natacha. *L'hôtel Aristocratique. Le Marché Du Luxe à Paris Au XVIIIe Siècle.* Paris, 1998.

Crafts, N. F. R. *British Economic Growth during the Industrial Revolution.* Oxford; New York, 1985.

Crossick, Geoffrey and Heinz-Gerhard Haupt. *The Petite Bourgeoisie in Europe 1780–1914: Enterprise, Family and Independence.* London 1998.

Crossick, Geoffrey. 'Meanings of Property and the World of the Petite Bourgeoisie'. In *Urban Fortunes: Property and Inheritance in the Town, 1700–1900.* Edited by Jon Stobart and Alastair Owens, 50–78. Aldershot; Burlington, VT, 2000.

'Metaphors of the Middle: The Discovery of the Petite Bourgeoisie 1880–1914'. *Transactions of the Royal Historical Society* 4 (1994): 251–79.

Crossick, Geoffrey, ed. *The Artisan and the European Town, 1500–1900.* Aldershot, 1997.

Crowston, Clare Haru. *Credit, Fashion, Sex: Economies of Regard in Old Regime France.* Durham, NC; London, 2013.

Dabhoiwala, Faramerz. 'The Construction of Honour, Reputation and Status in Late Seventeenth- and Early Eighteenth-Century England'. *Transactions of the Royal Historical Society* 6 (1996): 201–13.

Dancy, J. Ross. *The Myth of the Press Gang: Volunteers, Impressment and the Naval Manpower Problem in the Late Eighteenth Century.* Woodbridge, 2015.

Daunton, Martin. *Progress and Poverty: An Economic and Social History of Britain, 1700–1850.* Oxford, 1995.

D'Cruze, Shani. 'The Middling Sort in Eighteenth-Century Colchester: Independence, Social Relations and the Community Broker'. In *The Middling Sort of People: Culture, Society, and Politics in England, 1550–1800.* Edited by Jonathan Barry and Christopher Brooks, 181–207. Basingstoke, 1994.

de Vries, Jan. *The Industrious Revolution: Consumer Behaviour and the Household Economy, 1650 to the Present.* Cambridge, 2008.

Deane, Phyllis and W. A. Cole. *British Economic Growth, 1688–1959: Trends and Structure.* Cambridge, 1962.

Devereaux, Simon. 'England's "Bloody Code" in Crisis and Transition: Executions at the Old Bailey, 1760–1837'. *Journal of the Canadian Historical Association* 24, no. 2 (2013): 71–113.

Dickson, P. G. M. *The Financial Revolution in England: A Study in the Development of Public Credit, 1688–1756.* London, 1967.

Dingwall, Helen M. *Late Seventeenth-Century Edinburgh: A Demographic Study.* Aldershot, 1994.

Ditz, Toby L. 'Shipwrecked; Or, Masculinity Imperiled: Mercantile Representations of Failure and the Gendered Self in Eighteenth-Century Philadelphia'. *The Journal of American History* 81, no. 1 (1994): 51–80.

Dolan, Frances E. *True Relations: Reading, Literature, and Evidence in Seventeenth-Century England.* Philadelphia, PA, 2013.

Dorey, Margaret. 'Reckliss Endangerment? Feeding the Poor Prisoners of London in the Early Eighteenth Century'. In *Experiences of Poverty in Late Medieval and Early Modern England and France.* Edited by Anne M. Scott, 183–98. London, 2016.

Douglas, Mary and Aaron B. Wildavsky. *Risk and Culture: An Essay on the Selection of Technological and Environmental Dangers.* Berkeley, CA, 1983.

Earle, Peter. *The Making of the English Middle Class: Business, Society, and Family Life in London, 1660–1730.* Berkeley, CA, 1989.

Eastwood, David. *Government and Community in the English Provinces, 1700–1870.* Basingstoke, 1997.

Elias, Norbert. *The Civilizing Process: Sociogenetic and Psychogenetic Investigations.* Rev. edn. Translated by Edmund Jephcott, with contributions by Eric Dunning, Johan Goudsblom and Stephen Mennell. Oxford; Malden, MA, 2000.

Emmison, F. G. *Elizabethan Life*, vol. 2. Chelmsford, 1973.

England, Paula. 'Separative and Soluble Selves: Dichotomous Thinking in Economics'. In *Feminism Confronts Homo Economicus: Gender, Law and Society.* Edited by Martha Albertson Fineman and Terence Dougherty, 32–56. Ithaca, NY, 2005.

Erickson, Amy Louise. 'The Marital Economy in Perspective'. In *The Marital Economy in Scandinavia and Britain, 1400–1900.* Edited by Amy Louise Erickson and Maria Ågren, 3–20. Aldershot, 2005.

'Married Women's Occupations in Eighteenth-Century London'. *Continuity and Change* 23, no. 2 (2008): 267–307.

*Women and Property in Early Modern England.* London; New York, 1993.

Eustace, Nicole. *Passion Is the Gale: Emotion, Power, and the Coming of the American Revolution.* Chapel Hill, NC, 2008.

Ewen, Lorna. 'Debtors, Imprisonment and the Privilege of Girth'. In *Perspectives in Scottish Social History: Essays in Honour of Rosalind Mitchison.* Edited by Leah Leneman, 53–68. Aberdeen, 1988.

Fiebranz, Rosemarie, Erik Lindberg, Jonas Lindström and Maria Ågren. 'Making Verbs Count: The Research Project "Gender and Work" and Its

Methodology'. *Scandinavian Economic History Review* 59, no. 3 (1 November 2011): 273–93.

Fineman, Martha. 'The Vulnerable Subject: Anchoring Equality in the Human Condition'. *Yale Journal of Law & Feminism* 20, no. 1 (2008): 1–23.

Finn, Margot C. *The Character of Credit: Personal Debt in English Culture, 1740–1914*. Cambridge, 2003.

'Women, Consumption and Coverture in England, c. 1760–1860'. *The Historical Journal* 39, no. 3 (1996): 703–22.

Fletcher, Anthony. *Gender, Sex, and Subordination in England, 1500–1800*. New Haven, CT, 1995.

Flinn, Michael Walter, Duncan Adamson and Robin Lobban. *Scottish Population History from the 17th Century to the 1930s*. Cambridge, 1977.

Floud, Roderick, ed. *The Changing Body: Health, Nutrition, and Human Development in the Western World since 1700*. Cambridge, 2011.

Fontaine, Laurence. 'Antonio and Shylock: Credit and Trust in France, C. 1680–C. 1780'. *The Economic History Review* 54, no. 1 (2001): 39–57.

'The Circulation of Luxury Goods in Eighteenth-Century Paris: Social Redistribution and an Alternative Currency'. In *Luxury in the Eighteenth Century: Debates, Desires and Delectable Goods*. Edited by Maxine Berg and Elizabeth Eger, 89–102. London, 2002.

*The Moral Economy: Poverty, Credit, and Trust in Early Modern Europe*. New York, 2014.

Force, Pierre. *Self-Interest before Adam Smith: A Genealogy of Economicscience*. Cambridge, 2003.

Foucault, Michel. *Discipline and Punish: The Birth of the Prison*. New York, 1977.

Foyster, Elizabeth A. 'Boys Will Be Boys? Manhood and Aggression, 1660–1800'. In *English Masculinities, 1660–1800*. Edited by Tim Hitchcock and Michèle Cohen, 151–66. London, 1999.

*Manhood in Early Modern England: Honour, Sex and Marriage*. London, 1999.

French, Henry. '"Ingenious & Learned Gentlemen": Social Perceptions and Self-Fashioning among Parish Elites in Essex, 1680–1740'. *Social History* 25, no. 1 (2000): 44–66.

*The Middle Sort of People in Provincial England 1600–1750*. Oxford, 2007.

French, Henry and Jonathan Barry, eds. *Identity and Agency in England, 1500–1800*. Basingstoke, 2004.

Frevert, Ute. *Emotions in History: Lost and Found*. Budapest, 2011.

Froide, Amy M. *Silent Partners: Women as Public Investors during Britain's Financial Revolution, 1690–1750*. Oxford, 2016.

Garnot, Benoît. 'Justice, infrajustice, parajustice et extra justice dans la France d'Ancien Régime'. *Crime, Histoire & Sociétés / Crime, History & Societies* 4, no. 1 (2000): 103–20.

George, Mary Dorothy. *London Life in the XVIIIth Century*. London; New York, 1925.

Gibson, A. J. S. and T. C. Smout, *Prices, Food and Wages in Scotland, 1550–1780*. Cambridge, 1995.

Giddens, Anthony. *The Consequences of Modernity*. Cambridge, 1991.

Gittings, Clare. *Death, Burial and the Individual in Early Modern England*. London, 1984.

Glaisyer, Natasha. 'Calculating Credibility: Print Culture, Trust and Economic Figures in Early Eighteenth-Century England'. *The Economic History Review* 60, no. 4 (2007): 685–711.

*The Culture of Commerce in England 1660–1720*. London, 2011.

'"A Due Circulation in the Veins of the Publick": Imagining Credit in Late Seventeenth- and Early Eighteenth-Century England'. *The Eighteenth Century: Theory and Interpretation* 46, no. 3 (2005): 277–97.

Gowing, Laura. *Common Bodies: Women, Touch, and Power in Seventeenth-Century England*. New Haven, CT, 2003.

*Domestic Dangers: Women, Words, and Sex in Early Modern London*. Oxford, 2005.

'Gender and the Language of Insult in Early Modern London'. *History Workshop Journal*, no. 35 (1993): 1–21.

'Language, Power and the Law: Women's Slander Litigation in Early Modern London'. In *Women, Crime and the Courts in Early Modern England*. Edited by Jenny Kermode and Garthine Walker, 26–47. London, 1994.

Gráda, Cormac Ó. 'Neither Feast nor Famine: England before the Industrial Revolution'. In *Institutions, Innovation and Industrialization*. Edited by Avner Greif, Lynne Kiesling and John Nye, 7–32. Princeton, NJ, 2015.

Graeber, David. *Debt: The First 5,000 Years*. Brooklyn, NY, 2014.

Graham, Michael F. *The Blasphemies of Thomas Aikenhead: Boundaries of Belief on the Eve of the Enlightenment*. Edinburgh, 2008.

Greif, Avner. *Institutions and the Path to the Modern Economy: Lessons from Medieval Trade*. Cambridge, 2006.

Haagen, Paul. 'Eighteenth Century English Society and the Debt Law'. In *Social Control and the State: Historical and Comparative Essays*. Edited by Stanley Cohen and Andrew Scull, 222–47. Oxford, 1983.

Haggerty, Sheryllynne. *'Merely for Money'? Business Culture in the British Atlantic, 1750–1815*. Liverpool, 2012.

Hailwood, Mark. '"The Honest Tradesman's Honour": Occupational and Social Identity in Seventeenth-Century England'. *Transactions of the Royal Historical Society (Sixth Series)* 24 (2014): 79–103.

Halliday, Paul D. *Habeas Corpus: From England to Empire*. Cambridge, MA, 2010.

Harding, Vanessa. 'The Population of London, 1550–1700: A Review of the Published Evidence'. *The London Journal* 15, no. 2 (November 1990): 111–28.

Hardwick, Julie. 'Parasols and Poverty: Conjugal Marriage, Global Economy, and Rethinking the Consumer Revolution'. In *Market Ethics and Practices, c.1300–1850*. Edited by Simon Middleton and James E. Shaw, 129–49. New York, 2018.

Hall, Catherine. 'Gendering Property, Racing Capital'. *History Workshop Journal* 78, no. 1 (1 October 2014): 22–38.

Hannah, Hugh. 'The Sanctuary of Holyrood'. *Book of the Old Edinburgh Club* 15 (1927): 55–98.

Harris, Robert and Charles McKean. *The Scottish Town in the Age of Enlightenment 1740–1820*. Edinburgh, 2014.

Hartigan-O'Connor, Ellen. *The Ties That Buy: Women and Commerce in Revolutionary America*. Philadelphia, PA, 2009.

Harvey, Karen. *The Little Republic: Masculinity and Domestic Authority in Eighteenth-Century Britain*. Oxford, 2012.

Harvey, Karen and Alexandra Shepard. 'What Have Historians Done with Masculinity? Reflections on Five Centuries of British History, circa 1500–1950'. *Journal of British Studies* 44, no. 2 (2005): 274–80.

Hay, Douglas. 'Property, Authority and the Criminal Law'. In *Albion's Fatal Tree: Crime and Society in Eighteenth-Century England*. Edited by Douglas Hay, Peter Linebaugh and John G. Rule, 17–64. London, 1975.

Heal, Felicity. *The Power of Gifts: Gift-Exchange in Early Modern England*. Oxford, 2014.

Hindle, Steve. *On the Parish? The Micro-Politics of Poor Relief in Rural England, c. 1550–1750*. Oxford, 2004.

'The Shaming of Margaret Knowsley: Gossip, Gender and the Experience of Authority in Early Modern England'. *Continuity and Change* 9, no. 3 (1994): 391–419.

Hirschman, Albert O. *The Passions and the Interests: Political Arguments for Capitalism before Its Triumph*. Princeton, NJ, 1997.

Hitchcock, Tim. *Down and Out in Eighteenth-Century London*. London, 2004.

Hitchcock, Tim and Robert B. Shoemaker. *London Lives: Poverty, Crime and the Making of a Modern City, 1690–1800*. Cambridge, 2015.

Hoffman, Philip, Jean-Laurent Rosenthal and Gilles Postel-Vinay, *Dark Matter Credit: Peer to Peer Lending and Banking in France*. Princeton, NJ, 2019.

Holderness, B. A. 'Credit in a Rural Community, 1660–1800: Some Neglected Aspects of Probate Inventories'. *Midland History* 3, no. 2 (1975): 94–116.

Holdsworth, William. *A History of English Law*. London, 1938.

Hoock, Holger. *The King's Artists: The Royal Academy of Arts and the Politics of British Culture, 1760–1840*. Oxford, 2003.

Hoppit, Julian. 'Attitudes to Credit in Britain, 1680–1790'. *The Historical Journal* 33, no. 2 (1990): 305–22.

*A Land of Liberty? England, 1689–1727*. Oxford, 2000.

*Risk and Failure in English Business 1700–1800*. Cambridge, 1987.

Houston, R. A. 'Economy of Edinburgh, 1694–1763'. In *Conflict and Identity in the Economic and Social History of Ireland and Scotland since the 17th Century*. Edited by S. J. Connolly, R. J. Morris and R. A. Houston, 45–63. Edinburgh, 1992.

Popular Politics in the Reign of George II: The Edinburgh Cordiners'. *Scottish Historical Review* 72 (1993).

*The Population History of Britain and Ireland, 1500–1750*. Basingstoke, 1992.

*Social Change in the Age of Enlightenment: Edinburgh, 1660–1760*. Oxford, 1994.

Hudson, Pat. *The Genesis of Industrial Capital: A Study of the West Riding Wool Textile Industry, C. 1750–1850*. Cambridge; New York, 1986.

Humphries, Jane. *Childhood and Child Labour in the British Industrial Revolution*. Cambridge, 2010.

Humphries, Jane and Carmen Sarasua. 'Off the Record: Reconstructing Women's Labor Force Participation in the European Past'. *Feminist Economics* 18, no. 4 (2012): 39–67.

Hunt, Margaret R. *The Middling Sort: Commerce, Gender, and the Family in England, 1680–1780*. Berkeley, CA, 1996.

Hylland Eriksen, Thomas. 'Human Security and Social Anthropology'. In *A World of Insecurity: Anthropological Perspectives on Human Security*. Edited by Thomas Hylland Eriksen, Ellen Bal and Oscar Salemink, 1–19. London, 2010.

Ignatieff, Michael. *A Just Measure of Pain: The Penitentiary in the Industrial Revolution, 1750–1850*. New York, 1978.

Ingram, Martin. *Church Courts, Sex and Marriage in England, 1570–1640*. Cambridge, 1990.

Innes, Joanna. 'The King's Bench Prison in the Later Eighteenth Century: Law, Authority and Order in a London Debtor's Prison'. In *An Ungovernable People: The English and Their Law in the Seventeenth and Eighteenth Centuries*. Edited by John Brewer and John A. Styles, 250–98. London, 1980.

Jackson, Peter. 'The Cultural Politics of Masculinity: Towards a Social Geography'. *Transactions of the Institute of British Geographers* 16, no. 2 (1991): 199–213.

Jacob, Margaret C. *The First Knowledge Economy: Human Capital and the European Economy, 1750–1850*. Cambridge 2014.

Johnson, Lynn. 'Friendship, Coercion and Interest: Debating the Foundations of Justice in Early Modern England'. *Journal of Early Modern History* 8 (2004): 46–64.

Jones, Gareth Stedman. *An End to Poverty? A Historical Debate*. London, 2004.

Jones, Howard Mumford. 'The Colonial Impulse: An Analysis of the "Promotion" Literature of Colonization'. *Proceedings of the American Philosophical Society* 90 (1946): 131–61.

Joyce, Patrick. *The Historical Meanings of Work*. Cambridge, 1989.

Kadane, Matthew. 'Self-Discipline and the Struggle for the Middle in Eighteenth-Century Britain'. In *In Praise of Ordinary People: Early Modern Britain and the Dutch Republic*. Edited by Margaret C. Jacob and Catherine Secretan, 257–73. Basingstoke, 2013.

*The Watchful Clothier: The Life of an Eighteenth-Century Protestant Capitalist*. New Haven, CT, 2013.

Kadens, Emily. 'The Last Bankrupt Hanged: Balancing Incentives in the Development of Bankruptcy Law'. *Duke Law Journal* 59, no. 7 (2010): 1229–1319.

Kane, Hope Frances. *Colonial Promotion and Promotional Literature of Carolina, Pennsylvania, and New Jersey, 1660–1700*. Ann Arbor, MI, 1948.

Keibek, Sebastian A. J. and Leigh Shaw-Taylor. 'Early Modern Rural By-Employments: A Re-examination of the Probate Inventory Evidence'. *Agricultural History Review* 61, no. 2 (31 December 2013): 244–81.

Kelly, Morgan and Cormac Ó Gráda. 'Numerare Est Errare: Agricultural Output and Food Supply in England before and during the Industrial Revolution'. *Journal of Economic History* 73, no. 4 (December 2013): 1132–63.

King, Steven and Alannah Tomkins, eds. *The Poor in England, 1700–1850: An Economy of Makeshifts*. Manchester, 2010.

Klein, Lawrence. 'Politeness for Plebes. Consumption and Social Identity in Early Eighteenth-Century England'. In *The Consumption of Culture, 1600–1800: Image, Object, Text*. Edited by Ann Bermingham and John Brewer, 362–82. London, 1995.

Kramer, Matthew H. *John Locke and the Origins of Private Property: Philosophical Explorations of Individualism, Community, and Equality*. Cambridge, 2004.

Kuznets, Simon. 'Economic Growth and Income Inequality'. *The American Economic Review* 45, no. 1 (1955): 1–28.

Landers, John. *Death and the Metropolis: Studies in the Demographic History of London, 1670–1830*. Cambridge, 1993.

Langford, Paul. *A Polite and Commercial People: England 1727–1783*. Oxford, 1989.
  'The Uses of Eighteenth-Century Politeness'. *Transactions of the Royal Historical Society* 12 (2002): 311–31.

Laqueur, Thomas W. *The Work of the Dead: A Cultural History of Mortal Remains*. Princeton, NJ, 2015.

Lemire, Beverly. *The Business of Everyday Life: Gender, Practice and Social Politics in England, c.1600–1900*. Manchester, 2005.
  *Fashion's Favourite: The Cotton Trade and the Consumer in Britain, 1660–1800*. Oxford, 1991.
  'Petty Pawns and Informal Lending: Gender and the Transformation of Small-Scale Credit in England, circa 1600–1800'. In *From Family Firms to Corporate Capitalism: Essays in Business and Industrial History in Honour of Peter Mathias*. Edited by Christine Bruland and Patrick O'Brien, 112–38. Oxford, 1998.

Lemmings, David. 'Law and Order, Moral Panics and Early Modern England'. In *Moral Panics, the Media and the Law in Early Modern England*. Edited by David Lemmings and Claire Walker, 1–21. Basingstoke, 2009.

Leneman, Leah. *Alienated Affections: The Scottish Experience of Divorce and Separation, 1684–1830*. Edinburgh, 1998.
  'Defamation in Scotland, 1750–1800'. *Continuity and Change* 15, no. 2 (2000): 209–34.
  'Legitimacy and Bastardy in Scotland, 1694–1830'. *Scottish Historical Review* 80, no. 20 (2001): 45–62.

Leneman, Leah and Rosalind Mitchison. *Sin in the City: Sexuality and Social Control in Urban Scotland 1660–1780*. Edinburgh, 1998.

Lindert, Peter H. and Jeffrey G. Williamson. 'Revising England's Social Tables 1688–1812'. *Explorations in Economic History* 19 (1982): 385–408.

Lindström, Jonas, Rosemarie Fiebranz and Göran Rydén. 'The Diversity of Work'. In *Making a Living, Making a Difference: Gender and Work in Early Modern European Society*. Edited by Maria Ågren, 24–56. Oxford, 2016.

Linebaugh, Peter. *The London Hanged: Crime and Civil Society in the Eighteenth Century*. Cambridge, 1992.

Lloyd, Sarah. 'Cottage Conversations: Poverty and Manly Independence in Eighteenth-Century England'. *Past & Present* 184, no. 1 (2004): 69–108.

Lucassen, Jan. 'Deep Monetisation: The Case of the Netherlands 1200–1940'. *The Low Countries Journal of Social and Economic History* 11, no. 3 (2014): 73–121.

Lynch, Jack. *Deception and Detection in Eighteenth-Century Britain*. Aldershot, 2008.

MacKay, Lynn. 'Why They Stole: Women in the Old Bailey, 1779–1789'. *Journal of Social History* 32 (1999): 623–40.

Mann, Bruce H. *Neighbors and Strangers: Law and Community in Early Connecticut*. Chapel Hill, NC, 1987.

  *Republic of Debtors: Bankruptcy in the Age of American Independence*. Cambridge, MA, 2002.

Mascuch, Michael. *Origins of the Individualist Self: Autobiography and Self-Identity in England, 1591–1791*. Stanford, CA, 1996.

  'Social Mobility and Middling Self-Identity: The Ethos of British Autobiographers, 1600–1750'. *Social History* 20, no. 1 (1995): 45–61.

Mathias, Peter. 'Capital, Credit and Enterprise in the Industrial Revolution'. *Journal of European Economic History* 2, no. 1 (1973): 121–43.

  'Risk, Credit and Kinship in Early Modern Enterprise'. In *The Early Modern Atlantic Economy*. Edited by John J. McCusker and Kenneth Morgan, 15–35. Cambridge, 2000.

  'The Social Structure in the Eighteenth Century: A Calculation by Joseph Massie'. *The Economic History Review* 10, no. 1 (1957): 30–45.

Mauss, Marcel. *The Gift: The Form and Reason for Exchange in Archaic Societies*. New York, 2000.

McCormack, Matthew. *The Independent Man: Citizenship and Gender Politics in Georgian England*. Manchester, 2005.

McCusker, John J. *Money and Exchange in Europe and America, 1600–1775: A Handbook*. Chapel Hill, NC, 1978.

McGowen, Randall. 'The Body and Punishment in Eighteenth-Century England'. *The Journal of Modern History* 59, no. 4 (1987): 652–79.

  'Forgers and Forgery: Severity and Social Identity in Eighteenth-Century England'. In *Moral Panics, the Media and the Law in Early Modern England*. Edited by David Lemmings and Claire Walker, 157–75. Basingstoke, 2009.

  'From Pillory to Gallows: The Punishment of Forgery in the Age of the Financial Revolution'. *Past & Present* 165, no. 1 (1999): 107–40.

'Making the "Bloody Code"? Forgery Legislation in 18th-Century England'. In *Law, Crime and English Society 1660–1830*. Edited by Norman Landau, 117–38. Cambridge, 2002.

'The Well-Ordered Prison, England 1780–1865'. In *The Oxford History of the Prison: The Practice of Punishment in Western Society*. Edited by Norval Morris and David J. Rothman, 71–99. Oxford, 1998.

Mckay, Elaine. 'English Diarists: Gender, Geography and Occupation, 1500–1700'. *History* 90, no. 298 (1 April 2005): 191–212.

McKendrick, Neil, John Brewer and J. H. Plumb. *The Birth of a Consumer Society: The Commercialization of Eighteenth Century England*. London, 1982.

McLynn, Frank. *Crime and punishment in eighteenth-century England*. London, 1989.

Meldrum, Tim. 'A Women's Court in London: Defamation at the Bishop of London's Consistory Court, 1700–1745'. *The London Journal* 19, no. 1 (1994): 1–20.

Menke, Christoph. 'Law and Violence'. *Law and Literature* 22, no. 1 (2010): 1–17.

Meranze, Michael. *Laboratories of Virtue: Punishment, Revolution, and Authority in Philadelphia, 1760–1835*. Chapel Hill, NC, 1996.

Milanovic, Branko, Peter H Lindert and Jeffrey G Williamson. 'Measuring Ancient Inequality'. Working Paper. National Bureau of Economic Research, October 2007. www.nber.org/papers/w13550.

Mitchison, Rosalind. *The Old Poor Law in Scotland: The Experience of Poverty, 1574–1845*. Edinburgh, 2000.

Mokyr, Joel. *The Enlightened Economy: An Economic History of Britain, 1700–1850*. New Haven, CT, 2009.

Money, John. 'Teaching in the Marketplace, or "Caesar Adsum Jam Forte: Pompey Aderat": The Retailing of Knowledge in Provincial England during the Eighteenth Century'. In *Consumption and the World of Goods*. Edited by John Brewer and Roy Porter, 335–80. London, 1993.

Moore, Stanley Williams. 'Hobbes on Obligation, Moral and Political: Part Two: Political Obligation'. *Journal of the History of Philosophy* 10, no. 1 (1972): 29–42.

Morgan, Mary S. 'Economic Man as Model Man: Ideal Types, Idealization and Caricatures'. *Journal of the History of Economic Thought* 28, no. 1 (2006): 1–27.

Muldrew, Craig. 'Class and Credit: Social Identity, Wealth and the Life Course in Early Modern England'. In *Identity and Agency in England, 1500–1800*. Edited by Henry French and Jonathan Barry, 147–77. Basingstoke, 2004.

'Credit and the Courts: Debt Litigation in a Seventeenth-Century Urban Community'. *The Economic History Review* 46, no. 1 (1993): 23–38.

'The Culture of Reconciliation: Community and the Settlement of Economic Disputes in Early Modern England'. *The Historical Journal* 39, no. 4 (1996): 915–42.

*The Economy of Obligation: The Culture of Credit and Social Relations in Early Modern England*. Basingstoke, 1998.

*Food, Energy and the Creation of Industriousness: Work and Material Culture in Agrarian England, 1550–1780*. Cambridge; New York, 2011.

'Interpreting the Market: The Ethics of Credit and Community Relations in Early Modern England'. *Social History* 18, no. 2 (1993): 163–83.

'"A Mutual Assent of Her Mind"? Women, Debt, Litigation and Contract in Early Modern England'. *History Workshop Journal* 55, no. 1 (1 January 2003): 47–71.

'"Th'ancient Distaff" and "Whirling Spindle": Measuring the Contribution of Spinning to Household Earnings and the National Economy in England, 1550–1770?'. *The Economic History Review* 65, no. 2 (1 May 2012): 498–526.

'Wages and the Problem of Monetary Scarcity in Early Modern England'. In *Wages and Currency: Global Comparisons from Antiquity to the Twentieth Century*. Edited by Jan Lucassen, 391–410. Bern, 2007.

Murdoch, Alexander. 'The Importance of Being Edinburgh: Management and Opposition in Edinburgh Politics, 1746–1784'. *Scottish Historical Review* 62, no. 173 (1983): 1–16.

Murphy, Ann. *The Origins of English Financial Markets: Investment and Speculation before the South Sea Bubble*. Cambridge, 2012.

Myers, Milton L. *The Soul of Modern Economic Man: Ideas of Self-Interest, Thomas Hobbes to Adam Smith*. Chicago, 1983.

Nacol, Emily. *An Age of Risk: Politics and Economy in Early Modern Britain*. Princeton, NJ, 2016.

Nash, David and Anne-Marie Kilday. *Cultures of Shame: Exploring Crime and Morality in Britain 1600–1900*. Basingstoke, 2010.

Neal, Larry. 'How It All Began: The Monetary and Financial Architecture of Europe during the First Global Capital Markets, 1648–1815'. *Financial History Review* 7, no. 2 (2000): 117–40.

Neal, Patrick. 'Hobbes and Rational Choice Theory'. *The Western Political Quarterly* 41, no. 4 (1988): 635–52.

Nelson, Julie. 'Fearing Fear: Gender and Economic Discourse'. *Mind and Society: Cognitive Studies in Economics and Social Sciences* 14, no. 1 (2015): 129–39.

'Feminism and Economics'. *Journal of Economic Perspectives* 9, no. 2 (1995): 131–45.

Nenadic, Stana. *Lairds and Luxury: The Highland Gentry in Eighteenth-Century Scotland*. Edinburgh, 2007.

'Middle-Rank Consumers and Domestic Culture in Edinburgh and Glasgow 1720–1840'. *Past & Present* 145, no. 1 (1994): 122–56.

'Writing Medical Lives, Creating Posthumous Reputations: Dr Matthew Baillie and His Family in the Nineteenth Century'. *Social History of Medicine* 23, no. 3 (2010): 509–27.

Newman, Simon P. *Embodied History: The Lives of the Poor in Early Philadelphia*. Philadelphia, PA, 2013.

*A New World of Labor: The Development of Plantation Slavery in the British Atlantic*. Philadelphia, PA, 2016.

Nussbaum, Felicity. *The Autobiographical Subject: Gender and Ideology in Eighteenth-Century England*. Baltimore, MD, 1989.

Offer, Avner. 'Between the Gift and the Market: The Economy of Regard'. *The Economic History Review* 50, no. 3 (1997): 450–76.

O'Flaherty, Niall. 'Malthus and the "End of Poverty"'. In *New Perspectives on Malthus*. Edited by Robert J. Mayhew, 88–91. Cambridge, 2016.

Ogilvie, Sheilagh C. *A Bitter Living: Women, Markets, and Social Capital in Early Modern Germany*. Oxford, 2003.

Ottaway, Susannah R. *The Decline of Life: Old Age in Eighteenth-Century England*. Cambridge, 2007.

Overton, Mark. *Agricultural Revolution in England: The Transformation of the Agrarian Economy, 1500–1850*. Cambridge, 1996.

*Production and Consumption in English Households, 1600–1750*. London, 2004.

Park, Julie. *The Self and It: Novel Objects and Mimetic Subjects in Eighteenth-Century England*. Stanford, CA, 2009.

Paul, Tawny. 'Accounting for Men's Work: Multiple Employments and Occupational Identities in Early Modern England', *History Workshop Journal* 85 (2018): 26–46.

'Credit, Reputation, and Masculinity in British Urban Commerce: Edinburgh, C. 1710–70'. *The Economic History Review* 66, no. 1 (2013): 226–48.

'A "Polite and Commercial People"? Masculinity and Economic Violence in Scotland, 1700–60'. In *Nine Centuries of Man*. Edited by Elizabeth Ewan and Lynn Abrams, 203–22. Edinburgh, 2017.

Pearsall, Sarah M. S. *Atlantic Families: Lives and Letters in the Later Eighteenth Century*. Oxford; New York, 2008.

Peebles, Gustav. 'The Anthropology of Credit and Debt'. *Annual Review of Anthropology* 39, no. 1 (2010): 225–40.

'Washing away the Sins of Debt: The Nineteenth-Century Eradication of the Debtors' Prison'. *Comparative Studies in Society and History* 55, no. 3 (2013): 701–24.

Peltonen, Markku. *The Duel in Early Modern England: Civility, Politeness and Honour*. Cambridge, 2006.

Pennell, Sarah. 'Happiness in Things? Plebeian Experiences of Chattel "Property" in the Long Eighteenth Century'. In *Suffering and Happiness in England 1550–1850: Narratives and Representations: A Collection to Honour Paul Slack*. Edited by M. J. Braddick and Joanna Innes, 208–26. Oxford, 2017.

Phillips, Nicola. *The Profligate Son: Or, A True Story of Family Conflict, Fashionable Vice, and Financial Ruin in Regency Britain*. New York, 2013.

*Women in Business, 1700–1850*. Woodbridge, 2006.

Piketty, Thomas. *Capital in the Twenty-First Century*. Translated by Arthur Goldhammer. Cambridge, MA, 2014.

Pocock, J. G. A. 'The Mobility of Property and the Rise of Eighteenth-Century Sociology'. In *Virtue, Commerce and History: Essays on Political Thought and History, Chiefly in the Eighteenth Century*, 103–23. Cambridge, 1985.

Pointon, Marcia. *Hanging the Head: Portraiture and Social Formation in Eighteenth-Century England*. New Haven, CT; London, 1997.

Polanyi, Karl. *The Great Transformation: The Political and Economic Origins of Our Time*. Boston, MA, 2001.

Powell, Lucy. 'Doing Time: Temporality and Writing in the Eighteenth-Century British Prison Experience'. *Life Writing* 15, no. 1 (2 January 2018): 59–77.

Prior, Mary, ed. *Women in English Society, 1500–1800*. London; New York, 1984.

Rauser, Amelia. 'Hair, Authenticity, and the Self-Made Macaroni'. *Eighteenth-Century Studies* 38, no. 1 (2004): 101–17.

Reed, Michael. 'The Transformation of Urban Space 1700–1840'. In *The Cambridge Urban History of Britain*, vol. 2. Edited by Peter Clark, 615–40. Cambridge, 2000.

Reid, Kenneth and Reinhard Zimmermann. *A History of Private Law in Scotland. Volume 2*. Oxford, 2004.

Roberts, Michael. 'Recovering a Lost Inheritance: The Marital Economy and its Absence from the Prehistory of Economics in Britain'. In *The Marital Economy in Scandinavia and Britain, 1400–1900*. Edited by Maria Ågren and Amy Louise Erickson, 239–56. Aldershot, 2005.

Rollinson, David. 'Discourse and Class Struggle: The Politics of Industry in Early Modern England'. *Social History* 26, no. 2 (2001): 166–89.

Roper, Lyndal. 'Beyond Discourse Theory'. *Women's History Review* 19, no. 2 (1 April 2010): 307–19.

Rosanvallon, Pierre. *The Society of Equals*. Translated by Arthur Goldhammer. Cambridge, MA, 2013.

Rosenwein, Barbara H. *Anger's Past: The Social Uses of an Emotion in the Middle Ages*. Ithaca, NY, 1998.

Rozbicki, Michal J. 'To Save Them from Themselves: Proposals to Enslave the British Poor, 1698–1755'. *Slavery & Abolition* 22, no. 2 (2001): 29–50.

Rule, John. *The Labouring Classes in Early Industrial England, 1750–1850*. London, 1986.

'The Property of Skill in the Period of Manufacture'. In *The Historical Meanings of Work*. Edited by Patrick Joyce, 99–118. Cambridge, 1989.

Safley, Thomas Max, ed. *The History of Bankruptcy: Economic, Social and Cultural Implications in Early Modern Europe*. London, 2013.

Salinger, Sharon V. *'To Serve Well and Faithfully': Labour and Indentured Servants in Pennsylvania, 1682–1800*. Cambridge, 1987.

Sandage, Scott A. *Born Losers: A History of Failure in America*. Cambridge, MA; London, 2005.

Sanderson, Elizabeth C. 'Nearly New: The Second-Hand Clothing Trade in Eighteenth-Century Edinburgh'. *Costume* 31, no. 1 (1997): 38–48.

Sargent, Thomas J. and François R. Velde. *The Big Problem of Small Change*. Princeton, NJ, 2014.

Saville, Richard. *Bank of Scotland: A History, 1695–1995*. Edinburgh, 1996.

Schumpeter, Joseph A., *Business Cycles: A Theoretical, Historical, and Statistical Analysis of the Capitalist Process*, vol. 1. New York, 1939.

Schwarz, L. D. *London in the Age of Industrialization: Entrepreneurs, Labour Force and Living Conditions 1700–1850*. Cambridge, 1992.

Schwerhoff, Gerd. 'Criminalized Violence and the Process of Civilisation: A Reappraisal'. *Crime, Histoire et Sociétés* 6 (2002): 103–26.

'Early Modern Violence and the Honour Code: From Social Integration to Social Distinction?' *Crime, Histoire & Sociétés / Crime, History & Societies* 17, no. 2 (1 December 2013): 27–46.

'Social Control of Violence, Violence as Social Control: The Case of Early Modern Germany'. In *Social Control in Europe. Vol. 1, 1500–1800*. Edited by Herman Roodenburg and Pieter Spierenburg, 220–46. Columbus, OH, 2004.

Scott-Warren, Jason. 'Books in the Bedchamber: Religion, Accounting the Library of Richard Stonely'. In *Tudor Books and Readers: Materiality and the Construction of Meaning*. Edited by John N. King, 232–52. Cambridge, 2010.

Seaver, Paul S. *Wallington's World: A Puritan Artisan in Seventeenth-Century London*. Stanford, CA, 1989.

Shammas, Carole. 'Constructing a Wealth Distribution from Probate Records'. *The Journal of Interdisciplinary History* 9, no. 2 (1978): 297–307.

*The Pre-industrial Consumer in England and America*. Oxford, 1990.

Shannon, Timothy. 'A "Wicked Commerce": Consent, Coercion, and Kidnapping in Aberdeen's Servant Trade'. *The William and Mary Quarterly* 74, no. 3 (2017): 437–66.

Sharpe, J. A. *Defamation and Sexual Slander in Early Modern England: The Church Courts at York*. York, 1980.

*Judicial Punishment in England*. London, 1990.

'"Such Disagreement betwixt Neighbours": Litigation and Human Relations in Early Modern England'. In *Disputes and Settlements: Law and Human Relations in the West*. Edited by John Bossy, 167–88. Cambridge, 1983.

Shepard, Alexandra. *Accounting for Oneself: Worth, Status, and the Social Order in Early Modern England*. Oxford, 2015.

'Crediting Women in the Early Modern English Economy'. *History Workshop Journal* 79, no. 1 (Spring 2015): 1–24.

'Manhood, Credit and Patriarchy in Early Modern England C. 1580–1640'. *Past & Present* 167, no. 1 (2000): 75–106.

*Meanings of Manhood in Early Modern England*. Oxford, 2003.

'Minding Their Own Business: Married Women and Credit in Early Eighteenth-Century London'. *Transactions of the Royal Historical Society* 25 (2015): 53–74.

'Poverty, Labour and the Language of Social Description in Early Modern England'. *Past & Present* 201 (2008): 51–95.

Shimokawa, Kiyoshi. 'The Origin and Development of Property: Conventionalism, Unilateralism, and Colonialism'. In *The Oxford Handbook of British Philosophy in the Seventeenth Century*. Edited by Peter R. Anstey, 563–86. Oxford, 2013.

Shoemaker, Robert B. 'The Decline of Public Insult in London, 1660–1800'. *Past & Present* 169, no. 1 (2000): 97–131.

'Male Honour and the Decline of Public Violence in Eighteenth-Century London'. *Social History* 26, no. 2 (2001): 190–208.

'Reforming Male Manners: Public Insult and the Decline of Violence in London, 1660–1740'. In *English Masculinities, 1660–1800*. Edited by Tim Hitchcock and Michèle Cohen, 133–50. London, 1999.

Slack, Paul. *The English Poor Law 1531–1782*. Basingstoke, 1990.

*Poverty and Policy in Tudor and Stuart England*. London; New York, 1988.

Smail, John. 'Coming of Age in Trade: Masculinity and Commerce in Eighteenth-Century England'. In *The Self Perception of Early Modern Capitalists*. Edited by Margaret C. Jacob and Catherine Secretan, 229–52. New York, 2008.

'The Culture of Credit in Eighteenth-Century Commerce: The English Textile Industry'. *Enterprise & Society* 4, no. 2 (2003): 299–325.

Smout, T. C. *A History of the Scottish People 1560–1830*. London, 1969.

Snodin, Michael and John Styles. *Design and the Decorative Arts: Britain 1500–1900*. London, 2001.

Spacks, Patricia Meyer. *Imagining a Self: Autobiography and Novel in Eighteenth-Century England*. Cambridge, MA, 1976.

Spence, Cathryn. *Women, Credit, and Debt in Early Modern Scotland*. Manchester, 2016.

Spicksley, Judith M. '"Fly with a Duck in Thy Mouth": Single Women as Sources of Credit in Seventeenth-Century England'. *Social History* 32, no. 2 (2007): 187–207.

Spufford, Margaret. 'The Limitations of the Probate Inventory'. In *English Rural Society, 1500–1800: Essays in Honour of Joan Thirsk*. Edited by John Chartres and David Hey, 139–74. Cambridge; New York, 1990.

Spufford, Peter. 'Long Term Rural Credit in Sixteenth and Seventeenth Century England: The Evidence of Probate Accounts'. In *When Death Do Us Part: Understanding and Interpreting the Probate Records of Early Modern England*. Edited by Tom Arkell, Nesta Evans and Nigel Goose, 213–25. Oxford, 2000.

Standing, Guy. *The Precariat: The New Dangerous Class*. London, 2011.

Staves, Susan. 'Resentment or Resignation? Dividing the Spoils among Daughters and Younger Sons'. In *Early Modern Conceptions of Property*. Edited by Susan Staves and John Brewer, 194–218. London, 1995.

Stephenson, Judy Z. '"Real" Wages? Contractors, Workers, and Pay in London Building Trades, 1650–1800'. *The Economic History Review* 70, no. 1 (2018): 106–32.

Stirk, Nigel. 'Arresting Ambiguity: The Shifting Geographies of a London Debtors' Sanctuary in the Eighteenth Century'. *Social History* 25, no. 3 (2000): 316–29.

Stone, Lawrence. *Broken Lives: Separation and Divorce in England, 1660–1857*. Oxford, 1993.

*Road to Divorce: England 1530–1987*. Oxford, 1990.

Strathern, Marilyn. *The Gender of the Gift: Problems with Women and Problems with Society in Melanesia*. Berkeley, CA, 1988.

Stretton, Tim. 'Written Obligations, Litigation and Neighbourliness, 1580–1680'. In *Remaking English Society: Social Relations and Social Change in Early Modern England*. Edited by Steve Hindle, Alexandra Shepard and John Walter, 189–210. Woodbridge, 2013.

Styles, John. *The Dress of the People: Everyday Fashion in Eighteenth-Century England*. New Haven, CT, 2007.

'Involuntary Consumers? Servants and Their Clothes in Eighteenth-Century England'. *Textile History* 33, no. 1 (1 May 2002): 9–21.

'"Our Traitorous Money Makers": The Yorkshire Coiners and the Law, 1760–1783'. In *An Ungovernable People: The English and Their Law in The Seventeenth and Eighteenth Centuries*. Edited by John Brewer and John A. Styles, 172–249. New Brunswick, NJ, 1980.

Sweet, R. H. 'Topographies of Politeness', *Transactions of the Royal Historical Society* 12 (2002): 355–74.

Tadmor, Naomi. 'The Concept of the Household-Family in Eighteenth-Century England'. *Past & Present* 151, no. 1 (1996): 111–40.

Tarter, Michele Lise and Richard Bell, eds. *Buried Lives: Incarcerated in Early America*. Athens, 2012.

Temin, Peter and Hans-Joachim Voth. *Prometheus Shackled: Goldsmith Banks and England's Financial Revolution after 1700*. New York, 2013.

Thomas, Keith. 'Age and Authority in Early Modern England'. *Proceedings of the British Academy* 62 (1978): 205–48.

*The Ends of Life: Roads to Fulfilment in Early Modern England*. Oxford; New York, 2009.

'Numeracy in Early Modern England'. *Transactions of the Royal Historical Society (Fifth Series)* 37 (December 1987): 103–32.

Thompson, E. P. *The Making of the English Working Class*. New York, 1964.

'The Moral Economy of the English Crowd in the Eighteenth Century'. *Past & Present*, no. 50 (1971): 76–136.

Thomson, Karen Sander and Gordon DesBrisay. 'Crediting Wives: Married Women and Debt Litigation in the Seventeenth Century'. In *Finding the Family in Medieval and Early Modern Scotland*. Edited by Elizabeth Ewan and Janay Nugent, 85–98. Aldershot, 2017.

Timmins, Geoffrey. *Made in Lancashire: A History of Regional Industrialisation*. Manchester, 1998.

Todd, Margo. *The Culture of Protestantism in Early Modern Scotland*. New Haven, CT, 2002.

Tomkins, Alannah. 'Pawnbroking and the Survival Strategies of the Urban Poor in 1770s York'. In *The Poor in England, 1700–1850: An Economy of Makeshifts*. Edited by Alannah Tomkins and Steven King, 166–98. Manchester, 2003.

Tosh, John. *A Man's Place: Masculinity and the Middle-Class Home in Victorian England*. New Haven, CT, 1999.

Trollope, Anthony. *London Tradesmen*. London; New York, 1927.

Tyson, R. E. 'Contrasting Regimes: Population Growth in Ireland and Scotland during the Eighteenth Century'. In *Conflict, Identity and Economic Development: Ireland and Scotland, 1600–1939*. Edited by S. J. Connolly, R. A. Houston and R. J. Morris, 64–76. Preston, 1995.

Underdown, David E. 'The Taming of the Scold: The Enforcement of Patriarchal Authority in Early Modern England' In *Order and Disorder in Early Modern England*. Edited by Anthony Fletcher and John Stevenson, 116–36. Cambridge, 1985.

Vail, John. 'Insecure Times. Conceptualising Insecurity and Security'. In *Insecure Times: Living with Insecurity in Contemporary Society*. Edited by John Vail, Jane Wheelock and Michael Hill, 1–20. London, 1999.

'Insecurity'. In *The Elgar Companion to Social Economics*. Edited by John Bryan Davis and Wilfred Dolfsma, 44–56. Cheltenham, 2010.

Valenze, Deborah M. *The Social Life of Money in the English Past*. Cambridge, 2006.

Veblen, Thorstein. '"Conspicuous Consumption"'. In *The Theory of the Leisure Class: An Economic Study of Institutions*, 68–101. New York, 1902.

Vickers, Daniel. 'Competency and Competition: Economic Culture in Early America'. *The William and Mary Quarterly* 47, no. 1 (1990): 3–29.

'Errors Expected: The Culture of Credit in Rural New England, 1750–1800'. *The Economic History Review* 63, no. 4 (2010): 1032–57.

Vickery, Amanda. *Behind Closed Doors: At Home in Georgian England*. New Haven, CT, 2009.

'His and Hers: Gender, Consumption and Household Accounting in Eighteenth-Century England'. *Past & Present* 1, Issue suppl_1 (1 January 2006): 12–38.

Vincent, Susan. 'Men's Hair: Managing Appearances in the Long Eighteenth Century'. In *Gender and Material Culture in Britain since 1600*. Edited by Hannah Greig, Jane Hamlett and Leonie Hannan, 49–67. London, 2016.

Waddell, Brodie. *God, Duty and Community in English Economic Life, 1660–1720*. Woodbridge, 2012.

Wahrman, Dror. *The Making of the Modern Self: Identity and Culture in Eighteenth-Century England*. New Haven, CT, 2004.

Walker, David M. *A Legal History of Scotland, Vol. 5, The Eighteenth Century*. Edinburgh, 1998.

Walker, Garthine. 'Expanding the Boundaries of Female Honour in Early Modern England'. *Transactions of the Royal Historical Society* 6 (1996): 235–45.

Wareing, John. *Indentured Migration and the Servant Trade from London to America, 1618–1718: 'There Is Great Want of Servants'*. Oxford, 2017.

Weatherill, Lorna. *Consumer Behaviour and Material Culture in Britain, 1660–1760*. London, 1988.

Wennerlind, Carl. *Casualties of Credit: The English Financial Revolution, 1620–1720*. Cambridge, MA, 2011.

'The Death Penalty as Monetary Policy: The Practice and Punishment of Monetary Crime, 1690–1830'. *History of Political Economy* 36, no. 1 (1 March 2004): 131–61.

Wheelock, Jane. 'Who Dreams of Failure? Insecurity in Modern Capitalism'. In *Insecure Times: Living with Insecurity in Contemporary Society.* Edited by John Vail, Jane Wheelock and Michael Hill, 23–40. London, 1999.

White, Jerry. *Mansions of Misery: A Biography of the Marshalsea Debtors' Prison.* London, 2016.

'Pain and Degradation in Georgian London: Life in the Marshalsea Prison'. *History Workshop Journal* 68, no. 1 (2009): 69–98.

Williams, Samantha. *Poverty, Gender and Life-Cycle under the English Poor Law, 1760–1834.* Woodbridge, 2011.

Wiskin, Christine. 'Businesswomen and Financial Management: Three Eighteenth Century Case Studies'. *Accounting, Business and Financial History* 16, no. 2 (2006): 143–61.

Wood, Andy. 'Fear, Hatred and the Hidden Injuries of Class in Early Modern England'. *Journal of Social History* 39, no. 3 (2006): 803–26.

Wood, Cynthia. 'The First World/Third Party Criterion: A Feminist Critique of Production Boundaries in Economics'. *Feminist Economics* 3, no. 3 (1997): 47–68.

Wrightson, Keith. *Earthly Necessities: Economic Lives in Early Modern Britain.* New Haven, CT, 2000.

'Estates, Degrees and Sorts: Changing Perceptions of Society in Tudor and Stuart England'. In *Language, History, and Class.* Edited by Penelope J. Corfield, 30–52. Oxford, 1991.

'The Social Order of Early Modern England: Three Approaches'. In *The World We Have Gained: Histories of Population and Social Structure: Essays Presented to Peter Laslett.* Edited by Lloyd Bonfield and Peter Laslett, 177–202. Oxford, 1987.

'"Sorts of People" in Tudor and Stuart England'. In *The Middling Sort of People: Culture, Society and Politics in England : 1550–1800.* Edited by Jonathan Barry and Christopher Brooks, 28–51. Basingstoke, 1994.

Wrigley, E. A. 'British Population during the "Long" Eighteenth Century, 1680–1840'. In *The Cambridge Economic History of Modern Britain.* Edited by Roderick Floud and Paul Johnson, 57–95. Cambridge, 2003.

'The Divergence of England: The Growth of the English Economy in the Seventeenth and Eighteenth Centuries'. *Transactions of the Royal Historical Society* 10 (December 2000): 117–41.

*The Path to Sustained Growth: England's Transition from an Organic Economy to an Industrial Revolution.* Cambridge, 2016.

'Urban Growth and Agricultural Change: England and the Continent in the Early Modern Period', *The Journal of Interdisciplinary History* 15, no. 4 (1985): 686–8.

Wrigley, E. A. and Roger Schofield. *The Population History of England, 1541–1871: A Reconstruction.* Cambridge, 1981.

Zakim, Michael. 'The Best of Times and the Worst of Times'. *Common-Place* 10, no. 3 (2010). Available at www.common-place-archives.org/vol-10/no-03/zakim/

## *Theses and Unpublished Papers*

Burn, Andrew James. 'Work and Society in Newcastle upon Tyne, C. 1600–1710'. PhD thesis, University of Durham, 2014.

Corfield, Penelope J. 'The Social and Economic History of Norwich, 1650–1850: A Study in Urban Growth' PhD thesis, London School of Economics and Political Science [University of London], 1976.

Dingwall, Helen M. 'The Social and Economic Structure of Edinburgh in the Late Seventeenth Century'. PhD thesis, University of Edinburgh, 1989.

Haagen, Paul. 'Imprisonment for Debt in England and Wales'. PhD thesis, Princeton University, 1986.

Lineham, Peter J. 'The Campaign to Abolish Imprisonment for Debt in England, 1750–1840'. MA thesis, University of Canterbury, 1974.

Overton, Mark. 'Household Wealth, Indebtedness, and Economic Growth in Early Modern England'. International Economic History Congress. Helsinki, Finland, 2006.

Paul, K. Tawny. 'Credit and Social Relations amongst Artisans and Tradesmen in Edinburgh and Philadelphia, C. 1710–1770'. PhD thesis, University of Edinburgh, 2011.

Wakelam, Alexander Fensome. 'Imprisonment for Debt and Female Financial Failure in the Long Eighteenth Century'. PhD thesis, University of Cambridge, 2019.

## *Digital Sources*

The History of Parliament. The House of Commons, 1715–54, www.historyofparliamentonline.org/research/parliaments/parliaments-1715–1754.

The House of Commons, 1754–90, www.historyofparliamentonline.org/research/parliaments/parliaments-1754–1790.

*London Lives, 1690–1800.* http://www.londonlives.org/

*The Old Bailey Proceedings Online, 1674–1913,* www.oldbaileyonline.org/.

Oxford Dictionary of National Biography, www.oxforddnb.com.

The Statistical Accounts of Scotland, 1791–1845. http://stataccscot.edina.ac.uk/static/statacc/dist/home.

Carole Shammas, *Wealth, Household Expenditure, and Consumer Goods in Preindustrial England and America, 1550-1800* [data collection] (1993). UK Data Service. SN: 2994, http://doi.org/10.5255/UKDA-SN-2994-1

# Index

account books, 39, 87, 200, 234, 246
accounting, 183, 232
  and masculine household management.
    *See* married men
  as skill, 175
*Act of Grace*, 42, 106, 117, 120, 125,
    129
Acts for the Relief of Insolvent Debtors, 22, 23, 31,
    38, 42, 44, 47, 49, 54, 68, 79, 93, 103, 106,
    107, 108, 118, 126, 229
  applications for, 48
adultery, 160
age
  old age, 12, 17, 184, 185, 186,
    227
  young, 186, 187, 231
agriculture, 3, 237
anger, 116, 117, 118, 206
anxiety, 2, 32, 97, 116, 118, 122, 123, 124, 133, 148,
    171, 180, 240
appraisal, culture of, 215
apprentices, 54, 153, 176, 180, 181, 185
apprenticeship, 12, 165, 166
arrest, for debt, 27, 90, 142, 219
  as a form of shame, 203
  as strategy for enforcing debts, 35–6, 39, 54, 65,
    98–102, 104, 113, 125, 247
  evasion of, 40, 229
  experience of, 31, 40–1, 61, 110, 191, 196
  fear of, 122
  fees, 111
  legal process, 39–44, 114, 229
  legal reform, 38
  of corpses, 214
autonomy, 15, 17, 123, 153, 182, 206, 222, 223,
    224, 226
  and lifecycle, 184
  and work, 187
  as fiction, 17, 186, 200, 222, 247
  bodily, 217, 236, 244, 246
  loss of, 2, 157, 200, 202, 203, 245

bad debts, 81, *See* desperate debts
bailiffs, 40, 61, 103, 112, 113, 191, 196, 201, 229
bakers, 15, 129, 191, 230
bankruptcy, 5, 31, 32, 36, 37, 43, 55, 65, 98–9, 106,
    108, 114, 126, 148, 185, 246
  as a public insult, 156
  records, 33
Bath, 31, 128, 168
bedding, 1, 35, 62, 73, 75, 106
beggars, 33, 148
begging, 203, 239
bills, 80, 83, 84, 90, 92, 120, 128, 200, 201
Bloody Codes, 22, 207
bodies. *See* corpses
  as forms of investment, 231, 232
  as forms of value, 216–18, 222, 223
  for the poor, 221
  for women, 220–1
  under English law, 218–19
  under Scottish law, 219–20
  as resources for debtors, 227–8, 232
  autonomy, 206
bonds, 35, 71, 93, 203, 217, 231, *See* penal bonds
borrowers. *See* debtors
borrowing, 32, 71, 76, 105, 138
  and capitalism, 4
  and economic structures, 246
  and extravagance, 158
  and household status, 242
  attitudes towards, 174
  in form of delayed wages, 86
  networks of, 75
Boswell, James, 20, 31, 159, 210
Bourdieu, Pierre, 14, 194, 209
Brewer, John, 68
brewers, 2, 67, 80, 83, 95, 98, 119, 148, 157
Bristol Newgate prison, 230
brokers, 172, 231
builders, 105
building trades, 128, 176, *See* masons
burial, 48, 184, 214